Ceven Abi

A City Consumed

A City Consumed

**URBAN COMMERCE, THE CAIRO FIRE,
AND THE POLITICS OF DECOLONIZATION IN EGYPT**

Nancy Y. Reynolds

Stanford University Press
Stanford, California

Stanford University Press
Stanford, California

Printed in the United States of America on acid-free, archival-quality paper

Library of Congress Cataloging-in-Publication Data

Reynolds, Nancy Y., author.
  A city consumed : urban commerce, the Cairo fire, and the politics of decolonization in
Egypt / Nancy Y. Reynolds.
     pages cm
  Includes bibliographical references and index.
  ISBN 978-0-8047-8126-8 (cloth : alk. paper)
     1. Consumption (Economics)—Egypt—Cairo—History—20th century.   2. Cairo
(Egypt)—Commerce—History—20th century.   3. Nationalism—Economic aspects—Egypt.
4. Egypt—Politics and government—1919–1952.   5. Egypt—History—Revolution, 1952.
I. Title.
  HC830.Z7C348 2012
  381.0962'1609041—dc23
                                                                      2012001451

Typeset by Newgen in 10/14 Minion

For Dwyer, Anson,
and Graham

CONTENTS

ILLUSTRATIONS

Figures

Maps

ABBREVIATIONS

BOT	Board of Trade (UK)
CADN	Centre des Archives Diplomatiques (Center for Diplomatic Archives) (Nantes, France)
CNIB	Central Narcotics Intelligence Bureau (Egypt)
DOT	Department of Trade (UK)
DWQ	Dar al-Watha'iq al-Qawmi (Egyptian National Archives) (Egypt)
EC	*L'Egypte contemporaine*
EN	*L'Egypte nouvelle*
FO	Foreign Office series, UK National Archives
HMSO	His/Her Majesty's Stationery Office (UK)
IC Census	Industrial and Commercial Census (Egypt)
IFMCSMA	International Federation of Master Cotton Spinners' and Manufacturers' Association
LAB	Labour series, UK National Archives
MAE	Ministère des Affairs Etrangères (Ministry of Foreign Affairs) (France)
MAEP	Ministère des Affairs Etrangères, Quai d'Orsay, Paris (France)
MS	Maslahat al-Sharikat (Department of Corporations) (Egypt)
MW	Majlis al-Wuzara' (Council of Ministers) (Egypt)
NAUK	National Archives, UK
OHD	Oral History Department (Jerusalem)
SOP	Société Orientale de Publicité (Oriental Advertising Company)

ACKNOWLEDGMENTS

WHEN I FIRST chose to write on the history of Egypt's department stores, I expected to find a story about consumerism that would help explain women's changing status in twentieth-century Egypt. Shortly thereafter, the Egyptian government announced its intention to put the stores, which had been in the public sector for the past thirty-five years, up for auction to private bidders. The proposed reprivatization exploded into a public controversy about the legacy of the Nasserist state, collective memory of the ethnic basis of Egyptian identity, and the durability of conspiracy theories used to direct political criticism away from the state. That experience taught me to broaden my research on commerce into a study of politics and urban space, a process that took longer than I might have liked but no doubt enriched the book. It certainly expanded the intellectual and personal communities that have sustained the project. I did not expect to see echoes of my study appear so vividly in Egypt's 2011 political uprising. Some of my deepest debts lie with Egyptians and other close observers of Egyptian society and politics whose actions and analyses have helped me to formulate, and reformulate, the ideas and scope of this study.

Financial assistance from a number of sources greatly facilitated the research and writing for this project: an award from the Joint Committee on the Near and Middle East of the Social Science Research Council and the American Council of Learned Societies with funds provided by the U.S. Information Agency; grants from Stanford University's Department of History and School of Humanities and Sciences; a Geballe Fellowship from Stanford's Humanities Center; and research funds and sabbatical leave from Washington University in St. Louis. Numerous individuals and institutions assisted my research in

Egypt, Europe, and the United States. I thank the staffs at the following libraries for their professional and courteous assistance: in Cairo, the Dar al-Kutub, Centre d'Etudes et de Documentation Economiques (CEDEJ), the Dutch Institute, and the American University in Cairo's Main Library and the Creswell Rare Books Library; in France, the Bibliothèque Nationale, the Institut du Monde Arabe, and the Ministère des Affaires Etrangères archives in Paris and Nantes; in the United Kingdom, the National Archives and the University of Oxford's St. Antony's Middle East Centre and Bodleian Library; in Jerusalem, the Oral History Department archives of Hebrew University's Institute of Contemporary Jewry; and Stanford University's Hoover Institution. I particularly want to acknowledge the help of archivists at the Egyptian National Archives (Dar al-Watha'iq al-Qawmi), and especially Madame Sawsan ʿAbd al-Ghani, as well as Cynthia Nelson, Tim Sullivan, and the staffs of the libraries at Washington University in St. Louis and Stanford University. I presented versions of chapters to different audiences, whose feedback helped me refine and sharpen my arguments. I want to thank those at New York University's Kevorkian Center and the Junior Faculty Writing Seminar of Washington University's History Department for important comments that directed the final book in substantive ways.

Portions of this book appeared in modified forms in "National Socks and the 'Nylon Woman': Materiality, Gender, and Nationalism in Textile Marketing in Semicolonial Egypt, 1930–1956," *International Journal of Middle East Studies* 43, no. 1 (February 2011): 49–74; "*Sharikat al-Bayt al-Misri*: Domesticating Commerce in Egypt, 1931–1956," *Arab Studies Journal* 7, no. 2, and 8, no. 1 (Fall 1999/Spring 2000): 75–107; and "Salesclerks, Sexual Danger, and National Identity in Egypt in the 1920s and 1940s," *Journal of Women's History* 23, no. 3 (Fall 2011). I am grateful to the Johns Hopkins University Press, Cambridge University Press, and the *Arab Studies Journal* for permission to reprint.

It is a pleasure to thank, finally in print, individuals who have helped bring this book to fruition: Rizq ʿAbd al-Raziq ʿAbd al-Ghani, ʿImad ʿAbu Ghazi, Sophia Anninos, On Barak, Beth Baron, Miriam Beinin, Aimée Setton Beressi, Roger Beressi, Nancy Berg, Iver Bernstein, Shefali Chandra, Georges Chemla, Albert Cicurel, Yusuf Darwish, Raymond Douek, Beshara Doumani, Mine Ener, Anita Fabos, Khaled Fahmy, Nancy Fee, Ilana Feldman, Andrea Friedman, Margaret Garb, Will Hanley, Muhammad Hasan, Jacques Hassoun, Derek Hirst, Christine Johnson, Mona Kamil, Ahmet Karamustafa, Hillel Kieval, Samira Khalil, Noor-Aiman Khan, Krister Knapp, Steven Miles, Zizi Muhammad,

Linda Nicholson, Mohamed-Salah Omri, Jody Pavilack, Mark Gregory Pegg, Peter Platt, Lisa Pollard, Donald Quataert, Samir Raafat, Mario Ruiz, Mona Russell, Younasse Tarbouni, Elizabeth Thompson, ʿIman Saad, Mustafa Sadiq, Rifaʿat al-Saʿid, Jonathan Schoenwald, Relli Shechter, Raymond Stambuli, Sarah A. Stein, Corinna Treitel, Aviva Tuffield, Taha Saʿd ʿUthman, Robert Vitalis, Lori Watt, Lisa Wedeen, and Lisa White. Each has given valuable time and thought to various aspects of the project. Walter Armbrust, Joel Gordon, and Jaleh Fazelian showed me outstanding generosity in procuring copies of several important Egyptian films. Others offered crucial help on vexing points of the sources, among them Ahmed Abdalla, Pamela Barmash, Joel Beinin, Housni Bennis, Arthur Goldschmidt, Bruce Masters, ʿIman Saad, Samer Shehata, Loay el-Shawarby, and Chris Toensing. Students in several rounds of my classes on the history of colonial cities and consumption helped me think through some of the secondary literature for this book—in particular Parsa Bastani, Elizabeth Hague, Beverly Levine Tsacoyianis, Ava Marron, Martin Mintz, Kevin Parrish, Helen Pfeifer, and Michael Rapoport. Three anonymous reviewers for Stanford University Press generously gave detailed feedback from careful and knowledgeable readings of the manuscript that helped shape the book in crucial ways. Working with the Stanford University Press editors was wonderful. Kate Wahl provided gracious support and keen editorial insight through the various stages of revising and publishing the book. Joa Suorez, Emily Smith, and Rebecca Logan patiently and efficiently kept it all on track.

I have especially benefited from several colleagues' close readings of the manuscript. Zachary Lockman, Mary Louise Roberts, and Aron Rodrigue provided tremendously helpful feedback in the initial stages of the project and its later revision. Jean Allman and Tim Parsons mentored me with superb care during the final period of writing. Jean's generosity and expertise in commenting on multiple drafts and her support as department chair made this work possible as a book. Joel Beinin has shaped this book and my thinking about history and the Middle East more than anyone. For now over two decades, he has been an exceptional source of intellectual and moral inspiration, an advocate, and a trusted friend. He has read and commented on too many drafts of this material and always found suggestions, both imminently practical and profoundly philosophical, to refine its arguments and shore up its proof.

In many regards, this book is about the messiness of everyday life and efforts to clarify it. It is fitting, then, to end by thanking those who brought some order into my own life while I wrote it. Kathryn Love offered critical advice at the end of the project. I am deeply indebted to Trisha Singler, Sarah MacLaughlin, and Marcia Black, without whom the project would not have been completed. Friends and extended family have been supportive throughout the many years this project has traversed. Special thanks are due to Tate Brown for his love of words and engaging conversations. Three individuals provided extraordinary sustenance for the book. My parents, Herbert and Anne Reynolds, have modeled commitment to research and education throughout my life. With the eyes of scientists and mathematicians and the hearts of artists and readers, they supported my long years of education and encouraged me to think deeply and carefully. They also read drafts and provided important logistical support for the project itself. They have cared deeply about this book, and they have loved me well. I thank them both. Dwyer Brown has lived with this project on three continents, in five cities, and during most of our married life. His professional expertise about the care of objects, his sharp memory, and his ability to ask excellent questions have marked every page of the book. With good humor, personal generosity, and unflagging support, he made it possible for me to find the time and the will to write it at all. Our life together has been immeasurably enriched by our two sons, Anson and Graham, who grew up with this book. They tolerated many years of my long work hours, encouraged me to get it published, and kept me laughing with their love of funny stories. They may be as glad as I am to see it finally go to press.

NOTE ON TRANSLITERATION

I HAVE FOLLOWED the *International Journal of Middle East Studies* system for the transliteration of Arabic words, simplified by the omission of diacritical marks except for the *hamza* glottal stop (') and the letter ʿ*ayn* (ʿ). To emphasize the urban colloquial context, I have rendered the consonant *jim* as *g* instead of *j* (e.g., *gazma, ifrangi,* or galabiya). Very commonly used English spellings for well-known place and proper names (e.g., Nasser or Cairo) have been retained. This is a book about the changes over time in Egyptian usages of language and culture to represent social practices. To reflect the complexity, I have generally used the spellings of names of commercial firms as the companies themselves commonly transliterated them in published advertising or company materials, such as packaging, storefronts, and letterhead. These transliterations reflect the legal or ascribed French or Ottoman origins of many of the firms (e.g., Chemla, Sednaoui, or Cicurel). In these cases, I provide the standard or alternative spelling in the first substantive discussion in the text and in the index. I have retained alternative spellings in quoted material (e.g., Musky, galabieh).

A City Consumed

INTRODUCTION

DURING THE LATE MORNING and afternoon of January 26, 1952, much of downtown Cairo burned. Tensions had been building for several months because of escalating conflict between Egyptian popular groups and British troops stationed in the Suez Canal Zone, the site of lingering British colonial control that had officially begun in 1882. The ongoing British political and military presence in the country had persisted during the granting of limited sovereignty to Egypt in the aftermath of the 1919 Egyptian Revolution. The Suez Canal remained a crucial link in the British Empire, and Egypt's strategic location for Allied troop mobility had been pivotal in the Second World War. Egypt's cotton economy continued to bind the former colony to Britain as both an exporter of raw cotton and an importer of finished textiles, despite the trade's great reduction after the 1930s. The popular struggle in 1951–1952 encompassed a broad spectrum of opposition—university students, communists, religious activists, and paramilitary groups linked to several of Egypt's political parties, all increasingly mobilized since the end of the war. The collapsing old regime of vastly polarized social classes, ruled by a monarchy that played the various political parties off each other to retain power, was by the fall of 1951 grasping for any form of popular legitimacy. Encouraging guerrilla fighting in the canal zone seemed to deflect, at least initially, popular anger from the internal contradictions of Egyptian politics and society. On January 25 several state officials called on the Egyptian auxiliary police forces in the canal port city of Ismailia to make a heroic stand against British forces. British troops responded strongly, killing, wounding, and capturing large numbers of Egyptian police.[1]

On that Black Saturday of January 26, 1952, angry crowds responded by rioting through the streets of Cairo and attacking symbols of imperial power and privilege, including British banks, clubs, and companies. Ten British citizens, several of whom were high-ranking officials, died violently while locked in the exclusive, all-British Turf Club. Barclay's Bank exploded into flames as protestors nearby dragged Europeans from their cars and beat them. Rioters repeatedly accosted the doorman of the Lady Cromer Dispensary as they searched in vain for its "English matron."[2] The local correspondent from the London *Times* reported that "agents for British motor-cars had showrooms burnt out; new cars offered for sale were pushed into the streets and destroyed by fire."[3] The crowd also torched local nightclubs, hotels, and the cinemas along Fu'ad and Sulayman Pasha Streets, many "decorated with half-naked women that the demonstrators associated with the British and the corrupt King Faruq."[4]

Almost half the sites burned—three hundred in all—were commercial shops. Among the most prominent targets were eight of the city's luxurious department stores: Cicurel, Chemla, Orosdi-Back, Benzion, 'Adès, Chalons, ORECO, and Roberts Hughes. Specialty stores and smaller boutiques surrounding the department stores also burned, such as Pontremoli furniture store, Jacques nylon hose shop, and Schappino men's wear store. Commercial merchandise was widely pillaged, although rioters tossed much of it onto public roadways and lit it as bonfires. Most downtown streets remained impassable for days because of the acrid-smelling piles of burned merchandise. One observer noted that littered through the streets were "carcasses of automobiles still smoking" and "cardboard boxes from which were sticking out a pair of socks, a necktie or a scarf, [and] half-burned shirts."[5]

As a political struggle to control space and consumer style, the Cairo Fire in fact entailed the destruction of local society as much as imperial presence. Consumer goods such as socks, neckties, shirts, and cars figured visibly in the downtown ruins as targets of political protest, although they sat somewhat uncomfortably as both symbols of exploitation and items of consumption shared by local protestors and their foreign targets. Photographs of demonstrators and bystanders at the Cairo Fire and of the defendants in the trials that followed show many of them attired in trousers, shoes, jackets, and shirts; others dressed in a mixture of older, more local (*baladi*) styles, such as gownlike galabiyas or turbans, paired with various items of Western dress.[6] Ahmad Husayn, the leader of a fascist-style party who was initially charged with instigating the fires, wore a suit, suspenders, collared and button-front shirt, tie, and tarbush in the courtroom during his trial in May, as he did regularly in party meetings.[7] Trial testimony pivoted on conflicting eyewitness accounts of whether Husayn himself was in the vicinity of the primary buildings set afire just as they were being lit or only his car, driven by his chauffeur and carrying other members of his party. Reliable witnesses apparently saw Husayn, his driver, and his bodyguard together when the bodyguard threw "an Egyptian flag on top of one of the burning heaps of material from a store" later in the day and then disappeared. What was never called into question, however, was the identity of the car—it was a black Citroën.[8]

For many visiting observers, this represented the paradox at the heart of Egyptian colonial politics. Egyptians seemed to struggle against the very styles of clothing and the very commodities that they consumed: they rode in European cars to set fire to European car showrooms and stood trial for willful destruction of suits and silk ties attired in what looked like the same outfits. Many people derisively attributed the contradiction to Egyptian cultural incoherence and intellectual incompetence, arguing that Egyptians did not fully understand the meaning of their own consumption. Such observers tended to divide the world into two primary styles, focusing on a cultural duality that juxtaposed wholly separate spheres of urban culture: traditional versus modern, native versus foreign, Egyptian versus European, old versus new, *baladi* versus *ifrangi* (Western style). Fifteen years earlier, the Egyptian illustrated magazine *al-Musawwar* had used just such terms to disparage the variety of clothing styles visible on the streets of Cairo.[9] The lack of coherence in "outward appearance contradicts our nobility" as a nation, the writer warned, pointing a particularly harsh finger at Egyptians who "invented a mixed-up dress [*zayyan khalitan*]" by blending into the same outfit items of clothing from different national cultures, such as pairing the gownlike galabiya with a jacket and pants or wearing "western dress [*al-zayy al-ifrangi*] and a felt skullcap [*libda*]" together. The inconsistencies appeared especially stark in the case of a man photographed gazing into a "shop window filled with varieties of *ifrangi* clothes," himself wearing a jacket and pants with a skullcap and, even more "amazingly," wooden clogs (*qabaqib*) on his feet. Sartorial unity, the writer concluded, would reinforce a national linguistic unity—"the need to make Arabic the language visible to the eye in every place"—and contribute to a visual uniformity of space that could be a crucial platform for an emerging national politics.

Portraying Egyptians and other colonial subjects as national failures by focusing on their mixed-up dress was a remarkably common technique of metropolitan power. American traveler Finley Acker portrayed such a figure in 1899 (see Figure 1), remarking that "the dress of [Egyptian] men is frequently modified by the partial adoption of European fashions, the grotesqueness of which is quite striking when an Arab is seen wearing his conventional long skirt and fez, but, at the same time, displaying European gaiters [boots] and a short spring overcoat."[10] Derogatory descriptions of local dress participated in broader struggles over the direction colonial societies should take to modernize and thus "earn" national independence.[11] Mustafa Kemal Ataturk, Turkey's reformist and pro-Western ruler, publicly ridiculed a Turkish man's hybridized adaptation to new clothing laws in 1925.[12] European travelers and Chinese Americans bemoaned the "incongruous" and "inappropriate" mixtures of clothing styles in China in the same period, much as British officials opposed the wearing of caps by their Indian employees, since the caps "were not 'western' nor were they 'oriental,' and hence by application they were some kind of bastard concoction."[13] The mocking tone of colonial and elite accounts reveals the anxieties produced by mixed-up consumption practices that tended to defy the neat, binary categories on which colonial domination and nationalist revolt both rested.

om, which is usually
n
n
)r
æ

:e
's
g
d
h
1-
ie
ie
to
at

ilversmith bazaar is
nw lane not over four

Figure 1. An Egyptian man wearing mixed-up dress, including a galabiya, turban, short overcoat, and *ifrangi* boots. Drawing by C. P. Shoffner, in Finley Acker, *Pen Sketches* (Philadelphia: McLaughlin Brothers, 1899), 9.

Other colonial subjects eschewed rigid categories of difference and contrast, instead describing stylistic contests in the language of propinquity or contiguity. According to these consumers, different regimes of styles overlapped and coexisted, especially in the complexity of urban space; styles were available as an interlocking set of strategies or vocabularies when invoked in particular ways. Egyptian writer Yahya Haqqi, in fact, called the interwar mixed-up style "a morseling [taftit],"[14] in reference to the deliberate way that members of the lower-middle and lower classes acquired individual items of ifrangi clothing from the flea market (suq al-kantu)—"a jacket without its pants or pants without its jacket or an orphaned waistcoat."[15] The concept of morseling or a morseled style captures not only the discordant and interpenetrated bricolage Egyptians used to incorporate new or different types of clothing into their wardrobes or new uses of space into their experiences of the city. It also brings to the foreground the broader contexts of political and social power within which the fluid use of clothing style operated. New regional middle classes promoted modern cultural pursuits, forms of education, residential dwellings, and civic organizations to formulate novel forms of political and social power for themselves.[16] Poverty and need shaped many morselized consumption styles, however, and members of the upper and middle classes also mixed items of consumption or uses of space to signal cultural affiliation or their location in more regional politics.[17] Embedded in an unequal political culture, morseled consumption styles at times challenged and at other times accommodated political and cultural sovereignty. Although the mixing up of consumption styles could represent informal ways local subjects recaptured agency in the face of imperial power, the mixing also often signaled strategies with more local or individual goals, and thus we should be mindful not to romanticize them.[18]

As importantly, Egyptian economic nationalists such as Ahmad Husayn in political struggles focused on the origin of commodities—their "product-nationality"[19]—rather than particular styles. In the absence of locally made versions of some goods, practicing economic nationalism meant choosing a relatively neutral foreign product. In such a way, Egypt's lack of automobile manufacturing made French imports (such as Citroëns) preferable to British. Likewise, Egyptian dress could mean ifrangi-style clothing, such as trousers, jackets, ties, and collared and button-front shirts, if it was produced (the fabric woven or the outfits tailored) or sold in Egypt or Egyptian establishments. The relative complexity of determining what counted as nationalist consumption, then, both had consequences for and grew out of the complexity in ownership, geography, and merchandise of commercial space itself.

Disregard for the empirical intricacy of urban style and space helps explain why the Cairo Fire has remained poorly understood since 1952. Most investigation into the event has centered on the actors and political plots of January 1952: the short-term events, immediate causes, breaches of responsibility, and conspiracies that instigated the city's burning. As Anne-Claire Kerboeuf puts it, "Until today, the main question has been who set fire to Cairo and which political leader is to be blamed."[20] Although many histories of Egypt accord the fire the status of "death spasm of the monarchical regime,"[21] it usually figures as merely a self-explanatory bookend to periodize the recent past: the capstone of histories of the increasing opposition to entrenched political parties and the polarized class structure under Kings Fu'ad and Faruq, or the nadir of popular despair that invited the Free Officers' coup of 1952, thus launching the revolutionary era of Gamal 'Abd al-Nasser.[22] As an all-purpose explanation of why things changed in 1952, the fire remains in both the scholarly and the popular imaginations clouded by a static, dichotomous picture of the city that spawned it. This limitation has restricted its role in Egyptian historical memory to either a moment of national shame or a decisive step toward full national independence.[23]

Although questions of responsibility and recruitment are certainly important, many explanations of the fire rest on a premise of the dual-city character of Cairo imported from other colonial settings such as North and South Africa.[24] Kerboeuf, in her excellent history of popular mobilization during the fire, relies on such a description of Ismailia, the downtown commercial quarter that burned: "This elitist new neighborhood soon became a social enclave, complete with sartorial and linguistic markers. It became assumed that to enter one of the center's shops or coffee shops, one had to have an effendi look (shoes, a suit, and a tarboosh) and speak a foreign language. Financial means were consequently required. . . . [Thus], Isma'iliya was actually a European microsociety few Egyptians could frequent."[25] In accounts of the fire, the exclusivity of downtown commerce stands in as self-evident justification for Egyptian animosity toward and alienation from the district. This narrative strategy frames the fire as a purging of parasitical elements—a self-interested local elite colluding with foreign capital—from the otherwise whole and uncomplicated national fabric. Explanations of the 1952 fire that rely on such a tale of two Cairos thus risk portraying an unwarranted social consensus, a belief that all local residents could be clearly categorized as either foreign or native, in pre-1952 Egypt.[26] More than historical accuracy is at stake here. Erasing the ambivalences of pre-1952 Egyptian life has strengthened nationalism's self-justificatory, and at times quite coercive, claims to represent an authentic and eternal society.

A City Consumed instead takes a longer look back to the interwar period, to the changing space of the urban downtown and the commercial and sartorial practices that circulated there, to recast the Cairo Fire as both rupture and continuity—as a culmination of the hybridized society that grew in the first half of the century and a break with that world and its attendant versions of Egyptian nationalism. I argue that the specific materiality of the space of the colonial city and the goods purveyed there fostered a flexible and intimate culture of consumption in which local residents fluidly and even unpredictably moved through transitional spaces, combined items of sartorial style, and understood themselves to be Egyptian. The concrete and specific histories of retail space and everyday consumer objects ultimately demonstrate that the contours of colonial politics in Egypt formed as much by the particular trajectory of local consumption as the official dynamics of European rule.[27] Commercial practices worked to etch the colonial order onto consumer bodies, and commercial circuits tied areas of the city together in unexpected ways. Commercial penetration thus created a sense of captivity among many Egyptians, ultimately inscribing a discourse of self-destruction—of national suicide—into anticolonial resistance.

Space, or the ways power inhered in the built environment, thus comprises a central problematic for the book. Foucault argues that "the anxiety of [the twentieth century] has to do fundamentally with space" rather than time. "The problem of the human site or living space is . . . that of knowing what relations of propinquity, what type of storage, circulation, marking, and classification of human elements should be adopted in a given situation in order to achieve a given end. Our epoch is one in which space takes for us the form of relations among sites."[28] Part of the scholarly fascination with space has to do with its linkage to politics and, specifically, as David Harvey argues, "the relationship between the physicality of urban public space and the politics of the public sphere."[29] In Egypt during the first half of the twentieth century, the central political questions revolved around achieving national sovereignty.

Who and what was considered Egyptian in this period, a seemingly basic empirical and historical question, remains surprisingly mired in generalized, prescriptive thinking. The Arab nationalist view that emerged in the decade after the Cairo Fire projected back to the colonial and interwar periods a simplistic definition of *authentic Egyptian* as Arabic speaking and Muslim or, possibly, Coptic Christian. Conversely, alternative interpretations of Egyptian identity in this period have invoked a cosmopolitanism that, as Will Hanley explains, "consistently entails nostalgia for a more tolerant past" and tends to generalize elite experience over society as a whole.[30] Turning our analytic gaze on material structures of space and clothing offers a corrective to the more diffuse imaginaries of community formed by print capitalism and theorized by Benedict Anderson.[31] Objects of consumption acted as vehicles of community in ways that brought nationalism into completely different registers of corporeality and intimacy because of the effects of material objects on people.[32] Viewing Egyptian history through the lenses of space and consumption, then, provides an alternative to descriptions of modernity or nationalism that are based on the experiences of the upper and middle classes, commonly considered the bearers of new cultural practices and ideologies in the Middle East.[33]

CONSUMPTION AND COLONIAL POLITICS

Long considered the crucible for modernity, urban commercial space has been the focus of many studies in different national contexts. The particular growth of nineteenth-century European and American cities enabled the anonymity and mobility of the dandy, the flaneur, or the "woman adrift," consuming materially and visually what Marshall Berman calls "a great fashion show, a system of dazzling appearances, brilliant facades, glittering triumphs of decoration and design."[34] Newly opened spaces of cities, such as wide and well-lit Haussmanian boulevards flanked by sidewalks, arcades, plate-glass windows, cafés, and commercial goods, became accessible to crowds of spectators arriving from far-flung neighborhoods on novel modes of public transportation. Enormous department stores, designed to be both "palaces of consumption" and "cathedrals of commerce," anchored the new world, providing goods to outfit modern homes and wardrobes as well as space for spectatorship and cultural priming. Such stores were places for dressing up—for trying on clothing in stores without necessarily buying, as new policies of free entry disarticulated the processes of shopping and purchasing and new forms of display created imaginary geographies of consumption and place. They were also places to be seen, as new sorts of work and leisure subjectivities and alliances created a social world of urban spectatorship and "counter cultures" that overlaid most women and some men with sexual desire as part of the new urban spectacle.[35] The general plasticity and relative vacuity of commercial display in stores—department-store racks, for instance, offered shirts in different sizes, colors, and patterns or trousers in a variety of cuts and fabrics—could accommodate the projection of desire and the malleability of identity more easily than other institutions, such as schools, government offices, or most families. As Claire Walsh has noted critically, the department store functions, then, "to define our present age as distinct and 'modern' . . . as the analogue of 'industrial revolution,' Marxist alienation, and the beginnings of mass consumption."[36] Studies of consumption that have made "the spatial turn" away from institutions such as department stores, world's fairs, or retailer and trade associations to focus on contests of movement in public spaces have returned, perhaps paradoxically, to linking consumption to wider national identities of place in locally specific ways, and this overlaps with studies that link consumption to citizenship more directly.[37]

Although most studies of consumption have taken the Euro-American metropole as their analytic focus,[38] histories based in nonmetropolitan archives to reconstruct the specific ways that colonial economies shaped consumption cultures have offered a radical rethinking of the global flows of power and commerce. Novel metropolitan products flooded colonial markets, ultimately even altering the needs of colonial consumers, but preexisting local meanings shaped reception of the new, often creating consumption practices that contradicted prescriptive metropolitan marketing.[39] A growing literature about the history of Middle Eastern consumption has begun to outline some of the local specificities in regional trade and cultural practice that shaped the domestic trajectories of Egyptian consumption.[40] The inflection of Middle Eastern consumption regimes by religious politics has complicated broader narratives of the relationship of politics to economic change, especially as fatwa (religious advice) literature presented a unique intermediate public space to control— often in unexpected ways—the consumption of various goods and associated behaviors.[41] The history of colonialism has also helped call into question the notion that modernity is a chronological period, a condition, or a cluster of objective attributes. Scholars have increasingly relocated modernity as part of a more performative or "claim-making" process,[42] although few have engaged theoretically with tradition, implicitly relegating it instead to the role of static foil for the measurement of modernity's progress.[43]

Nuanced studies of nonmetropolitan consumption practices can sharpen our understanding of the complexities in the constitution and expression of membership, power, complicity, and resistance in colonial politics. Timothy

Mitchell's assertion that colonizing involves "the spread of a new political order that inscribes in the social world a new conception of space, new forms of personhood, and a new means of manufacturing the experience of the real" broadened the terrain of colonial politics into mundane spaces and practices.[44] Colonial politics were characterized, according to Partha Chatterjee and Benedict Anderson, by the state's emphasis on practices of governmentality in the absence of popular sovereignty. Classificatory divisions of the population made to facilitate the government's control through policy of the various groups under its jurisdiction tended to create a public sphere and political society based on clearly demarcated collective identities and ethnicities rather than, at least in theory, a more individualized sense of national belonging grounded in a discourse of equal rights and popular sovereignty in noncolonial states.[45] Colonial states engaged in the coercive process of ordering, enumerating, and classifying the heterogeneity of colonial societies through the census, taxation, military conscription, public health campaigns, regulatory and educational missions, property laws, land settlement schemes, and so forth.[46] This experience of governmentality ensured that development discourses about the emergence of a postcolonial "national economy" would fixedly regard "the state as the engine of progress."[47]

Expanding the analytic realm of the colonial public sphere to include consumption enables the recovery of alternative formations of collective identities and struggles for citizenship or legal enfranchisement made possible by boycotts and other consumer movements, by increasingly visible mass consumption, and by the circulation of people in new commercial spaces.[48] Specifically, it allows two important shifts in understanding colonial politics: first, to new nonstate actors and arenas, such as consumers, traders, and the commercial sector[49] and, second, to practices that blurred rather than inscribed classificatory categories, such as sartorial and domestic styles that mixed up objects commonly employed to differentiate groups, or to fluidity in urban movement that contrasted with static forms in the built environment. In fact, European colonization facilitated in most places, including Egypt, the movement of population and capital, which increased multiplicity in juridical status, categories of citizenship, languages, and customs among local residents, thereby frustrating colonial and postcolonial state efforts to "represent the country as a singular, national economy," as Mitchell reminds us.[50] Settler colonial regimes maintained "racial frontiers" by policing gendered intimacies, including sex and domestic arrangements, among their subjects. Yoking the intimate spaces of family and domestic life to the high politics of imperial rule—studying "their ambiguities as much as . . . their injustices"—brings the microphysics of race and the surveillance of the boundaries of public and private to the center of colonial politics.[51] Much as such studies take their analytic punch from depicting the implementation of colonial rule in nonpolitical spaces such as the home and popular storytelling, investigations of hybridized consumption practices in colonial societies can illuminate how commodities simultaneously condensed political power and fractured colonial rule. Hybridized styles of dress point, then, to a diffuse nature of power in colonial societies or its uneven concentration among different locations.[52] This spatialization of power scored colonial cities with fault lines more convoluted than the broad avenues usually associated with colonial urban planners.[53] The resulting sinuosity routed urban disorders such as the Cairo Fire in seemingly random directions.

Quotidian consumption practices and consumerist politics such as boycotts not only offered consumers a frame to imagine themselves as national subjects but also linked colonial subjects across political borders. Egyptians during the interwar period envisioned themselves in a broad field of colonial politics that included North Africans, the Irish, the Chinese, and Palestinians but most centrally featured Indians. The Egyptian press followed the emergence in India of locally produced cotton textiles as a national symbol in the anticolonial struggle, and Egyptian activists explicitly modeled some of their tactics, such as bonfires and boycotts, on Indian experiences.[54] "A visual vocabulary of the nation" deployed through live performance, courtly culture, religious practice, and newer artistic media such as film, photography, and postering became an especially important supplement to print capitalism to create community in India, a visuality that was also expanded by consumer objects such as homespun, home-woven cloth.[55] Ultimately, as I demonstrate in this book, the materiality of Egyptian raw cotton (its long-staple fiber in particular) imposed limits on the development of cotton as a vehicle for mass politics on the Indian model. In a similar way, critiques about the dual city of colonialism that developed most strikingly under French colonialism were imported to Egypt but failed to capture the more fluid mobility of Egyptians in urban space.[56] The prism of consumption thus allows us to see the Egyptian case as a model of colonial politics that differs from both North Africa and India.

The microphysical workings of colonial power through marking and classification techniques of governmentality thus extended to the corporeal and spatial practices of commerce and consumption. The Egyptian case specifically suggests that shopping and consumption bound the bodies of subjects to colonial regimes in very intimate ways and led to the framing of anticolonial protest as a project of self-destruction. A central argument of this book is that a sense of captivity, by regulatory, material, and discursive mechanisms, marked colonial consumption as distinctive from that in the metropole. Forced to overconsume certain imported goods or prohibited from consuming by the impoverishment caused by the extraction of resources and surplus, colonial subjects negotiated through economies of commercial desire that had been built on dramatic asymmetries in law and power.[57] As a poetics of protest, captivity narratives underlined how boycotts and other forms of opposition in commercial space and consumption could act as a "spiritual trial" and moral claim for Egyptians seeking national sovereignty.[58] Gender, family, and domesticity are important themes in captivity narratives, as they highlight the intensity and reach of the captor from the political sphere into the private realm.[59] Consumption's ability to link the public and the private worlds made it ripe terrain for such narrativizing. As claim-making devices, these narratives also trained attention to the physical sacrifices entailed by constrained consumption. Consumer captivity was, however, an ambiguous process. Commerce did not construct itself as coercive. Marketing and merchandise displays attempted to captivate consumers as much as to capture their spending power. The iteration of such displays in urban space and the local press worked at times to overwhelm consumers (and nonconsumers) with a sense of the profusion of available goods, although at other times excess helped regularize and routinize expectations and patterns of consumption, an important component in the ultimate translation of affective desires into mundane practices or acquisitions. Consumer spending could act as a pathway for upward mobility or at least secure a temporary confusion of status that individuals might exploit to challenge more rigid social stratifications based on class, ethnicity, nationality, age, or even gender. At the same time, many people were held captive by their inability to consume, a sense of entrapment intensified by the social heterogeneity of urban space that allowed easy comparison and competition.

Consumer desire helped fissure colonialism, then, in part by psychically blurring and yet reinforcing the "binary logic of colonial power" that underlay the ordering practices of governmentality.[60] To consider consumption a spatial practice, as I do in this book, is to acknowledge the important role shopping in commercial space played in the production of meaning about commodities as well as to focus on the ways that consumer goods, such as loose gowns, heeled shoes, or tight, fragile stockings, could discipline the physical body. Spatial relations of the colonial city, it is often argued, were influenced more by race than by class.[61] Hybridized cultures of consumption, forged in the relations of *both* class and race, most powerfully challenged the visual and spatial instantiation of colonial power in Egypt. As this book demonstrates, the mixed-up styles of dress and uses of space in local consumption imperiled the semicolonial state's efforts to classify and order the populations it controlled and channeled nationalist activism in specific directions. They also rendered the Cairo Fire an imprecise tool for decolonization. As an escape from colonial consumer captivity, the fire in fact left many Egyptians with deeply conflicting emotions. As leftist activist Anouar Abdel-Malek describes it, the fire produced "a vision of horror unforgettable to all who lived through that day of sorrow."[62] Tilting the analytic balance in understanding the Cairo Fire toward lived fluidity, as *A City Consumed* does, helps counteract both a narrow nationalist view of the past and a neo-Orientalist assumption that "what went wrong" (to use Bernard Lewis's popular phrase) was that Egyptians chose to remain mired in local tradition rather than embrace Western modernity.[63]

PEOPLE, PLACES, AND THINGS: ORGANIZATION OF THE BOOK

This book is a study of common commercial goods and space that had a profound effect on politics and community in Egypt in the first half of the twentieth century. While it seeks to understand the relationships among objects, especially as they were assembled into morseled or mixed-up regimes of style, it does not attempt a comprehensive study of objects or consumerism in Egypt. Rather, it investigates the histories of a matrix of commodities that operated in a coherent semiotic system in which the use of individual objects communicated locally understood meanings and status as part of a broader social logic.[64] Such a study demands simultaneous examination of prescriptions about the proper use of goods and the lived experiences of how they actually functioned in everyday life. To that end, the book uses a wide range of primary-source materials, including state archives in Egypt, France, and England; the Egyptian press; commercial and trade publications; speeches and autobiographical writings; and films, photographs, and literary sources. The Egyptian press expanded dramatically after the First World War, and in particular, illustrated magazines such as *Ruz al-yusuf, al-Ithnayn,* and *al-Musawwar* increased popular readership, which had been previously confined to a small, literate part of the urban and provincial strata.[65] While the reception of the magazines and their advertisements remains largely unknown, the marketing and satirical writings of the press can still offer historians an impression of the parameters of commodity politics and how people made sense of its changes. Likewise, films offered new frames for people to imagine themselves as consumers, social actors, and ultimately as national citizens, especially important in societies such as midcentury Egypt characterized by low formal literacy and a split between the spoken and written languages.[66] Although the exact ways that objects shaped the practices and habits of the self have been difficult for historians to track through archives, broader shifts in more public debates about the meanings of goods and their relationships to different members of society help identify significant changes that affected a wide array of people, the contours of ordinary perception, and how these altered over time.

The book's narrative arc from urban growth in the late nineteenth century through the first decade of Nasser's reign raises the question of defining *colonialism* in Egypt. In this book, I use *colonial* in several ways. On one level, I distinguish between the actual colonial situation of Egypt during 1882–1922, when Egypt was under the formal administration of Britain (it was actually a protectorate from only December 1914 to February 1922 but had been administered in all significant respects since the British invasion in 1882), and the semicolonial situation of the 1922–1956 period; throughout this second period British officials continued to wield considerable administrative and military power in Egypt, enshrined by the Four Reserved Points of the declaration that abrogated the protectorate, and although slowly renegotiated in 1933–1956, these powers were in large part retained. In a more general sense, however, I use *colonial* to describe the broader socioeconomic regime in Egypt during this entire period, when the Egyptian economy was based on monocrop agriculture (of cotton) intended primarily for export and the importation of vast quantities of finished goods for consumption. Differences in power between Europe and Egypt in this period also helped create a colonial situation with respect to "cultural capital" and social practices, in which the European assumed a certain hegemony over the local.[67]

Although the book focuses on making more complex a notion of the local, *European* was also not a monolithic term. Many Egyptian nationalists preferred French language and culture to English, in part for aesthetic reasons and in part because of the structure of education in Egypt but also as a sort of anticolonial protest against their British overlords. The use of French, especially after the 1867 World Exposition in Paris, became in Egypt (as elsewhere) its own autonomous cultural mode, reflecting an interest in France but not necessarily a desire for French rule or hegemony.[68] Some Egyptians under British colonial rule adopted French cultural mores and language to signal their modernity while still protesting the politics of the colonial situation. Later, more populist nationalists found the division between French and British cultures specious, arguing that there was a more generalized European cultural dominance, although by then many of the European practices and clothing styles were so engrained in Egyptian society as to make them local for many middle-class Egyptians. In general, I use *colonial* to refer to Egypt's relationship with Europe, rather than to other places with which it had what may be considered a colonial relationship. Egypt was, some would contend, a colonial province of the Ottoman Empire until 1914; it also commanded a certain colonial authority over neighboring areas such as Sudan and Nubia in this period.

The book thus follows the politics of colonialism and consumption through several Egyptian theaters as tension rose toward the 1952 Cairo Fire. Chapter 1 investigates the process by which the urban built environment under colonialism was framed as a dual city and juxtaposes this perception to the lived mobility of Egyptians through that space. I focus on morseled clothing styles and transitional neighborhoods between the two cities, spaces and practices historically disparaged because they fit into neither side of the double-city binarism but crucial, I argue, to the defiance of the binary logic of colonialism and the narrow conception of *Egyptian* that followed from it. Chapter 2 turns to shopping, with a particular focus on the people who circulated and worked in downtown commercial districts and the department stores that anchored them. Close examination of the histories of stores, their owners and employees, and their customers demonstrates the multiple ways that people identified as Egyptian in the interwar years.

Chapter 3 traces the politics of commercial boycotts in interwar Egypt. Boycotts were a moment when consumption emerged as a political arena to defy colonialism, and they helped initiate broad public awareness that colonialism was at least partially implemented through consumption. In so doing, boycotts popularized a language of dichotomies to understand Egyptian politics and encouraged the development of nationalist industries and commercial spaces. Chapter 4 examines the urgent campaigns to create a domestic market for locally produced cotton socks and shoes in response to boycotters. The cultivation and exportation of raw cotton had long driven colonialism in Egypt, and the development of a national cotton textile industry and the local consumption of its products were early and widely supported strategies of more elite Egyptian nationalists. The local footwear market grew in the interwar years under competition between *ifrangi* and *baladi* styles of shoes to create a dynamic set of commercial practices that propelled the consumption of new forms of footwear.

Chapter 5 turns to the transitional postwar years of 1945–1952, when mounting social and political tension put pressure on the old-regime society and a colonial politics that had been reinvigorated during the war. State-sponsored Egyptianization of the economy began to shift the terrain of commerce at the same time that cartoons, short stories, poetry, films, and other cultural texts developed a satirical focus on footwear and nylon stockings to expose anew the contradictions of negotiating the dichotomies that supposedly marked semicolonial Egypt. Finally, Chapter 6 retells the story of the Cairo Fire with a focus on its commercial and human targets to examine the complexity with which the foreign and the local remained imbricated after decades of nationalist activity. Rebuilding the downtown in the aftermath of the fire reinforced nationalization programs at the end of the decade that emphasized themes of public ownership, popular accessibility, and continuity in ways that only subtly altered the context of shopping and consumption.

The historically specific politics of describing different cultural and economic practices is contested terrain. This applies as much to historians writing today as to customers shopping in Cairo in the 1930s. People in Egypt marshaled terms such as *native, indigenous, local, European, traditional,* and *modern* to set certain practices off from others. For this reason, none of these terms can innocently serve as an empirically transparent description or label. Nevertheless, the act of writing necessitates lexical choices and the fixing of terms from their more fluid context. I have chosen in this book to use Arabic terms from Egyptian vernacular to describe different styles: I refer to more local styles as *baladi* ("of the country") and more European ones as *ifrangi* ("Frankish," or European).[69] I intend these terms to reflect the fluidity of Egyptian perception of these practices as Western or Eastern influenced, rather than focusing on whether in some objective sense they were actually or accurately copied from European or local practice. Capturing the fluidity of the practices of consumption and of the politics of naming, in the context of colonial politics, is the essence of this book.

1 THE "EVER-MELTING" CITY

IN EARLY OCTOBER 1922, a man calling himself "a Tramways Victim" complained in the local press about the poor quality of public transportation in Cairo.[1] The author described himself as "from the class of workers obligated to use public transportation," because he was "not rich" and had lived for the past fourteen years in a neighborhood ('Abbasiyya) far from downtown Cairo where he worked for a utilities company and socialized in the evenings. He claimed to ride the tram four times every day. In addition to commuting to work, he was also, "like not a few of the young people in my quarter, a lover of the theatre, concerts, cinema, etc.," as well as a member of many societies and associations that required his attendance downtown several evenings a week. Since the trams closed long before the cinema and theater showings were finished, he was frequently obliged to take a taxi home at a much higher cost. "What advantage do I have," he asked, "of living far from the city center and in a second-rate building except for the benefit of lower rent?" He declared that nighttime car and taxi fares cost him 50 percent more than his rent.

The Tramways Victim was not alone. In fact, his complaints centered precisely on the overcrowding and poor sanitary conditions of the tramways caused by the enormous demand constantly placed on them by the legions of mobile urban residents.[2] Massive population growth in outer areas of the city, such as 'Abbasiyya, Heliopolis, Shubra, Sakakini, Bulaq, and Sabtiyya, had recently expanded ridership exponentially. "Building had not stopped" for the past three years in 'Abbasiyya, the Tramways Victim contended, and "the population had surely grown by 50 percent." The Cairo Tramways Company, owned by Belgians, had not maintained its existing cars or replaced those damaged in the recent war and the nationalist and labor demonstrations that followed it.[3] "I dare you," he challenged the editor, "to arrive to take the tram from [Zahir to the city center] between 7:30 and 8:30 in the morning. It is a crowd, a crush, an unimaginable struggle." Trams arrived at their first stop full from the terminus and did not bother to stop again until reaching the train station plaza in downtown Cairo. Tram ridership in 1914 reached fifty-three million passengers a year; by 1917 ridership had grown to seventy-five million.[4] Since Cairo's population in 1917 stood at roughly eight hundred thousand people, many of these tram fares were likely purchased by the same people, who used the system several times a day as the Tramways Victim himself did.[5]

This testament to the daily crisscrossing of the city by hordes of residents evokes an urban mobility that differs completely from common images of interwar Cairo as a city radically divided and compartmentalized by its experience under colonialism. The idea that the force of colonialism most powerfully expressed itself spatially in the creation of a dual city comes from the experience of French settler colonialism, especially in North Africa.[6] There, French colonial planners deliberately sought to control local populations by containing and paternalistically preserving elements of indigenous culture through sharp demarcations in the built environment. Physical markers separated the old city from the new administrative and industrial city designed to lead the colony in modernization and development.[7] "The dual structure of the colonial city," Zeynep Çelik contends, "is a fragment of the broad discourse of colonialism which accommodates the exercise of colonial power by an 'articulation of forms of difference.' Separation plays an important part in defining otherness and allows for a critical distance needed for surveillance."[8] It was Frantz Fanon, spokesman for mid-twentieth-century decolonization, who did the most to popularize the notion that the "colonial world is a world cut in two."[9] The bifurcation between the contiguous towns of the settlers and of the colonized in what he called "the generic colonial city" revealed the disparities of power and of standards of living that sustained European colonialism:

> The settlers' town is a strongly built town, all made of stone and steel. It is a brightly lit town; the streets are covered with asphalt, and the garbage cans swallow all the leavings, unseen, unknown and hardly thought about. The settler's feet . . . are protected by strong shoes although the streets of his town are clean and even, with no holes or stones. The settler's town is a well-fed town, an easygoing town; its belly is always full of good things. The settler's town is a town of white people, of foreigners.

> The town belonging to the colonized people . . . is a world without spacious-
> ness; . . . their huts are built one on top of the other. The native town is a hungry
> town, starved of bread, of meat, of shoes, of coal, of light.[10]

Fanon forged his view of colonial urbanism primarily in French colonies such
as Martinique and Algeria. Although Egypt shared with Algeria many experiences of colonial rule, urban development in Egypt resulted less from deliberate planning enacted by colonial state policies than from the actions of complex
and shifting coalitions. Khaled Fahmy argues that the growth of Cairo into
what appeared to be a bifurcated city "happened by default rather than by design," if indeed it happened at all.[11]

Following Fahmy, this chapter also moves beyond the analysis of static built
forms, cartographical representations, and assumptions of division to understand the colonial city instead as a built environment defined by movement and
mutability, a space of complex navigations and rapid changes, one experienced
as interconnected despite its differences of architecture. Magdi Wahba remembered interwar Cairo in just this way for its "infinite complexity . . . crowded
with people of vastly differing backgrounds, rapidly changing class structures,
and heterogeneous cultural values. The experience of living in Cairo was . . .
one of constantly coming to terms with change. . . . Cairo, the physical place,
the changing metropolis, with its protean forms of vanishing communities and
social strata, is ever melting, ever taking on new shapes."[12] Wahba's experience
of the "melting" of "physical place" signals a violence and erasure enacted by
colonial urbanism, albeit with more causal opacity than Fanon's "lines of force"
drawn by "the policeman and the soldier."[13] This chapter likewise embraces a
less tidy focus on the dynamic use of space—the crowding and jostling of a
tram terminus, a dense commercial artery, or a square flanked promiscuously
by *baladi* and *ifrangi* shops—to reveal a microphysics of power more specific to
the complexity of British occupation and continued control during the interwar period. The elasticity and indeterminacy of space and style visible in the
lived experiences of many local residents ultimately worked to defy a colonial
politics premised on the notion of civilizational divide that was coded by the
dual city.

A discourse about the dual city of colonialism developed through dis-
crepancies in the material nature of building Egypt's main cities. The rapid
development of Europeanized neighborhoods and the relative inattention to
older urban cores created the impression of a new modern city grafted alongside, rather than integrated into, the older city. Rapid demographic changes in

immigration and urbanization seemed to reinforce this pattern. Many elite observers and later scholars disparaged the transitional spaces and neighborhoods between the two cities because their inability to fit into either side of a double-city binarism rendered the overall urban fabric illegible. For many less elite Egyptians, however, inhabiting and patronizing transitional city spaces helped them negotiate the asymmetries of a semicolonial society. A variety of contiguous commercial and consumption practices barnacled urban landscapes. Although such practices could compete with each other, local residents did not clearly or simply order them hierarchically. This chapter explores several prominent urban sites, such as transitional commercial districts, informal and itinerant commerce, and the hublike construction of city squares (*maydans*), to demonstrate the linkages among space, style, and politics. The material fluidity of Egyptian urban space and style underlay the specific contours of interwar colonial politics, particularly the absence of a monolithic Egyptian identity.

THE FORMATION OF A COLONIAL LANDSCAPE

By the time the Tramways Victim complained about the overcrowding of public transportation in 1922, Egyptians were beginning to emerge from a British colonial occupation that had restructured society in dramatic and significant ways since the nineteenth century. British rule formally began in 1882, although European economic, legal, and cultural encroachment had started much earlier. The export nature of the economy, first oriented toward Europe in the late eighteenth and early nineteenth centuries and emphasizing the cultivation of cash crops, most notably long-staple cotton, intensified after international cotton shortages caused by the U.S. Civil War pulled Egypt firmly into the world economy. The end of the nineteenth century witnessed the conversion of much of Egypt's prime and reclaimed agricultural land to cotton, sometimes replacing food crops but more often resulting from intensified use of the land through multiple cropping.[14] European imports of cheap manufactured goods flooded into Egypt in exchange for its raw exports, although population growth, local preferences, and lower prices allowed many indigenous artisans to maintain and at times expand their output of commodities such as shoes, textiles, clothing, furniture, brasswares, pottery, and matting.[15] The French development of the Suez Canal, which opened in 1869 and came under British control in 1875, made Egypt a strategic crossroads in global transportation, and particularly a crucial passageway to India in the British Empire. It also led to the expansion and redesign of Egyptian urban space, as Khedive Ismaʿil initiated a massive

facelift for Cairo for the canal's opening festivities, and Alexandria grew exponentially from its expanded cotton business and increasing seaborne trade and
tourist traffic throughout the nineteenth century.[16] These complex trends consolidated into a formal colonial presence once Egypt defaulted on repayment
of several European loans in the late 1870s, and by 1882 Britain occupied the
country and began to administer it as a veiled protectorate. Although Britain
would formally sever Egypt's connection to the Ottoman Empire and rule it
directly only during the First World War, the long implementation of informal
occupation generated a complex colonial situation.

Since the British administration prioritized the repayment of European
debt during its occupation, its effects on Egyptian society were contradictory. The state allocated massive funds toward the improvement of agricultural systems, including irrigation works and transportation networks, and of
standards of living in the countryside, especially with the abolition of forced
labor. Many large landowners benefited from this attention to agricultural
development. The British attenuated other state development projects, including educational opportunities for Egyptians, urban infrastructural projects,
and judicial reform. The first quarter century of colonial rule occurred under
Lord Cromer (Evelyn Baring; ruled 1883–1907), who was from a prominent
European banking family involved in financing Egypt's debt. It was Cromer's
administration that firmly entrenched the policies of colonial governmentality
in Egypt. "Most of Cromer's previous experience had been in the administration of financial affairs, first in the Dual [Anglo-French financial] Control of
Egypt and later, as virtual finance minister in the government of India. Aus-
tere, though undoubting and self-assured, he approached matters of government and administration from a neat bookkeeping point of view. Such an
approach tended to depoliticize politics and reduce all human affairs to questions of proper administration."[17] An Egyptian bureaucratic class developed
to execute policies through government departments and ministries, although
ultimately political control remained with British officials, backed by military
sanction.[18] Cairo itself housed a British garrison in the Qasr al-Nil barracks,
located between the embassy neighborhood of Garden City and the edge of the
commercial downtown.

Colonial political disenfranchisement overlapped with broader economic
and social disparities created by European imperialism. A system of legal asymmetries, in the form of state and consular protections, supported the colonial
and semicolonial states in Egypt and benefited locally resident foreign subjects

in intricate ways. Originally implemented as part of the Ottoman Capitulations, and still known as the Capitulations, the privileges allowed foreign residents exemption from Egyptian law and taxation, although universal tax reductions under British rule muted this latter benefit.[19] Foreign consular officials could interpret national laws and apply them to their subjects in Egypt, since consular courts retained criminal jurisdiction in cases involving foreigners. To consolidate their sovereignty, the British tried to rein in the capitulatory prerogatives of non-British subjects by curbing some inequalities in taxation, juridical status, and other extraterritorial privileges and founding the Mixed Courts to handle commercial and civil litigation between residents of different nationalities.[20] Considerable fluidity in claiming nationality existed among some segments of Egyptian society as a result of the workings of the juridical landscape and nationality status not being so firmly linked to national identity; before the 1920s no clear legal definition of nationality existed in Egypt.[21] The majority of Egyptians, exempt from its benefits, viewed the Capitulation regime as unfair.[22] It supported a more general colonial perception that foreign labor, products, and cultures were superior to their Egyptian counterparts.[23]

In addition to legal asymmetries, British occupation introduced important political economic arrangements that began to change the commercial and social landscape of Egypt's cities. These mechanisms solidified the varied legal practices around private property, particularly in agricultural land, and encouraged increasingly complex commercial relations, especially through the growing prevalence of joint-stock companies, property companies, commercial houses, stock exchanges, local and foreign banks, a uniform national currency, and paper money. As a result, statistics and economic calculation became the lens through which the state and businessmen made sense of commerce and consumption.[24] These novel economic and social forms tended to separate an *ifrangi* sector from more *baladi* practices around the turn of the century, although the wide circuits of people and money facilitated by European colonialism "made the very economic facts the statistics wished to fix far more elusive and difficult to define."[25] Through such mechanisms, a local bourgeoisie emerged out of Egypt's landed aristocracy and used foreign capital to grow alongside locally resident foreign subjects.[26] Although landowners and the new bourgeois elements benefited from British colonialism, they became increasingly cognizant of their vulnerability in the international market after the financial crash of 1907 and renewed the demands for political and economic representation that had been prominent in the 1880s.

By no means did colonialism dominate every aspect of Egyptian existence during the British occupation. Deep linkages existed in all spheres to social, legal, religious, and economic practices; bodies of knowledge; and institutions that predated the coming of European imperialism.[27] Moreover, as British policies helped over time to generate new social forms and social classes, the agents of change—as colonial or indigenous—became increasingly difficult to differentiate. In this context, an organized nationalist movement began to articulate its ideological opposition to colonial politics in 1906–1907. Spurred by the spectacular British repression of Egyptian peasants after a shooting incident in Dinshawai in 1906, moderate political reform and popular protest to colonialism led in 1907 to the establishment of several nationalist parties, each with its own newspaper. Recruitment among urban laborers through night schools and other organized nationalist activities began to funnel Egyptian anger at the asymmetries of Egyptian society into formal channels until their suspension at the outbreak of the First World War.[28] The war itself was a period of intense deprivation for most Egyptian subjects, as the British requisitioned commodities, animals, and transportation (including tramways) in the service of supplying Allied forces stationed in the Middle East.[29] This activism culminated in a nationalist uprising for Egyptian independence in 1919, although it resulted only in increased executive powers rather than full sovereignty for the nation.

BUILDING THE DUAL CITY: PATTERNS OF URBAN GROWTH AND COMMERCE

The complexity of colonial politics and economic reorientation led to a vast expansion of urban growth. As Egypt's cities burgeoned with rural migrants and workers from southern Europe, Mediterranean islands, and other Ottoman regions, renovation and development clustered in certain geographic areas. Structural changes concentrated on covered marketplaces, wide thoroughfares, orderly squares, and new transportation networks, while older urban cores witnessed less visible infrastructural work. Certainly connected to ideological currents about civilization and progress, the semantics of cultural difference were also in part extrapolated from this built environment, which appeared increasingly saturated with opposing architectural forms and streetscapes in the early twentieth century.

Although Egypt in the nineteenth and twentieth centuries remained overwhelmingly agricultural, the country underwent a demographic revolution of population expansion and urbanization between 1800 and 1957. The Egyptian population grew more than fivefold, from 4.5 million to 24 million people, but the population of the country's largest city, Cairo, expanded twelvefold. By 1960 more than a third of the nation's population lived in cities, which was double the number fifty years earlier; Egypt contained eighty-six urban-sized communities, up from seventeen in 1897.[30] Most urban migrants headed to Cairo, the capital city: between 1897 and 1960, the proportion of the Egyptian population living there increased from less than 8 to over 13 percent.[31] In Alexandria the population expansion particularly occurred in the second half of the nineteenth century: between 1848 and 1897 the population of the city more than tripled; between 1848 and 1927 it grew more than five times.[32] Other large cities included Tanta, with 89,712 inhabitants in 1927; Port Sa'id, which grew from 17,000 in 1883 to 104,603 in 1927; Mansura, 62,815 in 1927; and Fayyum, 52,372 in 1927.[33] This trend toward urbanization accelerated in response to economic growth, especially in services and industry. Major rural-to-urban migrations occurred during and immediately following the First and Second World Wars. Significant changes in public sanitation (drainage and sewer systems) in the 1920s also lengthened the life expectancy of city residents in Cairo, increasing the number of urban residents.[34]

An increase in the foreign-born or foreign national population also swelled Egyptian cities. The largest growth came from Greeks, Italians, North Africans, Maltese, and Ottoman subjects, many of whom came to Cairo in 1897–1907 during a speculative economic boom. In that period, the number of Cairo's residents who had been born outside Egypt increased from roughly 35,000 to 75,000; Alexandria witnessed a similar expansion (from 1897 to 1917, the foreign percentage of the population grew from 14.5 to 19 percent).[35] Egypt's Greek population, for instance, grew by almost 40 percent between 1897 and 1907, to 62,973 people. Alexandria claimed 39 percent of those residents in 1907, Cairo 30.8 percent, and other provincial areas the remaining 30 percent. The Italians in 1907 numbered almost 35,000, of which 83 percent lived in Alexandria or Cairo.[36] Most of these migrants thus remained in Egypt's largest cities, although a substantial number of Greeks moved to provincial cities such as Fayyum, Tanta, Port Sa'id, Suez, and Damanhur.

Expansion of the urban built environment both drew migrants to cities and resulted from these demographic changes. Alexandria witnessed a building boom in the 1830s and 1840s; new sections of the city, such as al-Manshiyya and Labban, were built on previously vacant land, so that "European architects and engineers could lay out the network of streets and buildings in accord with

European tastes."[37] The old town, known in Alexandria as the Turkish town, continued to be populated by Egyptians, North Africans, and local minority groups; this area developed a new, bourgeois residential zone during this time. A belt of less durable, mud-brick huts and houses built to accommodate the incoming rural migrants also coalesced along the western harbor, the Mahmudiya Canal, and east of the old city. The new European quarters of al-Manshiyya and Labban were contiguous with the old city but marked architecturally from it by the use of neoclassical architectural decoration, exposed balconies, and glass windows.[38] According to Michael Reimer, al-Manshiyya, "while not exclusively European, was nevertheless the citadel of European commerce and culture and certainly contained the city's most bourgeois neighborhoods."[39] The center of Manshiyya was Muhammad ʿAli Square, "the commercial and cultural hub of the city,"[40] which by the end of the nineteenth century was encircled by the offices of European shipping lines, Ciccolani's "Egyptian Bazar" department store, fashionable hotels and cafés, and the French consulate.[41] Robert Ilbert notes a local legend that people attired in galabiyas were prohibited from entering the square.[42] The 1870s witnessed further urban development, including street paving in the commercial districts and development of new forms of urban transportation that facilitated movement within the city. By 1929 shops for European goods were found in the eastern quarter, such as department stores Davies Bryan on Sharif Pasha Street or Sednaoui on Sidi al-Mitwalli Street.[43]

The transformation of Cairo and especially its commercial district began slightly later in the 1860s. Municipal development and public hygiene projects since at least the 1840s had straightened and opened Cairo's streets and its infrastructure. Khedive Ismaʿil's visit to Haussmann's remodeled Paris in 1867 prompted the urgent urban development plan that he instituted later that year in Cairo. Under the management of ʿAli Mubarak and other officials, this program of municipal improvement sought to create a European-style city within Cairo that would proclaim Egypt's parity to European powers during the ceremonies marking the opening of the Suez Canal in 1869.[44] The plan called for the development of new residential and commercial quarters to the west of the old city, on land that had been recently drained and reclaimed from the Nile floodplain. The plans of these new sections of town, eventually called the Ismailia, Tawfiqiyya, and ʿAbbasiyya districts, would come to include by the end of the century wide boulevards, public parks and gardens, grand cultural halls (for opera and theater), covered food markets and shopping arcades, a new tramways system, and sumptuous hotels, apartment buildings, villas, and commercial premises. Major government buildings such as the Mixed Tribunals, the royal palace, and consulates and ministries would soon fill out the new landscape. Most of the wide streets and spacious squares of the new quarters were laid out in straight lines, paved, and furnished with sidewalks and lighting.

Efforts to segment the new quarters from the rest of the city were ineffective in practice, however. Sections of the central streets could not be built as straight as planned because of existing religious buildings, very uneven topography, and the diversity of private interests that took over the project once the British colonial government, with its disinterest in nonagricultural development, took power in 1882.[45] Many of these limitations transformed the project of building neighborhoods such as Ismailia from one of adding new quarters outside the old urban fabric into "a project of joining the diverse elements of the urban space" by the end of the century.[46] The colonial state also established different regulatory codes for traffic, parking, building, begging, and vagrancy for various parts of the city, attempting to mark urban space with new juridical boundaries.[47] The state limited access to al-ʿAzbakiyya public garden, for instance, in the heart of the new downtown area, by stipulating an entrance fee and regulations for "appropriate dress."[48] Enforcement of such regulations was inconsistent, however, and turn-of-the-century photographs show crowds of hawkers, shoeblacks, fortunetellers, and tea servers installed along the fences of ʿAzbakiyya.[49] Officials waged a constant battle against residents who defecated and urinated on the sidewalks and fences ringing the park.[50] Nevertheless, such urban regulations contributed to the increasing intrusion of colonial authority into the daily lives and social spaces of Egyptians and sharpened economic differences by overlaying them with markers of social and legal distinction.[51]

Some infrastructural work was completed during this time on the medieval cores of Cairo and Alexandria, but large areas of both cities were left intact.[52] Space in the medieval cores tended to be organized around residential neighborhoods, markets (suqs), and religious institutions such as mosques, religious endowments, or schools. Although no longer gated or perhaps as ethnically homogeneous as once conceived, these older residential neighborhoods (haras) possessed a sense of interconnectedness, as the narrow, winding lanes, alleys, cul-de-sacs, and overhanging buildings rendered semiprivate the space of the street and tended to blend into the more private quarters of the household, especially in lower- and middle-class dwellings. Such spaces were shared for domestic labor and socializing. Often abutting the residential neighborhoods, the suqs comprised open-fronted stalls where merchants and small workshops clustered by type of trade (cloth, shoes, brasswares, gold, and so forth). Grocers, ironers, cafés, and other more regularly patronized establishments were interspersed through these market spaces. Although European tourists considered the Khan al-Khalili market in Cairo to epitomize these older suqs, local Egyptians more frequently patronized markets such as cloth merchants in the Hamzawi or the shoemakers in the Darb al-Ahmar in Cairo.[53] Much like the extension of domestic space into the streets of the *hara*, the street in the suq functioned as an extension of the shop, and as such was an important location for the display of goods. Moreover, it provided a space for the customer converse with other shoppers or merchants, without the obligation to purchase.[54]

The disparity in the pace of building between newly laid out quarters and the medieval cores in the second half of the nineteenth century caused contemporaries to view urban development in Egypt through a lens of the dual city. Jeremiah Lynch, writing during a several-month residence in Cairo in 1889–1890, remarked, for example, that "there are two Cairos—the Old and the New. New Cairo contains the Ismalieh and the Abbasiyeh quarters. The Ismalieh portion . . . is called the European quarter, and the streets running through it contain the shops where foreigners make their purchases. The thousands of Greeks, Italians, and Frenchmen who live permanently in Cairo inhabit this and the Abbasiyeh districts."[55] A visitor to Alexandria in the 1880s also saw that city as "divided in two completely distinct sections: the Arab city and the European city. The first include[d] the old quarters . . . [and, in the second,] the houses [were] built in the same style as the houses of Europe."[56] Even the provincial city of Mansura appeared in a popular European guidebook in 1929 in similar terms: "The town is regularly laid out and the crowded Arab quarter is gradually disappearing before modern streets."[57]

The commercial artery of Cairo's Muski Street—running on an east–west axis between the new Ismailia's modern shops and the artisanal suqs in the older Islamic quarter—functioned in many European accounts as the physical and metaphoric link between the capital's two cities. The British traveler Douglas Sladen described it in 1911 as "the chief avenue leading down to the native city, and not so many years ago [it] was full of picturesque native houses. Now it is as shoddy as it is squashy. . . . The street is absolutely packed with Arabs flowing from their city to goodness knows where. . . . [T]he whole effect is one of cheap shops kept by Greeks, to which the European goes for certain odds and ends, and the native for cheap splendour in his apparel."[58] The derivative nature of the merchandise for sale in the Muski district prompted Sladen to map the transition between the two cities in language inflected by social Darwinism. "Where it debouches into the Ataba [the Muski] has shops like the hosiers' and jewellers' in the Strand would be if they were kept by Levantines. But as it approaches the bazars it gets lower and lower in the scale of commerce. What scanty remains there are of the old mansions are faced with shallow shops of the toy, button, and baby-ribbon type; shops where German socks with undeveloped heels and music-hall umbrellas are flanked with scarlet cotton handkerchiefs and shoes on strings; shops of slop-tailors and chemists who live by the sale of noxious drugs and other less reputable commodities, for chemists cannot live by drugs alone in the Musky. Tarbush-sellers of course there are: that stamps a cheap street."[59] All accessories or tailoring details used as morsels in an outfit to mark their bearer as distinct from those in conventional local dress, *ifrangi* items such as socks, shoes, buttons, umbrellas, and *tarabish* (the plural of tarbush), appeared threatening in the Muski district for observers such as Sladen because they circulated detached from the full-body mannequin displays and complete Western outfits exhibited in the department stores just a few streets away in the *ifrangi* downtown. An east–west commercial artery, Muski Street represented for such viewers, then, the meeting of the two separate worlds in the colonial city. Europeans, venturing out from the Qasr al-Nil British military barracks or fancy hotels such as Shepheard's and the Continental around the ʿAzbakiyya Garden and Opera Square, just beyond the ʿAtaba, literally and metaphorically moved eastward toward the Muski's shops for small and cheap purchases they were reluctant to make at the more expensive oriental stores near the hotels, or they penetrated into the older bazaars for souvenirs or to view native life. For local Egyptians, passage down the street took them westward into the modern quarter, although travelers such as Sladen could not imagine what business the natives had with modernity (their destination westward—"flowing from their city to goodness knows where"—was simply unknowable and unthinkable) except to purchase "cheap splendour" for their apparel. Sladen's book is illustrated with numerous Kodak snapshots of what he saw as incongruities of cultural crossing: Egyptians lunching on the ground in front of a restaurant or galabiya-attired boys hawking newspapers. The captions accompanying the photographs suggest that such improvised uses of space were amusing mistakes by Egyptians who were so backward that they did not understand proper social or sartorial behavior. The pictures represent static views of lived experience and resonate with his more general focus on external architectural forms as markers of meaning.

By the turn of the century, many Egyptians themselves used a double-city discourse to criticize British power or as a class-based form of social control or critique of local policies and governance. Muhammad al-Muwaylihi's *Hadith 'Isa Ibn Hisham*, written between 1898 and 1907, made use of this duality to complain of the newer practices and corruption of the colonial period.[60] Architectural style was the initial focus for these dual-city models in travel literature and guidebooks, probably because for non-Arabic-speaking observers, static, exterior architectural forms were more legible and socially accessible than the interior or the use of that space. Attempts to spatially bifurcate the city thus carried broader implications about culture and history, and from the architecture, an entire semantics of cultural difference was eventually extrapolated: the dual city came to code for bifurcations in clothing styles, patterns of work and production, consumption styles, family relations, cultural orientation, and so forth.

ROUNDABOUTS OF URBAN COMMERCE

The idea of a radically dichotomized, or split, city was comforting and legible to foreign travelers, colonial officials, Egyptian elites, and liberal social reformers wishing to assert the power to maintain or critique European dominance. As Sladen's account of the Muski district suggests, more uncomfortable were urban transitional zones, those spaces where the two cities and sets of cultural practices or consumption styles met and intermingled. In Cairo, 'Ataba al-Khadra' (the green threshold) Square, located at the top of Muski Street, just two blocks southeast of the 'Azbakiyya Garden, formed such a liminal space in the city, as its name suggests. The neighborhood had been created by two major thoroughfares built to pierce the old urban fabric and link it to the area of the city developing to the west: Muski Street, first begun under Muhammad 'Ali and completed in the 1860s during Isma'il's reign, linked 'Ataba Square to the eastern edge of the city; in the 1920s the wider al-Azhar Street was opened up running south of and parallel to Muski Street, connecting 'Ataba Square and the Azhar Mosque, also nearly at the eastern edge of the city.[61] Like nearby Muski Street, 'Ataba often moved foreign observers to bewail its "unattractive mélange having neither the modernity of the Western zone nor the exotic charm of the Eastern bazaars: a place of crudely fashioned but brightly colored imitations of Western products."[62] Sladen again remarked in 1911, "The Ataba-el-Khadra is the epitome of the unmediaeval and unlovely native life. Here, instead of spending their lives in doing next to nothing for next to nothing in a dignified and picturesque way, every one is hurrying or touting. There are a

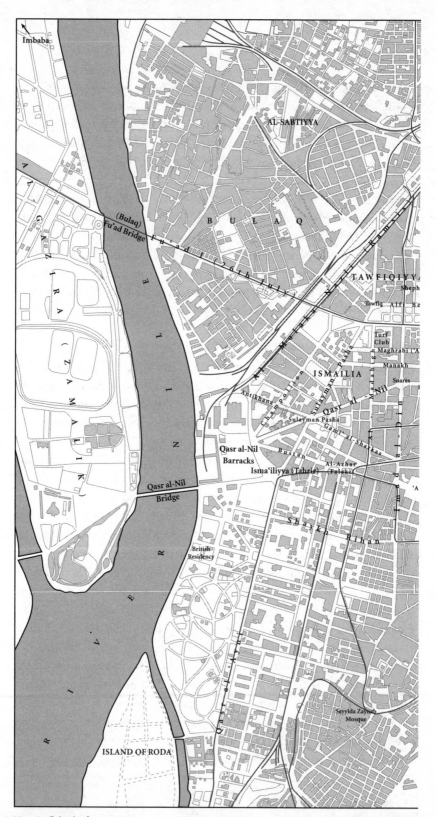

Map 1. Cairo in the 1920s

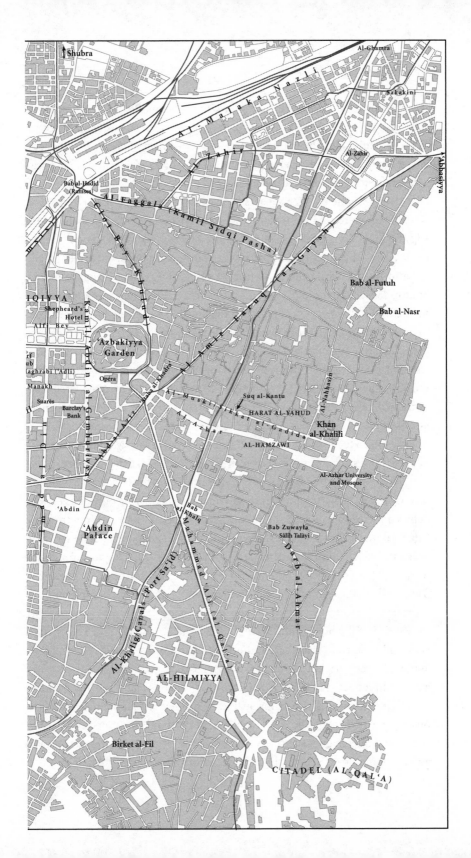

few immense shops kept by German Jews, which tempt the native issuing from the Musky with resplendent European hosiery; a jostle of nearly all the trams in Cairo—this being their chief starting-point; a crowd of *arabeahs* (carriages) and donkeys; and an ever-changing crowd of natives trying to sell European articles to each other, or to clean each other's boots."[63]

ʿAtaba was one of three squares (*maydans*) created adjacent to ʿAzbakiyya when it was converted from a lake to a formal garden in the late 1860s on the edge of the older city. A rectangular plaza attached to a roundabout, ʿAtaba made a perfect turnaround for carriages, trams, omnibuses, automobiles, and other forms of transportation. In fact, six of the city's original eight tramlines, built in 1898, commenced in ʿAtaba, and another local loop was added to the square in 1903. By 1917 "most points in the built-up zone were within a fifteen- to twenty-minute radius of the hub at al-ʿAtabah al-Khadra'."[64] Breaking down the isolation of previously self-contained neighborhoods in the city, the tramways led to the commercial development of the area around ʿAtaba Square and the new downtown district.[65] Although the tram barely penetrated large parts of the old city, it did connect the older market spaces of the Muski, Gamaliyya, and Hamzawi districts to the new area of Ismailia; in other words, it most directly linked the primary commercial sections of the city. Moreover, as a map of the tram system from 1937 shows, the layout of the system was more spoke-like than bifurcated (see Figure 2). The new tram lines thus linked the old commercial city to various points in the new, rather than offering only one corridor between them: one of the first lines installed (no. 3), for example, ran from the Citadel down Muhammad ʿAli Street through Opera Square, then down Fuʾad Street to Bulaq;[66] another line passed by the Khan al-Khalili and through the Muski to Opera Square and the start of Fuʾad Street. According to Muhammad Sayyid Kilani, the tram's popularity was due to its cheap fare, its long hours of operation (it ran from six in the morning until one a.m.), and its accessibility for women.[67] The horse-pulled omnibus, private horse-drawn carriages, donkeys, and pedestrian walks serviced other routes around the city. Automobiles appeared after 1903, but owing to the high costs of repair, became widespread among the upper classes only in the 1930s.[68] ʿAtaba's status as "the crowded converging point of all the tramway lines"[69] made it a stopping point for various itineraries through the city. Like the center of a hub, it connected the city's spokes and offered goods and services for city travelers passing through as well as an endpoint for those traveling up the various spokes. Thus ʿAtaba served as "the heart of the city."[70]

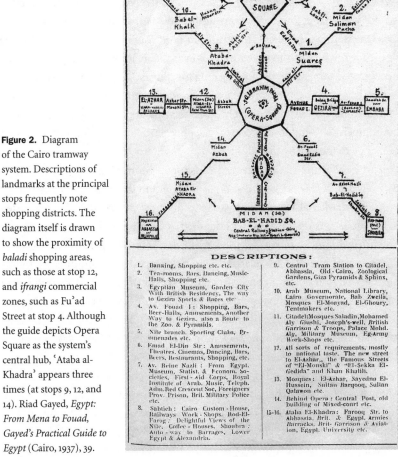

Figure 2. Diagram of the Cairo tramway system. Descriptions of landmarks at the principal stops frequently note shopping districts. The diagram itself is drawn to show the proximity of *baladi* shopping areas, such as those at stop 12, and *ifrangi* commercial zones, such as Fu'ad Street at stop 4. Although the guide depicts Opera Square as the system's central hub, 'Ataba al-Khadra' appears three times (at stops 9, 12, and 14). Riad Gayed, *Egypt: From Mena to Fouad, Gayed's Practical Guide to Egypt* (Cairo, 1937), 39.

Off one side of the square a road led into the Jewish quarter (*harat al-yahud*). From another, one could head down Muski Street into the bazaars of the old city, crossing by a small lane that paralleled Canal Street, called Bayn al-Nahdayn Street and known for its sellers of notions (*tujjar al-kurdawat*), and the nearby flea market (*suq al-kantu*).[71] In yet another direction, toward Opera Square, 'Ataba opened to the buildings that housed colonial power in the city, such as the Mixed Tribunals and the Public Debt Commission offices, as well as a variety of important municipal service buildings, including the post office and the police station.[72] The two-story Central Fire Station at 'Ataba had been constructed in 1905 to resemble those in Glasgow and Belfast.[73] Despite its staff of 103 firemen, its 13 "young English horses, specially imported," and its collection of steam-powered and manual fire engines and ladders, the fire service was unable to put out some of the city's worst fires. In 1909, just blocks from the station, a large fire gutted an acre of houses in the Muski, since "owing to the narrowness of the streets and to the limited supply of water, the brigade experienced some difficulty in attacking the flames."[74] A telephone exchange at 'Ataba was completely automated by the middle 1920s, providing the first such service in the city that did not rely on large numbers of young women switchboard operators, and it served more telephone users than any other telephone exchange in the city by 1927.[75]

Just behind the square between Muski and Muhammad 'Ali Streets were the New Market Halls that the municipality built in the 1890s to replace the old vegetable market at the beginning of Muski Street, which, *al-Ahram* reported at the time, "was unanimously condemned as harmful to public health."[76] Like other new outdoor markets for food, many of which were constructed between the 1890s and 1912 in Cairo in areas that served as stops or terminuses for multiple tramway and other rail lines, these "new types of markets . . . differed markedly from their traditional counterparts. Instead of convening once a week, they were installed in large permanent buildings equipped with the facilities to maintain health standards and they were open to the public six, and sometimes seven days a week."[77] 'Ataba market was built in a formal, *ifrangi* style "around two covered alleys, bringing together four principal pavilions, each of them having a specialty: butcher shops, a fish market, the sale of fruits or vegetables, and a spice/grocery market [*épicerie*]. Two smaller pavilions . . . housed bakeries."[78] In 1909 observers remarked on the animated scene the market stalls presented. "Camels being unloaded, Egyptian fellaheen squatting with their wives, a rich display of fruit and vegetables, streams of buyers, porters, Bedouins, and pedlars, are so grouped together as to make this corner of the capital one of the most interesting."[79]

A wide variety of commercial and professional services were available in the three- or four-story buildings that, with shade trees, flanked 'Ataba's central plaza and the covered platforms and open tracks of the tram terminus located nearby.[80] The names of their proprietors point to the ethnic variety and intermingling in this part of the city. In 1918 a customer could take refreshment in cafés and restaurants such as the Center of Cairo (run by the Heliopoulo brothers), the Citadelle (operated by the Stelianopoulos brothers), the Galossos, the

Mahroussa, the Parthenon, or the Grand Café de Ataba el-Khadra.[81] One could pray at a mosque, attend a concert at the Thousand and One Nights Theatre, and buy postcards and office supplies at K. H. Guzélimian, pharmaceuticals at the Joannides Chemists, or cigarettes from Melkonian. The Bazar Mourour, its name painted in large Latin characters on the top of the building and its distinctive balconies looking over the street, housed a diverse range of small shops, workshops, and services right at the entrance to the Jewish quarter of the city on the Muski side of the square. Although Bazar Mourour was populated by merchants whose names suggest many ethnic backgrounds, *murur*, which means "movement" or "passageway" in Arabic, has been identified recently as the quintessential feature of Islamic (and non-Western) business spaces.[82] The scale of activities and crowds at ʿAtaba could easily overwhelm its visitors. In 1909 Wright and Cartwright noted, "Without doubt it is the noisiest part of the city. What with the raucous shouting of the pedlars, the rattling of the water-carriers' tiny brass trays, the blowing of motor car trumpets, and the ringing of tram-car bells, the grinding of wheels, and clanging of iron-shod hoofs against cobbles—the uproar [was] heightened now and again by the voices of men and women in passionate controversy. . . . At the same time, and from a neighbouring crowded café, comes the monotonous tric-trac, tric-trac of backgammon."[83]

Four of the city's "largest drapery and clothing stores" dotted the square.[84] Two well-patronized establishments belonged to Ibrahim al-Mawardi and Hasan Bey Madkur, whose large store housed "a variety of merchandise in each department" and had been patronized in person by the Khedive ʿAbbas, report-edly the first time an Egyptian ruler had entered a commercial store in Egypt.[85] The Vienna-based Tiring Department Store, with its distinctive globe-topped cupola, four floors, and fin de siècle style, and Stein's Oriental Stores, stocking "every conceivable requisite for the complete outfitting of man, woman, or child," were visible presences on the square in 1909. Lined by fifty meters of front shop windows, Stein's boasted an electric lift, electric lighting through-out the store (provided by its own generator), and a staff of 180 employees.[86] The interior of the shop was spacious and organized by neat wooden shelving around large counters where goods were piled high for customer inspection. Numerous large lamps, broad mirrors, and glass cases reflected light on the mannequin and tabletop displays throughout the shop. Stein's sold a range of goods, some imported from England, France, and its own factories in Vienna, "where particular attention [was] given to the local requirements of Egypt."[87] The store drew many local customers but also served clients in the broader region and would deliver purchases over a certain price "free of charge to any part of Egypt or the Soudan" in 1909. By the early twentieth century, Stein's had branch stores in Alexandria, Mansura, Tanta, Minya, and Asyut and in Istanbul, Salonica, and Vienna, although many of these would be sequestered in the First World War.[88]

The Waqfs Building at ʿAtaba no longer held the religious Ministry of Pious Endowments, which by 1918 was located farther west on Gamaʿ Sharkas Street, but rather housed various services—the offices of the Syndicat des Ouvriers, the Ibrahim al-Mawardi department store, the coiffeur Gad Abdel-Azziz, the offices of at least six physicians (Ali Rassikh, Selim Bahgat, A. Chirinian, Hamid Chaker Bey, Hasan Mahmud Bey, and Husayn Mahmud Bey), several branches of city pharmacies, and the import-export offices of Ghanem and Chahin.[89] The Household Cooperative Society for Government Employees in Cairo was housed on the building's second floor and held "normal business hours." According to its 1926 catalog, the cooperative offered an inventory of "indispensable everyday commodities [al-hajiyat al-daruriya]" that combined European imports and local products.[90] Government employees epitomized the effendi status group, educated but not simply Westernized professionals who struggled with the rising cost of living.[91] Unlike the glitzy advertising catalogs of the department stores, its catalog—titled a fihris ("index")—was simply a listing of products for sale through the cooperative. Although the catalog divided commodities between foodstuffs and clothing, goods appeared in those sections arrayed alphabetically rather than grouped functionally. The clothing and accessory styles offered by the store ranged from baladi styles such as the sudayri (a men's short, sleeveless vest), shawl, and kufiya (men's headscarf) to more modern items such as suits (bidal), silk neckties, and cigarette cases. The cooperative purveyed Rosetta rice, Syrian hazelnuts, Yemeni coffee, rosewater, and dates alongside European pastilles, Castor Cream biscuits, shortbread cookies, Four O'Clock biscuits, and French bonbons. Gillette razors; Swiss tea services; library clocks; school bags; sets of forks, spoons, and knives; suspenders for pants and socks; collar pins; and men's "ifranki" shirts mixed with shibshibs (slippers), camphor oil, and an entire section devoted to various styles of the tarbush and its accessories.[92] In 1909 the Waqfs Building was prominently (and some observers thought ironically) topped by "the huge signboard of a well-known whisky firm."[93]

Although few parts of Egypt's cities matched the scale of ʿAtaba as a hub, other roundabouts of commerce and residential life were important in the urban fabric. Covered food-market spaces were also built in Cairo at Tawfiqi-yya in the 1890s, at the Cairo train station (Bab al-Hadid) in 1910, and at Bab al-Luq in 1912.[94] The Alexandria New Market, outfitted in white Carrara marble with nickel-plated fittings, opened at the turn of the century "in the very heart of Alexandria, [where] the principal thoroughfares converge at its gates."[95] The master plan for the old city of Cairo drawn up in the late 1870s envisioned a series of thirteen or more squares scattered throughout the old and new sections of the city, each acting as a hub in a wide system of thoroughfares. Those in the denser urban neighborhoods were more difficult and expensive to execute, however, because of the need to acquire and demolish many residential, commercial, and monumental properties.[96] These hublike squares included ʿAtaba, ʿAbdin, Khazindar, Bab al-Hadid, Bab al-Luq, Muhammad ʿAli, Opera, al-Azhar (later Falaki), Sultan Hasan, Qasr al-Nil (later Tahrir), Birkat al-Fil, Bab al-Futuh, and Sayyida Zaynab. Despite the initial difficulties in executing the master plan, its vision continued to "exert a lasting influence on later attempts to open up the old city, and a number of projected streets and *maydans* were eventually constructed almost as" master planners had envisioned.[97] Sayyida Zaynab Square, for example, lay to the south of ʿAtaba Square, at the bend of the old canal bed that was filled and transformed into Cairo's first "centrally located north–south thoroughfare" for the tram and a wide variety of other forms of transportation by 1900.[98]

Fathi Radwan, a well-known writer, professor, and eventually minister of culture under the Nasser regime who founded Young Egypt (a political group) with Ahmad Husayn in the early 1930s, has argued for the profound influence these transportation and commercial hubs had on the subjectivity of individual Cairenes. The squares at ʿAtaba, at Sayyida Zaynab, and in Giza feature prominently in his memory of Cairo during the 1910s and 1920s. Radwan's family had owned moderate amounts of land in the Delta, and before he was born, Radwan's father became a government employee in the Irrigation Department, a job that took the family to Upper Egypt, Giza, and finally back to the center of Cairo while Radwan was a young boy. Radwan inflected his memoir of this childhood with a deep sense of the interlocking of urban geography, commerce, and subjectivity, clearly linking space and style in nonbinary ways. *Khatt al-ʿataba: hayat tifli misri* (The Line of the Threshold: The Life of an Egyptian Child) presents a series of vivid tableaux, often describing at length the houses, neighborhoods, and people that shaped him or small objects and aspects of appearance that struck him (e.g., his mother's handkerchief, a pack of cigarettes, different types of ice cream) in an uncluttered and focused way typical of many young children's perception.[99]

The memoir's title alludes to the interconnectivity of urban space as a factor shaping individual subjectivity. In addition to meaning "the line of the threshold," *Khatt al-ʿataba* refers to the Cairo tramline (*khatt*) to ʿAtaba Square. The ʿAtaba line prominently links Radwan's experience of the city to his coming of age. It introduced him to literature, because when relatives taking the tram to ʿAtaba "on an outing to work or for amusement" brought him along, he spied and later bought his first literary journals and newspapers, hawked by merchants near the tram terminus. It created the bustling commercial and pedestrian activity around Sayyida Zaynab Square near his home. It sustained the kiosk next to his tram stop in Giza—that "magic box" where a Greek woman merchant sold candy, bottled water, newspapers, toys, and other small merchandise—that he remembers most vividly from this young age.[100] The tramline works to stitch together Radwan's memories, which are dispersed through time and the space of the city, providing striking evidence of the power of transitional spaces and mobility as crucial experiences of city life.

Radwan's description of commercial and urban space as cultural markers in the memoir relies more on a language of contiguity or propinquity (although clearly hierarchialized) than of one of radical duality or dichotomy. He depicts spaces of transition as central hubs rather than as dividing lines in the city. His portrayal of the transportation available in Sayyida Zaynab Square is one such example. The tramways, he argues, occupied the top rung among the various modes of urban transportation, but these were intermingled in the square rather than spatially separated in different parts of the city. "In the square, five eras exist in the form of five modes of transportation: a stand for donkeys, Caro cars, horse-drawn victorias [*hanturs*], Suares buses, and the stop for the official tram. For each of these modes, a customer exists: the donkeys represent the seventeenth century; the Caro car represents the beginning of the eighteenth century; the *hantur* carriage represents the mid-eighteenth century; the Suares is the omnibus led by mules, and it was owned by a Jew who grew so exceedingly rich that he gave his name to a square in Cairo where it remained until the name Mustafa Kamil replaced it; and the tram represents the nineteenth century."[101] Radwan's chronological and nonbinary listing is not without conflict. He refuses to give the Jewish-owned mode of transportation, the Suares omnibus, a historical presence in time. Its elision and narrative replacement by a nationalist sign, Mustafa Kamil, is characteristic of his brand of ultranationalism in the 1930s and 1940s.[102]

Clustered around the tram stop in Radwan's depiction was an equally wide array of clothing styles. These styles, composed of different combinations of discrete items of clothing, such as headgear or suits, evoked class differentiation but represented it as a fluid semiotic code. Despite the coverage of their bodies by long black wraps, the women emerged as differentiated by the cuts and qualities of the fabric of their clothing.

> At the tram stop stand women dressed in *milaya* [long, plain wrap], and women dressed in *habara* [black silk or velvet outer wrap] and *tazyira* [black wrap worn by middle-class women]. The white *burquʿ* [face veil] covers some of their faces. . . . In addition to all these, the twentieth century appears in the picture of the women students of the Saniyya School, demanding knowledge.[103]

The men's clothing offered an even wider variety of morseled styles.

> Next to them are a group of men as if they are figures in a museum, wearing the turban, the *jabba* [buttonless, long outer robe], and *quftan* [caftan], or the turban and *gallab baladi* [galabiya], and wearing the *tarbush* with the *jabba* and *quftan* together, and with the *gallab baladi* at another time, and wearing the *libda* [felt skullcap], the *taqiya* [white skullcap] and the *lasa* [white wrapper of fine silk or linen worn around the skullcap; i.e., a turban] with an *ifrangi* suit. Some wear this suit not convincing by it proof of their westernization if they pull up the tops of their socks [*shawaribihim*] like the edge of a knife.[104]

Details of sartorial style point to how consumers used dichotomies such as *ifrangi-baladi* to convey subtle messages about status and cultural affiliation. Combining a Western-tailored suit with socks pulled up too high or incongruously wearing a tarbush and a galabiya and shifting to tarbush and *jabba* or turban and suit made only a certain statement because such items of apparel participated in a shifting semiotic code.

Much like his description of urban transportation systems and dress, Radwan's description of the commerce in Sayyida Zaynab invoked dichotomized language but did not map that onto a spatial separation. Radwan wrote, for instance, that "scattered around the square are a number of commercial stores [*al-mahall al-tijariyya*] and coffee shops, each one of which represents an era. . . . [There is a] shop of an *ifrangi* barber . . . and next to him is a *baladi* barber . . . who not only beautifies hair and heads but who is more than a doctor [selling leeches and removing teeth]."[105] Radwan attributed this "haphazard" and "scattered" arrangement in the square to a paucity of "organization [*tanzim*]." "Thus, we see shops [*hawanit*; sing. *hanut*] adjoining each other without logic or guiding principle."[106] He cited by way of example, "a bookstore that sells school books, such as Riyad bookstore, [that] is next to a *masmat*, a shop that sells trotters [*kawari*ʿ], tripe, and brains, and next to the mortician [*hanuti*] of Sayyida Zaynab, who undertakes funeral services, such as shrouding the dead, the presentation of biers, and the provision of a kind of worker [professional mourners] whose era is extinct and vanished."[107] More elaborate still is Radwan's description of a textile store next door to the funeral shop.

> Next to this shop [*dukkan*] is an eminent store [*mahall wagih*], whose front windows [*wagiha*] were decorated with electric lights for the Prophet's birthday and religious and national holidays. Standing at its door is a man with broad shoulders and a wide chest, of medium height, wheaten colored . . . wearing a caftan and *jabba*, which emanate a special scent, and [sporting] a thin mustache arranged on his face like a sentinel of elegance. . . . That is al-Ziftawi's store [*mahall al-Ziftawi*], which achieved great fame and profit, and whose owner seduces the rich of the neighborhood among the women who wear a *milaya* with . . . the "exquisite qualities" of what he purveys to them.[108]

In al-Ziftawi's store the seeming contradictions of shop windows and electric lights mingled easily with *baladi* merchandise, the *milaya*-clad customers, and a traditionally attired merchant, whose name recalls that of an old style of hand-woven cloth produced in Zifta, a Delta town near Tanta.[109] Radwan's description of city space is notable for its complexity. Its reflection of the morseling consumption style of a variety of urban classes challenges didactic portrayals of two juxtaposed cultures of consumption. Using time rather than culture, Radwan specifically articulates different forms of transportation, clothing, and commercial premises. Radwan's observations resonate with slightly later marketing surveys that noted such an interweaving of styles of commerce; Abdel Aziz El Sherbini and Ahmed Fouad Sherif argue that "central shopping districts constitute the core of the retailing structure in urban centers. They are typically a mixture of the old and the new."[110]

Others remembered Cairo also as a more complex urban entity than the dual city that supposedly appeared on maps. Magdi Wahba's memoir deliberately invokes a triple-city model of overlapping spaces, all of which were moving. He writes:

> The Cairo of my childhood in the early 1930s was one of three converging cities. The first was middle-class and residential, with nervously centrifugal tendencies, moving out of the traditional residential quarters of Abbassia, Ezbekia, Helmia, and Moneera, to the relatively new ones of Heliopolis, Zamalek, Garden City and Giza. . . . The second city was the commercial centre, consisting of a triangle of three tree-lined streets—Kasr-el-Nil, Soliman Pasha, and Fuad. . . . The third city was nomadic. Like amoebae regrouping, it wandered from the narrow alleys of the area between the Citadel, the Azhar and Abbassia, to the outskirts of Shubra, Zeitoun, the island of Roda and the loose conurbation of Giza behind the Zoo. The lower-middle class lived here, . . . and also the small shopkeeper class, . . . the impoverished ulema of the Azhar, and the lower rungs of the clerical hierarchies in the Ministries.[111]

Wahba's description echoes Radwan's focus on hubs and depiction of urban elasticity scored by social conflict. The intermingling of spatial style and cultural orientation recounted by Radwan and Wahba points to how the modern, or *ifrangi*, depended on the traditional, or *baladi*, for meaning within urban commercial zones.[112]

BALADI DIMENSIONS OF THE IFRANGI SECTOR

While market researchers would come to associate the interweaving of commercial styles with neighborhood or transitional retail districts, more densely packed and smaller merchant areas that closely resembled the scale of commerce in the "old city" were interspersed as well among the sleek and large-scale commercial buildings of downtown areas.[113] "Commercial Alley [*al-mamarr al-tijari*]," for example, was a tiny but incredibly densely populated passageway that ran between Fu'ad and 'Adli Streets in Cairo's Ismailia district. The alley, only 6 meters wide and 150 meters long, formed in 1910 when two large buildings were built on either side. In the 1910s, "when commercial activity in the area became brisk," the owner of the buildings converted the alleyway into a warehouse for the merchandise of nearby merchants. New owners in 1928 remodeled the space into a thoroughfare by demolishing the barrier at one end and established shops and workshops along both sides of the passageway. By 1948 Commercial Alley contained 119 commercial stores and workshops: twenty tailors, fourteen seamstresses for women's clothing, twelve sellers of notions, nine vendors of women's handbags and suitcases, nine shoe shops, eight grocers, eight photography studios, seven cloth shops, six sellers of trinkets and women's jewelry, six cafés, five tobacconists, four sellers of ready-made clothing, four restaurants, four sellers of children's toys, and three vendors of radios. All told, 714 people worked in the passageway (in addition to the 320 residents of the eighty apartments upstairs from the shops).[114] Although much of the merchandise retailed in the alley connected to the *ifrangi* goods proffered by the larger stores nearby (fancy goods, handbags, radios, and cigarettes, for example), a photograph of the alley in 1948 shows goods such as bags and cookware displayed hung up outside open-front shops or piled on tables in the street, in a manner usually associated with the suqs of the medieval cores or areas such as ʿAtaba. Several food stores crowded together featured large, open canvas sacks of nuts, grains, and spices; another advertised jams and sweets from Damascus.[115]

Even on the main commercial boulevards, small-scale and informal commerce crowded the modern building facades. Hawkers peddled wares on Fu'ad Street, even though selling on the street without a fixed shop location, an activity that went against a modern, clean, and rational style of commerce associated with the new downtown, was illegal. "Some [hawkers] . . . spread out [their merchandise] on the sidewalk in a fixed or permanent manner and made for themselves on the pavement a spontaneous store for their merchandise."[116] ʿUthman Muhammad al-Maliji was a thirty-year-old vendor of sweets and dates from a cart in front of the modern Saʿidiyya School in the 1930s. He had inherited the trade from his father, and he and his father had originally worked together at another school in Cairo.[117] Some of the Alexandrian newspaper publishing houses provided new jumpsuits to their itinerant newspaper vendors. They hoped that these new clothes would cause the salesmen to renounce their conventional galabiyas and thus appear more in tune with "the [modern] spirit of the age" that the newspaper strove to represent.[118] Informal salesmen often sold *ifrangi* merchandise, such as the men who in 1914 retailed stationery supplies "to the public writers residing in the back of the Mixed Tribunals" in ʿAzbakiyya Square from their "cupboards" of roughly one meter in length.[119] A "Union of Itinerant Salesmen [*niqabat al-baʿa al-mutajawwilin*]" claimed in 1944 that its members generally carried goods worth merely £E1, which consisted of novelties and "foreign goods that do not weigh more than two or three kilos, such as eyeglasses, pens, eastern knickknacks, and writing instruments that are light in weight." These salesmen stationed themselves in areas of high consumer and tourist traffic in upscale commercial districts, such as "in front of shops" or "on verandahs of hotels," or advertised their goods "while acting as guides."[120]

Individual merchants also alternated or interwove different styles of commerce, sometimes emphasizing a more Islamic or Egyptian identity, while at other times employing more *ifrangi* commercial practices. ʿAwf Department Store, specializing in the wholesale and retail of textiles, was founded in 1914 near the Husayn mosque in the center of the old commercial zone of Cairo. The store catered to the more *baladi* and lower-middle-class residents of the area, as well as the students at the nearby Islamic university of al-Azhar; one of its specialties was outfitting Muslims to make the pilgrimage to Mecca.[121] Nevertheless, the store's organization and spatial layout were quite modern and rational. The store, which employed about twenty-five people in the 1930s, consisted of two floors, and despite its relatively small size, it had goods arranged in departments or sections of the store. On the first floor were departments for women's veils and hosiery; upholstery; sheets, napkins, blankets, and towels; and even a separate section devoted to special clothing for the pilgrimage. Its wholesale business was located on the second floor, creating a separate department. Transactions were based on fixed prices rather than bargaining.[122] ʿAbd al-Karim Hasan's sweet shop in the Muski offered "Eastern" sweets and "European-style" chocolates and bonbons (*mulabbasat ifrangiyya*), as well as tea and "all the latest sweets of the season." The shop promoted itself in the local press and even offered "rapid home delivery of its selections." Despite these *ifrangi* products and services, the store advertised itself in a *baladi* calligraphic script and closed its advertising texts with Islamic religious injunctions.[123]

While intermingling *baladi* and *ifrangi* commercial practices represented one strategy, another was the translation or adaptation of *ifrangi* articles in local materials or new sartorial relationships. The used clothing market, *suq al-kantu*, provided in particular the opportunity to purchase morsels of clothing that were ordinarily sold downtown as an entire set. The market lay near the Muski close to the opening of ʿAtaba Square, or in the heart of the transitional zone. Its merchants displayed used clothes hanging on racks under informal shelters, and the market hosted regular auctions of clothing.[124] Probably named after the Italian word for song (*canto*), the market's name, according to local lore, derived from the combined songlike calls of its merchants or for its cheap prices by which it retailed goods for a song. Ever on the lookout for authentic souvenirs, Douglas Sladen noted in 1911 that the market sold "for mere songs the lovely old Persian shawls which are hand-worked as close as if they were woven, and the gossamer veils of silk coloured like the rainbow worn by dancing women, and wonderful Arab dresses which have done duty for *bedawin* sheikhs and will do duty for many fancy-dress balls. Embroideries, too, can be bought here, the patient embroideries of the harem, done before harem doyleys and cushion-covers became a regular line with London drapers."[125] The flea market was best known for selling the used but fashionable clothing of the local elites to lower-class and lower-middle-class urban employees trying to ascend or at least maintain a position in the urban business world, where competencies in *ifrangi* culture were valued as a marker of qualification. In a slightly satirical comparison of local markets selling used merchandise to the poor in Cairo, Yahya Haqqi described the flea market in the following terms.[126] Haqqi peopled the *suq al-kantu* with devious merchants, procuring their wares from thieves and undertakers, and with poor, recently urbanized employees. One such character was "a gaunt, wan boy (suffering from bilharzia, or schistosomiasis), attired in striped galabiya with an oily jacket over top. Perhaps he is an accountant in a *wakala* [a commercial warehouse in the medieval city]," who is persuaded to purchase a new jacket in the market. The merchant tells him the jacket is "from the house of a Pasha, who only wore it for a few months, then bestowed it on his cook. He then sold it in an hour of need." Displaying "the jacket begging on his hand, while he pulls it into shape with his other hand . . . [the merchant] grabs [the customer] in the middle of the crowd to whisper in his ear" about the history of the item. The market specialized in a range of *ifrangi* secondhand clothing: "Egyptian suits, effendi suits, and sometimes the suits of beys and pashas. Some even had the signature of the most famous [*ifrangi*] tailors of the time, Delia and Fista. But rarely would you find a complete suit. You would buy a jacket without its pants or pants without its jacket or an orphaned waistcoat [*sudayri*], having lost its mother and father. This morseling was the secret reason for the [successful] sales of the flea market, for you cannot imagine how many people were on tight budgets. For the many people who wore over a galabiya a jacket purchased without pants or a vest, the *suq al-kantu* was the only place in Cairo to acquire it."[127] Thus, like Radwan's residents of Sayyida Zaynab Square, flea-market customers mixed sartorial morsels in seemingly incongruous ways.

On the other end of the spectrum of informal *ifrangi* commerce was an active trade in couture dresses from the personal wardrobes of elite women to their family members, acquaintances, or tailors. In 1947 the French commercial agent complained to French officials about the contraband and counterfeit of French haute couture in Egypt. He testified that "numerous Egyptian women . . . on a trip in France . . . stuff their suitcases with Parisian dresses, to resell" in Egypt to their relatives or local designers.[128] About a dozen "society women" had returned in recent years to Egypt with "30, 40, or even 50 models" of dresses even though he noted that he had "rarely encountered, even among the most elegant, an Egyptian woman . . . appearing in the course of the season in more than five or six different dresses or coats."[129] Usually purchased at seasonal sales and "very often paid for with francs acquired on the black market at an advantageous price," these dresses received exemption from customs because they were declared as "personal effects."[130] As a result, "these dresses become here two times less expensive than those imported normally."[131] This smuggling was indicative of a larger problem of the production of knockoff fashion goods, he argued.

> Counterfeiting of these models of Parisian dresses and hats is here a very common practice among local designers and milliners, and it is relatively easy to have the copies accompanied by origin stamps. They sell, also, in certain stores in Cairo or Alexandria, fabrics serving the collections of our large [couture] houses. Clients can thus have made, in the same fabric even that worked in the original creation, whichever model they had admired in French fashion magazines.[132]

The agent in 1946 had confidentially named "Mme. Charles Zagdoun and Mme. Efflatoun" [Aflatun] as two women "indulging themselves in the trafficking of models [of fashion]."[133]

Salha Aflatun, a member of the upper class (her father had been a pasha) and a divorced mother, had opened a workshop and boutique called Salha's Shop (*mahall salha*), located in Sharwarbi Street in downtown Cairo, in 1935 or 1936 with nationalist financial assistance from Tal'at Harb and Bank Misr.[134] Her daughter reported that Salha "traveled frequently abroad and especially to France to follow fashion and to select models of the big famous couture houses, such as . . . Dior."[135] A local magazine claimed that her shop "governed aristocratic fashion in Egypt" and that it "resemble[d] the biggest Parisian houses that are distinguished in international couture."[136] Mme. Salha eventually employed thirty seamstresses and two *premières* (to do the cutting) and acted as the exclusive agent for Christian Dior, Jacques Fathes, and Balmain in Egypt.[137] The translation, then, of European designer fashions into the local Egyptian economy was effected through the personal wardrobes of women travelers and boutique owners.

Unlike large, urban department stores, which modeled entire outfits on display-window mannequins, market spaces such as the *suq al-kantu* or Salha's Shop made available a variety of disparate articles of clothing that could be assembled more complexly to signal a wide range of status levels among urban residents, even poorer ones. Members of the lower-middle and middle classes who wanted to make a modern appearance on a budget—lower-level government employees, teachers in government schools, students, and commercial employees in department stores, shops, banks, the lower levels of company administration—might all have availed themselves of the assemblage of used clothing in flea markets, just as divorced or middling-elite women might have had recourse to designer knockoffs to maintain their places in high society. Rarely visited by Europeans, these sorts of market spaces defied the dual city by outfitting a continuum of clothing styles that came to code for broad patterns of work and production, consumption styles, family relations, cultural orientation, and so on. Fluidity in style and space paralleled and reinforced elasticity in Egyptian identity.

Rather than marking particular streets as boundaries between two cultures, the *maydan*, or square, as a hub or roundabout came to represent the complexity of urban social and cultural movement. Originally an *ifrangi* architectural feature imported to regularize and Parisianize Egypt's cities, *maydan*s in fact developed a more complex urban fabric that defied the dual city usually envisioned by colonial officials. The ultimate growth of the old and new cities into a continuous urban network—what sociologists call *conurbation*—thus resulted not simply from random population pressures that filled in all available space and not from the growth of a middle class spatially expressing its economic and cultural status by living in the middle. Rather, conurbation followed the already existing use of the city, its well-worn grooves and pathways, particularly the commercial circuits of people's quotidian routines. These commercial and spatial crossings, not without conflict, suggest that there was not a single way to define "Egyptian" in the interwar period. The histories of the department stores that anchored *ifrangi* commercial districts in fact provide something of an inventory of the ways urban residents could be Egyptian.

2 DEPARTMENT STORES AND DOWNTOWN SHOPPING

DEPARTMENT STORES, at the heart of newly constructed urban space, epitomized for many people the temptations offered by the commercial sector as it expanded under the colonial and semicolonial regimes of the late nineteenth and early twentieth centuries.[1] The wide plate-glass shop windows of department stores visually and spatially marked them off from smaller shops nearby and from the open-front stalls of the suqs in the medieval urban cores and in the lower-class or *baladi* shopping districts in other neighborhoods. Even the glass-front shops of the Muski lacked the pristine clarity and enormity of the vitrines of the new downtown stores that lay to the west of ʿAtaba Square in Cairo or around the central squares in Alexandria and provincial cities. Running for entire blocks and outfitted with mannequins, props, and display racks for goods, these department-store display windows held up metropolitan merchandise in a partitioned space above the dusty, active street—encasing and enshrining *ifrangi* consumer goods to represent the modern world "in miniature" for shoppers and passing spectators.[2] A writer for the local French-language magazine *L'Egypte nouvelle* dramatized in 1923 the commercial spectacle offered by such windows.

> On ʿImad al-Din Street, in front of the store window [*vitrine*] on the corner of a department store. There, in this plate-glass window, is a ravishing girl, all pink and white. . . . Adorned in a small dress of white silk chiffon, hair arranged and feet shod with exquisite taste, she lifts toward onlookers the naïve look of her faïence eyes, which give to her small wax face a natural and lively expression. Oh, the delicious child!

Right in front of her, but on the other side of the plate-glass window, a young gentleman contemplates her. . . . His head, closely cropped, retains [a] large forelock . . . ; his handsome face, all round, is lit up by two big black eyes, bright with health; the rags that serve as his only clothing no longer have any shape, nor color, nor name, and reveal a small brown body, solidly built. . . .

The young brown man cannot take his eyes off the beautiful pink and white child; and in order to see her better, he presses himself to the pane of glass [*il se colle à la vitre*] and puts his little hands, brown and chubby, on it. Between them is only the thickness of a strip of glass; but what infinite distance separates them in reality! The little gentleman has a vague feeling of this; he has the impression that the pretty girl and he belong to two races, to two completely different species . . . between them, no relation, no contact is possible.[3]

Full-sized mannequins wearing "natural and lively expressions" and fully dressed in elegant, new clothing captivated passersby with alluring offers of consumption and portrayals of bourgeois culture. These vivid scenes could activate a visceral response from viewers, drawing a fleshy hand to the pane of glass in a tactile effort to see better. They could ignite a deep longing, a sharpened awareness of difference and exclusion, a sense of personal validation, or even a bored sense of comfort. That the spatial boundary of the window—"only the thickness of a strip of glass" but "infinite distance . . . in reality"—could appear to mark a physical and social separation of class, race, and gender difference so shrilly suggests that tangled in commercial space was a complex relationship between ethnicity and national belonging.

Downtown department stores, with their enormous staffs, wide array of imported and local goods, and links to various components of urban space, acted as focal points in the surrounding built environment and in the mental topographies of many downtown residents. In contrast to the more morseled styles worn by many Egyptians, downtown department stores self-consciously prescribed for their customers a unified subjectivity associated with *ifrangi* urban modernity. As composite goods stores, they offered a broader range of items for sale—from hats and veils to shoes, underwear, dresses, suits, coats, and even furniture, linens, china, and appliances—than any other single retail outlet in the country.[4] Prestigious department stores tended to furnish items for important transitions in people's lives, such as a special outfit to celebrate the birth of a first child, school uniforms, or wedding trousseaux, thus perhaps commanding a disproportionate amount of social and cultural importance in middle-class and lower-middle-class people's consumption identities. The stores were also highly visible in public life. With their bold depictions of store premises, provocative and anonymous costumed figures, and detailed descriptions of goods, department-store advertisements appeared prominently in the expanding print media of the early twentieth century, and the stores even provided the settings for short stories, movies, and cartoons.

Nevertheless, the inequalities of colonial power and local specificities of Egyptian society inflected and modulated this self-proclaimed department-store modernity. The stores themselves, through their histories, customers, marketing, merchandising, and other retail practices, often actually linked to a more *baladi* commercial culture carried from their early years in older urban core areas through their moves into the newer downtown centers of commerce. Retail stores' ability to depict themselves as both local companies and emporiums of *ifrangi* culture reflected the hybridized nature of Egyptian national belonging in the interwar years. Egyptians who worked and shopped in downtown stores hailed from a mix of ethnic, religious, and regional backgrounds that defied the more narrow views of Egyptian-ness that would become hegemonic by the 1950s and 1960s. Although these subjects were recognized by other Egyptians and by themselves as different from rural peasants or lower-middle-class *baladi* urbanites, Egyptian national community in the prewar and interwar eras was an entity marked, much as the public space where it was enacted, by propinquity, contiguity, and diversity.

THE ALLURE OF SHOPPING

Although many elite families provisioned themselves on a mundane basis with goods from department stores, it was the culture of display and spectatorship—of merchandise, lifestyle, desire, and even shoppers themselves—that drew most people to downtown commerce. In 1925 Morums Department Store ran an illustrated advertisement for a big sale that it held on the occasion of the closing of its older branch in 'Ataba Square and the consequent expansion of its new shop on Fu'ad Street in Cairo.[5] The advertisement listed French-style and luxurious goods for which the store had slashed prices, including "500 complete men's suits in the latest styles and with fashionable tailoring," "100 dozen pairs of white cotton socks," "200 dressing gowns [*rub di shambir*]," "our special brand '999' of muslin ladies' stockings, very fine with reinforced heel and foot, in different modern colors," and "famous Parisian cologne." A large drawing of the facade of the new store ran as a banner over the text copy. It showed the wide store windows, lit by lamps and filled with elegant models of hats and cloth and male and female mannequins dressed in the latest fashions. Below the windows, the sidewalks overflowed with a huge crowd of shoppers, laughing, mingling, and looking guardedly at each other. Women in black cloaks and thin white veils stood shoulder to shoulder with women dressed in narrow, short-sleeved dresses and cloche hats; men in suits and brimmed hats squeezed in alongside men wearing *tarabish* and spectacles, some with a female companion on their arm, but many entering the store alone. Uniformed store porters directed shoppers to the store entrance or helped them manage their boxes and parcels of merchandise as they departed. A thick column of shoppers flowed through the store's open front doors and deep into the central cloth departments. Emblazoned above the shop windows, the store's name appeared in Arabic, Latin, and Cyrillic characters.[6]

The sleek visuality of the store space contrasted with the kinetic and corporeal energy of the shoppers themselves. As another department-store owner remembered about nearby Chemla in the 1920s, "When we held sales, these were so successful that we had to shut the doors, because people rushed forward in a frenzy . . . roaring and yelling. We had to close the doors so that each person could have a turn. . . . People knew there was something [there] for everyone. In the luxury departments, there was something for the elegant man and woman. Even in the departments where there were less expensive items, everything was well chosen and of good taste."[7] Chemla's clearance sale in October 1934 reduced the price of merchandise by 50 to 60 percent, resulting in large crowds for two weeks.[8] A five-day display of winter fashions at Orosdi-Back in 1934 reportedly drew daily crowds of five thousand to seven thousand people.[9]

The allure of shopping in Egyptian department stores thus lay in a particular mixture of sophistication and worldliness, spaciousness and luxury, coupled and juxtaposed with a sense of profusion and insistent demand created by bargain prices and wide-ranging selection. "There is no boat or airplane landing in Egypt that does not carry all the latest creations for Cicurel stores. In Paris, London, and New York, as well as other major capitals, Cicurel's buying houses rapidly route toward Cairo that which is the finest," a Cicurel advertisement boasted in the 1940s.[10] The intoxication induced by the opportunity to imagine a new self in the store's merchandise was integral to the economy of desire the stores produced. Most essential to evoking commercial desire was the display window, that "transparent mirror," according to René Péron, "neither outside nor inside, space of mediation between desire and its satisfaction. Intimate space: through it, objects move from the interior of the store into the customer's head . . . where presentation transforms into representation, the virtual reflection of someone looking at him/herself in the outfit . . . the screen where projection liberates itself in the urge to purchase or withdraws in frustration."[11] In his 1947 novel *Zuqaq al-midaq* (Midaq Alley), Naguib Mahfouz captured this appeal of "the transparent mirror" in shopping even for more modest clothing in his description of Hamida walking down Muski Street in the late afternoon, "enjoying her daily promenade and looking in the shop windows, one after the other. The luxurious clothes stirred in her greedy and ambitious mind bewitching dreams of power and influence."[12]

Titillated by the power to command both merchandise and service from deferential salesclerks, customers could realize a fantasy of authority in retail stores denied to them elsewhere. Another character in Mafouz's *Midaq Alley* purchases a dozen socks from a small shop on Azhar Street near the Muski. It is his third purchase from the shop in three days, as the thrill of summoning the shop's salesman—"gentle, humble and well-mannered" as he tediously displayed, wrapped, and rewrapped socks at the whim of the customer—keeps pulling him to return to the store.[13] John Hayes, an impoverished Englishman working for the Nile Construction Company in Khartoum, Sudan, came to Cairo in November 1920 and had a similar experience of power during a buying spree at Davies Bryan Department Store.[14] Hayes first selected a dozen Viyella-brand shirts and six pairs of pajamas. He next demanded a leather suitcase "with the necessaries"—a brown canvas kit bag, lunch basket, and thermos. Although the salesman brought him a valise worth £E22, Hayes declared "it was not good enough," so another bag, nearly twice as expensive, was proffered instead. He then went to the store's footwear department, where he chose three pairs of boots and asked the salesman to fetch him first a dressing gown and then a selection of overcoats. When a salesman from the ready-made clothes department brought him down four overcoats, "he chose one which he put on and took a seat." As all purchased goods had to pass through the Control Department before they could be released to customers, Hayes was forced to remove the overcoat while he continued shopping. Hayes also picked out a walking stick, a dozen handkerchiefs, two pairs of suspenders, two undershirts, two pairs of pants, two body belts, and three pairs of slippers. Finally, he selected six silk neckties and three pairs of gloves from yet another salesman at the shop. As Hayes claimed he needed to return to his lodging to obtain funds for his purchase, a clerk in the accounting office and a store *farrash* (servant) accompanied him and the merchandise in a hired taxi. The store clerk was forced to have a drink and watch Hayes play cards for three hours while he politely waited for Hayes to produce the cash to settle his bill. All in all, Hayes had obtained a ready-made wardrobe and commanded extensive service from at least seven or eight store employees over the course of five hours.[15]

Although Davies Bryan advertised itself as "English outfitters," the employees who attended Hayes came from a world of Mediterranean ethnic entanglements: men such as Maurice Carasso, Nicola Peter, Dolore Dimiani, Amin Michel, Nicolas Mavridis, Simon Axelroud, and Galal Abdallah were neither Anglo-Saxon nor all clearly ethnically Egyptian, although unlike Hayes, they spoke some Arabic as well as English and probably other languages such as French and Italian.[16] Stores such as Davies Bryan profited from their customers' intoxication with the power to command and enact authority that encouraged them to binge on store merchandise.[17] For Hayes, the store floors of Davies Bryan became an opportunity to assume, however temporarily, a new class and imperial identity—that of the colonial gentleman—denied to lower-class British men serving the empire in more menial and less powerful occupations in remote areas. The glimpse of "power and influence" promised by shopping and the merchandise displayed in commercial spaces enhanced the allure of shopping.

The colonial display window, like those in Egypt's urban department stores, held an even more specific cultural role than merely mediating objects from commercial space to the self. Just as powerfully, it shepherded the passage of goods from the metropole to the colony.[18] In this regard, department-store shopping in colonial Egypt challenged the nonmetropolitan gendering of urban space and consumption that marked the broader society, bestowing on its customers a certain independence from older social codes and practices. The mixing of men and women in department stores complemented the modernity associated with the new kinds of goods the stores sold and increased their marketability. The Egyptian nationalist-feminist Huda Sha'rawi's memoir perhaps most famously reports a woman's shopping trip to an Alexandrian department store as an upper-class and, in this period, secluded woman. Her family's anxiety about the public exposure such an experience would cause her reflected the era's upper-class concerns about women and public space.

> I remember the first shopping trip to Chalon[s]. The mere prospect of it threw the entire household into an uproar and provided the main topic of

conversation and heated debate for days. They looked upon me as if I were about to violate the religious law or commit some other crime. After considerable persuasion on my part, however, my mother gave in to my wishes and, along with everyone else around me, issued endless orders and instructions for my correct behaviour. They insisted it was not proper for me to go alone, but I must be accompanied by Said Agha and my maids. The day of the outing, Said Agha made doubly sure I was completely hidden with wraps and veil.[19]

Such concerns gradually eroded, Sha'rawi believed, after families saw "the advantages of shopping in person. Not only was there a wide range of goods to choose from but there was money to be saved through wise spending. From then on [my mother] resolved to do her own shopping and permitted me to do my own as well."[20]

Displays of power in department stores could provide shoppers with temporary and "bewitching" escape from class and customary behaviors in which the intimate spaces of the body and its desires could become public spectacle. The intoxication of the temporary suspension of class, gender, or colonial identity provided by shopping also fostered a broad social anxiety. In his play *al-Hawiya* (The Abyss), written in 1920–1921, Muhammad Taymur, for example, likened the allure of department-store shopping to an addiction to drugs, with similarly destructive effects on family life. "When a man thinks of nothing but women, wine, and cocaine, women's thoughts naturally turn to drinks, silk handkerchiefs, laces and other trifles picked up at Cicurel's, after which they turn to [adultery]!"[21] With their offers of escape, fantasy, and power, department stores struggled to balance their reputations as emporiums of sophistication and sites of personal and social decadence. The ambiguities of social status and class relations that department-store shopping could create provoked social anxieties and ultimately encouraged scrutiny of their practices.

"ROUND THE MOUSKY, ATABA, AND AZHAR" TO FU'AD STREET: THE HISTORICAL GEOGRAPHY OF DEPARTMENT STORES

In April 1923 the International Union of Commercial Establishment Employees of Cairo organized a Grand Corso Carnavalesque, a public festival of decorated cars presented by commercial companies (see Figure 3). With the Egyptian prime minister, foreign and domestic ministers, and large crowds in attendance, the floats paraded through the Cairo International Sporting Club in

Figure 3. Decorated floats of Cairo department stores in the 1923 Grand Corso Carnavalesque. Al-Marwardi's entry is pictured on top and Cicurel's on the bottom. *Al-Lataʾif al-musawwara* 9, no. 430 (7 May 1923), 9.

Bulaq district and were judged by a committee that included the famous nationalist sculptor Muhammad Mukhtar. Twenty-five companies participated, including retail stores such as Cicurel; the Bon Marché; Mawardi; Salamander; Paul Favre's shoe store; and Palacci, Fils & Hayam.[22] Several stores "artistically" expressed the overall style of their particular merchandise or re-created the layouts of their premises through the tableaux on the floats. The Cairo branch of the French department store Au Bon Marché, which took the grand prize, presented a boat with a French rooster at the prow and filled with "beautiful young women" each representing a different department of the store—fashion, dresses, perfume, notions, and so forth.[23] Cicurel built a copy of Mukhtar's famous and already iconic nationalist sculpture *Nahdat misr* (Egypt's Renaissance), which displayed the Sphinx and a "beautiful young woman, high on a pedestal, representing Egypt."[24] The company, known for its luxury products, adorned the participants on its chariot in "rich costumes," including a "sumptuous cape" for the woman representing Egypt.[25] An elaborate social event, the Corso celebrations included a dance after the ceremony at the Cinema Metropole. Stores in the city sold tickets, promotional films of the event circulated in cinemas, the local press carried extensive coverage, and the official event photographs appeared in the vitrines of a downtown jewelry store, Maison Sussmann. A local newspaper "congratulate[d] warmly the commerce of Cairo which seems to have understood that it is able, in festivals of this type, to serve the general good and its own proper interest at the same time."[26]

The sense that for-profit department-store commerce could "serve the general good," and specifically the nation's interest, grew from the way that the stores created a unique public space in the city. Department stores occupied a large amount of nearly contiguous physical space in Alexandria, Cairo, and several provincial cities, such as Tanta, by the first decades of the twentieth century. In Alexandria, large department stores such as Davies Bryan, Chalons, Stein's, Hannaux, and Sednaoui clustered in the area of Sharif Pasha and Sidi al-Mitwalli Streets and around Muhammad ʿAli Square. In Cairo many of these stores were located in Ismailia and around ʿAtaba Square, which connected the older commercial zones of the city with the newer downtown quarter. Major local or regional stores included Cicurel, Chemla, Orosdi-Back, Sednaoui, Hannaux, Chalons, Palacci, ʿAdès, Gattegno, Madkur, Ahmad and Yusuf Gamal, and Benzion as well as Morums, Stein's, Raff's, Roberts Hughes, Mayer, Tiring, and Salamander. Unlike the smaller shops in the older commercial districts, department stores were enormous enterprises with sumptuous and spacious premises that relied on large sales forces to move their merchandise. In the late 1920s less than 1 percent of retail stores retained ten or more employees. These few big stores, however, employed a large percentage of the country's commercial workforce. In 1909 Sednaoui employed 150 salespeople and clerks; Orosdi Back listed 239 employees in 1914 in its Cairo store.[27]

Several branches of western European department-store chains also opened in Egypt in this period. Davies Bryan and Company was established in 1886 as a branch of Bryan Brothers Drapers of Carnarvon, North Wales, although the entire business eventually moved to Egypt.[28] At least four branches of French department stores operated during this time: Au Bon Marché, Au Printemps, Aux Galeries Lafayette, and Les Grands Magasins du Louvre.[29] Several of these, including Printemps and Trois Quartiers, functioned much as samples showrooms.[30] Other branches offered more complete lines of merchandise and more variety in their stock, although they were only a fraction of the size of their Paris headquarters. Au Bon Marché, for example, sold in the middle 1920s a wide array of cloth; ready-made clothing and haberdashery for men, women, and children; hats; bedding and table linens; soaps, perfumes, and toiletries; clocks; cutlery; and even some furnishings, including rugs.[31] The French stores assumed an ambivalent role in Egyptian commercial culture. On the one hand, their marketing appeal depended on their French identification, and they actively participated in the French expatriate community. The Bon Marché was a strong proponent of French culture in Egypt and lavishly and patriotically decorated for Bastille Day.[32] On the other hand, the stores often took part in local events. The Bon Marché prominently advertised that King Fu'ad patronized its Cairo store and even displayed in its ground-floor windows the "nationalist" pottery produced by Huda Sha'rawi's vocational school for women in the 1920s.[33] Most (if not all) of the French branch stores closed their operations in Egypt in the 1930s.[34] Davies Bryan in March 1929 had stock valued at more than £E57,000 but was regarded by a competitor as a "decaying" concern.[35] In the 1910s and 1920s, however, European department stores played a central role in Egyptian commerce, as the 1923 Corso demonstrated.

The clustering of department stores in newly expanded urban commercial zones contributed to both the stores' and the districts' cultural power and provided a register of many of the ways people considered themselves Egyptian in the century before 1956. By the 1920s, shoppers on Cairo's Fu'ad Street in the Ismailia district or the nearby Khazindar Square would have faced several large, elegant department stores stationed almost side by side in which to make their purchases. Cicurel (*Shikuril*), at 3 Fu'ad Street, had moved to these premises in 1909 from the Muski district and had grown to include about eighty employees. The ornate Cicurel store, originally designed by a well-known Levantine architect and completely rebuilt after a devastating fire in 1920 (caused by a neglected electric iron), encompassed two buildings, each taking up a city block

Figure 4. Cicurel's main store on Fu'ad Street in Cairo, 1924. Cicurel catalog for winter 1924–1925 (Paris: Léon Ullman, n.d.), inside front cover.

and looming four stories high (see Figure 4). Shoppers could pass from one part of the store to the other through the sets of large doors on the ground level or by an enclosed bridge over the side roadway. Many shoppers undoubtedly lingered over the displays in the large glass windows that ran the length of the ground-floor sides of the building.[36] Once inside, shoppers could view an array of goods in departments that supplied the king of Egypt as well as other elite and more middle-class families, could purchase goods and have them delivered to their homes, and could even return goods that were not bought during sales for a full refund.[37]

The firm's history reflected its imbrication in multiple sites of urban commerce and its owners' Mediterranean-Egyptian roots. A poor, Sephardi Jew holding Italian nationality, Moreno Cicurel came to Cairo from Izmir (in today's Turkey) when both were part of the Ottoman Empire, and he worked as an assistant in the mid-1880s in a haberdashery located in the Muski and owned by a Mr. Hannaux.[38] After acquiring the business in 1887, Moreno added new lines of inventory over the next decade. Within a few years, the store's name changed from Au Petit Bazaar to Les Grands Magasins de Nouveautés Cicurel/*Mahallat al-kubra shikuril* to reflect its evolution from "a small store in the Arab quarter . . . to a new store, very luxurious, which . . . occupied the entire building."[39] After Moreno's death in 1919, the Cicurel business transferred to his three sons, Solomon, Yusuf, and Salvator, who in the next two decades expanded the company into a retail empire that included a cheaper bargain-basement line of stores called ORECO, branch stores in Alexandria and Asyut, and Trémode shops.[40]

The Cicurels, who probably spoke French among themselves, were by 1920 important local capitalists and widely considered Egyptian. When Solomon Cicurel was killed during a robbery in 1927, nationalist leader Saʿd Zaghlul formally offered his condolences and dispatched his personal secretary to assist Mrs. Cicurel in any way necessary. (Zaghlul, himself quite sick at the time, died shortly thereafter.)[41] Solomon's younger brother Yusuf served in 1920 as a founding board member of Bank Misr, the Egyptian bank established by Talʿat Harb during the nationalist uprising to spearhead Egypt's economic independence. It was probably around this time that the family took Egyptian nationality; the family members on the board in 1947 all held Egyptian citizenship.[42] Salvator Cicurel (1894–1976) held leadership roles in a range of cultural, administrative, and commercial capacities in Egypt. He served prominently on various Egyptian trade missions, commercial courts (including the Mixed Tribunals), and from the 1920s through at least the 1940s, the Egyptian Chambers of Commerce, where peers praised his "competence, his proverbial integrity, authority, and prestige."[43] He helped found the Association of Department Stores and Wholesalers, a group whose mission was "to encourage the sale of locally produced goods."[44] From 1946 to 1957 he also presided over Cairo's Sephardi Jewish community. In addition, Salvator was a champion fencer. He represented Egypt as captain of its fencing team, reaching the finals in the 1928 Olympic Games. The king gave him the title of bey in the middle 1930s.[45] His personal prestige and connections undoubtedly not only helped the company withstand the multiple rebuildings of the store premises and continue to grow in the first half of the twentieth century but also contributed to the reputation of the store as "the most elegant in Egypt."[46] His is also a story of national leadership in sports, commerce, and civic organizations that calls into question ethnically based definitions of Egyptian identity.

Next door to Cicurel was the Chemla (*Shimla*) department store, designed in a fin de siècle French style by the same prominent Ottoman architect who planned the Cicurel stores but built a year or so earlier and on a slightly smaller—although still quite grand—scale. Once past the enormous plate-glass display windows facing the ground floor, shoppers entering the Chemla store would have encountered vast marble halls supported by columns topped with acanthus leaves and finished in a Louis XVI style. Right in the middle of the store, glass display cases of French-style goods (such as bottled perfume, gloves, and fancy goods) caught the eye of customers as they perhaps headed to the counters of polished mahogany wood where the ever-popular notions selections lay in vitrines, there to find buttons or trim to accent ready-made clothing or to give to one of the many tailors in the city who made clothes to measure inexpensively. From this counter a shopper could look right and see the piles of bolts and wide tables signaling the cloth department. The company was well known for selling imported silks and fine cottons and more modest fabrics for everyday wear. Turning left, the shopper would find the hosiery departments for men and for women, while even deeper in the store lay women's lingerie. Traveling all the way to the back of the store, the customer would find the furniture and shoe departments. The next floor housed the spacious haute couture atelier, which employed "two important women designers from Paris"; an extremely large ready-made clothing department "where they sold dresses, from the most simple to the most beautiful"; a "corset-maker from Paris"; and the millinery departments. A customer in search of a hat could browse either the department of hats imported from Paris or the more general hat department under the direction of a Parisian milliner. The store also elegantly displayed ready-made clothing and even had a separate department of flowers for use in women's dresses, for evening gowns, and for hats.[47] Shoppers in search of holiday presents could find options as diverse as children's tricycles and scooters of many styles, an array of dolls and tea sets, musical toys and instruments, table tennis and other games, blackboards, swings, highchairs, desks and chair sets, electric trains, porcelain figurines, clocks and watches, crystal fruit bowls, liqueur glasses, and even a film projector or a decorated Christmas tree.[48]

The Chemla family had a branch or buying house in Paris by the 1920s that helped them acquire and market this merchandise. The Chemlas' status as French subjects and their familiarity with French culture and commerce traced back to their origins in French-occupied Tunisia. Sons of an Arabic-speaking, Jewish olive oil producer in Monastir, a city on Tunisia's eastern coast, the Chemla brothers began their clothing business in the mid-1880s in Tunis, peddling door to door fashionable merchandise imported from France, such as cloth, scarves, blouses, and lingerie. Eventually establishing a fixed shop front in the 1890s, the brothers expanded their product line to include shoes, pants, and ready-to-wear clothing. By the turn of the century, their small department store Au Petit Louvre specialized in the outfitting of trousseaux and in ready-to-wear *ifrangi* clothing for the modernizing middle class of Tunis: Jewish families, Muslim families beginning to consume European goods, Francophile professionals, and commercial and industrial employees. Hoping to capitalize on the cotton booms of the early twentieth century, the family moved its operations in 1907 from Tunis to Cairo, although the store's fortunes remained precarious, suffering under tremendous debt, until the business profited from the inflation caused by the First World War. Chemla especially benefited from its large stock of merchandise (and from buying up some stocks of bankrupted competitors) during the blockades of the First World War. Even after the war, when Chemla became known as one of Cairo's top department stores, the business remained modest and never opened retail branches, although the store retained many of its initial customers through the middle of the 1930s.[49]

Just on the other side of the ʿAzbakiyya Garden from Chemla and Cicurel stood the Sednaoui (*Sidnawi*) brothers' flagship store, opened in 1913 and designed in a classical fin de siècle architectural style to resemble the Paris stores of Au Printemps and Galeries Lafayette.[50] Its distinctive cupolas flanking the front entrance and its spacious interior atrium onto which all the selling floors opened heralded the success of the Sednaoui enterprise, which had grown within the past decade, much as its competitors had, from a tiny tailoring and clothing shop in the Muski into a full-scale department store employing 150 salespeople and clerks (in addition to other workers in support services) and drawing goods from buying houses in Paris and Lyon. Sednaoui carried much the same lines of goods as the other major stores.[51] Like Cicurel (but not Chemla), Sednaoui had begun to open branch stores in Alexandria and major provincial Egyptian cities such as Tanta, Mansura, Asyut, and Fayyum by the 1910s, making it accessible to customers outside the capital city.

The Sednaouis hailed from a Greek Catholic family originally from Sidnaya in Syria (also under Ottoman rule) that had moved to Damascus in the early nineteenth century and engaged in trading. The brothers Salim and Samʿan, both born in Damascus in the 1850s, respectively worked as a tailor, specializing in European clothing, and as a low-level employee for the Ottoman government and carpet salesman. Samʿan migrated to Egypt in 1877 to work for his uncle, Nicola Sidnawi, a merchant in the Hamzawi district of Cairo selling silks and notions. Shortly thereafter, Samʿan managed the liquidation of a Hamzawi shop run by another Syrian merchant, from whom he learned about the different merchandise on the market and its pricing; for his work, Samʿan received half the sale's profits. He used this capital to import European silks and scarves (*manadil*) from merchants in Istanbul and later prospered when he established trading relations directly with European merchants, who offered him lower prices. Salim came to Cairo about the same time as Samʿan to work as a tailor, and with Samʿan's financial backing, Salim and "a foreigner" named Mitri

Salhani opened a tailoring and retail shop. After that business burned down, the Sednaoui brothers opened a new small shop (*hanut*), measuring only four square meters, in Cairo's Muski district at the head of Mansur Pasha Street;[52] the brothers lived in a simple room at the *wakalat* (caravansary) Ya'qub Bey in the Hamzawi. In 1878 or 1879, they founded the Association of Salim and Sam'an Sednaoui.[53] A chance business deal with members of the royal court helped expand upper-class patronage of the store, and in 1881 the brothers moved to a larger shop in the Muski on the old canal where they specialized in carpets and furniture; they also kept the original shop in the Hamzawi. The firm began to expand significantly after a medical trip to Europe introduced Salim to the variety of products available in the European market, and the company began to organize yearly buying trips to Europe. The company later established fixed buying agencies in Europe, notably in Paris and Lyon and eventually in Manchester.[54] Like the Cicurels, the Sednaouis had come to Egypt as part of an internal Ottoman migration, and by the 1940s the Sednaouis serving on the company board held Egyptian citizenship.[55]

Other prominent department stores reflected different aspects of Mediterranean regional diversity. The grand Cairo premises of Orosdi-Back (Urusdi-Bak/'Umar Effendi) on 'Abd al-'Aziz Street, built in 1909, occupied another busy shopping corner. Tall and dramatic, it too was topped by a steep cupola and had wide display windows running along both sides of the building. Controlled by Ottoman subjects of Hungarian and Jewish descent, the company sold a variety of products purchased by its buying house in Paris, as well as items from Italy, Austria, Germany, and Spain acquired by intermediaries.[56] The Cairo store, founded in 1856 and originally located on Muski Street, was one in a chain of department stores that the company established throughout the Middle East in the second half of the nineteenth century.[57] Department-store magnate Vita Palacci (*Balatshi*), who opened a shop in 1897 on Bayn al-Nahdayn Street in the Muski, clearly exemplified the Egyptianist world of national belonging in the interwar years. By 1909 Palacci had partnered with A. Hayam, and their shop had grown into a three-story, 1,200-square-meter store, employing 20 office clerks and 120 salespeople in at least thirteen departments, and was doing "a large share of the wholesale and retail trade in Egypt and the Soudan."[58] The company had opened additional branches on Fu'ad Street and in the new suburb of Heliopolis by the middle 1920s.[59] The family was of Sephardi Jewish heritage and came to Cairo from Istanbul in the sixteenth and seventeenth centuries.[60] Although in the late 1930s the family lived in a villa in the new upper-class neighborhood of Garden City, Vita Palacci's granddaughter remembered him as part of the local merchant community of the suqs of the old city. "At lunchtime, merchants sitting on stools outside their open stores greeted my grandfather loudly in Arabic. He, in turn, inquired about their health or their family. Often he would bring a bolt of cloth from his store as a present for someone's daughter who was getting married. My grandfather loved Egyptian food, especially street food."[61] Palacci, like Egypt's other primary department stores, blended the allure of *ifrangi* shopping with an elastic ethnic and national identity that challenged rigid or dichotomous views of urban space. As microcosms of the Egyptianist public sphere of the interwar years, the stores fostered social practices in which people could temporarily assume different identities.

Surrounding the larger downtown shops were smaller boutiques that offered the accessories and ancillary services to maintain the new outfits offered by the department stores: tailors and seamstresses, jewelers, leatherworkers, shoe shops, and so forth. These stores also participated in the multiethnic character of urban commerce. Although the *baladi* shoe trade was centered in the old city's Darb al-Ahmar, *ifrangi* shoe stores clustered in the downtown commercial district. "Cordonnerie Française, Paul Favre" opened in Cairo in 1902. A Frenchman, Favre had entered the *ifrangi* shoe trade six years earlier as a twenty-two-year-old employee at La Cordonnerie Française of Alexandria. By 1922 his stores were headquartered on the chic Fu'ad Street in the Continental building and regarded as "among the most important in Cairo"; Favre himself was proposed to serve as the French foreign trade counselor at Cairo.[62] I. Hornstein, another important independent shoe store nearby in downtown Cairo, was reputed to be "one of the leading boot and shoe stores in Egypt." Born in Cairo in 1865, Isidore Hornstein was a son of the jeweler to Khedive Sa'id; he attended local schools and worked for almost fifteen years for a shoe merchant named L. Juster before founding his own small shoe store in the Muski in 1893. By 1918 the store had moved to 9 Fu'ad Street, in the Egyptian Telegraph building, nearly adjacent to the Cordonnerie Parisienne (at no. 7) and the Chemla department store (at no. 11). Hornstein moved easily in the multiethnic world of Egyptian trade; fluent, both writing and speaking, in eight languages, he was also a Freemason.[63]

"Matton and Debono—Cordonnerie Parisienne," with stores in Cairo and Alexandria, was another upscale, *ifrangi* shoe firm that capitalized on the cultural mixture of downtown commerce in a slightly different way. In 1896 the company offered "an extraordinary amount of good shoes in different styles and types" in addition to a range of other products, including socks, underwear, shirts, hats, perfume, toys, children's clothing, and handkerchiefs—in short, "everything families need" at "moderate prices" that were "fixed and avert all competition."[64] The partners' alliance was certainly strategic, as each had connections to different foreign communities: Vincent Debono was Maltese and a British subject, and A. Matton likely held or acquired French citizenship.[65] This gave the company a foot in both the culturally dominant French community and the politically dominant British one. Despite the dissolution of the Matton and Debono partnership by 1917, when the Debono family took over the entire business, the company continued to manage several shops in Cairo, on al-Bawaki Street and Fu'ad Street.[66] The Bawaki store burned in December 1926, probably during a period of financial difficulty; some local merchants at the time accused the Debonos of arson to collect on their fire insurance.[67]

That many of the luxurious department stores and upscale shoe shops that opened in Cairo's Ismailia district or Alexandria's Sharif Pasha Street in the 1910s and 1920s actually had their commercial roots in the older urban cores deeply affected their relationship to the city and allowed them to bridge the various cultures of consumption in colonial urban Egypt. In his memoir on Cairo, Magdi Wahba recalled "the commercial centre . . . [of] Kasr el-Nil, Soliman Pasha, and Fuad. Here were the department stores (guarded by the moustachioed Albanian doormen, in their fustanella and high boots) which had emerged from the hinterland of crowded medieval Cairo, round the Mousky, Ataba, and Azhar."[68] Marius Schemeil remarked in 1949 that the Muski origins of the department stores created a series of overlapping commercial communities: "As for the Muski, it has always formed an inextricable maze of small streets and of stores, of boutiques and alleys. There debuted the Sednaouis as well as the Omar Effendis–Orosodi Backs, the Madkours, the Kramers, the Hornsteins, etc."[69] Like Radwan's sense of the propinquity of commercial cultures, the embedded relationships of physical space marked collective memory of the department stores' Muski origins:

At Khazindar Square, we notice that in the building that replaced the Sednaoui stores and where previously the Barbier bookshop was located (which now has been moved to 'Imad al-Din Street in the Davies Bryan building), there was, in the south-east corner of the building, a very small ground-floor alcove, measuring perhaps ten square meters, where the founder of the grand stores of Cicurel began his commerce and from where the millionaires of today emerged.[70]

Such itineraries of memory traced the changes of commerce onto the built environment, etching ever deeply locally inflected retail practices onto the high *ifrangi* culture of downtown areas.

Egyptian belonging thus took many forms in this era, in part because the dominant strain of Egyptian nationalism in the 1920s and early 1930s, Egyptianism, was a territorial nationalism predicated on a common connection to place rather than more integral forms of supranational identity based in a shared ethnicity, language, or religion (Arabism, Islamism, neofascism, etc.) that expanded their institutional base in the 1930s and 1940s.[71] As department-store histories suggest, Egypt acted as a hub for merchant migration around the Mediterranean Basin.[72] Many Egyptian merchants, along with industrialists such as Tal'at Harb, held what Joel Beinin has described as "a business-oriented conception of the national project" that particularly highlighted participation on the Executive Committee of the Egyptian Chambers of Commerce as a mark of contributing to the Egyptian national economy; department-store owners such as Yusuf and Salvator Cicurel served as members of this committee and others like it.[73] For many of these naturalized Egyptians (*mutamassiruna*), who had migrated internally from other areas of the Ottoman Empire in the nineteenth century and participated enthusiastically in intercommunal business relationships, it was not long residence or connection to Arab culture that formed the primary rubrics for national belonging. Rather, these merchants "did not believe that their lack of these attributes made them any less Egyptian. . . . As Ottoman subjects, they were not juridically foreigners. They were Arabic and, occasionally, Turkish speakers. Their 'Eastern' culture allowed them to acclimate easily."[74]

The broadly intercommunal society that included the downtown department stores defined itself in terms of language that connected more with a notion of culture than with either ethnicity or nationality. Many Egyptians in the elite and middle classes considered French culture a sign of and vehicle for modernity rather than a conflict with Egyptian nationalism.[75] This "loose, almost classless," community was, according to Wahba,

> not the French but the French-speaking—a complex diversity of people, cutting through race, community, nationality, and religion. To be French-speaking in Cairo before the 1952 Revolution was to belong to a group of people who felt themselves deeply rooted in Cairo as a place, and probably believed that their lives would be spent in that city until death disseminated them to their various

cemeteries, distinguished only by religion or religious rite. This rootedness did not imply a sense of belonging in any way to the world of culture, politics, and religion which informed the rising nationalism of the Egyptian middle classes. To be French-speaking was to think of Cairo as home, but to believe that Paris was the navel of the world. You could be French-speaking and yet feel patriotic, regardless of your origins.[76]

Wahba gives pride of place to Cairene Jews such as the Cicurels, Chemlas, Palaccis, and many of their employees in this French-speaking world; in it he also includes the "Syro-Lebanese Christians," such as the Sednaouis, "who spoke French with equal fluency [but] had retained a link with Arabic."[77] The effect of these disparate yet interconnected groups was to render Cairo a city of "infinite complexity . . . crowded with people of vastly differing backgrounds, rapidly changing class structures, and heterogeneous cultural values."[78] The clustering of department stores in urban sites that gave rise to these cultural communities recalled the organization of commerce in the older suqs yet created a public space of cosmopolitan, homegrown fashion that seemingly could uplift the city "for the general good." At the same time, the commercial geography and the movement of stores within the urban fabric positioned them well to link, hub-like, the subcultures of the urban fabric.

MULTILINGUAL ENTANGLEMENTS IN COMMERCE

As Wahba's memoirs suggest, language formed a primary arena to express the multicultural character of downtown commerce and the *ifrangi* cultures of consumption associated with it. Patriotism and language were not bound in a unilateral relationship. Stores used linguistic registers to craft the complex and shifting portrayal of modernity and national identity with which they were associated. Marketing materials and promotional signs used multiple languages, and multilingual salesclerks drew a variety of customers into stores.

Illustrated catalogs made this use of language particularly visible. Such catalogs, a mainstay of European and American stores, distinguished the ability of department stores to prescribe a totalizing vision of cultural identity. Several Egyptian stores published illustrated catalogs, sometimes even designed and produced in Europe in line with European trends in graphic design. Cicurel's catalog for winter 1924–1925 was a hundred-page, lavish affair that included several plates printed in multiple colors. Published in France, the catalog projected the drama of shopping: its table of contents appeared as a sign on a stage,

Figure 5. The cover of the Cicurel catalog for winter 1924–1925 used pharaonic motifs and *ifrangi* dress to signal the drama and glamour of shopping. Cicurel catalog for winter 1924–1925 (Paris: Léon Ullman, n.d.), cover.

and its front cover displayed two women and a man, adorned in evening dress, exiting an automobile and entering a theater or a formal hall (see Figure 5). The designer incorporated pharaonic motifs, popular in Egypt in the middle 1920s; the front cover in particular displayed broad templelike columns painted with pharaonic designs and figures. When the catalog appeared, a local French-language magazine, *L'Egypte nouvelle,* heralded its "bold modernity" and "harmony" of decoration, declaring that "certain plates seem almost transposed directly from the admirable fashion magazine *Art, Taste, and Beauty* [*Art, goût, et beauté*], so bold is their modernism."[79] The local branch of Bon Marché also received similar acclaim for its color winter 1924 catalog, designed by "Maitre" Bréval. *L'Egypte nouvelle* called it "a small wonder" and "an enchantment" from "the first to the last page" and proclaimed that it reflected "an admirable spirit of modernism" that reigned at the store.[80]

At the same time, catalogs revealed the stores' nonmetropolitan location in the multiethnic society of Egypt. The text of the Cicurel and Bon Marché catalogs was bilingual Arabic and French. The Cicurel winter 1924–1925 catalog even sported as a result two front covers (as French was read left to right and Arabic right to left), thus creating something of a mirrored effect in the book. Although many of the models in the drawings appeared to be white Europeans and some of the tableaux recalled European countryside scenes, the majority of the pages promoted fabrics, trimmings, and sewing accessories to make clothing. An entire section displayed veils and veil fabrics, and other pages featured a variety of fabrics tailored to Middle Eastern markets, such as silks for *milayat* (women's black coverings).[81] The bilingual nature of commercial catalogs disrupted the sleek modernity depicted in their illustrations but signaled the local conditions of their circulation. A similar bilingual promotional strategy structured store signage and print advertising. In Arabic advertisements for the Matton and Debono shoe stores, for example, the company's name— Cordonnerie parisienne—was printed in French (in Latin characters) and then transliterated, rather than translated, into Arabic. The merchants' names— *Mattun wa-dabunu*—were listed immediately below the store's name, printed in Arabic and occasionally in Latin characters as well.[82] Multilingual typographical strategies not only widened audiences but also turned foreign words into recognizable signs of *ifrangi* culture.

Linguistic versatility aided department-store commercial workers in their ability to connect the various groups of shoppers who entered stores. One of the cosmopolitan competencies required of salesclerks in colonial department stores, speaking multiple languages reinforced a familiarity with *ifrangi* consumption patterns and social practices.[83] Local Greek and Italian saleswomen spoke French and Arabic in addition to their native languages in the 1920s.[84] Two decades later, Cairo department stores still required salesclerk proficiency in "Arabic, English, Italian, Greek, and always French."[85] Some Arabic-speaking Egyptians attended language classes at local cultural institutes so they could enter *ifrangi* commercial employment.[86] Code switching between Arabic and French (or other European languages) resonated with a more fundamental aspect of Egyptian linguistic structure, the diglossic nature of classical and colloquial Arabic, in which speakers pitched linguistic registers as a form of power and status.[87]

Like store owners, salesclerks came from a variety of ethnoreligious backgrounds. Although some store owners may have preferred to hire staffs from among their own ethnic or religious group, on most store floors locally resident foreigners worked alongside Muslim, Coptic, and Jewish Egyptians. A 1914 letter written by Leon Orosdi listed the 245 men and women employed in

Orosdi-Back's Cairo store; they fell into at least thirteen distinct ethnonational categories.[88] At least thirty Muslims appeared in this list, and "local subjects," an elastic category that included people born in Egypt (both Muslims and local minorities such as Jews and Christians), represented the largest group of people in the company's employ.[89] "Ottoman" subjects and Greeks made up the next two major groups, followed by Italians. Other employees held French, Algerian-French, Austrian, Swiss, Russian, Rumanian, Spanish, and English protection.[90] The list included at least thirty-nine Jews and a number of Armenians in the local and Ottoman categories. Many "foreign" employees bore names suggesting long residence in Egypt.[91] By 1947 about a third of the sales force at Cicurel and its branches held foreign citizenship and about a quarter of the Egyptian employees had recognizably Jewish names; another 8 percent were Christians, and quite a few Armenians were also employed.[92] The vast majority of Cicurel salesclerks used non-Arabic first names (such as Regine, Albert, Henry, Alegra, or Jack), although this did not necessarily indicate a particular ethnic, religious, or national identity.[93] While about half Chemla's salesclerks in 1947 probably were local Jews, Italians and Muslim Egyptians were substantially represented.[94] Evidence suggests that members of different religious, ethnic, or national communities often worked together in specific departments or on the selling floor. Sednaoui's hosiery (*shurrabat, bonneterie*) department at the Khazindar Square store in 1947 employed four Muslim Egyptians, four Italians, three Greeks, two local Jews, and thirteen Arab Christians, most born in Egypt to parents who had emigrated in the late nineteenth or early twentieth century from other parts of the Ottoman Empire.[95]

Many store employees formally associated in trade unions with memberships that encompassed an array of ethnic, religious, and national backgrounds and with platforms that promoted labor activism in nationalist terms. Salesclerks participated with other industrial and commercial workers in the nationalist strikes of the 1919 Revolution and formed several unions in August 1919.[96] The International Association of Commercial Employees of Cairo remained active through the early 1920s. The union's general secretary, Robert Goldenberg, edited the local French-language magazine *L'Egypte nouvelle*, and the magazine published weekly updates on the union's activities and meetings.[97] The union protested unfair labor practices at local stores.[98] During and after the Second World War, union activity among commercial employees again surged, as part of the wider nationalist movement. The International Union of Commercial Establishment Employees, a Marxist group led by Da'ud Nahum and "based on the clerks of the large and fashionable department stores in the European section of Cairo"—including Cicurel, Chemla, Sednaoui, 'Adès and Benzion—participated in the strikes of 1946.[99] This labor activism demonstrated that many workers in *ifrangi* commerce, including local minorities such as Jews, Armenians, or *shami* (Syrian) Christians, considered themselves Egyptian and wanted to work within the broader nationalist movement. The hybridized nature of Egyptianist national belonging accommodated the ethnic and linguistic entanglements of department-store workers, and the performance of cosmopolitan competencies linked the stores—bastions of *ifrangi* culture—to other transitional commercial spaces in the city.

DOWNTOWN SHOPPERS

Scholars have generally depicted Egyptian department-store shoppers as from the Europeanized middle and upper classes.[100] Although these groups certainly provided important, regular patronage of the stores, photographs, drawings, memoirs, and police reports reveal a more diverse shopping crowd.[101] One effect of department stores' origins in older city neighborhoods was the retention of many of their *baladi* customers, whom stores were able to draw into new urban spaces. Moreover, *shopper* or even *consumer* quite elastically connoted people actually entering a shop and buying merchandise but also included those who consumed less literally, those just looking, and those accompanying or observing someone else's consumption.[102] The elasticity of shopping also refers to its uneven temporal nature for most people. Many shoppers patronized a range of commercial sites rather than doing all their shopping at one store. Antoine and Victoria Micallef, for instance, in the mid-1930s shopped at Chemla, the Bon Marché, and Cicurel, as well as various tailors.[103] Not remaining confined to one "city" of commerce or another, shoppers formed a series of interwoven and overlapping communities. The lack of formal marketing studies renders tracking and quantification of shoppers in Egypt a very difficult endeavor. Nevertheless, understanding the complexity of retail practices warrants an examination of the general characteristics of and changes in Egypt's shopping public.

Although precise and nuanced information about the distribution of income and the spending habits of Egyptians in the first half of the twentieth century is difficult to retrieve, that time generally witnessed a significant expansion in consumption, usually attributed to a slow but constant expansion of the middle class.[104] Roger Owen estimates that Egypt "increase[d] its purchase of foreign imports by nearly 350 percent" in 1880–1910 and that "the value of imports per head of population . . . increase[d] from an average of just under £1 [sterling] in the early 1880s to over £2 in 1913 [and] at the latter date, it was well in excess of such countries as Greece and Japan and more or less the same level as Spain."[105] A rebuilding of the economy after the First World War expanded the middle sectors of society, especially those working in government and in the growing local commercial and industrial sectors. In 1931 the British commercial agent estimated "the potential customers for the larger number of western manufactured products" to be about two million people; "the fellah," or peasant, he added parenthetically, "of course, requires cotton for his clothing, fertilizers for his fields, and is either directly or indirectly a consumer of various petroleum products, but beyond these his requirements of western products are very small, and in the present economic crisis his consumption is reduced to a minimum."[106] By the early 1950s a UK trade mission estimated that roughly 36 percent of the Egyptian population belonged to the middle class.

> Those in the middle income bracket—small farmers, clerks and the better paid industrial workers—are sufficiently well off to be able to afford some non-essentials—such as tobacco, imported foodstuffs, European-style clothing, or durable consumer goods—and saving is a possibility. At the top of the scale come merchants, industrialists, property owners and professional men, whose consumption habits are similar to those of their counterparts in Western Europe. The effective value of an income in the provinces where food and lodging are cheaper is probably 30 percent above that of a similar income in the towns, but purchasing power is concentrated mainly in Cairo because of the large numbers of clerical and commercial employees in the middle income groups who live there.[107]

The commercial agent suggested, however, that cultural preferences skewed the effect of population and income numbers in the market. "Egypt, with her cosmopolitan cities and international tourist traffic, rapidly becomes acquainted with the latest ideas and fashions in consumer goods, and is very receptive to them. Taste tends to the flamboyant, and to the purchase of minor luxuries even at the expense of more essential articles; hence there is a bigger demand for better class goods than the general standard of living might lead one to expect."[108] Despite their urban base, most department stores employed commission agents who carried store merchandise to provincial and even rural customers.[109] Department stores in Cairo also served as regional shopping venues for the upper classes of more provincial parts of the Middle East, including the royal house of Saudi Arabia and other Persian Gulf clients.[110]

Certain seasons and events in the life cycle prompted people to shop who might otherwise have made do with homemade or used goods; specific events also called for the patronage of stores in different parts of the city or with more pronounced cultural identities—e.g., European bookshops for school needs or *baladi* confectioners for holiday treats. Many wealthy consumers purchased clothing during summer trips to Europe and from the large department stores in Cairo and Alexandria but galabiyas for home wear from the Muski and groceries from a neighborhood shop. Middle-class and lower-middle-class customers usually made special purchases such as wedding dresses and school uniforms at local department stores, saving their mundane clothes shopping for the cheaper shops or tailors or the flea market in 'Ataba and the Muski or their neighborhood. Xanthippi Christoforou was such an occasional shopper. A twenty-two-year-old maidservant, she had been sent to Orosdi-Back's Cairo store during a March 1928 sale to price cheap children's shoes for her mistress. Although she did not find any suitable shoes in the basement department, she made her way upstairs to the dress department, where she inspected several silk gowns for herself, despite not having any money in her wallet. The submanager of the store testified that "on that day there was a sale and a big crowd in the shop," and merchandise from the vitrines spilled in the chaos onto store floors.[111]

Although stores themselves set some consumption "seasons" artificially, such as annual winter white sales or seasonal sales that liquidated old stocks to create space for new inventory, other seasons were set by events more extrinsic to the stores, such as the September return to school or religious holidays. In 1943 Sednaoui held a special back-to-school sale of children's clothing and school supplies, including several different gray flannel suits and pants, khaki pants, blue and red wool blazers, and black satin smocks for uniform wear.[112] Cicurel also carried school uniforms used by middle-class and upper-middle-class children in private and parochial schools, as well as "the complete equipment for the schoolchild for the new school year [*rentrée des classes*]: smocks [*tabliers*] and uniforms for various schools; all clothing for schoolchildren; complete outfits [*trousseaux*] for boarding-school students; leather satchels and briefcases; and pens."[113]

Ramadan had long been a holiday associated with gift giving and the purchase of new clothing and was especially commercially significant because it affected a large segment of the population. Chabrol, one of the chroniclers of Napoleon's army in Egypt, wrote in the late eighteenth century that "Ramadan is the most appropriate time for the sale of wool and silk cloths: at this time, all the individuals and nobles of the country purchase new clothing for themselves, their wives, and their servants."[114] In the twentieth century, people who might not have shopped much the rest of the year patronized stores selling cloth and clothing around Ramadan and the month's final feast day, ʿid al-fitr, in particular.[115] Stores extensively advertised their goods and offered sales to respond to this seasonal surge of consumer demand.[116] In September 1910, for example, Chemla ran an enormous sale to mark the end of Ramadan. The store offered its special bargains from the "biggest factories in Europe" as a "gift for this blessed holiday" to its "noble customers" and also "the general public." The sale particularly featured an array of silk, woolen, and cotton fabrics that the store suggested could be made up into women's coverings (*milayat*), dresses, shirts, suits, nightgowns, and other clothing.[117] Ramadan sales were so important to local businesses that the British trade official in 1929 attributed the stagnation of the cotton piece-goods market "to the fact that Ramadan this year fell between two crops and consequently the fellaheen were short of money, with the result that importers and merchants found themselves overstocked."[118] The ʿid al-adha, or Feast of the Sacrifice, also customarily involved the purchase of cloth or clothing. For this holiday in 1925, al-Mawardi offered price reductions in all its departments.[119] Christian holidays formed important selling days for many stores as well.[120] The French commercial agent advised in 1929 that the "important thing is that [French imports to Egypt] arrive *before* the holidays of Christmas and the days of the Catholic and Greek [new] year."[121] Jewish holidays such as Passover also prompted occasional department-store promotions.[122] The increased sales volume of holidays remained so important to retailers that extra hours in these seasons were legally required of commercial employees, especially of department and clothing stores, throughout the first half of the twentieth century.[123] Holiday seasonal purchases created an irregular but significant contribution to store sales by the lower-middle urban classes that widely expanded the reach of department stores and their popular visibility. They also point to the multiethnic and multilingual character of Egypt's urban commercial culture in this period.

The multicultural character of urban Egypt caused department stores to struggle to stock goods that could appeal to their customers. Unlike the morseled styles available at the flea market, stores' floors and windows featured mannequins dressed completely in *ifrangi* costumes. New ready-made clothing was relatively rare in Egyptian markets, because of the availability of cheap labor for tailoring, especially for women's apparel, and the variety of vestimentary styles that resulted from the plurality of Egyptian urban society at this time. Sherbini and Sherif noted as late as the middle 1950s that the congeries of distinct communities in Egyptian society generally discouraged the sale of ready-made clothing: "The diversity of dress ranging from 'rags to riches' . . . reflects the influence of several cultures on different segments of the population. Wide differences in habitual dress make a complete assortment of made-up garments an unprofitable business from the standpoint of the Egyptian manufacturer."[124] In such local conditions, piece-good textiles and notions, more than ready-made clothing, played a central role in department-store merchandising, and interior layouts of department stores reflected this emphasis.

Although shopping became increasingly associated with women's work for the family, men and women patronized stores throughout the first half of the century. In the 1920s Chemla offered a bonus to its "loyal and numerous male clients" who shopped for men's goods in the store. The store identified a "masculine toilette" as comprising "cloth, men and boys' clothing and underwear, shirts, wool sweaters (and vests), undershorts, neckties, suspenders, hosiery, hats, gloves, etc."[125] Sednaoui prominently sold men's clothes in the 1920s (see Figure 6). Men remained important as shoppers throughout this time, purchasing food, furniture, and clothing for themselves and their families.[126] Advertisements targeted men and women, usually separately, in the 1920s and 1930s; in the 1940s, however, department stores also began to depict their customers in advertisements as small, companionate-style families made up of a husband, wife, and child (see Figure 7).[127] Women's role in neighborhood shopping varied by class in the nineteenth and early twentieth centuries. Lower- and middle-class women had longer or more frequent experience of public work and movement in market spaces than upper-class women, who more commonly bought goods brought into their homes by itinerant peddlers or sent their servants or male relatives to the market. Nevertheless, many of the upper- and middle-class Muslim and Coptic women who had been secluded in the previous decades began to shop in big stores in the first decades of the twentieth century.

Complex economic and social changes pushed women into department stores, including the active women's press that developed in the 1890s, increased education in household sciences, and the diffusion of the ideal of the bourgeois home, with its functional differentiation of space. Reformers concurred that

Figure 6. Sednaoui advertised its selection of men's clothes in 1929. Views of store branches are from, counterclockwise from top right, Tanta, Cairo, Alexandria, Mansura, and Asyut. *Ruz al-yusuf*, no. 351 (12 November 1934), 29.

Figure 7. The Egyptian Products Sales Company advertised winter clothes for men, women, and children. The family gazes into a display window featuring bolts of cloth produced by Bank Misr companies. Printed cloth was particularly popular in the middle 1930s. *Al-Ahram*, 1 November 1938, 10.

specific rooms furnished for dining, sleeping, or sitting would cultivate morally strong and nationalistic children, as opposed to multipurpose rooms filled with mats, pillows, and low tables. The "New Woman," according to Mona Russell, became "the general administrator and purchasing agent for her home. Whether wealthy or middle class, she was responsible for the careful and efficient running of her household."[128] Middle- and upper-class women claimed an expanded public role by framing their shopping and consumption as crucial work to transform "urban homes [into] building blocks of the nation."[129]

Stores increasingly catered to these women shopping in person. Department stores employed women salesclerks to prevent the exposure of customers' bodies during the intimacy of shopping in public space. Huda Sha'rawi, the Egyptian nationalist-feminist cited earlier, recounted in her memoir the accommodations stores made for upper-class and secluded women in the 1910s when such women were beginning to enter public shops. "When I entered

Chalon[s], the eunuch proceeded straight to the store manager and brusquely demanded the place for the harem. We were led to the department for women's apparel, behind a pair of screens hastily erected to obscure me from view. A saleswoman was assigned to wait on me and to bring whatever I wished."[130] The creation of a secluded area in the public space of the store helped Sha'rawi's family feel more comfortable about women's shopping and physical exposure, especially as maintaining class status in new store spaces was a complex process. In the 1910s and 1920s, local department stores also provided their services in customer homes to address upper-class concerns about the public exposure of women's bodies. Stein's Department Store in 'Ataba Square had in 1909 ateliers on the second floor that made up men's, women's, and boys' clothing to measure or "in accordance with directions given by customers on the self-measurement forms which are . . . so popular."[131] Morums in the 1920s advertised its *atelier de couture* in the women's ready-made clothing department, which offered the special service of making up customers' own material into garments (*travailler à façon*) and offered the services of its designer to give advice on the style and cut of dresses; she was also available to come to customers' homes.[132] That downtown stores attracted a wide variety of shoppers provides evidence of the stores' transcultural identity as well as the insufficiency of dualistic models for understanding colonial consumption. Store merchandising practices both responded to the diverse array of shoppers and cultivated them, thus becoming a crucial link among overlapping urban commercial communities.

Department stores formed a central space in interwar Egyptian public life, one which self-defined as radically demarcating two distinct cultures of consumption but in actual practice served as a hub for the different groups living in Egypt's cities. As purveyors of a much wider range of goods than other commercial venues in Egypt, department stores and their promotional marketing in shop windows, interior layout, advertising, and catalogs reached to various communities of shoppers. Department stores positioned themselves as "cultural primers" for a certain cosmopolitan modernity based on metropolitan, and especially French, culture.[133] The stores' ability to marshal goods as diverse as dining-room sets, table and bed linens, *ifrangi* clothing, popular and imported cloth, shoes, toys, and perfumes to construct prescriptions made them relatively powerful and totalizing cultural agents. In the late nineteenth century, European and American department stores also proclaimed themselves the creators of a new bourgeois lifestyle,[134] and many Egyptian stores self-consciously modeled themselves on these stores. Egyptian department stores did not, how-ever, simply channel an undigested French culture into Egypt, even if store architecture deliberately attempted such a mimesis. Certain features of the Egyptian commercial landscape—its cultural and linguistic diversity, the resul-tant range of styles in clothing and household furnishings among the popula-tion, the availability of cheap labor—altered and modulated the impact of store prescriptions. Egyptian catalogs were distinctive in reflecting the multilingual and multiethnic context of the commercial world in which they operated, and a merchandise focus on cloth and tailoring accessories rather than ready-made goods provided stores with the flexibility to accommodate shoppers from the cultures of consumption current in Egyptian cities. The experience of depart-ment stores also points to the complex way many Egyptians understood French culture to be an aspect of modernity rather than a threat to national sover-eignty. That nationalists such as Sha'rawi would promote shopping in depart-ment stores and even consider the local Bon Marché a suitable venue for the display of nationalist policy reflects the prevalence of this view.

Flexible in their marketing and merchandising, Egyptian department stores participated in a hybridized consumer culture that challenged the dichoto-mous image of the dual city perhaps more unexpectedly than transitional urban hubs such as 'Ataba and Sayyida Zaynab. The diversity of migration tra-jectories among store owners and employees, coming from points throughout the Mediterranean Basin, illustrates the many ways people could be Egyptian in the prewar and interwar periods. Shopping for momentous occasions in life—marriage, promotions, births, or important trips—brought a wider va-riety of people into department stores than those who could afford to shop there for their more mundane consumption needs, thus suggesting the need to recast the stores as more than upper-class enclaves. The stores' ability to bridge different constituencies, then, enlarged and ensured a broad customer base. At the same time, department stores with their vast stocks of luxurious goods, sumptuous premises, and "bewitching" display windows dominated the urban spaces in which they were situated. Many Egyptians, such as the fictional brown street urchin on 'Imad al-Din Street pressing himself to the store win-dow "in order to see . . . better," felt both captivated and held captive by the profusion and richness of the goods displayed to enthrall them. The ambigui-ties of the stores' cultural affiliations would increasingly become liabilities as nationalist rhetoric turned to a series of dichotomies to call for the remaking of local commerce.

3 ANTICOLONIAL BOYCOTTS AND NATIONAL TRADE

IN "AN OPEN ADDRESS to the British in Egypt" that she wrote in English in December 1924, Esther Fahmy Wissa criticized the numbing overconsumption of foreign goods among Egyptians. She began by sarcastically thanking the British for the benefits of English rule. "You have improved our financial position," Wissa continued. "You have regulated our government, you have helped to make us wealthy and prosperous, and you have introduced Western Civilization in Egypt. You have taught us how to speak English, how to wear European clothes, how to use a knife and fork, how to take tea in the afternoon, how to dance, and lots of other little things, but unfortunately we are not any the happier. Do you know that although we thank you for all this, yet we are not quite satisfied." Instead, Wissa argued, British rule had transformed the nation into a bloated, immobile captive, dutifully overconsuming in the service of the empire and awaiting sacrifice. "We say among ourselves that you are making 'fois gras' of us," Wissa continued in her address. "'Fois gras' is a Western invention you know, and I am sure you all know how it is made. If you don't, I'll tell you. To make 'fois gras,' you tie the geese to a post, so that they don't move much, then you feed them on the best and richest food. You stuff them and stuff them, until their liver expands to a huge size, then before they die out, you kill them to make 'fois gras.'"[1]

Like other activists, Wissa portrayed nationalism as an "awakening." Literally tightening its belt under self-imposed spending austerity, the nation in her vision was rising from the torpor of overconsumption. Only by starving could the nation gain independence and political self-expression:

We tried to break away from our bonds, but you held us back. You said, "Silly creatures to run away from this lovely food we are giving you; you will starve if you break away from us." But we want to starve! It will take us a long while to get rid of this fat, this unhealthy liver, and if we don't hurry up and move, we will die. . . . Don't you see that a goose that has been fattened, has to pay for her fattening and has to be slaughtered to give up the lovely delicious "fois gras," and do you blame it when it cries out that it does not want to be slaughtered? . . . Fortunately, we are wide awake now, and although our lives are fatty and we feel somewhat heavy after your feeding up, yet we have run away from you, and we are not afraid of starving. We know that you will try to starve us, to make us long after the "fois gras" fattening, but we have seen the slaughter, and we want anything but that![2]

Narrating colonial relations as the forced consumption of excess, rather than the appropriation of surplus (the exploitation of labor or the extraction of resources), reflected Wissa's class and gender position, although her assertion tapped into a fundamental concern that was widely shared in Egyptian society: consuming colonialism could be deadly.

Consumerism became a primary theater of anticolonial politics in Egypt as elsewhere in the opening decades of the twentieth century. Wilsonian rhetoric about the self-determination of nations combined with the model of consumerist politics advocated most prominently by Gandhi in India to put pressure on colonial empires across the globe in the 1920s and 1930s. In Egypt this led to a series of boycotts—self-starvings in Wissa's language—spearheaded by elite women first exercising their political muscle and encompassing broad swaths of rural, provincial, and university groups. Boycott committees instructed consumers and merchants on how to distinguish the local from the foreign and emphasized the reach of colonialism into the mundane areas of personal and household provisioning. Since consumption was crucial to the implementation of colonialism, boycotters argued, nationalist protest had to extend into the kitchens, wardrobes, and pocketbooks of everyday Egyptians to be effective. By the early 1930s, world economic contraction renewed pressure on global colonialism and increased the repression of local regimes, and Egypt again engaged in widespread boycotts in 1931–1932. The boycotts spurred local efforts to industrialize, most prominently in textile manufacturing, and to create new, nationalist marketing spaces. As a pivotal moment in the nationalist struggle, boycotts made consumption visible as a site of politics.

Boycotts and their industrial and commercial responses warrant scholarly attention because they expanded the political field by drawing nonpolitical social groups and realms of activity into nationalist movements. What distinguishes boycotts of metropolitan goods in colonial settings such as Egypt, India, or China—societies subject to the colonial rule or aggression of a society that defined itself as culturally different and superior—is the way those actions foregrounded the link between culture and consumerism. Wissa's metaphor of the "'fois gras' fattening" signaled explicitly the power of commodities to "introduce[] Western Civilization" to Egypt. The growing cultural focus of Egyptian boycotts would strengthen a public discourse of bifurcation, a sharpening that would increasingly narrow the definition of what counted as Egyptian and intensify scrutiny and censure of those who crossed between the two dominant poles of culture. Also notable in Wissa's critique is its focus on the corporeal and intimate nature of consumption and the consequences this held for colonial and consumer agency. Confined and captive, the Egyptian herself consumed and thereby cultivated the outcome desired by colonialism.[3] The "'fois gras' fattening" thus represented the creation of a colonial subjectivity premised in self-destruction: by capitulating to increasing consumer desire, the goose amplified its own desirability as a commodity, transforming itself into the "lovely delicious" product so craved by colonial societies. The force-feeding of bound colonial economies with metropolitan products and culture, and the eventual longing for these objects that gradually developed, emphasized the intimate and embodied reach of the colonial market and the consumerist politics mobilized in response to it. The metaphor of colonial rule as cruel animal husbandry thus threw into relief how the corporeal consumption practices of captured bodies could nourish colonial power. This corporeality marked a deeper intrusion of colonialism than that imagined and circulated by the culture workers of print capitalism.[4]

Although Wissa's protest used commodities and cultural forms common among elites, her own biography illustrates the complex but crucial linkages among social groups that formed under colonialism and consumption in this period—linkages ultimately responsible for the success of the boycotts. Dismissed by some British officials as "a nuisance" and "a bit loonie," Wissa (1895–1990) was well known for her outspokenness on public issues and her leadership in Egyptian society.[5] She actively supported the nationalist movement and was an early leader in the Wafd Party; she served as vice president of the Wafdist Women's Central Committee (WWCC) during the boycotts of the 1920s and later helped found the Saadist Women's Committee.[6] In addition to her role in national politics, she worked diligently for social reform and advances in education for Coptic Christians and women; in 1924 she founded the Work for Egypt Society, a charitable organization in Alexandria, and directed it until 1962.[7] The hotel stationery that she used to write her personal petitions to British officials reveals her ability to move across Egypt and Europe. She seemed to feel equally at home in Asyut, Cairo, Alexandria, and even London. Her childhood home was furnished with Khedive Ismaʿil's furniture sold at liquidation in the 1870s and 1880s, and she was educated in the American Mission School.[8] Beth Baron has noted that "as a Coptic notable and from a family that had converted to Protestantism, Esther had a degree of mobility, excellent English language skills, and access to officials, which made her eminently suited to represent the Wafd."[9]

As important for her political success was her link to merchants. Wissa came from a family with its roots in the textile trade. The family fortune traced back to the mid-nineteenth century when two brothers (Wissa Wissa and Hanna Wissa) began to go door to door along the Nile villages in Upper Egypt selling notions. According to family lore, a chance river salvage of cases of silk cloth enabled the brothers to open a textile shop, which gradually expanded into a vibrant business outfitting the Sudan trade and servicing a wide network of traders south of Asyut with merchandise from Cairo. The Wissa brothers eventually moved into trading agricultural produce, including cotton, and slowly began to acquire large parcels of land in Upper Egypt, especially in the 1890s.[10] Asyut itself was well known for the production of cotton textiles, woven on handlooms by the 1910s from thread imported from Lancashire in England. Used to make a common and customary form of Egyptian dress, the galabiya,[11] this Asyuti fabric was sold in Cairo and other towns in Egypt, as well as locally.[12]

Esther Wissa in the 1920s would not herself have worn a galabiya at the public events over which she presided. The *ifrangi* commodities included in her protest point to her elite status (French foie gras, afternoon tea, European-style dancing and clothing fashions, silverware), and pictures of her depict her in European clothes.[13] Yet her nationalist protests resonated with the widest popular mobilizations against the British presence because textile politics played a central role in the broader colonial "'fois gras' fattening." Merchants, and especially textile merchants, acted as the common thread that knit the upper and lower classes into commercial networks. The webs of connection among commodities mobilized a wide array of Egyptians, and as a result, commercial goods became the lynchpin of political activism in the anticolonial struggle.

PURCHASING POWER: BOYCOTTS
AND ANTICONSUMERISM IN COLONIAL POLITICS

Commercial boycotts emerged in the first decades of the twentieth century as a common and powerful instrument of anticolonial protest worldwide.[14] Although eighteenth-century Americans first demonstrated the power of nonimportation and nonconsumption movements, by the 1910s boycotts formed an acknowledged staple in anticolonial movements from China to Africa.[15] Timothy Breen refers to the boycott as "the distinguishing mark of colonial protest, what cultural anthropologists would call its signature."[16] Excluded from participation in formal political processes, colonized subjects turned the marketplace into a forum for public culture and "made goods speak to power."[17] A "weapon of the weak" for political outsiders, boycotts thus invited participation from groups, such as women or the middling classes, historically without access to political decision making and were commonly portrayed as political tools in the service of a nation, a region, or a social group.[18] Over time and in different political economic contexts, boycotts have emphasized either the act of purchasing or the act of using (or not using) certain goods as the key political moment of consumption. Although some scholars have mapped these changing emphases over time onto changing models of economic thought,[19] targets of boycotts also differed in colonial and noncolonial contexts. In colonial situations in which the struggle for recognition as a nation-state and national community predominated, the crucial political act lay in the use or nonuse of merchandise rather than its purchase. Consumption functioned as an arena of symbolic politics in which the use of particular, locally made goods, such as homespun clothing, acted foremost as a claim of membership in the national community, even if it was also designed to damage colonial trade.[20] Boycotts thus played a crucial role in promoting a sense of community, trust, and communication among people from various backgrounds, regions, and classes because "ordinary consumer goods . . . [could] bring strangers together in common cause."[21] A substitute for formal participation in politics, colonial boycotts worked, then, both to define the boundaries of a new polity and to stimulate awareness of the link of colonialism to commerce and consumption.

As a result, consumer politics charged the marketplace with a particular and new moral valence. Morality became increasingly associated with the goods in the marketplace rather than the character of the marketplace as a whole, which assumed the status of a neutral space and therefore became a critical site of political and moral struggle and intervention.[22] Boycotts also challenged the existence of a public-private division in society as they were premised on a belief that consumption acted as a vector to transmit the morality of actions from one side of the divide to the other. According to Lawrence Glickman, "Consumer activists stressed that shopping, often understood as the quint-essentially private act in capitalist society, was in fact an unavoidably public responsibility. . . . Radiating inward in the web of consumption, goods brought into the home took with them the very real, if undetectable, congeries of re-lationships and forces that made their production, distribution, and sale pos-sible. . . . The outward radiation of shopping decisions . . . [meant] that every individual consumer action had powerful social repercussions, which also were generally invisible to consumers but no less their responsibility."[23] As boycotts heightened awareness of the ability of consumption decisions to link consum-ers to broader political and social communities, they fostered a new model of citizen-consumer, responsible on the one hand for protecting the welfare of the nation by monitoring the market and on the other for building, through its purchases, a strong nation and national economy.[24] By the 1950s and 1960s, this new role had transformed into an idea of economic citizenship: that consumers had become a political class with rights that should be protected.[25]

Colonial boycotts highlighted the relationship between individual consum-ers and particular material goods in the marketplace, especially their ability to link the intimate space of the home or self with the broader arena of pol-itics. In other words, the colonial boycott marked the bodies of individuals as crucial sites of nationalism.[26] In the world economy of the first half of the twentieth century, "boycotts played a pivotal role in instilling the notions that every product had a nationality and that product-nationality should deter-mine purchasing decisions," Karl Gerth has observed.[27] In China's twentieth-century National Products Movement, boycott language popularized a sense of national community by inscribing material culture with a radical duality between the foreign and the national.[28] National products came increasingly to be defined "by content rather than by style; Chinese labor, management, raw material, and capital and not the shape of the garment made it Chinese."[29] Like China, Egypt lived under semicolonial status for most of this time, and its boycotts reflected a similarly fractured nature of political power. Ultimately, both states would draw on the logic and social acceptance of boycott rhetoric to create compliance with nationalization programs in the 1950s and 1960s.[30] As Wissa's protest made clear, and as will emerge from a closer examination of Egyptian boycotts in this chapter, a combined emphasis on cultural bifurcation and the corporeality of colonial and national symbolic politics marked late-colonial consumer protests as different from boycotts in other global and historical settings.

Boycotts proliferated as a political tool across the Middle East and South Asia in the first decades of the twentieth century. The 1908 Ottoman boycott of Austrian goods to protest the annexation of Bosnia-Herzegovina powerfully mobilized patriotic sentiments against the penetration of European capital into the Ottoman Empire, and it spread from Istanbul to Tripoli in North Africa.[31] Boycott actions frequently accompanied collective resistance among Palestinians to the British and Zionists in the 1920s and 1930s.[32] The most widely publicized use of anticonsumerism as a political tool was the Indian case. The 1906 Bengali boycott of British goods and the ongoing *swadeshi* ("home industry") politics associated with Mohandas Gandhi during the interwar period of mass nationalism particularly inspired Egyptian nationalists to move their struggle into the realms of economy and culture.[33] Egyptian nationalist party leaders had formed important relationships with Indian activists in the prewar period in metropolitan centers such as London, Lausanne, Paris, and Geneva, and these experiences helped form a common culture of anti-British protest.[34] Gandhi launched the noncooperation movement in India and the Indian National Congress adopted the principle of *swadeshi* in 1920, at a time when Egyptians and other colonial subjects demanded representation at the postwar settlement conferences. In September 1925 *al-Ahram* published a long interview with a visiting Muslim Indian physician on the principles, strategies, and effectiveness of economic boycott.[35] The Society of the Eastern Bond regularly brought Indian leaders to Cairo, and Indian and Egyptian leaders met during Islamic and caliphal congresses of the 1920s; Egyptian women probably had contacts with Indian women through some of these events, and certainly Indian women were frequently profiled in the women's press.[36] It was Gandhi's stopover on the Suez Canal during his trip to London in September 1931, however, that would generate some of the most ardent inspiration for Egyptians to boycott British goods.[37] By the middle 1930s Egyptian satirists used images of Gandhi and homespun cloth to denounce local elites and government officials as tools of imperialism (see Figure 8).

Figure 8. Misri Effendi, symbol of middle-class Egypt, addresses Gandhi. "Naked and Naked. The Ministry failed to solve the problem of mortgage debts and the crisis remains as it was. Misri Effendi says, 'What! Why are you naked like that—is your finance minister also Hasan Sabri Bey?'" *Ruz al-yusuf*, no. 332 (2 July 1934), back cover.

Egyptian patriots would use both the boycott model of refusing to purchase British products and the *swadeshi* model of supporting indigenous goods in the fight against ongoing British imperialism. As in India, the Egyptian campaign's two-pronged nature, appealing to both public and private interests, allowed a broad spectrum of political support; calls to encourage native industry appealed to domestic textile manufacturers and others in the political elite as well as to local workers who would benefit from expanded demand. As Indian nationalist leader Subhas Chandra Bose put it in 1931, "When one buys an indigenous product, probably of worse quality or at a higher price than the imported product, he does this for the good of the nation as a whole."[38] As in India and China, Egyptian boycotters protested both the cultural and the economic encroachment of the colonial economy into the marketplace, the home, and the body.

NATIONALIST BOYCOTTS IN THE AFTERMATH OF THE 1919 REVOLUTION

In March 1919 Egyptians took to the streets to protest the British presence in Egypt. In what would become known as the 1919 Revolution, transport workers, students, judges, lawyers, and eventually peasants and upper-class women joined in protests that expanded from Egypt's major urban centers and large provincial cities to rural areas. Sparking the protests was Britain's opposition to the delegation (or *wafd*) of Sa'd Zaghlul and other leaders to represent Egypt at the Versailles Peace Conference in the aftermath of the First World War. The mass mobilizations and petition campaigns in support of the *wafd* demonstrated the vibrancy of the nationalist movement and the deep opposition to British rule. The "ladies' demonstrations" in March 1919 played a particularly powerful symbolic role in articulating the depth of Egyptian discontent and ultimately unity.[39] Nevertheless, the 1919 struggle only partly succeeded. The British granted limited independence in 1922. By the following year, the country had a constitution that allowed the establishment of a parliament but reserved key powers for the British, including retention of British troops in Egypt, of the system of juridical protection for minorities and foreigners, and of British sovereignty of Sudan and the Suez Canal.

The British also continued to refuse reentry to the exiled Wafdist leaders, including Sa'd Zaghlul. To maintain pressure on the government, the Wafd's women's auxiliary, the WWCC, initiated a widely publicized and successful boycott of British goods, merchants, and banks that complemented the subscription campaign for a new national bank, which would become Bank Misr, to fund local industry. Serving as WWCC president was Huda Sha'rawi, whose earlier struggle against the patriarchal confines of her upper-class family had strengthened her determination to shop in person at downtown department stores such as Chalons. Writing (in French) on "behalf of the women of Egypt," Sha'rawi telegraphed the British government and British newspapers on January 21, 1922, that

> Egyptian women hold a special meeting. . . . They decide to boycott everything English—merchandise, merchants, artisans, bureaucrats, doctors, pharmacists, dentists, etc. No cooperation with them. Took an oath if the English people do not intervene to redress the conduct of their government and bring it to a resolution more compatible with honor and justice, [they will] instill in their sons hatred for their oppressors that they will transmit to future generations.[40]

The women's committee cited several political demands, including the return of Sa'd Zaghlul, the suppression of martial law, the abolition of the protectorate, and the resignation of British officials such as Foreign Secretary George Curzon and High Commissioner of Egypt Edmund Allenby. The women's collective "religious oath" to be steadfast in their actions underlined their seriousness of purpose: "to boycott the British aggressor, to deny to ourselves and to the people close to us everything that those usurpers have manufactured. By God, their shops are forbidden to us. By God, their factories are forbidden to us. By God, all that is connected to them is forbidden to us." The oath appealed ecumenically to a monolithic "God . . . and all his bountiful messengers," since the WWCC included both Christian and Muslim women.[41] The women linked up with their networks in elite charitable organizations such as the Muhammad 'Ali Society and the New Woman Association and broadcast their plans by telephone.[42]

The days of the boycott found women regularly meeting to discuss strategies and products, sanctioning local merchants and consumers in urban shopping areas, and overseeing the production at home of many of the imported products they usually purchased. On the first day, "a squad of twenty women were out in their motors and carriages interviewing the principal shopkeepers of Cairo and Alexandria."[43] Grace Seton, an American woman visiting Egypt during this time, observed prominent Egyptian women serving homemade cakes at tea and remarked on the ability of these women to enforce the boycott:

At first they were laughed at, but before a week had passed a delegation, this time of the shopkeepers, had waited upon the women and asked for their co-operation. They organized Women's Committees in the big cities and in the provinces, and . . . held a meeting in Cairo of over 2,000 women who made political speeches and vowed continued effort to boycott the British and British goods. . . . The boycott affected the English merchants very seriously for several months, and then the change of government . . . lessened public opposition. The merchants have been able to carry on a volume of business with foreigners which helps them to get on without the native trade. But there can be no doubt that the business of many firms was crippled much more than they are willing to admit. Some firms closed, some suspended business and others had liquidation sales.[44]

One boycott committee member had personally confronted "a shopkeeper, an English haberdasher. She was on the opposite side of the street when she saw two Egyptian gentlemen enter the English shop. At once she went across and addressed the two men in Arabic, asking them not to buy English goods. . . . The two Egyptians left their expensive purchases of neckties on the counter and walked away from the furious haberdasher."[45] Boycott committees also formed among upper-class and upper-middle-class male students from universities and secondary schools; delegations of these groups visited important Egyptian provinces, such as Asyut, al-Minya, and Bani Swayf, and advocated the transfer of funds from British banks into the new Bank Misr and the boycott of British stores in favor of "national stores," which explicitly included the Cairo department stores of al-Gamal, al-Mawardi, and Cicurel.[46] Egyptians abroad also supported the new movement. Sha'rawi received a letter from "the Egyptian society in Paris . . . saying, 'We greet your patriotism and support your demands. We call upon you to publish this among the parties, and we hope you will carry on with the implement[ation] of the idea of boycottage.'"[47]

The call to boycott apparently reached broadly into Egyptian society. The Ladies' Awakening Society of Zifta, an important textile center of the Delta, called for the boycott of English trade. The Zifta committee included school administrators and teachers.[48] Safiyya Zaghlul wrote to her exiled husband, Sa'd, in April 1922 that "the people in different quarters ha[d] refrained from dealing with English merchants and founded national markets which they called Saad's markets. The government opposed these last named which opposition resulted in the death of some and the wounding of many specially in Shandawil."[49] The newspaper *Misr* reported on January 31, 1922, that "a new market" had been established "by the people" of Girga to replace the "English company's market and its name is Sa'd's market [*suq Sa'd*]. It is held the Wednesday of every week instead of on Tuesday, which was the day for the Company market." The paper also reported a similar market in Samnud.[50] In Buhayra the boycott of the English Markets Company was also reported to be strong in mid-January and was especially supported by the "wearers of blue *galalib*," or in other words, peasants.[51]

As the establishment of nationalist markets suggests, the primary goal of the boycotts in 1922 was commercial and financial—to boycott British firms and representatives. Although a strong part of the boycott platform was the call for local industrialization, large-scale Egyptian industries were not widespread and little emphasis was placed on the purchase of indigenous goods. Rather, the boycott strategy was essentially to buy non-British items (i.e., items imported from other countries) and to purchase from national stores. Many merchants probably simply put away their stocks of British cloths and advertised their French, other European, or local merchandise. French government officials, noting that support for the boycott was widespread, even hoped that the boycott would enhance French trade in Egypt, although they cautioned that the outcome of the boycott would be complicated by the general stagnation of business.[52] Some storeowners clearly advertised their citizenship or national origins; Salamander's Fashionable Stores announced, for example, that their owners were not English but rather local minorities.[53] Other stores still advertised their stocks of "Egyptian clothes" and "national soap" several months after the boycott had been called.[54] Thus one effect of the boycott was to force a specific and public definition among merchants about what it meant to be Egyptian.

Many merchants complained, however, about the hardships the boycott placed on them. One newspaper article argued that "most of the goods that are in our markets are of English origin, [and to move] to a new stage in which all we need is [met] by other goods in our markets, we must provide Egyptian merchants a respite to sell what they have of English goods."[55] The writer suggested that an adequate delay would be six months for textiles and building supplies and three months for food stuffs and fuel; he also called for new methods to make information available to Egyptian merchants about products from other countries, such as garnering help from local chambers of commerce to bring in agents from other countries.[56] Another man, identifying himself as

"Muhammad Ghali Fawda, the merchant in Shubra," worried to *al-Muqattam* at the end of January 1922 that if Egyptian merchants could not respond to the demands of their customers, many of whom might in fact be British, other foreigners, or simply not participating in the boycott, local merchants might be driven out of business altogether. "Doesn't it suffice that [opinion leaders] have prohibited the display of English goods in [the Egyptian merchant's] store, while he doesn't know what fate has in store for him?" he asked. If his customers are not supportive of the boycott, "should he reduce his work, close his shop, and become unemployed so that his business transfers as a result to the hand of one of the foreigners? Or what is the solution?"[57] Other merchants did, however, create special marketing spaces for their locally produced goods. Al-Mawardi department store announced in *al-Muqattam* in February 1922 that it had "founded a branch of the store for national textiles [*al-mansujat al-wataniyya*]."[58] A man named Husayn al-Halabi claimed in January to have established a cooperative society to distribute locally produced goods throughout Egypt that "did not involve politics . . . or foreigners."[59] He had solicited the textile handworkers of Mahalla, Samnud, and Kum al-Nur for his society, as well as a cigarette company and some other local producers.[60]

Merchant and customer complaints about a dearth of alternative goods did lead to some calls for Egypt to develop national industries to produce locally many of the products imported from Britain and Europe. In January 1922, for example, an anonymous writer from Alexandria urged the founding of companies to manufacture glass and pottery, tan leather, and do spinning and weaving.[61] In February 1922 Mustafa Muhammad al-Ray'a promoted his efforts to weave textiles on mechanical looms and sell them in Cairo. He wrote to the newspaper *Misr*, "I have dedicated my life to the service of my beloved country and brought my talents and mental powers toward improving the manufacture of local textiles [*sina'at al-mansujat al-ahliyya*]. . . . I committed myself to the good idea of supporting the industry and encouraging Egyptian trade." Al-Ray'a's solution was to

> procure the most modern mechanical machines for weaving that run on electricity. I chose the workshop of our textiles on Husam al-Din Street no. 13 in the Sabtiyya district near the Cairo train station market, and we established there as a trial year. It is a large factory plant [*fawariqa*] that [will] expand with the rest of the machines that have been ordered. We chose for its technical direction the greatly talented Muhammad effendi Husayn Sadiq who practiced the

art [of weaving] and excelled at it at the famous schools of Lyon in France; the newspapers constantly speak of him with praise and display his picture. . . . Our center is the Ghuriyya [district]. Since it is difficult for people to travel, we have established a branch in ʿAtaba al-Khadra Square at number one ʿAbd al-ʿAziz Street, to display all the textiles. It is small now, but by the grace of God it will grow large.[62]

Al-Rayʿa politely "invited" his compatriot readers "to look at the first building in the creation of our economic renaissance, or, more clearly, the first Egyptian factory established in Egypt in the modern era."[63]

Saʿd Zaghlul was freed in the spring of 1923, but the WWCC renewed its anti-British boycott efforts in the fall of 1924 during Egyptian government negotiations with the British over the status of Sudan.[64] The women's boycott committee in 1924 continued to "boycott . . . everything English whether in Egypt or abroad and to demand of the Egyptian Government that they should share with the nation in that boycottage," as well as to protest issues regarding Sudan.[65] The WWCC resolved "to form a committee from among Egyptian Ladies to be known as 'the boycottage committee,' and to voice the demand for another committee to be formed from among Egyptian men, so that both committees may carry out the resolutions of the assembly."[66] The 1924 boycott kept an array of men and women involved and active in the Wafdist nationalist struggle.

The boycotts of 1922–1924 offered, then, a pivotal moment in which the deep imbrication of political economy and culture inhering in cloth, tea biscuits, neckties, and other commodities became visible. As economic nationalists had hoped, the events of 1922–1924 opened up economic and political space for the establishment of local industry and companies to distribute their products. Although a novel tactic, the boycott fit in well with the overall nationalist program, which advocated economic independence from both British capital to finance the development of the economy and British imports of manufactured goods. Blocked by the British and their local allies from participation in international politics, the Wafd Party and its supporters turned to their power as consumers to protest colonial subordination. Local newspapers promoted new market spaces and manufacturing concerns, and publicized consumption practices linked people in newly visible ways. The boycott actions also point to the imbrication of the local and the foreign in urban commercial culture: goods intermingled in shops, Egyptian store owners purveyed British goods, boycott adherence was broadcast on telephones and enforced in motor cars, and even newly established local industry used imported machines. As a new forum for creating common cause, Egyptian boycotts in the 1920s were intended to speak to power in a united voice but at the same time revealed the complex contours of consumption politics and the meanings of Egyptian identity.

ENCOURAGING EGYPTIAN GOODS:
1930S ECONOMIC NATIONALISM

In the early 1930s, the nation replayed the boycotts of the 1920s, but on a somewhat smaller scale with a slightly different focus.[67] Again led in part by supporters of the Wafd Party, the 1931 boycotts were primarily organized by youth and university groups, although they received support from women's committees as well. In the context of the early 1930s, the creation and support of local industry became the primary aim of the boycotts. Whereas the 1922 boycott had been specifically anti-British, by the 1930s the campaign focused on buying Egyptian instead of foreign products, although anti-British themes still resonated loudly. One reason for the shift was that British dominance in textile imports had severely declined by the early 1930s.[68] Egypt had finally achieved tariff independence in 1930 and could thus create barriers to British imports, which were simultaneously being undercut by cheaper textiles, first from Italy and increasingly from Japan. The 1931 boycott thus responded to the changed realities of the by-then semicolonial political economy.

In 1931 the Wafd was again out of power, and its political enemy, the palace-backed government of Isma'il Sidqi, had abrogated the 1923 constitution and enacted a new level of authoritarian rule. Perhaps paradoxically, Sidqi advocated the protection and fostering of new local mechanized industry, including textile factories. In the context of the international economic crisis of the early 1930s, Sidqi's cabinet undertook extensive internal public works projects, including wells for village drinking water, electrification, government kitchens for the poor, medical relief, and pond drainage. At the same time, it increased repression in the countryside through new security measures and restricted popular suffrage.[69] To discredit the Sidqi regime as a tool of imperialism, the Wafd called simultaneously for a political boycott of Sidqi's government and an economic boycott of British commerce. Elite women, including Esther Wissa and Safiyya Zaghlul, were again visibly involved in the boycott of British goods. "The British high commissioner reported that the boycott was supported by 'Egyptian ladies of the higher classes.' Boycotts were balanced by fund-raisers, as the power of female notables stemmed in great part from their collective purse: the Sa'dist committee, for example, raised funds for workers shot by the police during Sidqi's tenure."[70] The British high commissioner also noted that Egyptian women were issued a booklet "giving them the names of all British institutions, shops, etc. in Cairo, in order that the boycotters may not, through ignorance, have recourse to them."[71] Many nationalist stores avidly promoted their textiles, furniture, and foodstuffs "made in Egypt."[72]

The immediate impetus for the 1931–1932 boycotts, however, was the nationalism that attended the 1931 Agricultural and Industrial Exposition at Gezirah. Although the fair had been held frequently in the 1910s and early 1920s,[73] the 1931 fair was the first since 1926, and as a result it attracted substantial attention and enthusiasm. The French commercial attaché noted that whereas in 1926 the fair had prominently displayed agricultural and industrial machines of "foreign provenance," the exhibition in 1931 almost exclusively displayed Egyptian items, produced locally. "Egyptian industry" was of three types at the fair: "long-established industries" for commodities such as sugar, cement, cigarettes, alcohol, soap, oil, and mineral water (several of which industries were owned by local minorities or had foreign capital, as was congruent with nationalism in this period); "artisanal industries" for furniture, shoes, clothes, rugs, and cookies and pastries; and the "Bank Misr industries," including the press, the cinema and theater group, the fishery, linen, silk and cotton weaving plants, and the mother-of-pearl button plant.[74] Safiyya Zaghlul, still known as the Mother of the Egyptians, was among the political elite who toured the exhibition to encourage nationalist sentiment.[75] Although the British at the time considered that the "stimulus of the Exhibition [would] give this movement a certain temporary, fashionable vogue,"[76] historian 'Abd al-Rahman al-Rafi'i credited the 1931 Agricultural and Industrial Exposition with launching the youth movement for economic nationalism. The fair made obvious, al-Rafi'i noted, the country's ability to produce good-quality industrial products and sparked the economic boycotts and a broader industrial renaissance.[77]

The 1931–1932 boycott was primarily directed toward product nationality, although *national* came increasingly to mean "Egyptian" in a vaguely ethnic way. This corresponded to a wider trend in Egyptian nationalism, which shifted from a liberal territorial nationalism in the 1920s, drawing largely on pharaonic symbolism, to several "supra-Egyptian" ideologies grounded in ethnic, linguistic, or religious determinism.[78] This shift began to bifurcate Egyptian culture and society in increasingly politicized ways. Boycott committees asked

Egyptians to swear, "I will only deal with Egyptians and only use Egyptian goods unless I am sure that no Egyptian and no Egyptian goods exist which can replace the foreigner or the foreign goods." Other circulars called on Egyptians to substitute specific goods for those manufactured by the British: "Boycott all British goods. Boycott Thornycroft cars. Boycott Shell oil and benzine. Use Vacuum benzine and Mobil oil. Boycott Dunlop tires. Use Michelin Tyres."[79] Boycotters repeatedly referenced noncooperation tactics against the British being deployed in India, including the *swadeshi* campaign and British bus boycotts.[80] A local boycott of the British omnibus system did lead to dramatically reduced profits, especially in the Cairo suburb of Shubra.[81] A British official noted that "the boycott [was] . . . in no way directed against French, Italian, American, or German products, but solely and particularly against England,"[82] but in reality the primary thrust of the movement was to support nascent local industry.

In particular, the boycotters juxtaposed foreign silks and local cotton cloth to mark a boundary between Egyptian and non-Egyptian communities. The Committee of the Young Wafdist Volunteers for the Purpose of Encouraging Egyptian Goods, for example, ran a public notice in several Arabic-language Egyptian newspapers on March 3, 1931, declaring, "We have all seen the results of Egyptian brains at the [1931 Agricultural and Industrial] Exhibition and this has caused us to love and encourage home-manufactured goods and to be prepared to put all our energies into propaganda in its favour. This we consider to be a sacred duty to each Egyptian, male or female."[83] To reach the goal that "all Egypt become a single commercial unit, in which Egyptians individually and collectively will find all they require, summer and winter clothing and other necessaries," the committee appointed itself as a public guide to assess and locate appropriate sources of local goods. The committee thus exhorted "all owners of factories and workshops to supply it, at the earliest possible date, with information regarding their goods, with samples of them giving places where they are made and sold and lists of prices so that the Committee may be able to give guidance to the public."[84] One of the campaign's regional branches, the Giza boycott committee, which included a tailor, a shoemaker, and at least one merchant, announced specifically, "It is better for a native to wear coarse clothes made in Egypt than to wear silks of foreign manufacture."[85]

By the following spring (1932), the boycott had broadened to include well-publicized burnings of European clothes. Bonfires were held in the provincial town of Benha, and at Cairo University.[86] The police reported that "a number of students belonging to the Faculties of Law and Letters gathered in the University Yard and set on fire some old European suits. . . . Three students took off their jackets, threw them into the fire and cheered for the boycott of British goods."[87] A few days later, the nationalist magazine *Ruz al-yusuf* ran a cartoon depicting large bonfires surrounded by crowds of Egyptians, with an enormous statue of John Bull—symbol of England—looming behind. John Bull had been tacked with many nails, but one large nail, protruding from his cleaved chest, read "the boycott" (see Figure 9).[88] In the same issue, *Ruz al-yusuf* featured a poem, "Egypt Addresses the Egyptian," on the bonfires that again called on Egyptians to reject "foreign silks" and to consume coarser local cotton cloth.[89]

> The silk garment [*thawb al-harir*] is from your enemy, take it off and trample
>   on it.
> Light the fire and burn his old clothes in it.
> By your blood he amassed his capital and money . . .
> If the son of the nation [*ibn al-watan*] weaves canvas [*khaysh*],
>   wear it and embrace it. . . .
> Boycott [the foreigner's] trade and encourage the production of your
>   compatriots!
> Your lame donkey will allow you to do without the horse of your enemies.
> It is forbidden to you from now on to transact business with people
> Who offer a glass of poison mixed with honey.
> You have had enough insults and wounds to your feelings.
> Break off your relations with them, and the garment—Burn it!
> And show that the noble and honest [man] is not trampled upon.[90]

Like Wissa's "'fois gras' fattening," the poem's assertion that colonialism offered Egyptians "a glass of poison mixed with honey" pointed to the way increased consumption was meant to sweeten colonial domination. That foreign merchants profited "by your blood" also resonated with the theme of intimate and bodily transformations and sacrifices being demanded by colonial commerce and politics. Even though indigenous manufacturers may feel as though they are "lame donkeys" compared to the fine horses of imports, the nobility and honesty of using indigenous substitutions would restore "wounded feelings" and mitigate national shame.

Bodies were marked as sites in this new nationalist symbology. The boycotters produced a red tin buttonhole badge depicting an Egyptian spindle to be worn by people wishing to encourage national industry by indicating that the clothes they wore were "spun and woven in Egypt."[91] In the mid-1930s a popular name circulated among Egyptians for a locally produced cloth, a cheap, plaid

المقاطعة

مسمار يفلق

Figure 9. The boycott as the single nail that destroyed England's John Bull. *Ruz al-yusuf,* no. 221 (9 May 1932), 11.

cloth used for women's clothing that was sold primarily in the countryside and probably imitated Scottish plaid. The new local cloth was called "'*uskut—ma' skutish* [be quiet—I won't be quiet],"[92] which suggests the popularity of the belief that locally made textiles could give voice to anticolonial resistance.

The boycott and campaign to promote local industry expanded into a new phase in the development of local import-substitution industries to manufacture popular consumer goods.[93] Muhammad Yasin established his National Glassworks in 1934 to produce common items such as tea glasses, lamp chimneys, and eventually sheet glass.[94] Food processing industries were founded or expanded, especially in the flour market, in which companies such as the Grands Moulins d'Egypte were able to benefit from new tariff protections to reduce the country's reliance on imported foodstuffs.[95] The most widely popularized of these new industrial projects was known as the Piastre Plan (*mashru' al-qirsh*), a mass-based movement organized by university students to gather money—in subscriptions of a piastre—from Egyptians to develop national industries.[96] Encouraged by economic leaders such as Tal'at Harb, the group was led by Ahmad Husayn and Fathi Radwan, both of whom would use the success of the Piastre Plan to launch their political group Young Egypt several years later (Husayn's popularity from these days even carried up to the 1952 Cairo Fire). The group developed into one of the "most important youth-organized economic movements" of the time.[97] Collection drives nationwide in 1932 included a large two-day celebration in Cairo's 'Azbakiyya Garden that raised £E17,000 and reportedly included 85,000 people. This money and the government's donation of land in 'Abbasiyya enabled the group to found a factory.[98]

The Piastre Plan committee chose the tarbush (pl. *tarabish*) as the article to be manufactured by this new national factory, since *tarabish* were mostly imported from Austria or North Africa even though they were a popular and symbolic item of local dress (see Figure 10). A head covering that had replaced the turban for most middle- and upper-class Egyptian men (except religious scholars), the tarbush became an indigenous or Islamic alternative to the European brimmed hat for middle- and upper-class men. The precise meaning of the tarbush varied among people and situations: some considered it "a symbol of the East facing West";[99] others argued that with the advent of *ifrangi* fashions in Egypt, "the tarbush became a nationalist sign to distinguish those who wear Western clothes from Westerners."[100] The Piastre Plan's new tarbush factory, "equipped with the most modern machinery," began production in 1933 or 1934 and continued until at least October 1951.[101] Al-Rafi'i notes that the factory reduced the value of annual imports of *tarabish* from £E79,000 to merely £E600 by 1939.[102] The marketing of the Piastre Plan's *tarabish* linked the nation regionally and historically: different models of *tarabish* sported names of major Egyptian textile centers or momentous events in national tarbush production

Figure 10. Converting coins into national headgear, the Piastre Plan's tarbush factory offered different models named for prominent milestones in local production. *Al-Ahram*, 10 November 1938, 6.

history, such as the "Muhammad ʿAli," after the ruler who introduced the head-gear to Egypt, the "Fuwwa" or the "Qaha" for towns with *tarabish* factories, and the "Mahalla" in reference to the famous Delta textile center.[103] *Tarabish* and tea glasses formed important consumption items that began to unite Egyptian consumers into self-conscious communities and to mark out commerce and consumption as arenas of politics. Cotton cloth would be the commodity that most decidedly altered the public politics of private consumption, because cloth spoke most directly to the basis of British power.

FOREIGN SILKS AND LOCAL CANVAS:
THE POLITICS OF CLOTH AND NATION

Although the goals of Egyptian boycotters and new industrialists were broad, cloth became their primary idiom of protest because the relationship of cotton to cloth had encapsulated Egypt's economic and ultimately political dependency on Britain since the mid-nineteenth century. A British textile expert in Egypt described the paradox of the cotton economy in 1928: "The growing of cotton is Egypt's staple industry; the wearing of cotton fabrics in some shape or form is almost universal in the country; and yet this cotton grown on the banks of the Nile is despatched thousands of miles away to be manufactured and then ret[u]rned a like distance until it reaches the hands of those who grew it as a woven fabric. Needless to add [that] the expense of such transport is paid for by the ultimate consumer."[104] At the time Egypt achieved formal independence in the early 1920s, Britain bought nearly 45 percent of Egypt's exports of raw cotton and supplied almost 90 percent of the 201 million square meters of cotton textiles imported annually into Egypt.[105] Although British cloth in the following decade dropped from 90 to 42 percent of total cotton textiles imported into Egypt and the country achieved tariff independence in 1930, allowing diversification in the import market, the inability to furnish the local market in textiles plagued Egyptian cotton growers.[106]

Despite perception that the cotton economy presented a simple paradox of moving the same cotton out and then back into Egypt in different forms, the reality of the relationship of Egyptian raw cotton to Egyptian textile consumption had actually been more complicated for the past century. Egypt had a long history of artisanal textile spinning, weaving, and dyeing, and the sector remained strong into the early twentieth century by furnishing part of the demand of local markets and households for Egypt's ever-growing population.[107] Although short-staple cotton had been cultivated in Egypt in the early nineteenth century, most textiles were at that time made from locally cultivated linen or wool or from cotton imported from Syria. In 1820 Muhammad ʿAli, the viceroy of Egypt, promoted the growth of a new variety of cotton, known as Jumel or Mako, which had a very long staple; Lancashire's demand for this fine cotton particularly accelerated during the shortages caused by the U.S. Civil War. Continual British demand for long-staple raw cotton from Egypt eventually encouraged the conversion of most prime agricultural land to the cultivation of long-staple cotton for export. The varieties of long-staple cotton grown in Egypt in the 1910s (most notably Mit-Afifi, Janovitch, and later, Sakel, Nubari, Maarad, and Nahda) competed only with American Sea Island and later Pima cottons in the production of fine, silky cloth for the upper reaches of the global luxury cotton textile market. Egyptian long-staple cotton was suited especially for "high-quality cotton textiles" such as poplins and fabrics for men's shirts, women's fine lingerie, "other high grades of ladies' apparel, blouses, satins, voiles and mock-voiles, as well as pongees for ladies' robes and linings for their clothes" and also gloves and stockings, towels, dining and bed linens, and tapestry.[108]

Staple length in a fiber could affect the nature of the cloth woven from it in several ways. A long staple created a silky finish and a strong yarn. As one British textile expert noted in 1927, "Generally speaking, the more silky a fibre is, the rounder and more compact a yarn it produces, and a lack of silkiness and lustre in the fibre is reflected by a lack of lustre in the cloth, which becomes very marked if either the yarn or cloth is subjected to the process of mercerising."[109] Egyptian cotton thus formed "quite a specialised trade," as it was "especially suitable for . . . all kinds of cotton goods with a smooth surface and a fine luster. For this reason Egyptian cotton is largely employed in weaving along with silk."[110] While this silky quality added value to the crop, it also limited it to the more volatile luxury market.[111] In addition to imparting a silky sheen to fabrics, long-staple fibers produced exceptionally strong cloth. Egyptian Sakel cotton was used in the early 1930s in the production of sturdy industrial fabrics, such as sewing thread, ropes, tents, tarpaulins, belting, fishing and trawl nets, umbrella cloths, car and cab hoods, artificial leather for car seats, mailbags, and electric cables.[112] European customers favored Egyptian cotton for its durability and silkiness. In the words of one British consumer, "The use of Egyptian cotton materials, by reason of their being less costly than silk, easily laundered at home, and exceedingly durable, would seem to provide an excellent way of economising while keeping up a good appearance and achieving that 'well-dressed' look so desired of every woman for herself and her children."[113] French trade officials noted that French customers often requested fabrics made with specific growths of long-staple Egyptian cotton.[114]

A large portion of both locally produced and imported cloth in the Egyptian market was sewn up into galabiyas, the full-length, loose gowns worn especially by peasants and lower-class men and women in urban areas but also at home and in their local neighborhood by those middle classes who wore *ifrangi* dress at work.[115] Since the quality of galabiyas varied according to the occasion and the purchaser's income level, styles ranged through different types and weights of cloth for different seasons. For example, a galabiya worn at weddings and feasts would have been crafted from silk or a fine imported cotton cloth, whereas a more durable galabiya for use during manual work would have been made from either coarser cotton fabric or a wool or wool-blend fabric.[116] In 1910 in Asyut, cotton was woven into articles of "several qualities according to the quality of thread used, and to the nature of the work. The common quality [was] known as *Ghazli*, which may be of different colors, and there [was] a finer quality known as *Ghazli Mazwi*. Both [were] used for clothing, mostly for gallabiehs. The white cotton stuff known as *Dammur*, [was] also made to some extent, but not . . . largely, though the amount [was] apparently on the increase."[117] The Asyuti production of *ghazli* used European raw materials, primarily from Lancashire, England. Weavers worked on hand looms in workshops, and the fabrics retailed in Asyut and to a lesser extent in Cairo and other towns. In Fayyum Province around the same time, American cotton, which might have been coarser and cheaper, was used to weave fabrics for men and women's clothing, including *deffiyeh*s (robes resembling galabiyas), *dammur*, and "a large quantity of loosely woven fabric, white or black, almost resembling fine knits, and this serves for the clothing of women."[118] Gray, or unfinished, cloth in a variety of weights was also imported widely from Great Britain and India (India supplied the cheaper varieties). Most often dyed blue in Egypt by local dyers, this fabric was frequently used to make galabiyas.[119] In 1923, for example, over half the textiles imported from the United Kingdom were gray or bleached fabrics; these fabrics cost less than half the price of finished fabrics, such as printed or dyed fabrics.[120]

The short-staple cottons and yarn used locally to weave fabrics that supplied "mainly the ordinary local consumption" and some export to Turkey were mostly of imported "cheap yarn" of which three-quarters came from England and east India in 1913. Some shorter-staple varieties of cotton were also grown locally, and many village spinners worked Egyptian cotton "principally from the very last picking and . . . of quite an inferior fibre . . . [woven into] Galabieh material for the gowns of the native population."[121] A German-managed mill at Alexandria (the Filature Nationale d'Egypte) in the 1910s used "mainly cheap Upper Egyptian cotton . . . along with a very small quantity of Indian cotton" to manufacture plain shirtings sold in Egypt and Turkey and yarn supplied to local hand-loom weavers.[122] In the first decades of the twentieth century, some shorter-staple brown cottons, known as Ashmuni, Zagora, or other Upper Egyptian varieties, were cultivated on a small scale in Egypt,[123] but this local crop could not fully furnish domestic needs.[124] The problem of obtaining suitable raw material was exacerbated after 1916, when the Egyptian government forbade the importation of raw cotton into the country. Designed to protect local growers from foreign competition and to prevent infestation of local crops by foreign pests, the law seriously constrained domestic industry, especially for peasant galabiya cloth.[125]

It was in this context that boycotters in the 1920s and 1930s urged development of a new mechanized textile industry to make locally grown raw cotton into cloth for the domestic market. Talʿat Harb, the founder of Bank Misr and its group of industries, argued that a robust local mechanized textile industry would resolve the cotton paradox and spearhead Egyptian economic independence.[126] "By using our cotton in our clothes, and especially the clothes of the poor, for which there is great demand, we would be able to create a new use for this cotton, and greatly aid in the increase of the amount of consumption of Egyptian cotton inside Egypt. And this is the true promotion—or rather active encouragement—of agriculture and industry at a single time."[127] A variety of industrial concerns emerged to support the goal of textile self-sufficiency, and many were funded by Egypt's new national bank. Established on April 13, 1920, and declaring itself "an Egyptian bank for Egyptians only," Bank Misr was the first bank completely financed and administered by Egyptians. Intended not merely to offer commercial banking services but to provide industrial credit to establish large, Egyptian-owned enterprises and thus break the monopoly of foreign capital, Bank Misr was "to be the motor force behind the creation of a modern industrial sector in the Egyptian economy."[128] Although the bank founded printing, paper, cinema, and fishing companies initially, its expansion into industries connected to cotton finally made it profitable: in 1924 it established cotton ginning and transportation companies, and in the late 1920s the bank founded silk- and flax-weaving companies, cotton-trading and cotton-export companies, and its most important firm, the Cotton Spinning and Weaving Company, established in al-Mahalla al-Kubra in al-Gharbiya province in 1927 and beginning production in 1930.[129] The Mahalla enterprise encompassed all the processes of textile manufacturing (spinning, weaving, and dyeing) and employed fifteen thousand workers by 1930.[130] "During its initial period of operations between 1930 and 1936, the firm increased its consumption of local

cotton by over 90 percent, from 22,308 to 281,803 qintars. During the same period the firm increased its yarn production from 843,744 kilograms of yarn
to 10,716,894 kilograms and its piece-goods production from 148,324 square
meters of piece-goods to 1,499,586 square meters."[131] In time, the bank would
also found the Misr Fine Spinning and Weaving Company at Kafr al-Dawwar
(1938). These textile giants were supplemented by many smaller ventures that
received Bank Misr funding as well as prominent industries founded by other
groups of capitalists in Egypt.[132] The Filature Nationale was the most important textile factory among these, but numerous smaller knitting and weaving
factories, especially to produce hosiery and underwear, also began operation.[133]

The 1930s marked a new moment in the politics of cloth in Egypt. Shortages
caused by the world Depression lent new urgency to textile production, which
was becoming increasingly viable from a technical standpoint. Textile factories
quickly refined their technologies and rationalized their workforces to increase
output.[134] Competition especially raged over the coarser fabrics used to make
galabiyas, and price competed with other factors, such as a thicker feel to cloth,
durability, and preferences about design, color, or print, to influence changing
styles and tastes. Modifications in local fashion were aided by international
changes in cloth manufacture and the material nature of cloth, such as Japanese factories' use of short fibers to weave thicker fabrics and improvements in
dyeing techniques, not simply reducible to issues of price. The primary competition for new Egyptian fabrics was a series of heavy Japanese cloths known
as cabots and drills that, even though made of a lesser quality cotton, were
"cleaner" and of better color than similar British textiles.[135] Cheaper grades
of short-staple cotton (mostly Indian) gave a thicker and more durable feel to
this drill fabric, and its twill weave, with a diagonal rib, created cloth "looser
and more flexible than plain cloths with the same yarns and set [because it]
permit[ted] coarser yarns . . . to be more tightly packed, than is possible with
a plain weave; and so twill cloths can be heavy and compact, yet flexible."[136]
"This style," the British trade agent in Egypt in 1929 explained, "has established
itself in Egypt as no other has ever done, for it is cheap and durable. Whereas
before its appearance the poorer consumer paid an average of 17 piastres for his
galabieh, he now spends 12 piastres and the cloth lasts him twice as long. These
Japanese qualities do not compete with other coloured goods only, but they
have, in fact, reduced the consumption of many other styles."[137] The dominance of this drill fabric over imported grays, cabots, and coarse white shirtings was nearly complete by 1931.[138] The cheaper price of Japanese fabrics was

attributable not only to cheaper labor costs and government subsidies but also to the starch treatment many Japanese fabrics received to make the thinner fabric have more shape.[139]

Local mechanized cloth companies fought against this new Japanese drill using a barrage of tactics that included steep tariffs imposed by the state, harsh labor conditions to keep down production costs, heavy advertising in the local press, and the grassroots work of local boycott committees.[140]

> The local mills can normally produce the coarser grey cloth from the medium count of yarn (i.e. 16, which nearly corresponds to the yarn used by Japanese manufacturers of this quality) by employing a low grade Egyptian cotton.... It should also be said that hundreds of spinners using old hand-looms, principally in Lower Egypt, produce the coarser qualities similar to the Japanese drill. These spinners purchase their yarn, dye it in their own primitive fashion, and weave it into the cloth most appreciated by the poorer classes of the population.... It is understood that the local production of cotton and silk goods represents only 15 per cent. of the market's requirements.[141]

The improvement in the local production of cotton piece goods and the standardization of prices made the local industry lucrative by October 1936, and at that point it "commenced seriously to affect imports from both the United Kingdom and the Continent. Thus the last quarter of 1936 may be termed the Egyptian era."[142] The nation-state categories that commercial consuls used to describe this struggle in the cloth market indicate the growing acceptance of product nationality that allowed local industries to appeal to consumers in nationalist terms.[143]

"ONLY BUY WHAT YOU NEED FROM AN EGYPTIAN":
COMMERCE IN NATIONAL TEXTILES

The project to reconfigure the local market as Egyptian or national after 1930 also emerged through the establishment and promotion of retail sites for new national commodities, especially textiles from the new Bank Misr factories established in the late 1920s. The commercial response to the growth of local industry and the boycotts of the early 1930s provided concrete fulfillment to the more rhetorical calls of boycotters about the social and national responsibility of the consumer and visions of national unity and economic independence anchored in particular historical memories and national narratives. Moreover, the articulation of new national commercial practices and philosophies attempted to clarify the commercial and political ambiguities in the retail landscape that had grown since the last decades of the nineteenth century. In the process, many stores intensified a discourse about product nationality and the use of the language of dichotomies.

Many small national stores emerged in the early 1930s. Al-Nahhas, a shop in the Muski, was one of the first commercial sites to publicize that it offered the kinds of goods demanded by boycotters who had been spurred into action by the 1931 Agricultural and Industrial Exposition and the Wafd's social networks. In December 1931 it advertised itself as "100 percent Egyptian" and purveying "Egyptian cotton in all sizes and colors" and "all the white goods of the Misr company at al-Mahalla," in addition to cotton flannel (*kastur*) and velvet plush (*'utifa*), socks and underwear, and towels from al-Mahalla (*fuwwat wa-bashakir mahallawi*), and mother-of-pearl buttons from the Misr fishing company at Suez.[144] Al-Nahhas intensified its advertising in May 1932, actually depicting men re-dressing in their store after burning their foreign clothes in the boycott bonfires.[145] In other places, the company used overtly nationalist symbols such as flags to signal that the store "assume[s] her place in the place of the foreigner" (see Figure 11).[146] The Egyptian Products Store (*Mahall al-Muntajat al-Misriyya*) was directed and owned by graduates of the Higher School of Commerce, and it advertised in May 1932 that it displayed the "hidden manufacturing talents of Egyptians—at unbeatable prices."[147] One magazine article described the store as located in "one of the most sumptuous squares in the capital [Opera Square], within sight and earshot of foreign merchants";[148] it claimed the store carried "samples of cloths amazing in quality and price" and "varieties of good-quality silk clothes at reasonable prices . . . of Egyptian manufacture," in addition to reasonably priced cologne, "delicious" fruit jams, and high-quality shoes, silk socks, and other silks.[149] The venture probably suffered from insufficient funding, however, as it was criticized for employing too few salespeople (so that customers had to wait in long lines to be helped) and providing too few chairs in which women customers could rest.[150] Other stores in the 1940s used similar types of company names to market local goods. The Egyptian Textiles Company (*Sharikat al-Mansujat al-Misriyya*), located on Fu'ad Street in Cairo, advertised in April 1940 that it offered a selection of spring fabrics, including silks, cottons, and linen, as well as an "excellent selection of shoes"; in the early 1950s, the company claimed to be a "national Egyptian establishment."[151] The Egyptian Company for Local Products (*Sharikat Misr li-Mantujat al-Ahliyya*) opened its third branch in July 1948 on Fu'ad Street in Bulaq across the street

Figure 11. Using the motif of flags, the al-Nahhas store in the Muski proudly displayed the wares of Egyptian factories that provided substitutes for imported products. *Ruz al-yusuf*, no. 224 (30 May 1932), 25.

from the 'Ali Baba cinema. The press referred to the company as a "popular establishment [*al-mu'assa al-sha'biyya*]," and *shaykh* Ma'mun al-Shinawi, rector of al-Azhar, cut the ceremonial ribbon and offered prayers at the opening. The store purveyed a "wide selection of cloth, items for weddings, and rugs at moderate prices" and advertised in 1952 that it was owned by Muhammad 'Uthman Bayumi. Its central store comprising at least several departments was located in Khazindar Square in Cairo, and it had a branch in 'Abbasiyya.[152]

The most sustained and institutionalized response to the demand to make local goods available to consumers, as the 1930s boycotters demanded, came from the Egyptian Products Sales Company (*Sharika Bai' al-Masnu'at al-Misriyya*), a retail venture founded by Bank Misr on October 9, 1932, to sell the products of the bank's industries, and in particular its textiles.[153] In February 1933 the company opened its main store on Fu'ad Street in downtown Cairo, in the corner building at the top of the street, a space previously occupied by Morums Department Store.[154] Projected as a crucial link in developing the national economy, the new store received substantial state support. Major politicians of the primary political parties of the era visited the opening on January 3, 1933. Isma'il Sidqi, at the time prime minister and head of the Sha'b Party, and his entourage toured at ten o'clock in the morning, followed at noon by the prominent Wafdists Mustafa al-Nahhas (former prime minister and party leader), Makram 'Ubayd, and Mahmud al-Nuqrashi.[155] In the early 1930s the store specialized in "silk and cotton clothing and varieties of calico [*bafta*], plain white calico [*dabalan*], cotton flannel [*kastur*], and other [products] from the Misr Spinning and Weaving Company at Mahalla."[156] By 1934 its inventory included cloth, "towels [both *fuwwat* and *bashakir*], cloaks [*baranis*], socks, suitcases, shoes, and aromatic perfumes [*rawa'ih 'itriya*]," as well as brass bedsteads, neckties, sterile medicinal cotton, and underwear and hosiery.[157] Its products, the company advertised, befitted modern Egyptian consumers—its cloth was "appropriate for the climate"; its silk cloth could be used "for dresses, shirts, and neckties"; and its cotton fabrics were of "renowned durability and good taste."[158]

In an advertisement for the store's opening in February 1933, the company explicitly linked individual consumption through the store with national development and asserted its own ability to mark objects of consumption as national. It was not the style of its retail premises, the kinds of marketing practices it used, the interior decor of the store, or the designs of its merchandise that made the store Egyptian; instead, the store began to associate national consumption with the nature of the company itself and the characteristics of the production of its merchandise. "Only buy what you need from an Egyptian—in that way the wealth of your country will grow. Visit the stores of the Egyptian Products Sales Company: its employees are Egyptian, its wares are Egyptian, its raw materials are Egyptian, and [its products are] made by the hands of Egyptian workers."[159] The advertising narrative invoked different images of the nation as a single commercial unit, framing the individual consumer at the center of an ever-widening series of concentric circles.

Visit the store and learn that what you spend there comes out of your right pocket to enter your left pocket. That what you spend from your private budget returns to the budget of the nation (your big family). That what you pay returns to your brothers, sisters, and families for which you, as a citizen guarding his nation, are responsible. That what you buy does not [merely] follow the market with respect to moderation of price, and sturdiness and excellence of type. In all of this *you* will be the one to benefit in the end, and at the same time you will have participated in building Egypt's economic mosque.[160]

From the most intimate space of an individual's clothing (the closed private pockets tucked close to the body) through the household and state to the sacred realms of nation and religion, the advertisement's images underlined the outward radiation of "private" consumption into the public sphere. The deployment of an excess of imagery—figuring the nation as a garment, a family, a state, and an economic mosque—indicates the intensity of anxiety that had surfaced in the past several decades about the resilience of department stores such as Cicurel, Sednaoui, or Chemla to meet and shape local demand. The gendered association of the nation (*al-watan*) with the family (*al-usra*) is well known,[161] although the specific correlation of the national budget to the household budget appealed to new discourses of scientific domesticity and linked the new store directly to the state rather than only to a more abstract notion of the nation, one peopled by citizen-consumers "guarding the nation" through their purchases. The "economic mosque" perhaps attempted to localize the European metaphor of department stores as cathedrals or temples of consumption and, specifically, to differentiate what the company's marketers considered authentically Egyptian products from *ifrangi* commerce. Linking into a particular narrative of the Egyptian nation—that of its role as Islamic capital in the Middle Ages and its fame for housing the most prominent centers of Sunni Islamic learning, such as al-Azhar—the mosque metaphor seems particularly pointed at the Jewish and Christian ownership of Egyptian department stores such as Chemla, Cicurel, or Sednaoui.

Funded by Bank Misr and supported by the Ministry of Commerce and Industry, the company's expansion throughout the country was rapid in the 1930s and 1940s. In the first two years, five stores opened in Cairo (the main branch on Fu'ad Street and branches in the Muski district, al-Bawaki Street, Sayyida Zaynab district, and Nahhasin Street), along with stores in Suhaj,

Alexandria (at Muhammad ʿAli Square), Shibin al-Kum, and Asyut. Between 1935 and 1938 the company moved aggressively into the central and Delta provinces, with store openings in Fayyum, Minya, Tanta, Zaqaziq, Damanhur, and Suez. Through the 1940s the company established branches in smaller provincial towns such as Zifta, Qina, Aswan, Buhayra, Dissuq, Port Saʿid, Mallawi, and Minya al-Kum, bringing the total to thirty-seven branch stores by 1954.[162] The company's strategy of buying existing cloth firms, such as al-Nahhas and al-Sayufi, an old Egyptian house that in the early 1930s had aggressively marketed its own brand of "famously sturdy calico," manufactured in Manchester, against the rising emphasis on locally manufactured goods, fueled its initial expansion.[163] In the 1940s and 1950s the company included independently owned stores, many of which were explicitly identified with Muslim individuals or religious institutions. The Benha store listed al-Hajj Gharib al-ʿAzim Siraj as owner; the Girga store, the *shaykh* Ismaʿil Mustafa al-Tahtawi; and Cairo's Bab al-Shaʿriyya neighborhood branch, opened in 1945, the *waqf* (pious endowment) of the deceased woman Zaynab al-Mahshayiba. Several branches were owned by Muslim women, such as Fatima al-Shafʿi of the shop in Bani Mazar.[164] The regional visibility of the company also grew in the 1930s, as it exhibited at trade fairs in Damascus and Jerusalem.[165] The firm's downtown store on Fuʾad Street was quite large by 1947, employing nine department heads, forty-seven salesclerks, and seventy other employees.[166]

The celebrations marking the opening of the Tanta branch store on February 12, 1937, demonstrated the discursive and material ways that the company intersected with certain state and anticolonial authorities who sought to use the store to clarify the commercial landscape. The opening of the store coincided with Faruq's birthday, the first celebration for the then eighteen-year-old Faruq, whose father, King Fuʾad, had died the previous April and who would himself be crowned king in July. The newspaper *al-Ahram*, which provided extensive coverage of the event, noted that "thousands of invitees from among the leaders, notables, merchants, and politicians from Gharbiyya and Minufiyya provinces as well as important employees and directors of Bank [Misr]" had gathered in a large tent set up for the celebrations.[167] Many flags, electric lights, chairs, and banquettes provided decoration, although the focal point was a "large picture of Faruq at the heart of the pavilion, and a high podium for the speakers . . . equipped with a microphone to magnify the voice." In addition to the directors of the company, the event's speakers included important local and national officials: the deputy of the province, a member of the Chamber of Deputies, a famous popular (*zajal*) poet (Badiya' Khayri),[168] a well-known Qur'an reciter, and the minister of commerce and industry.

The commerce and industry minister, 'Abd al-Salam Fahmi Pasha, gave a long speech in which he linked the company's mission and expansion to the "start [of] a political renaissance . . . and an economic renaissance" in the country and drew on a supraprovincial national identity to promote the store. As he delivered his speech, Fahmi proclaimed that he was himself dressed "in a cotton and wool suit and a tarbush [both] of Egyptian manufacture and Egyptian raw materials and [made] by Egyptian hands." This outfit, he declared, was "the most chic," although he argued (much as had the 1931–1932 boycotters) that "by God, if I wore canvas [*khaysh*] made by my country and by the hand of my brother the Egyptian, it would be good that I was wearing it." Fahmi specifically posited the store's mission as liberation from European commercial intrusion. "I know, gentlemen, that some foreigners in our country have decided against [the company] and its nationalism, although [such economic nationalism] is considered appropriate in their own countries. . . . For what do we think when they, the leaders of trade, come to our country to display their goods—no, rather to our houses—and then do not entrust us with the task of coming to them?" The store, he contended, would enable Egyptians to use their bodies to display a new level of political loyalty.

> Shame . . . after today on an Egyptian who wants to honor his community [*umma*] and be faithful to his nation [*watan*] and does not dress in Egyptian-made clothes. . . . I have full confidence that Egyptian merchants are nationalist like the rest and that they will create sales for their stores from what they acquire from Egyptian manufacturers, which they will display to their customers and present to others, if it is a duty of the Egyptian not to purchase foreign goods of which exists a similar product made in this country.

Fahmi also called on Egyptian commercial nationalism by connecting regional identity to the larger nation-state. He praised the city of Tanta for its contributions to the Egyptian nation—making explicit reference to the nearby Bank Misr textile mills at Mahalla al-Kubra and to the province's fame as the birthplace of nationalist leader Sa'd Zaghlul. He linked different regions of the country in an imagined unity, referring to his recent trip to Fayyum to see local support for the branch store operating there. "I can assure you," Fahmi noted, "that if the city of Fayyum forbade its people to acquire anything other than national Egyptian manufactures, then the city of Tanta will outstrip the rest of the country in this field." Finally, the timing of the store's opening to coincide with the king's birthday conjoined yet another symbol of the nation to the economic venture.

The Egyptian Products Sales Company, then, positioned itself in this celebration as the vehicle through which individual Egyptians as consumers could assert their patriotism and thereby connect themselves to Egyptian producers and capitalists as well as politicians and national symbols. The opening speeches by Fahmi and 'Abd al-Hamid al-Bannan, the managing director of the company, emphasized that public good rather than private gain motivated the venture. Both men positioned the company's work as one of national service and downplayed the economic benefits that would accrue to shareholders. "The company is content," Fahmi declared, "with a reasonable profit and to serve the national economy by offering to you manufactures of the nation that were made by the hand of the son of the nation, raw materials of the nation, and capital from the nation." The morning celebration concluded with the invitees touring and purchasing from the new store.

In addition to the explicit state support and overtly political nature of the morning celebration attended by male notables, the Tanta store's opening included several different events designed to incorporate a range of Egyptian consumers. At three o'clock in the afternoon, "a swarm of ladies and young women in popular processions crowded the store and visited the many departments. They saw its displays and purchased what they liked from them, [thereby] encouraging Egypt's manufactures and products." The "popular carnival or festival" celebrations that drew thousands of people from "all the classes" began in the tent at five o'clock. The carnival included more Qur'anic recitations, the cinematic advertising of the Bank Misr Publicity Department, and the performances of two famous musical troupes, Salah 'Abd al-Hayy and Zakariyya Ahmad. The company showed films about Faruq's return from Europe to claim his crown and the "popular welcome" he received, as well as a promotional film on the salt markets (an industry in which the bank was involved). Popular attention was especially focused on the troupes, which performed numbers in honor of the King's birthday, as well as nationalist songs and a "song about the sale of national products, by the title 'Oh Egyptian, why is the piastre squandered?'"[169]

Buoyed by the boycotts and the broader climate of economic nationalism, the Egyptian Products Sales Company filled the commercial niche of a landscape increasingly populated by state and organizational structures to support wide nationalist efforts in trade and production. The Egyptian Chambers of Commerce, first founded in Cairo in 1913 by indigenous Egyptian merchants, had established twenty-three chambers by 1926; by 1938 even the more cosmopolitan Egyptian chamber in Alexandria had become solidly nationalist and had begun to issue a journal. "Unlike the foreign chambers of commerce on which they were modeled," Tignor noted, "the Egyptian chambers self-consciously and aggressively sought to represent native Egyptian interests."[170] The Department of Commerce and Industry, founded in 1920 to introduce new industries and encourage their production, was reorganized into the more prestigious and powerful Ministry for Commerce and Industry in December 1934.[171] The new ministry was divided into five departments, overseeing commerce, industry, labor, tourism, and weights and measures, with the commerce section supervising "questions of tariff, commercial treaties, commercial legislation and registration, inland markets, export trade, commercial intelligence, statistics, and chambers of commerce."[172] In the first few years of its existence, the new ministry undertook a variety of projects, including reorganizing the chambers of commerce and trade unions; the unification of weights and measures; drafting new laws on patents, trade marks, women and children's labor, hours of work, and worker compensation; the reorganization of domestic fruit, vegetable, and grain markets; instituting export control on commodities; creating an official Commercial Register; and investigation of "commercial fraud and adulteration of foodstuffs."[173]

Although reducing the debilitating overreliance on flimsy, cheap fabrics among the poor formed the core of the economic nationalist agenda as expressed by men such as Tala't Harb and new industrialists, other boycotters focused on eliminating the numbing overconsumption of foreign luxury goods among the elite. Wissa's opposition to the "'fois gras' fattening" reminds us how colonial consumerist politics differed from those in established nation-states. Consumers navigated a fine line between captivation and captivity in their consumption practices and commercial habits. Boycotters targeted everything English because of the link of certain commodities to the British economy and also because of their influence in shaping broader cultural loyalties. As a political language, consumerism particularly resonated with upper-class Egyptian women who only decades earlier had claimed a public space for themselves through scientific domesticity.

During the 1922–1924 and 1931–1932 boycotts, nationalist rhetoric repeatedly turned to the language of dichotomies to shape the boycott struggles, juxtaposing the "foreign silks of colonialism" with the "coarse canvas" of local weavers or nationalist stores with British agents. Although the actions of protestors reveal the insufficiency of such dichotomies, the boycotts, especially that of 1922–1924, have prominently functioned in the historiography and in national imagination as historical evidence of women's entrenchment as consumers, the catalyst for their emerging political might, and the proof of the resonance of the national movement to wide constituencies of supporters. In this telling, the boycotts acted as steppingstones toward the establishment of a completely independent nation-state.[174] The bifurcating language the boycotts popularized persisted with the recollection of the actions themselves, especially marking the local footwear and hosiery markets in dramatically new ways.

4 SOCKS, SHOES, AND MARKETING MASS CONSUMPTION

DESPITE THE INJUNCTIONS of nationalist boycotters, acquiring a piece of fine fabric and a pair of good shoes remained a major consumer goal for many ordinary Egyptians in the interwar period. Fikri al-Khuli, a young peasant-turned-worker in Bank Misr's new cotton textile plant, the Misr Spinning and Weaving Company at al-Mahalla al-Kubra, dreamed of "the future" in such terms after one of his first workdays in 1927. "My wages increase," he imagined, "and I earn well. I will buy a piece of silk [*maqtaʿ al-harir*] and good shoes [*gazma kuwayyisa*] and walk with the men. I will wear a tarbush."[1] Al-Khuli and other workers returned repeatedly to the dream of buying shoes and silk, and these consumer goals kept them at work despite the factory's harsh conditions that threatened their health, their intraclass alliances, and their sense of connection to the nation.[2] As a sign of maturity and prosperity, ownership of such goods signaled social independence and power. The persistent longing for fine textiles and footwear must also be situated, however, in the broader context of the nationalist marketing of locally made cotton textiles and in particular of expectations of cotton's performance as a political vehicle in the anticolonial struggle.

Bourgeois nationalists, such as Talʿat Harb, who established the factory at Mahalla, believed firmly in the potential of local cotton textile production to act as a pillar of the nation's economic independence, as well as in the transformative power of mechanization to modernize Egyptian society.[3] Mechanization, such economic nationalists hoped, could create a rationalized production sector staffed by efficient and disciplined workers with strong purchasing power and a commitment to a paternalistic national community that provided it for them. Just as importantly, mechanization would produce cheaply priced, standardized commodities that could deepen the domestic market and foster mass consumption in a regularized and controllable manner.[4] Such an expanded national market would in turn benefit large landowners, who could more easily control prices on their cotton crops, and the nascent bourgeoisie, who had invested in the new textile industries.

The wider mobility of Egyptians because of changes in the building and use of urban space, such as the increasing prevalence of paved streets, public transportation, and industrial workplaces, and new marketing and educational campaigns in the countryside expanded demand for footwear and hosiery and propelled certain changes in style during the interwar years. Shoe stores proliferated across the urban landscape, their displays packed tightly with high-heeled women's shoes, sturdy laced-up men's shoes, and a variety of less formal slipperlike styles. Such *ifrangi* shoes began to increase demand for socks and stockings to finish the look of or add comfort to new styles. Unlike galabiya cloth, socks and shoes were made and sold as finished items in specific styles and rarely produced at home.

Marketers worked through the popular press and more informal media to convince Egyptian consumers to purchase textiles and footwear manufactured by new national factories and styled according to *ifrangi* conventions. Their promotional campaigns attempted to redirect consumer desire for comfort or upward mobility into a patriotic desire for belonging in a modern polity. This chapter examines the development of the shoe and hosiery industries in the interwar years and looks closely at several marketing campaigns for men's socks and new shoe styles that promoted the consumption of particular sartorial items as vehicles to increase the political maturity of citizens, entitling them to walk with the men and participate in the new nation. Responding to the urgent calls of boycotters in the 1920s and 1930s to make available locally produced textiles and other goods to replace foreign imports, industrialists and their marketers drew increasingly on the dichotomized language of foreign silks and local canvas as well as the modernity of mechanized production to promote the vision of an authentic and tightly knit national public. The markets for footwear and hosiery evolved in tandem, as new production technologies and materials emerged to differentiate shoes from socks, and Egypt's growing regulatory independence transformed the landscape of trade.

This chapter demonstrates that the drive to create a national market independent of colonial domination developed as much from the particular trajectories of the expansion of local consumption as from the dynamics of

European colonial dominance in trade and culture. The nationalist production sector, and the local elites who operated it, attempted in the late 1920s and 1930s to siphon the growing demand for ready-made footwear and hosiery to capture and control the mass consumption regime inaugurated by colonial forces in preceding decades. The elevation of Egypt's long-staple cotton as a national unifier would struggle, however, against religious and class injunctions against silk and other luxury fabrics. Interwar shoe marketers also attempted to capture consumers with the promise of upward mobility, in this instance employing directly the language of foreignness, so maligned by boycotters. That commodities as prosaic as shoes or cloth could challenge Egypt's social, religious, and political regime so directly suggests the need to take seriously these sartorial realms long underinvestigated by scholars.[5]

NEW MARKETS FOR NEW STYLES

In the nineteenth century, footwear and hosiery had great overlap as productive sectors and items of consumption since most socks and shoes were made of leather. Egyptians did not widely consume knitted socks and stockings, as they were expensive and not necessary in the mild climate or under the long, modest clothing worn by both men and women.[6] Although a limited amount of textile hosiery existed, it was not until the early twentieth century, when socks and stockings were increasingly made from cotton, wool, and silk, that hosiery became an item of underwear rather than footwear. Much as foreign silks and local canvas in the textile market, *ifrangi* and *baladi* styles would emerge in new marketing campaigns in complex, contiguous ways that reflected the uneven process by which shoes and hosiery became differentiated.

In the early nineteenth century, Egyptian footwear consisted of a mix of styles shared with other parts of the Ottoman Empire and Mediterranean Basin or transformed from earlier Mamluk periods. The urban upper and middle classes preferred light leather or wooden slip-on shoes: slippers, ankle boots for riding, and wooden pattens. M. de Chabrol, one of the ethnographers of the Napoleonic expedition to Egypt in 1798, observed that

> the shoe is no less complicated than the other parts of dress: it is composed first of the *mest*, a type of leather sock, that covers the entire foot; next the *babouche* and the *sarmeh*, shoes of leather in which one puts the foot covered with the *mest*. Upon entering an apartment adorned with carpets, one removes the *babouche* and the *sarmeh*: politeness demands such. To ride a horse, or even

to walk in the city, one puts on the *khouff*, a type of ankle boot in red or yellow leather, which are common to men and women.[7]

He added that women's shoes also included "a type of wooden shoe called *qobqab* [patten], which they use in the interior of their houses."[8] The soles of Egyptian shoes were usually made of water buffalo hides, tanned locally, and cut flat.[9] Writing in the late 1820s and early 1830s, Edward Lane found a similar prevalence among Egyptians of layering slip-on leather shoes and a general disregard for textile hosiery. For men of the middle and higher classes, "stockings are not in use, but some few persons, in cold weather, wear woollen or cotton socks."[10]

Unlike galabiyas, shoes rarely entered the wardrobes of the urban and rural poor. Although Lane observed that among men of the lower classes "shoes are of red or yellow morocco, or of sheep-skin," he frequently depicted lower-class men barefoot in his etchings.[11] Many peasant men undoubtedly acquired their first pair of shoes after conscription into the state's new modern army. In an 1840 commercial report, John Bowring noted that the dress of the newly outfitted army included "loose slippers, which have both an unmilitary look and are very inconvenient for marching, or for rapid evolution of any sort."[12] European portraits of Egyptian soldiers depicted them wearing either backless or low-backed leather slippers, such as the *bulgha, sarma,* or *markub*.[13] Although the army issued orders on how soldiers were to care for their shoes, budgetary limitations probably kept many barefoot. In the Syrian campaigns of the 1830s, uniforms and especially shoes wore out and were not replaced.[14] Light, pliable, slipper-style shoes thus dominated nineteenth-century footwear design because of their suitability for the mild climate; the ease with which they could be changed to cross thresholds or reinforced by layering with other shoes for protection, warmth, or status; and their inexpensive cost.

Footwear consumption, like many sartorial changes, shifted in the late nineteenth century from a mode that emphasized layering to display higher status or different function to one in which separate styles signaled particular meaning and purpose.[15] As new *ifrangi* shoe styles rapidly entered the market, several important material changes in footwear contributed to the increasing differentiation between socks and shoes. Heels, a common element of *ifrangi* styles, radically altered the nature of shoes and made them less malleable for layering. "Heels changed the whole idea of shoemaking in that the flat shoe could be cut single, but the heel necessitated the shaping of a right and a left."[16] Imported knitted hosiery became increasingly prevalent with new styles of fashion and colonial policies favoring European imports. A 1911 French commercial report noted, "The importation of hosiery has increased in the past twenty years; this is because the native is becoming slowly accustomed to European underwear. He begins, in the provinces, to abandon roughly woven products to purchase imported items which are sold to him at extremely advantageous prices. As for the native in the city, one may say that he now dresses almost entirely in European articles. He wears undershirts, undershorts, socks, etc."[17] Germany and Japan dominated the Egyptian cotton hosiery trade in the 1920s, and higher-end products were imported from France and the United States, as well as several other European countries.[18]

A pronounced expansion of shoe consumption also occurred in the first two decades of the twentieth century, although the precise extent of consumption remains unknown. In 1911 the French commercial attaché remarked, "With the considerable growth of the population and the taste for luxury which is gradually developing among the natives, the consumption of [shoes (*chaussures*)] has become very important in Egypt. One can find evidence for that in the quantity of shoe stores of which the number has increased tenfold in the past decade in Cairo and Alexandria."[19] The importation of shoe polish increased nearly five-fold between 1913 and 1920 (local production was minimal), and the number of shoeblacks reported in the commercial censuses grew between 1927 and 1947, especially in the provinces.[20] In 1925 the country, with a population of roughly fourteen million people, consumed approximately seven million pairs of new shoes. Of these, about 6.5 million pairs were produced domestically, and at least 624,397 pairs were imported. Upper-class urbanites consumed more than their rural and poorer counterparts.[21]

In addition to growth in the absolute size of the market, these decades also witnessed a change in shoe style from the slipper to a closed-back, heeled shoe. In 1907 the Belgian consul general in Egypt, Baron E. de Gaiffier d'Hestroy, noted a turn to "European fashions" in shoes. "The natives increasingly abandon the old national shoe, the red and yellow babush, for the ankle boot and the shoe."[22] Demand for new styles also stimulated, d'Hestroy claimed, an expansion and change in the Egyptian production of shoes, evidenced by increased imports of new fabrics, such as canvas, hemp, and linen, to replace leather in shoe uppers and of laces and other accessories typical of more fitted footwear fashions.[23] Moroccan imports of leather native slippers suffered most visibly in these changes. Long dominant in the import market in sheer numbers and in affordability, averaging about half or a third the price of leather-shoe imports from Europe, Moroccan slippers began to face serious competition by 1920–1921, when France and Germany increased their imports of cheaper leather-soled shoes with canvas or textile uppers; by the mid-1920s, the threat came primarily from cheaper Italian shoes.[24]

DRESS IN THE PRESS

The fashion pages and advertisements of the local press aimed at the upper and middle classes quickly picked up on changing footwear and hosiery styles and promoted them aggressively. Fashion columns in the Arabic and foreign-language press regularly featured *ifrangi* shoes, such as high-heeled pumps and oxfords, to complement the "latest modes" in clothing they presented.[25] An article on the 1927 fashions in women's accessories lauded the season's "beautiful and elegant shoe [*hidha' rashiq jamil*] in all colors, the most modern creation of Parisian taste. It combines the styles of Louis XV and Louis XVI in beautiful harmony."[26] Several designers in the 1920s modified French dress styles to suit the Egyptian market by including sheer face veils on hats and constructing draping shawls, soft jackets, or long veils to cover the upper body (see Figure 12). Such creations regularly appeared, however, with pointed, narrow, high-heeled, and strapped pumps, lifted directly from the pages of European fashions.[27] Although less prevalent in the press, men's fashion advice also endorsed European styles of shoes, such as oxfords or wing tips.[28]

Fashionable advertising reinforced the focus of advice columns on imported footwear styles, the shoes often bearing names that referred very specifically to European culture, historical periods, or places. In 1910 Chemla Department Store advertised a sale in *al-Liwa'* in which it offered only imported pairs of shoes (*gizam*) or shoes in imported styles and materials, such as "fine American men's shoes, white linen," or "finely made shoes, patent leather, American-shaped heel."[29] Chemla continued to promote these styles in its marketing in the 1920s. Its advertisement in *al-Ahram* in March 1927 offered women's pumps (*gizam dikulatayh* [*décolleté*]) with "Louis XV" (*lu kanz*) heels.[30] Its December 1928 catalog also featured only European shoes or styles: among them, the store's "series of 25 models of women's shoes in kidskin, fashionable colors and black patent leather, Cuban Louis XV heel, European manufacture guaranteed";[31] "men's wingtips [*Richelieu*] in black patent leather"; and slippers (*pantoufles*) for both men and women.[32] Cicurel's winter 1924–1925 catalog offered an even more elaborate array of European-style shoes, such as the Goliath, the

احدث الازياء

Création *Chic Oriental*

الرسومات من « شيك اورينتال »

معطف لبق جداً من القطيفة «تيرسيس» يطبق على بعضه بلطف ويـمـدل باسـتدارة من تحت الإبطار من الجهة اليسرى متجهاً نحو اليمين وتتألف الطويلة من ثلاث قطع متراصة فوق بعضها البعض تحت مشرط «اتوديه» واما الخبرة فبطة لون فاتح

معطف من الكريب ليفر بشكل مستقيم يطبق على بعضه من الجهة اليسرى تحت زركير . واما الخبرة فطارقة بشريط قماش مرصوص فوق بعضه على ثلاثة ادوار

معطف من الحرير الطري جداً يقفل على من الامام وهو مكشكش كشكشة خفية عقدة وطرف الجونيلا مزخرف بـ مكشكش

Figure 12. "The latest creations" in Egyptian fashion paired modified *ifrangi* dress styles with European-style pumps. *Misr al-haditha al-musawwara*, no. 4, 25 January 1928, 28.

Rivola, the Matador, and the Bagatelle for women and the Richelieu, the Balmoral, gaiters, and elastic-sided boots for men; it featured only these styles on its models.[33] Local luxury cobblers also capitalized on the trend toward European styles. Ahmad Kamal's shoe store, on Buwaki Street in Cairo, for example, advertised in 1920 the excellence of its custom-cut shoes, made on "equipment imported from the most famous *fabricats* in Europe."[34]

Although shown with *ifrangi* shoes in the press, women's sheer hosiery remained an expensive luxury through the Second World War because it was primarily produced from natural silk. In mid-1920s Egypt, silk stockings cost from three to eight times the price of cotton stockings, twice as much as wool hosiery, and considerably more than men's socks. The demand in women's fashion for sheer stockings escalated with the popularization of shorter dress cuts in the interwar years.[35] Using the language of light and reflection, *al-Musawwar* advertised imported Kayser stockings for their beauty under short hemlines: "Cover your legs with Kayser Miroclear stockings so that the world's spotlight will shine on them, especially under the short dress styles in fashion this year."[36] The sheerness of these stockings implied a new mobility and visibility of women's bodies in society (shorter, leg-revealing skirts) and a new adornment of such bodies to express luxury as a reflection of class aspirations. Such fashions represented a substantial change from older status markers in women's public sumptuary practices, which tended to link covering, rather than revealing, with upper-class status. Advertisements for women's silk stockings through the 1930s played on similar associations of luxury, rarely mentioning prices, but rather emphasizing the fine quality and elegance of the products and the potential for these attributes to pass on to consumers.[37] Popular stories in the press parodied the upward mobility women believed silk stockings could confer. One such story in 1942 depicted the social snubbing of a lawyer's wife for bragging about the cheaply priced (and as it turned out, cheaply made) silk stockings she found in a local department store.[38]

The local press had long advertised imported goods and the wares of larger commercial establishments such as department stores for their quality, beauty, elegance, and appropriateness for modern life or bourgeois status.[39] Advertising generally "demonstrated a concern for modernity and modern products," Mona Russell asserts, and constructed "the fashionable male . . . [as] clad in a European suit, wing-tip shoes, fancy tie, tarbush, and sometimes carrying a walking stick and/or cigarette."[40] Interwar advertising increasingly depicted women adorned in narrowly cut frocks, high-heeled pumps, and stylish hats, although modest styles such as draping shawls and sheer veils continued to mark women as local, much as the tarbush did for men.[41] In the 1930s most advertisements "remained product oriented, with uncomplicated text, few slogans, and simple illustrations."[42] Some began to provide a more definite context for commodities' consumption by using increasingly elaborate captions and illustrations to link goods with particular lifestyles and consumer identities.[43]

Print advertising expanded dramatically after the First World War, fueled in part by the popularity of illustrated magazines such as *Ruz al-yusuf*, *al-Ithnayn*, and *al-Musawwar*, whose circulation went beyond the small, literate audiences in Egypt's cities and towns.[44] Although precise figures are hard to obtain and probably lower than actual readership, Arabic press circulation in Egypt grew from an estimated daily 180,000 in 1928–1929 to over 500,000 in the second half of the 1940s.[45] The new illustrated, popular magazines, according to Relli Shechter, "introduced the concept of reading for leisure, and promoted a new style of journalism that highlighted fashion, sports, tourism, and local and international cinema. They featured attractive layouts and high-quality illustrations, caricatures, and photographs."[46] Uniformity in advertising—whether repeating ads over several issues of the same periodical or promoting different products with similar ads—resulted from the monopoly character of the press into which the advertising business itself was integrated.[47] Individual presses produced most advertising, and some journal publishers formed advertising agencies. Preliminary studies of the reception of the magazines and their advertisements point to the complex ways that readers interacted with them, including clipping advertisements and other images from journals and compiling them into private scrapbooks in ways that "anchored [the images] in visual discourses of fashion, elegance, and beauty."[48] The marketing advertisements and promotional articles the new magazines published reveal crucial elements about changes to local industry and the scope of Egyptian commodity politics.

Press accounts demonstrate how certain elements of style shifted from the 1920s to the 1930s, especially the cuts of suits, the size and shapes of lapels, the lengths of skirts, and the structure of hats. Fabrics, colors, and prints also varied from season to season. The look of the tarbush changed considerably over time. In the middle of the nineteenth century, it had been fashioned short and wide, almost covering the ears, whereas by the first decade of the twentieth century, it was cut higher, well above the ears.[49] Although *tarabish* in Egypt were generally worn in "garnet or red more or less dark," the precise tint varied from place to place, and other colors such as white were used for turbans.[50] The use of printed fabrics increased during the first three decades of the century. Before the First World War, locally produced patterned fabrics largely consisted of nonfigurative designs woven directly into the cloth. Among weavers in al-Mahalla al-Kubra in 1909, for example, "all the patterns were based on simple geometrical forms, such as squares, triangles, and combinations of these, and were used generally in stripes. There seemed to [have been] little or no attempt to use floral forms or simple sprig patterns."[51] By 1931, however, printed cloths had largely come to replace coarse white cloths in women's wear.[52] Local merchants at the time frequently had popular textile patterns copied, suggesting that demand for patterned cloth existed in lower-priced markets.[53] ʿAdès featured floral prints in women's wear in the spring of 1935, offering "original designs in fabric,"[54] and al-Farnawani, another prominent textile merchant in the Muski, displayed fabrics printed with bold flowers and other floral and striped designs, alongside bolts of plain fabric, in its spring 1934 advertisements.[55]

Baladi clothing did not receive the same journalistic promotion as *ifrangi* items but was nevertheless an important part of the clothing market and people's everyday sartorial identities. Many lower-class men who worked in manual labor or in crafts wore galabiya, coat (*miʿtaf*), and skullcap (*taqiyya*) as a daily dress.[56] Even effendi men, such as government or bank clerks, who wore *ifrangi* or "business dress" to work—a suit or jacket and trousers, a button-front shirt, a necktie, a tarbush—often changed into more *baladi* styles such as a galabiya and skullcap once at home in the afternoon.[57] Industrial workers of rural origin, such as al-Khuli, dressed simply and owned a single galabiya, a shirt made of coarse cotton (*dammur*), and a pair of underwear (*libas*), which "they wore all day and night, in sleep and in work."[58] For such consumers, clothing was not usually purchased for specific functions or activities; rather, its temporal status marked it as either formal or informal: a new dress or galabiya served as a best outfit, last year's dress as a second-best outfit, and an even older one as dress for chores or manual work.[59] Thus advertising provided no single typical portrait of Egyptian dress in the first three decades of the century. As with household furnishings, foods, and other items of consumption, dress varied among Egyptians primarily according to class status but also region, gender, and generation, not to mention individual style and, for those above the poverty line, occasion and season.

SELLING NATIONAL TEXTILES AND OTHER
COMMODITIES IN THE 1930S

Although buy-local and other nationalist campaigns surfaced in the press around the 1919–1924 nationalist upsurge, most local producers did not have the resources to allocate funds to large advertising campaigns before the 1930s. The majority of advertisements even then continued to promote imported products or those of foreign-owned firms, since "under normal conditions, established local businesses did not feel they needed to advertise in order to increase sales, and they would usually do so only under pressure of competition."[60] New nationalist goods such as the textiles produced by Bank Misr's firms and affiliated companies received prominent publicity, however, to help them gain a foothold in the market. As the giant new textile factories began to produce and advertise galabiya cloth that could compete with British, Japanese, and other imports, smaller textile companies developed other items of dress, such as hosiery, that could be manufactured from Egyptian cotton and marketed to Egyptian consumers.

Since the local cotton industry was premised on import substitution, marketing campaigns for locally manufactured textiles of Egyptian cotton addressed external competition and tried to convince Egyptians to buy locally made products instead. To do this, textile marketers capitalized on Egyptian cotton's reputation as a material that could produce exceptionally fine and strong cloth with its long-staple fibers—"all kinds of cotton goods with a smooth surface and a fine luster."[61] The long-staple length of most Egyptian raw cottons confronted their mass marketing, however, with a peculiar dilemma. *Silkiness* connoted a complex array of meanings commonly drawn on to mark social differentiation rather than the national unity so sought after by new industrialists-cum-economic-nationalists. The material nature of Egyptian cotton thus compromised its potency as a political vehicle for anticolonial politics.

In Egypt the nationalist call to reject foreign silks resonated with a strand of Islamic discourse that had singled out silk cloth, and especially its use by men, to represent degenerative luxury and the need for moral and religious reform. Popular opinion in the nineteenth century considered abstention from silk consumption a marker of piety among local 'ulama' and other exemplary men.[62] By the middle twentieth century, Islamist leaders viewed luxury textiles as a cause of the decadence of the entire community. Although it is not clear that Islamist leaders themselves, or the industries they established, entirely avoided silk, Hasan al-Banna, the founder of the Muslim Brothers (or the Muslim Brotherhood), invoked hadiths about the moral corruption caused by luxury fabrics and railed in his sermons against "luxury" in dress and consumption.[63] In the 1940s Sayyid Qutb wrote explicitly against silk in *Social Justice in Islam*. Citing a hadith forbidding the use of silk by men, Qutb explained that although generally the commands of the Prophet should be understood in their own context, the injunction on silk should be followed literally. "In fact, the wearing of silk, or saffron-dyed or embroidered cloth often detracts from the worth of men [*qimat al-rijal*]. It moves them to softness [*tarawa*], especially in the era of struggle [*jihad*]."[64] Silk—like "huge automobiles" and imported bottled water—exemplified excessive consumption that, Qutb asserted, was an individual crime capable of ultimately corrupting the broader community that tolerated it.[65]

The increased consumption of printed fabrics, especially those decorated with human figures, also drew religious opposition in the 1930s. Administrators from al-Azhar University petitioned Egyptian customs officials in 1937 about the threat to public morality caused by imported cotton flannelette fabrics printed with pictures of women wearing bathing suits.[66] Including a sample of the offensive cloth, the petition asserted, "This fabric is of a nature to encourage virtuous young girls and women, as the season of summer approaches, to ask either their parents or their husbands to allow them to go to the beach and wear indecent bathing suits."[67] Customs officials, in consultation with the Department of Public Security, ultimately supported the university's call and banned the importation of the "morally endangering" cloths.[68]

Class conflict also often found expression through reference to the quality of cloth, and silk acted as a primary cultural marker of class differentiation. The French commercial attaché described the widespread effects of the economic boom preceding the spectacular crash in 1907 in such terms. Even the small farmer, "up til now so thrifty," he asserted, began to spend part of his earnings on ameliorating his situation with "a relative luxury," such as a silk robe or silk scarf for himself, his wife, or his children.[69] Al-Khuli frequently used silkiness in his memoir to illustrate the disparity between prosperous craftsmen and unskilled workers in the textile industry at al-Mahalla al-Kubra. One of the primary sources of conflict in Mahalla at the time was between the more urban, experienced, and relatively affluent hand weavers from the town itself (the *mahallawiyya*) and the untrained peasants recruited to work in the factories alongside them (the *shirkawiyya*, or company men). Al-Khuli remarked that although the cloth manufactured in the factory was as fine as "flowered calico that brides wear in the village," the factory workers dressed in "canvas [*khaysh*]."[70] The *mahallawi* weavers, however, wore "foreign silk [*harir ifrangi*]."[71] Expensive silken clothes, whether made of real silk or fine cotton, and cloth stamped with certain representational designs thus connoted a complicated interweaving of immorality, class difference, foreignness as an import, complicity with authority or colonialism, and un-Islamic practices.

The early 1930s marketing campaigns for cotton cloth made from local, long-staple cotton responded to the cluster of meanings attached to silkiness with a variety of strategies to promote their goods. One concerned the issue of price. Long-staple cotton worked most effectively as a luxury material, woven into fine but expensive textiles. Egyptian textiles from the new cotton weaving factories could not beat out cheaper Indian and Japanese textiles in terms of price unless the state imposed high tariffs on imports, which it could do after 1930, but this still made local textiles expensive. As a result, industry leaders, such as Tal'at Harb, exhorted consumers to pay the higher prices: it was, Harb argued, "necessary that the Egyptian understand that the piastre that he paid extra in the price of Egyptian cloth profits him in the durability of the cloth, and from the other perspective, it is a national sacrifice in the service of Egyptian industry and Egyptian workers who are present now in Egyptian factories working to earn their bread after they had been unemployed."[72]

The difficulty of creating consumer desire for locally produced fabrics exacerbated the problem of price. Technical limitations of Egyptian mechanization hampered marketing the silkiness of new nationalist textiles. Secondhand imported machinery and inexperienced mill workers, whom companies tended to recruit from among local peasants rather than skilled hand weavers to keep labor costs low, could not make full use of the properties of Egyptian long-staple cotton.[73] "The cotton piece goods produced in Egypt [in the 1920s and early 1930s], at first of a poor quality, had a thick weave and were plain whites and yellows. With the passage of time, Egyptian weaving and dyeing became more expert, but the quality of the finished Egyptian product was not as fine as that of European and Asian imports," Robert Tignor notes.[74] An Egyptian textile expert at the time lamented that low-grade textiles made with the shortest available growths of cotton, even if durable, did not appear tempting when displayed in shop windows.[75] Moreover, cloth had long been marketed by trademark, and Egyptian industrialists found it difficult to compete with established brands. The "Egyptian consumer," according to Roger Owen, "had already come to believe that foreign goods were always preferable to those produced locally. . . . Where products like cotton-piece goods were concerned the consumer was accustomed to protect himself against inferior articles by purchasing only those which carried the familiar trade mark of one of the large, reputable importers."[76] Local factories turned to the popular press for help in improving their market share through a variety of advertising campaigns that promoted the quality and patriotic value of their goods.

Although marketers in the 1930s emphasized the "elegant" merchandise produced by the Bank Misr industries,[77] most advertisements explicitly argued that the consumption of locally produced textiles would lead to overall national progress. Along with nationalist symbols such as flags, drums, and uniforms, the imagery of steps and hills frequently marked the upward trajectory of national development in such promotions.[78] Promotions also emphasized that consumers could have national cloth tailored into a wide variety of dress styles. The Misr Spinning and Weaving Company depicted its cotton cloth as an instrument to bring unity to the diversity of local residents. One illustration portrayed the inside of a shop, where a smiling saleswoman displayed a long swath of fabric to four customers standing side by side at the counter. The caption identifies them as "the Egyptians," and the image highlights their differences in dress: an upper-class woman wearing a thin veil; a balding, bareheaded man dressed in a light-colored *ifrangi* suit; another man in a dark suit and tarbush; and finally a man clothed in a caftan, turban, and spectacles. Framed by long draping displays of fabric, the advertisement's text conveyed the Egyptians' astonishment at the beauty of locally crafted cloth.[79] Arrayed equally at the cloth counter, despite their heterogeneity, consumers would be bound together, this advertisement suggested, by national textiles.

Another solution to the dilemma of how to market the rather coarse, locally produced textiles made of longer growths of Egyptian cotton was to transform the cotton's reputation for fineness and silkiness into one about durability. Harb himself positioned Egyptian cotton textiles as "authentic" and "pure," unlike cheaply made imported textiles that used finishing processes, such as adding cornstarch or glue, to achieve a temporary silky or smooth look.[80] He repeatedly stressed that one Egyptian garment equaled three or four of foreign manufacture because the former lasted longer.[81] The promotion of Egyptian cotton as more durable and authentic than other imported yarns and fabrics encouraged the use of pharaonic imagery in textile trademarks. Although some companies used a variety of imagery, the iconography of ancient Egypt featured prominently in several important local textile brandings: the Filature Nationale's depiction of a crocodile in front of pyramids, the Ahram Weaving Company's use of the pyramids at Giza, Bank Misr's Spinning and Weaving Company's profile of a pharaoh, Shurbaji's portrayal of a felucca on the Nile in front of a pharaonic temple, and the scarab of al-Kahira textile factories.[82]

Narratives about pharaonicism and durability coincided with a masculinist nationalist rhetoric associated with strength that became increasingly popular in the 1930s. One advertisement, for example, featured a drawing of the Shurbaji cotton hosiery factory in front of the Giza pyramids, flanked by a young man dressed in a scouting uniform and a tarbush, holding an Egyptian flag in one hand and a pair of socks in the other (see Figure 13). The 1930s Shurbaji pharaonic logo (a falcon with outstretched wings, the pharaonic symbol of royal protection) hung prominently over the factory door. The text declared, "Egypt's ancient glory is expressed in building the pyramids. Her modern glory is expressed in al-Shurbaji's hosiery factory. Durable like the pyramids; strong like boys [al-shabab]—Shurbaji's socks."[83] The emphasis on the strength and durability conferred by long-staple fibers to local cloth remained, however, barnacled with associations of silkiness that ultimately tinged the consumption of durable local fabrics with expectations of upward social mobility and a concomitant moral ambiguity. The anxiety that surfaced about silkiness would come to mark the masculine market in socks knit with local cotton, as the broader effort to create a united national cloth community struggled with the submerged tendency of silkiness to create social differentiation.

KNITTING COTTON HOSIERY AND A MALE CITIZENRY

Positioning cotton textiles, and especially hosiery, as part of a narrative linked to the durability and duration of the Egyptian national community was part of an explicit promotion to create and expand markets for new local goods, such as men's socks. Although growing in the 1920s, the sock market still remained import based. Purveying both men's socks and women's stockings in silk, lace, and silk blends, Holeproof Hosiery was a leader in the 1920s market, with promotions for its "incomparably" "sturdy," "elegant," and "economical" socks and stockings. An Alexandrian agent, Baruda Brothers, imported Holeproof goods from Great Britain and retailed them at "all department stores."[84] Advertisements for Holeproof men's socks varied, depicting a sock-clad foot next to an elegant shoe or a man in a dressing gown pointing out the reinforced toe and heel of his sock;[85] at other times ads featured the enormous Holeproof factory

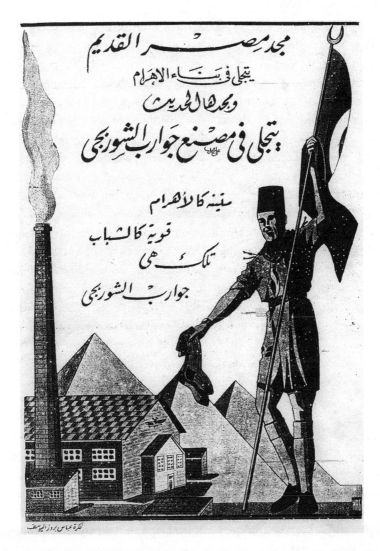

مجد مصر القديم
يتجلى في بناء الاهرام
ومجدها الحديث
يتجلى في مصنع جوارب الشوربجي
متينة كالأهرام
قوية كالشباب
تلك هى
جوارب الشوربجي

نكلة عباس بروز اليوسف

Figure 13. Shurbaji proclaimed its factory's socks to be Egypt's "modern glory" by likening them to the building of the pyramids, "the glory of ancient Egypt." *Ruz al-yusuf*, no. 349 (29 October 1934) (special issue), 27.

in England.[86] Stores also commonly sold hosiery without reference to brand. In the winter 1924–1925 catalog, Cicurel advertised five types of men's socks in cotton, mercerized cotton, and wool, all of which were described simply by material, color, and pattern.[87] Other companies simply promoted hosiery by price.[88]

Responding to the growing domestic market in imported socks and increasing support for new factories, the local hosiery sector exploded in the 1930s and 1940s.[89] Knitting hosiery required machines and labor processes that differed from those for weaving cotton galabiya fabrics. The state sponsored expanded training in the new knitting (or *tricotage*) technologies. The Ministry of Commerce and Industry established a technical school for knitting hosiery, underwear, and dress fabrics in 1935. Many women enrolled in its six-month course and then worked as contractors at the department's workshop to produce fabrics until they eventually saved enough to purchase knitting equipment for their homes.[90] Bank Misr specifically promoted small-scale development of this niche in the textile industry (hosiery, underwear, upholstery) to compete against foreign merchandise, in part by urging the immigration of several Muslim families to Egypt from Syria in the late 1920s and 1930s.[91] By 1943 a local textile expert estimated that "the bonneterie industry has attained sufficient development to satisfy and at times surpass the needs of local consumption."[92] Much of this growth came from the establishment of small local hosiery factories, most of which employed hand knitting, although several large mechanized factories were also founded. Among the most important was the Egyptian Hosiery Company/La Bonneterie, established in 1924 and registered as a joint-stock company in 1935. Half-owned by the Filature Nationale, it had by 1937 an "up-to-date factory" in Alexandria with 560 workers operating 420 machines to make underwear and another 80 knitting machines to manufacture socks and stockings. These machines worked "coarse cotton yarn" from the local spinning mills, "fine cotton yarn (spun from Egyptian cotton)," wool yarn imported from the United Kingdom, and rayon yarn procured from the United Kingdom and Germany. Annual output was estimated to be 96,000 dozen pairs of socks and stockings and 72,000 sets of underclothes.[93] Although few hosiery companies consistently showed a profit,[94] the sock market continued to grow faster than the output of local industries. A Ministry of Commerce and Industry report in 1948 "estimated that tricotage factories and workshops employed 6,000 workmen and produced 70 percent of local consumption."[95] In 1954 local production reached 600,000 dozen socks per year, although strong imports continued at least through the 1940s, with 458,000 dozen socks imported in 1950.[96]

Among the numerous hosiery enterprises founded in this period, the Shurbaji (*Chourbagui*) Hosiery Factory stood out for its aggressive marketing of itself as Egyptian, probably on the basis of the company's ties to Bank Misr and the Shurbajis being Muslim, though the family had emigrated from Syria only in 1932. Muhammad Shurbaji owned one of the largest weaving factories in Damascus; it manufactured natural and artificial silk textiles that it exported to Iraq, Anatolia, the Balkans, and Egypt. The family expanded into a variety of industrial concerns throughout the Middle East in the 1920s and 1930s, establishing a cigarette paper factory in Aleppo in 1923 or 1925, match factories in Damascus in 1927 and Baghdad in 1928, and an oil and soap factory in Damascus in 1939. In Egypt the Shurbajis founded textile factories: a knitting factory for hosiery in Cairo in 1932, a silk weaving and upholstery factory in Cairo in 1937, and two spinning and weaving factories in 1940 (one in Alexandria and another in Cairo).[97] The family received an industrial loan from the Egyptian state in 1937 to expand their textile operations, although "taking the loan was not evidence of [financial] need," as the family had large holdings in Egypt and Syria.[98] The company was privately owned until it registered as an Egyptian joint-stock company in April 1947, capitalized at £E50,000.[99] Although the family retained significant commercial interests in Syria through at least the 1940s, the local Arabic press always referred to them as Egyptians.[100] Journalists reported that they "never saw a single foreigner in this authentic national factory; all of the workmen were Egyptian."[101]

The press specifically promoted Shurbaji's mechanized Cairo factory at Bulaq as an example of Egyptian industrial—and therefore national—progress. The factory, one article declared, was "actually considered an industrial school respected for the education of boys and girls in hosiery manufacture, and as such is considered an important part of establishing an industrial renaissance in Egypt."[102] Support of the factory was "a national duty incumbent on the people and the government,"[103] which would lead, another article argued, to the "release of the Egyptian heart from the stranglehold of foreign factories."[104] Owned and directed by Salah al-Din al-Shurbaji (whom the press dubbed the "king of Egyptian hosiery"), the factory was managed by his three younger brothers, one of whom had been trained in hosiery production in Germany. Promotional articles carefully detailed the mechanization in Shurbaji factories, focusing on the "modern machines," assembly-line production, and interdependent division of labor that knit together all areas of the factory in the production of a single sock.[105] In 1940 the Egyptian architectural review al-'Imara featured the company's new Imbaba factory as a "model modern factory," in which production materials moved "in one continuous direction" through the factory and to the warehouse, connecting the factory's workers and administrators.[106] In 1934 the Bulaq factory employed roughly two hundred people, including specialist engineers and young children working in knitting and sewing.[107] Factory operations had grown considerably by 1948, with 625 workers and 42 employees, all Egyptian.[108] Despite its portrayal as an engine of national uplift, the Shurbaji Company was renowned for its unjust treatment of its workers.[109]

Echoing the new marketing discourse of locally manufactured textiles of Egyptian cotton, promotional material in the 1930s and 1940s on the Shurbaji hosiery factories heralded the ability of its hosiery to foster patriotic belonging. Its cotton socks for men and boys received praise for their "durability and tasteful colors" and their superior quality compared to foreign imports of comparable prices.[110] Moreover, the press depicted the manufacture of cotton hosiery as knitting together various social groups and geographic regions into a national community.[111] In January 1933 a *Ruz al-yusuf* advertisement connected producers and consumers: a peasant man on top of the frame looked over a field of cotton; below him a worker leaned against a small drawing of the factory; and spreading out from the factory were cotton threads that metamorphosed into socks—a commodity awaiting a consumer (see Figure 14). "Oh Egyptian!" the text exhorted. "The cotton of Egypt. From it, the Egyptian worker manufactures fine socks—socks that are Egyptian by their raw materials, manufacture, and capital."[112] Other Shurbaji advertisements in the 1930s focused on tying together diverse groups of male consumers. One portrayed different generations of customers—a middle-aged effendi, a young upper-class man, and a boy—clustered around a pair of al-Shurbaji socks, which "the old and the young prefer" (see Figure 15).[113] Al-Shurbaji specifically marketed different types of socks for "people of various classes," some made of "the finest type of Egyptian cotton—Sakellarides,"[114] others matching "the most modern types of suit cloth."[115] In 1935 the company also planned to launch several "durable, good-quality, and cheaply priced" lines for the general middle-class public—"student socks [*jawarib tilmidh*]" and "government employee socks [*jawarib muwazzaf*]"—as well as a more expensive, deluxe (*fakhir*) model for the "special class of people [*tabaqa khassa min al-sha'b*]" who prefer and could afford it.[116]

Although differentiated, these male identities became linked in marketing materials through a universal consumption: socks, like the tarbush, formed part of a modern national dress required of men from all groups and classes of Egyptians. One promotional article asserted, "Socks are almost the only type of clothing that all people share in wearing—from a suckling infant to an

Figure 14. Shurbaji's socks were Egyptian by their raw material, their manufacture, and the firm's capital, a chain that linked company administrators, peasants, factory workers, and hosiery consumers. *Ruz al-yusuf*, no. 258 (23 January 1933), 37.

Figure 15. "The old and the young" men consumed Shurbaji hosiery, the company proclaimed. *Ruz al-yusuf*, no. 343 (17 September 1934), 18.

old adult, from a worker to a government minister."[117] Another asked, "How many Egyptians, in their differences of class and contrasts of income, finances, and creed, don't plunge their feet and legs into socks?"[118] Echoing the diversity of the market, such publicity generally depicted men's whole bodies or faces rather than just their stocking-clad legs. This promotional connection of different male identities—based on class and occupation (peasants, workers, government employees, students), consumption culture (elite, practical, elegant), and age—projected a single, stratified but conflict-free national community. Shurbaji's 1933–1935 sock campaign made the most deliberate use of the imagery of interlinked male identities, although several other firms promoted men's socks in similar ways during this time.[119] The Ahmad Halawa Stores advertised that they offered the "largest storehouse of hosiery" for men, women, and boys, depicting elegantly dressed upper-class adults and a young schoolboy.[120] Bata Company also marketed lines of imported men's socks, including more luxurious styles made from silk and "refined cotton" and less expensive ones bearing names such as the "cotton screen" and the "practical."[121]

Thus the local production and sale of Egyptian textiles in the early 1930s—responding to the calls of Egyptian boycotters and the interests of economic-nationalists-cum-industrialists—attempted to bind together the Egyptian nation as a diverse community of postcolonial consumers in ways that differed in scope and metaphor from similar attempts on the part of literary figures and politicians who increasingly focused their bifurcated language on supranational identities, such as Arabism, Islamism, and neofascism.[122] Marketing Egyptian textiles as symbols of the Egyptian nation through their association with Egypt's primary national resource, long-staple cotton, and its new niche industry, cotton hosiery, linked textiles into a multilayered series of national narratives and a view of the heterogeneity of local society. The material nature of Egyptian cotton—famed for the silkiness and durability its long staple length imparted to fabrics—helped shift nationalist marketing from the home-spun and anticommercial rhetoric espoused by Indian nationalists and their use of short-staple Indian cotton under similar circumstances.

FROM "FLIMSY SLIPPERS" TO "PROPER SHOES"

Like cloth, footwear appeared to state-sponsored industrialists in the 1930s to be a commodity that could fuel a national economic renaissance. A basic element of proper dress, heeled and fitted shoes could be produced locally, they argued, to deepen the domestic market, support a new regime of mass consumption, and modernize Egyptian culture. A 1921 report on shoe consumption among Egyptians estimated that "75 percent of the population is rural and not accustomed to wearing shoes of any kind, while a large percentage of the urban Moslem population use flimsy slippers of native manufacture."[123] The interrelated problems of shoeing the barefoot and shifting Egyptian taste away from "flimsy slippers" to sturdy, modern styles structured elite efforts to fashion the footwear sector as another pillar of the nation's economic independence. Promotions of *ifrangi* shoes employed material and semiotic strategies that used elements of older footwear styles and lexical class markers to transition to new models. Foreignness circulated in these promotions in complicated ways that seemed to defy the bifurcated categories popularized by boycotters. Expansion of the footwear market also rested on a belief that mechanized production would standardize shoes and make them affordable in ways that would move national unification from the terrain of economics into cultural and visual registers.

Despite the growing trend in the early twentieth century toward footwear fashions originating in Europe and the United States, certain material elements of *baladi* styles continued to be in demand in newer *ifrangi* models. Consumer preference for slipper styles of *ifrangi* shoes provides one example of the complex and locally inflected nature of market change. Slipper styles had dominated Egyptian footwear styles in the nineteenth century due in part to the cultural importance accorded to preserving the sanctity and cleanliness of domestic and sacred space. In households, people conventionally sat on the floor around low tables or on low couches to eat or visit. Sitting in such a cross-legged position was easier and cleaner if shoes were slipped off at the threshold of the house or the room.[124] Shoes were also taken off for prayer, especially at the thresholds of mosques.[125] Contemporary observers noted that the frequent removal of shoes to enter domestic or religious space factored heavily into Egyptians' preference for slip-on shoes. A 1905 report, "Egypt's Boot and Shoe Trade," for the British Chamber of Commerce in Egypt remarked that "in a Mohammedan country such as Egypt, it is obvious that a strong demand must exist for a boot which can be taken off with a minimum of trouble, since the strict follower of the Prophet has to remove his boots a number of times a day in connection with the performance of his religious duties."[126] Although Egyptian social practices were likely not as monolithically shaped by a static notion of Islam as Europeans tended to portray them, foreign-trade statistics and commercial reports did suggest that the most widely consumed new shoe styles were successful precisely because they resembled the slipper forms of the more indigenous backless leather *bulgha* or the slip-on red or yellow *sarma* and *markub*. Switzerland and Austria were among the largest early European importers into the Egyptian market, as they exported shoes that could easily be removed and put on, such as "half-shoes for women," or "a 'Spring-side' boot, the article being made in one piece with elastic sides."[127] Other popular styles included felt slippers from Bavaria and the cheap, slip-on canvas "Espadrille" from Spain.[128] In a similar way, the most prevalent colors in shoe polish remained red, coffee, and especially yellow and black, suggesting that local slippers of these colors were still very much in use and preference for wearing the new styles in familiar colors continued strong.[129]

The success of European imports in styles similar to native slippers lay, however, in more than their functional suitability for Egyptian social mores. Marketers also overlaid the material familiarity of shape or style of such shoes with a new nomenclature that connoted elite status and a modern sartorial consumption style. Both French and Ottoman terminologies were used to represent certain shoes this way for the upper and urban cosmopolitan classes, as well as for the more middle-class *effendiyya*. The success of the *pantoufle*, a term that appeared by the mid-1920s to denote several styles of European slip-on shoes, may be attributed to this new lexical practice. A light, flat style of shoe with a closed back, it essentially retained an older slipper or loafer shape, without significant lacing or buckles, although it was often modified by the addition of a medium or high heel. The 1928 Chemla catalog, for instance, offered *pantoufles* either in camel hair with leather soles for men or felt with silk tassel and piping for women.[130] In the Cicurel catalog for winter 1924–1925, *pantoufles* in both leather and felt were advertised under the store's exclusive brand name, Chaussures Royale. The bilingual catalog directly transliterated the French word *pantoufle* into Arabic as *bantufl* rather than translating it as "slipper" through use of an Arabic equivalent. In addition, Cicurel offered several styles of mules, a slip-on shoe with a heel, in leather and in lamé under the French names *mule* or *sandale* but universally translated them into *bantufl* or *bantufli* in the Arabic captions.[131] Even the Czechoslovakian Bata Company used such terminology. An advertisement in 1931 promoted a variety of closed and flat slippers as well as high-heeled, open-backed mules under the name *bantufla*.[132] The associations with French fashion retained through transliterating *pantoufle* directly into Arabic, rather than translating it as *bulgha* or *babush*, partook in the wider cultural capital of French as a language of modern sophistication used by retail spaces in bilingual advertising and by wealthier Egyptians, increasingly schooled in foreign languages and mannerisms (such as eating foie gras), to signal status.[133]

Another semantic transformation enabled the assimilation of new footwear styles in middle- and lower-class markets. In this case, adaptations of Ottoman words for footwear came to designate the new styles of closed and heeled shoes associated with Europe, as well as accord open, local styles a more modern connotation. Nineteenth-century footwear terminology primarily included terms such as *bulgha, khuff, sarma, markub*, and *qubqab*, many of which were Arabic words long current in Egypt. A rather cumbersome, formal, and descriptive terminology rendered European-style shoes into formal Arabic: boots were denoted "shoes with a neck [*hidha' bi-raqabi*]" and lower, lace-up oxford or wing-tip shoes were termed "half shoes [*hidha' nusf*]."[134] *Sarma, bulgha*, and *markub* were the primary Egyptian words for low or flat slipper-type shoes in the eighteenth and nineteenth centuries, while *khuff* designated short boots.[135] The 1927 Industrial and Commercial (IC) Census identified these latter terms with native, or *baladi*, shoe styles. Its category for "the manufacture of native footwear" appeared in Arabic as "*san'a al-ahdhiyya al-baladiyya (al-marakib wa'l-bulagh)* [the manufacture of native footwear (*markub*s and *bulgha*s)]."

By contrast, the same 1927 census identified European, or *ifrangi*, styles with a new set of colloquial words: "the manufacture of European footwear" appeared in Arabic as "*san'a al-ahdhiyya al-ifrangiyya (al-gizam wa'l-shabashib, ila-akhari)* [the manufacture of Westernized footwear (*gizam, shibshib*s, and so forth)]."[136] The terms *gazma* (pl. *gizam*) and *shibshib* (pl. *shabashib*) would become the more colloquial and contemporary terms used in Egypt for shoe styles in the twentieth century.[137] Both terms derived from Turkish or Ottoman. From the Turkish word for "boot" (*çizme*), *gazma* came to designate the newer, more closed and backed European-style shoes such as the oxford or the pump, which were more substantial, sturdier, and bootlike compared to *baladi* forms such as the *bulgha*, although shorter than true ankle boots (*khuff*).[138] As noted earlier, the 1924–1925 Cicurel catalog used *gazma* to denote pumps of various styles, *souliers* (shoes), oxfords, ankle boots, and wing tips. Boots and gaiters ("balmorals") were called *gazma butt* and tennis shoes, *gazma kawitch*. In addition, *shibshib*, the Turkish word to denote a backless slipper, came to replace *bulgha* and *qubqab*.[139] These Ottoman Turkish words, familiar to Egyptians because of the long Ottoman occupation and the persistence into the twentieth century of Turco-Circassian elites, especially in the army, entered Egyptian colloquial although not Modern Standard Arabic by the 1910s.[140] These terms did more than merely distinguish new styles from old. Perhaps their success lay in their ability to encode these shoes as "foreign-yet-familiar": they did not appear as distant—and thus as intimidating—as French words to ordinary Egyptians, although they still retained an appealing aura of cosmopolitan fashion.[141]

Such terminology appealed most directly to the upwardly mobile and modernizing members of the *effendiyya*, such as government employees and others in the middle and lower classes, educated (but not simply Westernized) professionals who struggled with the rising cost of living.[142] The 1926 catalog of the Household Cooperative Society for Government Employees in Cairo, discussed in Chapter 1 reflected this.[143] The catalog listed no *bulgha*, *babush*, *markub*, *sarma*, or *qubqab* or any *pantoufles*, *décolletés*, or *Richelieus*. Rather, it offered a variety of shoes—all designated *gizam*—for men, women, and children in assorted styles and colors. In addition, the catalog included several much cheaper styles, including several pairs of slip-on shoes: a children's sandal (*sandal*) imported from Europe; women's rubber shoes (*kawitch gizam harimi*); and a palm-frond slipper with a rubber sole (*shibshib khus bi-naʿil kawitch*).[144] Some of these shoes were made in nontraditional materials, such as rubber, linen, or black patent leather, or nontraditional styles, with two-toned uppers, or laces and buttons. The catalog even included a separate category for long or short shoelaces (*ribat al-gizam*) in a variety of colors. The presence of new materials and footwear elements suggests the stylistic resemblance between the catalog's shoes and European forms of heeled and backed shoes with complex, closed uppers. Thus newer styles of footwear designated with Ottoman names such as *gazma* and *shibshib* corresponded to a familiar modernity that most appealed to more-conservative middle-class employees. Their incorporation into the variety of Egyptians' wardrobes contributed to a linguistic morseling.

Older *baladi* styles continued to sell in the Egyptian market in this period. Shoes from Morocco—"the whole of [its] trade . . . practically confined to [generally red or yellow leather] native slippers, which are the ordinary footgear used by the Arabs"[145]—were imported through the 1920s, despite a steady decrease in annual imports after 1908. Morocco's imports of native slippers would not disappear from Egyptian import figures until 1939.[146] *Baladi* slipper styles also continued to be manufactured locally. The family of al-Hajj Mukhtar ʿAbd al-Karim al-Bannani made and sold *bulgha*s (what they called "*des chaussures egyptiennes* [*Bolaghs*]") in Cairo in 1926.[147] Like many native cobblers, the family lived in the Darb al-Ahmar district and owned and operated a workshop (*atelier*) and a store (*magasin*). Part of a "very respectable family," they were French subjects who had been residing in Egypt since 1914. The Bannanis represented a healthy segment of the shoemaking industry, as census figures attested. The 1927 IC Census documented the continued production of these shoes in Egypt (although not the quantity of their output): "the manufacture of native footwear/*al-ahdhiyya al-baladiyya* (*al-marakib wa'l-bulagh*)" and of pattens (*al-qabaqib*).[148] Although establishments manufacturing *ifrangi* shoes (6,415) well outnumbered those of *baladi* cobblers (978) in 1927, the census most likely underrepresented *baladi* cobblers.[149] A decade later, however, the census no longer even differentiated between *baladi* and *ifrangi* types of footwear, instead collapsing them both into the more comprehensive category of "boot making and repairing/*san' wa-taslih al-ahdhiyya wa-ku'ubaha*."[150]

Changes in census reporting of the local footwear industry were part of a broader push by interwar economic elites toward the mechanization of shoe production. Mechanization of the sector had been a stated goal since at least the First World War, when the Egyptian government's Committee on Commerce and Industry called for an expansion in local mechanized footwear production to create cheaply priced and standardized shoes, because of "the low prices that machines and assembly lines allow to maintain, and against the style of which modern equipment allows to ensure perfection."[151] The new mechanized industry struggled against the persistence of "hundreds of small workshops—owned chiefly by Armenians—who manufacture[d] a low priced but presentable article which appeal[ed] to the lower class Europeans established in Egypt."[152] The one large-scale attempt to manufacture boots and shoes in the mid-1930s—"a factory equipped with [an] up-to-date plant" and "a substantial increase of capital"—failed against the "very numerous small producers with limited overhead expenses."[153] The state tried to support large mechanized factories through a variety of methods, such as tariff protection, a series of industry loans, and stipulations that government contracts for military and police footwear, once the exclusive purview of British uniform "ammunition" boots, be awarded only to local factories.[154] Nevertheless, the Department of Commerce and Industry remained deeply concerned in the middle 1930s about "overcoming the idea of competition between the process of mechanized production and hand production."[155] It even proposed the establishment of a "cooperative union for shoe production" that would centralize hand producers by relocating them into "a factory" "reserved for the mechanical production of semi-manufactured [materials] prepared for the specialized artistic and technical finishing by the masters [*arbab*] of hand production."[156] The project would provide machinery for the production of footwear parts that could be purchased and assembled by individual shoemakers and even include an affiliated workshop to research "the new fashion designs in cutting" and offer them to members at a special rate. The government hoped that through this new cooperative union a "semi-mechanized industry" would develop to ensure that "machines would become an encouragement to hand crafting, facilitating an increase in production instead of being obstructive to the means of livelihood from the perspective of hand workers."[157]

Local cobblers by 1930 were, however, "feeling the effects of strong competition by Czechoslovakian shoemakers who, in 1927, opened their own retail shops in Cairo and Alexandria for the sale of smart but cheap footwear, which [was] in great demand in the Egyptian market."[158] From the 1930s through the 1950s, the Bata Company, known for its inexpensive, standardized, *ifrangi*-style footwear, dominated the mechanized side of the industry as well as large-scale retail distribution.[159] Originally based in Czechoslovakia but decentralized in the 1920s into several independent subsidiaries in different countries, Bata operated an empire of stores throughout Egypt, selling shoes produced in their local factories as well as imported, perhaps from Bata factories abroad, and eventually it produced shoes for export.[160] Bata opened its first shoe store in Egypt in October 1927. The subsidiary registered as an Egyptian joint-stock company in November 1930, and within the next year, it operated numerous stores in Alexandria, Port Sa'id, Mansura, Cairo, and Tanta, in addition to branches in Jerusalem, Tel Aviv, and Nablus.[161] It advertised in 1933 fourteen branch stores in Egypt, and in 1938 the company built its first factory in Egypt.[162] The number of retail venues and factories grew substantially, so that by 1943 Bata operated two factories (one in Old Cairo and the other in Alexandria) and was planning to build another (near Cairo, to manufacture rubber products), in addition to 133 retail stores, of which 43 alone were in Cairo and 24 in Alexandria. At that time, the company also had branch operations in Palestine, Syria, Lebanon, Iraq, Sudan, Saudi Arabia, and Cyprus.[163] Bata focused its footwear production in Egypt by 1947 in a single factory, located at Mafrouza in Alexandria. Considered the "largest shoe factory in the Middle East," it employed more than a thousand workers and produced roughly one million leather and linen shoes in 1950, a production level that nearly doubled the following year.[164] Through the

1950s, the Egyptian Bata Company remained nominally under the direction of Bata family members, and the general management and many of the top-level employees of the company—including the general director and the heads of departments and warehouses—were Czechoslovakian.[165]

Much like other nationalist enterprises, such as the textile plant at al-Mahalla al-Kubra, Bata paternalistically offered modern goods and services to customers and employees. Shops furnished pedicures and manicures to customers, as well as darned socks and repaired and refinished shoes.[166] The factory provided services to "uplift" its workforce: a cafeteria "of the most modern style, which offer[ed] good food"; an athletic department emphasizing "the importance of bodily exercise" and organizing tournaments and parades for workers and their families; special funds for health care; "high wages"; bonuses for seniority; and child subsidies.[167] By 1950 the company had 140 stores "spread throughout different parts of Egypt from Alexandria and Port Saʿid to the heights of Aswan" and located in small towns such as Bilbis, Bilqas, Shibin al-Kum, Dayrut, Dissuq, Girga, Kafr al-Shaykh, Kafr al-Zayat, Mit Ghamr, Samnud, and Suhaj.[168] These shoe stores were most likely fairly standardized in interior design and layout—flanked "by a wide vitrine, with signage in both Arabic and French, artfully displaying an array of the latest shoe models"—and resembled Bata retail sites throughout the world, which also gave them an air of modernity.[169]

The shoes Bata produced in its large factories in Egypt received acclaim as "a sign of quality and prestige [ʿunwan liʾl-juda waʾl-wajaha]," in part by their association with the company's mechanization.[170] Promotional material depicted large drawings of the Bata factory at Alexandria that emphasized the factory's vastness and sleek modernity by portraying it as isolated from its surrounding context of buildings, populated with only long rows of machines rather than workers, and sanitized by the clean lines of the drawing. Much like the rational technology of its plant, Bata used "scientific methods," it proclaimed, to design and market its shoes.

[As] Bata care[d] for the interest of the public, it made its shoe production into an art with rules. Before it manufactured any style in its large selection, the company tested it on a large number of people and [evaluated] its production from the results of these tests. Bata's technical preparation is regarded as exemplary in a modern factory. Special technical machines study the strength of the wear of each part of the shoe and verify its overall durability.[171]

The modernity in Bata's shoes accrued also from their standardization and affordability. In particular, Bata became known for its cheaply priced but stylish shoes, competitive in the local market since they were affordable to the middle and lower-middle classes. "The Bata Company's wish for service to the Egyptian consumer peaked when it decided finally to produce new shoes for the poor classes, carrying the name '*munafis*' (rival or competitor) and offered them for sale at an unbeatable price. It is a sturdy and good-looking shoe, made of good leather and with a sole of compressed rubber that is appropriate for all occasions . . . [and stronger than] the sole made of the best types of leather."[172] Bata marketing thus drew on official attitudes about the superiority of mechanization and the importance of creating cheaply priced, *ifrangi* footwear to portray its shoes as proper for and a service to contemporary Egyptians.

State and industrial elites tried to force lower-class Egyptians to wear *ifrangi* shoes at various times. Entry into new work and educational institutions became contingent on the use of particular styles of shoes. The Mahalla textile workers initially wore *baladi* shoes—*qabaqib*—to the factory, to protect their more expensive shoes from the wear and tear of the workplace. In an effort to save on wage costs by instituting a system of harsh fines and to introduce modern discipline into the factory, the Mahalla factory management issued a new set of regulations designed to formalize the workspace, including a prohibition against "the wearing of *qabaqib* on the factory floor."[173] Although al-Khuli does not explain the reasoning behind the administration's decision, the management likely did not consider *qabaqib* modern enough to correspond to the factory's self-image, as they recalled village life. The shoes were raised, clunky, and open-toed and thus may have caused the workers to walk and stand in undisciplined ways.[174] Whatever the reasons, the workers resented the new sartorial regulation. "They even want us to walk barefoot at work. They don't even want us to wear *qabaqib*. Do [they think] we have money to buy shoes [*gizam*]? This is the *only* pair of shoes one has, which is kept for going [to the village] every two weeks. Do [they think] if we wear them out we will be able to buy other ones?"[175] The harsh nature of the Mahalla factory restrictions, including those on *qabaqib*, and the drastic dockings in worker pay they caused, ultimately helped propel the workers to demand wage increases from the administration and undertake their first strikes.[176] The coercive induction into new "modern" consumption practices, such as this type of footwear prescription, on the lower classes in new workspaces was echoed in military and educational policies in Egypt that required students and conscripts to dress in appropriate uniforms, including shoes. The state undertook "barefoot campaigns" in the 1930s and 1940s to encourage shoe consumption among peasants as public health measures against parasites and used the labor of orphans and street children to make cheap *ifrangi* shoes available to potential students as part of its expansion of free elementary education.[177] Such sartorial coercions perhaps paradoxically fostered the spread of hybridized, or morseled, styles of dress.

Socks and shoes acted as instruments, then, by which new industrial elites tried to unify diversity of the national community in the face of continued colonial domination. Both material and linguistic transformations in footwear had helped launch Egypt into the beginnings of a mass consumption regime. Unlike didactic and official portrayals of the total annihilation of traditional crafts from the influx of cheap and seductive foreign goods,[178] the process of change was slow, using already established patterns of consumption and consumer preferences—for customary styles such as slippers, particular colors such as red and yellow, or familiar nomenclature such as Ottoman terms—to insinuate the new styles into Egyptian use. The contrasting styles of traditional slipper-style footwear and more modern closed and backed shoes emerged quite interconnectedly and contiguously in Egypt in this period, as an example of the fluid way the lived experiences of subjects of colonial modernity incorporated new sartorial practices. The increased mobility of urban residents, and especially the prevalence of transportation systems such as trams, buses, and automobiles, brought shoes into the public spotlight.

Despite expectations that locally produced industrial products would provide a key platform for full national liberation, cotton textiles failed to produce a mass politics of anticolonialism as they did in India, in part because the peculiar material traits of Egypt's long-staple cotton pushed producers to market new national textiles as vehicles for upward mobility and the attainment of luxury. The expense of using long-staple cotton fostered a rhetoric of consumer sacrifice but eventually pushed marketers toward stratified versions of the new national social order, thereby bringing class more than race to the center of Egypt's anticolonial struggle. Shurbaji sock promotions provide a glimpse of the more complex ways that the press and local politicians viewed Egyptian national identity in the interwar years. The local context constrained shoe marketing, too, and new styles drew on lexical markings of status that referred to Egypt's various colonial pasts rather than its new national present. Locally resident foreign companies such as Shurbaji and Bata convinced segments of local society that the companies could produce public good with their commercial success. Mixed-up practices of sartorial style contravened the neat and ordered vision espoused by nationalist industrialists who attempted to harness emerging mass consumption for the growth of their privately owned factories. The consumer preferences evident in shoe and hosiery wearing in fact demonstrate that interwar fashion defied the injunctions of nationalist boycotters.

Rather than heed the recommendations of women such as Esther Wissa, the nationalism of the interwar years promoted a domestic fattening that quickly escaped the control of the elites who so delicately wanted to balance the growth of a local market for domestically produced goods with the perpetuation of a social control they perceived as essential to their own interests. In the 1940s, when late colonialism and Egypt's monarchical regime came under increasing pressure, the fault lines along which it would crack had been in many ways established by the contradictions of new developments in interwar commerce, consumption, and urban space. As Jacques Berque recalls of the late 1930s: "On the city pavements, dress assumed a classificatory and indeed almost a philosophical importance. Visitors and citizens were alarmed at its heterogeneity. Witnesses have described the University as a fashion show, where the most diverse forms of dress were seen side by side. . . . Some men wore Western dress, the *badla*, topped with the tarboosh, as a sort of compromise between the national and the imported, a reconciliation of the *qadim* [old] and the *jadid* [new]. And beside them other men walked bare-headed, or wearing berets, or clad in turbans and robes to assert their loyalty to Islam. Needless to say, this variety also implied inequality. The brougham or the motor-car in which the bourgeois rode at ease cut its way through a poverty-stricken crowd. In the neighborhood of Darb al-Ahmar, it was not uncommon to find the bodies of beggars who had died of hunger during the night."[179] This climate of heterogeneity and inequality became increasingly untenable as Egypt responded to the Second World War.

5 POSTWAR COMMODITY PARABLES
AND THE CRACKING OF LATE COLONIALISM

THE INCREASING USE of heeled shoes and tight hosiery caused changes to Egyptian bodies that alarmed postwar health activists. One author, writing in the popular press in 1945, bemoaned the structural deformities in feet and legs as well as skin and joint inflammations that resulted from new forms of urban spatial mobility: "The shortening [of the nerves and muscles of the legs and feet] stems from the fact that we live in an age in which the streets are paved with smooth, even asphalt. We use cars and public transportation that allow us to do without walking, and thus our feet and legs do not enjoy the benefit of adequate movement in order to help our muscles grow strong."[1] Unlike older footwear practices in which flexible shoes could be easily and casually removed at frequent intervals, the prolonged wearing of sturdy shoes in new fashions further crippled Egyptian feet. "This confinement in the prisons of shoes [sujun al-ahdhiyya] is among the most important factors leading to the weakness in the growth of [leg and foot] muscles." Not only do they wear them too young, the author continued, but "most children wear ready-made shoes [al-ahdhiyya al-jahiza] that are fitted to conform to average feet." To repair the health of their feet, Egyptians should eschew poorly fitting footwear, especially ready-to-wear fashion shoes, and walk barefoot. "The truth about shoes," the author concluded, is that "they are among the biggest factors that deform feet."

In the postwar climate of mounting social and political tension, footwear became a crucial metaphor for the paradoxical nature of late-colonial consumption. The increasing mobility of Egyptians on paved roads and public transportation, resulting from decades-long development of the urban built environment and the expansion of the economy, had not in fact liberated and empowered Egyptians, some local residents argued. Instead, footwear caused a fundamental immobility of Egyptian feet, held captive in heavy, laced, heeled shoes made impersonally in "average" dimensions. In part, this represented anxiety about the possible upending of existing class relations by the social mobility offered by shoes. In debates over compulsory-education bills in the middle 1930s, several parliamentarians explicitly linked increased peasant consumption with disintegration of social control over the rural labor force. Deputy ʿAziz Abaza reported his shock that peasants in the village of Mit Ghamr go "out to their fields wearing coats, stockings and shoes."[2] Another deputy, ʿAwad Ahmad al-Gindi, put the problem even more bluntly several years later: "The day the fellah puts the tarboosh on his head, it becomes difficult for him to hold the hoe with his hand. . . . [He will wear] a suspender and shoes, which is useless; even extremely dangerous for social and economic life in the country."[3]

Thanks to interwar marketing campaigns and the expansion of local industry, the domestic shoe market had indeed drastically expanded in the late 1940s, so that by 1951, Egypt produced nearly enough footwear to shoe its urban population and about a quarter of its rural residents, although about 5 percent of the uppermost end of the market in luxury shoes was still furnished from abroad.[4] Expectations of consumption had shifted accordingly, so that shoes were included among the necessities for which the state fixed prices in the face of the rising cost of living in 1948.[5] Consumption of women's hosiery also skyrocketed in the immediate postwar years, as the spread of new artificial materials and industrial technologies made stockings affordable and accessible in urban markets.[6] Although, writing from Algeria, Fanon would soon condemn the asymmetries of colonial power that ensured that the "settler's feet . . . are protected by strong shoes although the streets of his town are clean and even, with no holes or stones,"[7] some Egyptians regarded the plethora of ready-made footwear, intimate "prisons" put on daily by local residents, as proliferating microphysical sites of colonial power or, more specifically, of the corrupt and fractious alliance among the monarchy, British officials, and the political parties that by the late 1940s was struggling to remain in power.

This chapter examines the multiple ways that a pair of shoes (*gawz gazma*) and nylon stockings came by the late 1940s to represent new kinds of conflict and new forms of community emerging from the rise of mass consumption in the preceding quarter century. The concurrent growth of artificial silks and social mobilization in Egypt between 1945 and 1952 were two processes that unseamed the national fabric marketers had attempted to produce with long-staple cotton in the 1930s. The chapter also offers a study of the storytelling that made popular sense of the tensions of late colonial cultures of consumption. Works of imagination supplied new parables about the role of consumerism in Egypt's transformation during more than six decades under various forms of British rule. Although street protests and party meetings became increasingly the sites of debates about the parameters of commodity politics in Egypt, the popular press and cinema were crucial media for rendering new narratives about Egypt's consumption. In a society marked by low formal literacy and a diglossic split between a high written language and a popular colloquial dialect, Egyptian commercial cinema functioned, Walter Armbrust argues, as "a powerful force for constructing nationalism and, by extension, modernity"—a sort of "screen capitalism" akin to the print capitalism behind the novels and newspapers identified by Benedict Anderson as drivers of nationalist imagination.[8] The old-regime commercial cinema of the 1940s and early 1950s built "an intricate architecture of references designed to evoke not an alien film tradition but Egypt's own tradition," one that characterized "a middle-class bourgeois nationalist identity" by linking "vernacular authenticity, high tradition, and modern technique."[9] Indeed, like the mass consumption it often portrayed, commercial postwar cinema suffused Egyptian popular culture. Between 1945 and 1952, domestic industry churned out over four hundred films.[10]

The theme of doubling would particularly capture postwar literary and filmic representations of footwear and national cloth. Parodying Egyptian consumers as both captive and captivated in their desire for mass-produced goods, popular films, short stories, and press satire increasingly used the image of pairing left and right shoes, the trope of mirrors, or the double casting of actors in two roles to fashion the single embodiment of "the binary logic of colonial power."[11] The story of captive consumers who, unaware, fueled their own moral corruption thus became a template for understanding the paradoxical role that Egyptians played in their own late-colonial oppression and the growing pressure the regime faced from it. The doubling terms through which footwear and other goods menaced Egyptian society in postwar texts helped transform a widespread belief in colonialism as an external force into a view that emphasized its deep imbrication in the Egyptian social and physical landscape. This postwar vision would stoke anticolonial sentiment by shifting it toward the fluidity of urban commercial space and the morseled styles associated with it, sentiment that would literally burst into flames in January 1952. Once imagined as riven between colonized and colonizer, Egyptian

society, popular view acknowledged by the late 1940s, was a complex entangle-
ment of mirrored subjectivities and hybridized practices constituted by both
ifrangi and *baladi* influences. Cutting through the layers of complexity to the
truth about footwear and other consumption and commercial practices thus
preoccupied postwar culture, sharpening the internal contradictions of Egyptian society along the way.

A POSTWAR POLITICS OF PROTEST

The Second World War was in many ways a watershed for Egypt. A base for
Allied troops stationed to protect the Suez Canal and ultimately mobilized to
fend off Rommel's invasion in 1942, Egypt appeared reoccupied in its everyday
spaces during the war years. By spring 1941 Cairo's population of roughly one
and a half million people expanded with the addition of 35,000 British and
Empire troops, many of whom found Egypt a haven of consumption and gaiety
from the grim wartime conditions in Europe.[12] For most Egyptians the immediate effects of this troop presence were a relentless acceleration of prices for
basic goods and a rise in unemployment due to the disruption of the import-
export trade by transportation closures and international rationing. Ultimately,
however, the war would fuel the growth of large-scale industry and the working
classes to run it.[13] Wartime import shortages encouraged the further development of local factories, such as in the textile, ceramics, rubber, paper, footwear,
and tanning sectors,[14] making calls to Egyptianize the economy appear increasingly feasible. In the political field, the Palace, the Wafd Party, and other leaders
were compromised during the war as a result of making expedient alliances
that betrayed their political ideals or of public exposure for venality while in
office.[15] In part to compensate for its installation in power behind British tanks
in 1942, the Wafd enacted a series of nationalist measures, including abolishing
fees for primary education, establishing a national auditing office to supervise
public funds, "converting the Old Public Debt into a National Debt," establishing the independence of the judiciary, and mandating Arabic as the official
language in all commercial transactions.[16]

Despite these efforts to shore up nationalism against the country's escalated
occupation by foreign troops, the aftermath of the war fell heavily on Egypt.
Jacques Berque calls the years between 1945 and 1950 "a dark period, during
which Egypt experienced disappointments as great as her hopes, the anger
of the under-privileged flared up in violence, and the contrast between the
matureness of men's demands and the indefinite postponement of solutions

reached its highest pitch."[17] Egyptians faced food shortages, caused by stagnant grain harvests and the return to widespread cotton cultivation, which had been limited during the war.[18] The immediate postwar years witnessed important changes in global politics and colonialism that would shape Egyptian perceptions of their situation. By 1948 a fully-fledged Cold War had developed out of the disintegration of wartime alliances between the United States and the Soviet Union.[19] The polarization of international politics between two superpowers "who both were eager to disassociate themselves from European colonialism, opened up new possibilities for aid and support" to anticolonial movements that were able to play into Cold War rivalry.[20] After the Allied landing in North Africa in 1942, Algerians appealed to the United States for aid in their decolonization bid, and at the Allies' European victory in May 1945 open insurrection erupted in large parts of the country, although French repression staved off the formal war for independence until 1954.[21] Two of the British colonial situations most closely watched by Egyptians also shifted significantly by 1947–1948. In India, partition marked the British exit from colonial rule, which was further clouded by the assassination of Gandhi. The British departed the Palestine Mandate in the context of the United Nations' call for partition, thereby transforming civilian fighting into an Arab-Israeli war that would leave Israel an internationally recognized state, the Palestinians as refugees, and the Egyptian old regime, although an occupier of Gaza, held largely responsible for the humiliating defeat. The scandal over faulty arms that emerged in the aftermath of the Palestine war would ultimately unseat the monarchy itself four years later when the Free Officers, embittered by what they saw as their betrayal on the battlefield, would stage a full-scale coup.

Demonstrations and bombings in the winter of 1947–1948 and in the summer and fall of 1948 brought home the changing context of global colonialism. The UN decision on the partition of Palestine provoked large demonstrations in December 1947 in Egypt's main cities, including attacks on commercial properties owned by Jews and also Copts, Greeks, and other Europeans.[22] Lethal explosions occurred in Cairo's Jewish quarters; prominent department stores, including Cicurel, ʿAdès, Benzion, and Gattegno; and the premises of a prominent advertising firm, the Société Orientale de Publicité. The state also placed several Jewish-owned stores under temporary sequestration that year, including Chemla, ʿAdès, and Gattegno, in response to the Arab-Israeli war in Palestine.[23] Foreign officials worried about the "extremist elements such as the 'Ikhwan el Muslimeen' [who] . . . for some time past [had] been deliberately working up the feelings of the populace against Jews in a way which was obviously bound to end in mob violence."[24] Even Egyptian officials privately attributed the bombing of Cicurel to "a bomb or a mine deliberately placed in the street by local hands,"[25] despite the official story that blamed a dropped land mine. Several French subjects (who were not Jewish) were "savagely attacked after the Cicurel bomb incident and one of them, the French trainer of the Egyptian Olympic team," died.[26] Smaller stores in Cairo's commercial downtown also were attacked, including the English bookstore W. H. Smith, which had its door and window panes smashed by police and a staff member assaulted and robbed, and "the shop of a Cypriot named Eliades," which was broken into by a crowd that "beat him up severely."[27] In addition, "a British subject was accosted by four men on his way to . . . the Turf Club and instructed to wear a tarboosh."[28]

The French Embassy reported that fifty or sixty North African Jews holding French nationality had been arrested and beaten since June.[29] Sami Schperberg, a locally engaged Jewish clerk in the British Information Services Middle East Films division, suffered violence on his way to work in July 1948. While "waiting for the office bus in Ataba Square at about half past seven [in the] morning," Schperberg "was set upon by a large number of youths, who beat him over the head with chairs borrowed from a nearby coffee shop, and robbed him of his wallet, wrist-watch and a number of other personal possessions."[30] The Cairo Association of Merchants and Importers met in July 1948 because of widespread alarm caused by the events of that year. The director of Roberts Hughes Department Store reported to the British Embassy, "There was no feeling of public security. The police were inclined to be spectators at attacks made by hooligans on individuals. The Arabic press was inflammatory, and, while organized attacks were mainly against Jews, there was no saying that they would not be turned in future against all foreigners indiscriminately."[31] The events of summer 1948 induced, he felt, "a paralysis of the commercial life of the country. Merchants are now hesitating to place orders for imports, and the prospects are that there will be various commodities in short supply in future which will lead to a rise in prices."[32] Such occurrences began to shape a new definition of what constituted *foreign* in Egyptian commerce.

In this charged political climate, a new official rhetoric of Egyptian nationalism congealed. Moving away from a more territorial nationalism often referred to as *wataniyya* to a more overtly ethnically Arab one, often intertwined with a religious component and known as *qawmiyya*, the ideological change corresponded to a variety of socioeconomic and political transformations.[33] The state slowly dismantled the system of extraterritorial legal and economic privileges that benefited foreign residents in Egypt. The 1937 Montreux Convention curtailed the Capitulations in phases until the abolition of the Mixed Courts in 1949. The elimination of these foreign privileges "paved the way for the government to exert more control over the economic activities of local foreigners and to move towards a more ambitious programme of Egyptianisation."[34] Laws in 1942 and 1946 mandated the use of Arabic in commercial bookkeeping and government correspondence, as well as in shop signage, all of which resulted in the employment of more Arabic-speaking Egyptians in local commerce.[35]

After many years of parliamentary debate and partial and piecemeal legislative efforts, the Egyptian government passed Law 138 of 1947. Known as the Company Law, it mandated a high proportion of Egyptian capital and labor in joint-stock companies and instituted a new supervisory body, the Department of Corporations (*Maslahat al-Sharikat*; MS) in the Ministry of Commerce and Industry, to oversee implementation and compliance over the next decade through a complex series of inspection procedures.[36] Between 1947 and 1959 MS inspectors scrutinized the business practices of stores and companies such as Cicurel, Chemla, Sednaoui, the Egyptian Products Sales Company, Shurbaji, and Bata. Officials repeatedly interviewed employees, copying or at times even requisitioning their identity cards, asking for paperwork on their parentage, location of birth, religious affiliation, education, and so forth, to determine nationality status and making surprise inspections to store floors to verify whether particular employees were required to write in their jobs, a task the state used to distinguish higher-paid employees from workers. Many companies tried to claim that Muslim Egyptians retained in menial jobs such as office servants (*farrashin*) were higher-paid employees (such as assistant salesmen or clerks) to meet their quotas. MS inspections placed extra work on company clerks required to document the details of monthly salaries; in the case of department stores this included not only base salaries but also commissions earned from sales and other bonuses.[37] The law provoked the most fear in lower-level employees who were locally resident foreigners or without documentation, since they were most vulnerable to firing.[38] The new regulations substantially reduced locally resident foreigners in Egyptian commerce and other sectors, especially in middle-level positions such as those occupied by salesclerks. Sednaoui lost many foreign employees between 1947 and 1951 (a decrease from 34 to 21 percent of total employees); at Chemla the difference was even more dramatic, as the percentage of Egyptian employees increased from 21 to 82 percent between 1947 and 1950.[39]

Although the 1947 Company Law itself did not define *Egyptian*, the legal definition that emerged from the work of state inspectors was that of "Egyptian nationals," meaning, according to one MS official, "those who had been born in Egypt, and whose name left no doubt that they were Egyptian, and those who had an official Egyptian nationality certificate issued prior to 4 November.... Egyptian passports or military service certificates were not regarded as valid proof of naturalisation."[40] Egyptian nationality until 1950 was granted on the basis of a 1929 law that facilitated naturalization of immigrants from the former Ottoman territories or Arab or Muslim countries, although the acquisition by other groups was more complex. "Foreigners born in Egypt qualified for Egyptian nationality within a year of reaching their majority and long-term residents could apply after 10 years of proven continuous residence in Egypt.... These people were known as Mutamassiruna."[41] Although the 1929 law clarified Egyptian nationality requirements, most locally resident foreigners did not see the advantages of Egyptian citizenship until after the phasing out of Capitulation privileges between 1937 and 1949; after that time, Egyptian nationality was difficult for many non-Muslims to attain.[42] These legal initiatives helped reduce the privileges of foreign citizens in Egypt's economy and politics and ultimately the communities of permanently resident foreigners themselves.[43] The state interned many Italians as enemies during the war, and most left Egypt by the early 1940s. Although some Greeks remained after the 1950s, many relocated to mainland Greece during the Greek Civil War of 1946–1949.[44]

The Wafd's signing of the 1936 Anglo-Egyptian Treaty, which allowed continued British military presence in the country and especially in the Suez Canal Zone, seemed to signal the failure of liberal constitutionalism and called the Wafd's nationalist credentials into question among many of its supporters. This opened up political space for the operation and growth of several more-radical groups, whose membership swelled with youth disaffected by Wafdist compromise.[45] Student political activism ran especially high in 1945–1946, as organized university students built linkages with political organizations.[46] Vying for adherents were three main oppositional social movements at the heart of the unrest of the postwar years: the communists, the Muslim Brothers, and Young Egypt. Although very different in political goals and orientations, all three engaged in tactics that directly addressed Egyptian consumption and other economic practices. Each group became increasingly vocal in local politics by demanding radical restructurings of Egypt's subjection to "foreign domination" of the economy and tried to mobilize supporters by claiming to know "the truth" about Egyptian relations of commerce and consumption.[47] The communists allied with trade unionists during large strikes in 1946–1948 at major textile centers, including the Bank Misr textile factory at al-Mahalla al-Kubra, at the Bata shoe factory in Alexandria, and among the workers in Cairo's public transportation (trams, buses, and metro), a strike wave that by 1948 had expanded to include government employees, nurses, public utilities workers, and the police.[48] The textile workers struggled with the "volatility of the market for all but the most common textiles (known as 'popular cloth') and the introduction of more labor-efficient machinery into the industry."[49] The strikes were symptomatic of the deep crisis of the old-regime government that could not improve popular standards of living or achieve complete independence from the British.[50]

The Muslim Brothers (*al-Ikhwan al-muslimun*), a religious association founded in 1928, addressed political and social problems in Egypt in moral terms, using the language of consumer austerity, cultural authenticity, and anti-imperialism. In the area of social and educational reform, Hasan al-Banna, the group's founder, called for "a campaign against ostentation in dress and loose behavior; . . . consideration of ways to arrive gradually at a uniform mode of dress for the nation; an end to the foreign spirit in our homes with regard to language, manners, dress, governesses, nurses, etc.; all these to be Egyptianized, especially in upper-class homes."[51] The group mingled calls for Egyptianization of the economy away from "the hands of foreigners" with campaigns to increase "respect for public morality . . . and the imposition of severe penalties for moral offenses," of which the foremost concerned "the problem of women" and gambling, drinking, dancing, singing, and recreation associated with urban culture.[52] Al-Banna recommended to the society's members in 1939 that when accused of being revolutionaries they should respond, "We are agents of the truth."[53] Sayyid Qutb, whose condemnation of silk and excessive consumption helped direct textile marketing, particularly denounced the employment of women in commerce, diplomatic administration, and information services as "a form of slavery and servitude" and the "exploitation of the sex instinct of customers."[54] The Muslim Brothers mobilized many Egyptians in the postwar period, with active membership estimated between one hundred thousand and five hundred thousand in 1944.[55] The group founded several local business enterprises designed to aid the growth of the national economy and provide revenue so that Egyptians would not have to work in non-Muslim enterprises. These ventures included a short-lived and small textile mill, the Muslim Brothers' Company for Spinning and Weaving, established in the Shubra al-Khayma neighborhood of Cairo in 1947; a commercial company founded in 1952 at al-Mahalla al-Kubra; and other small companies in the fields of advertising, transport, and construction. The commercial company "produced textiles, household goods, clothing—ready-made men's clothing and accessories, including ties and scarves—notions, office and school supplies, and electrical equipment."[56] Although the companies were not likely very profitable because of their small scale and the severity of state repression after 1948, these commercial and industrial activities demonstrate the close binding of politics and economy in the Muslim Brothers' postwar ideology.

The other primary movement to campaign for a purification of Egyptian social and political practices in the 1930s and 1940s was Young Egypt (*Misr al-fatat*). Founded by Ahmad Husayn and Fathi Radwan in 1933 out of their success with organizing the Piastre Plan, the group became the Islamic Nationalist Party in 1940 in response to the growing popularity of the Muslim Brothers. It finally renamed itself the Socialist Party of Egypt in 1949 after struggling to regain a wide following after its wartime suppression. A youth movement with a patriotic orientation and a paramilitary organization, Young Egypt "ideologically . . . was a fervently Egyptian nationalist movement preaching the necessity of uncompromising nationalist struggle against the British occupation of Egypt. Young Egypt defined the anticolonial struggle in comprehensive terms, not just the termination of the political and military presence of a foreign occupier on Egyptian soil but also as the need totally to purge the alien economic and cultural influences that had taken root in Egypt under the umbrella of foreign occupation."[57] Radwan penned biographies of Gandhi in 1932 and of an Irish nationalist in 1937, although the group became increasingly sympathetic to European fascism by the late 1930s.[58] Radwan himself would withdraw from active participation in the group in 1939, finally officially resigning in 1942.[59] Young Egypt mobilized primarily youth in Cairo and Alexandria. Its core membership fluctuated in the 1930s from several hundred to a thousand people, although its events and publications reportedly drew much larger crowds; by 1951 it claimed to have sixty-five branches in Egypt.[60]

In the 1940s Young Egypt's attacks on centers of foreign influence came to define national identity by the ethnic status of individuals rather than the targets of their actions as the boycott rhetoric of the 1930s seemed to imply. "In competition with the surging Muslim Brothers, from late 1938 onward, Young Egypt's rhetoric had taken a more Islamic coloration, its demands for greater social justice in Egypt now being articulated as the realization of authentic Islamic values. . . . [Its] new party program [of 1940] simultaneously called for the enforcement of Islamic mores in Egypt and for a closer Egyptian orientation with the neighboring Arab and Muslim countries."[61] In practice, this meant militant surveillance of urban commerce and public space for traces of "Western and 'unIslamic' social practices."[62] Ahmad Husayn called on Young Egypt's members to "wage war against wine, and against gambling, and against prostitution, and against all forms of sin," launching a series of directed attacks against bars and taverns.[63] It drew on many of the organizing tactics used in association with the nationalist movement in the 1930s. "Young Egypt's anti-Jewish activism went beyond rhetoric in mid-1939. The movement attempted to organize a boycott of Egyptian Jewish merchants, establishing a 'Committee for the Boycott of Jewish Commerce,' sending activists to preach in mosques in support of the campaign, publishing lists of Jewish Cairo merchants to be boycotted, and distributing anti-Jewish literature in provincial cities."[64]

The party campaigned for less-formal actions by the state and ordinary citizens to transform the everyday social and commercial practices of ordinary Egyptians: Arabic was to become the official commercial language; Friday rather than Sunday to become the day of weekly commercial closure; government purchasing "always to give preference to local products, whatever their price"; and government employees and pupils of government schools to wear only "clothing made in Egypt." Party members were "constantly enjoined to 'speak only in Arabic,' to 'eat only Egyptian foods,' to 'wear only Egyptian clothing,' to 'buy only Egyptian goods,' and generally to 'scorn anything foreign, each of you, and cling steadfastly to your nationalism, making it an obsession.'"[65] During the group's revival as the Socialist Party from 1949 to 1952, Husayn advocated an instrumentalist, nondialectical, and non-Marxist form of socialism "[that] consistently presented itself as being based on the principles of revealed religion."[66] Never leftist in orientation, the group emphasized by the 1950s a pan-national anti-imperialism that increasingly drew on dichotomized language—"the Manichean image of 'them' (the Western imperialists) versus 'us' (all other states and peoples of the world)."[67] Thus during the postwar years, a growing gap between the rich and the poor coupled with the increasingly visible corruption and decadence among the upper classes to swell wide-scale opposition movements that spanned the political spectrum and mobilized university students, workers, and the lower-middle classes in particular.

The changing tenor of nationalism also began to inflect postwar commerce. By 1948 a store's being Egyptian had become more to do with the nationality and religion of its employees and owners than with the assortment of goods it purveyed. Advertisements for the Egyptian Home Company (*Sharikat al-Bayt al-Misri*) illustrate some of the ways that commercial practices were being reoriented through an image of the nation as public home. A medium-sized composite goods store, or a small department store, the al-Bayt al-Misri company had been operating since at least the mid-1940s under the Cairo-based administration of Muhammad ʿAbd al-Salam al-Banna.[68] Al-Bayt al-Misri's mixture of products in 1948 included merchandise from a variety of origins: English and other imported woolens and even imported cotton fabrics, in addition to unspecified textiles, shoes, men's shirts, ready-to-wear clothes, pajamas, towels, and stockings.[69] Nevertheless, the store advertised that same year that its "primary goal is to lift up the head of every Egyptian in pride of his country and its establishments," and that "hopes have been realized—and it is an Egyptian stock company preparing for you all of your requirements and the requirements of your households at reasonable prices."[70] In keeping with the new postwar legal and political environment, the national identity of the store, then, accrued from its Egyptian ownership—what the store's 1948 advertisements labeled its being "Egyptian by its owners and employees."[71] In practice, this meant both the company's registration in Egypt and its operation by a Muslim Egyptian, rather than the product nationality of its inventory. Press advertising in 1948 reinforced this assertion of the Egyptian identity of the store by an oblique geographic reference to its occupation of the former site of foreign commerce in Egypt—its location in the Tiring Building in ʿAtaba Square. Such occupations of foreign sites by native Egyptians began to play an integral symbolic and fiscal role in the larger discourse of nationalism in this period. Other merchant houses prominently advertised their Muslim owners. Soon after the al-Tarabishi store opened in late 1947 on Fuʾad Street in downtown Cairo, for example, the store claimed to be "conquering" the primary merchant street in Cairo and drew attention to its Egyptian and Muslim ownership in its actual advertising text and by publicizing photographs of its employees and administration in prayer and breaking the fast together during Ramadan.[72]

THE ADVENT OF ARTIFICIAL SILKS

The textile sector also witnessed the changing tenor of commodity politics as the definition of *Egyptian* began to alter in the postwar period. Despite improvements in local textile technologies in the 1940s, manufacturers such as Shurbaji began to protest that yarns made from Egyptian cotton were too expensive and often too physically defective for the production of hosiery for the rapidly expanding middle-class and lower-class markets.[73] By the end of the 1940s, Shurbaji had turned to producing nylon hosiery and claimed to be the first local factory to do so in Egypt. Nylon utterly transformed the postwar hosiery market, altering both the products available to consumers and the advertising that promoted them. The Shurbaji hosiery factory in Imbaba alone produced nearly eight hundred pairs of nylon hosiery (*jawarib*) a day in 1950.[74] By 1954 the French commercial counselor in Egypt noted that "it appears that in the hosiery industry, nylon has practically replaced all other fibers."[75] Despite, or perhaps because of, its break with the nationalist model of manufacturing locally grown cotton into hosiery, the Shurbaji Company used its press promotions to cast its new endeavor in nationalist terms by arguing that the production of nylon had previously been "monopolized" by the United States.[76] Thus nylon production began to preview a new Cold War inflection of anticolonialism that would become increasingly significant in the 1950s as American influence came to replace British and French colonial power in the Middle East. Artificial silk fibers, including nylon, possessed characteristics similar to long-staple cotton as well as natural silk and thus proved to be an easy substitute for both in many fabrics. Nylon stockings, more than any other postwar item of clothing, came to signify a complex new relationship of technological ingenuity, consumer subjectivity, and state polity. The "material fragility and sexual vulnerability" that stockings represented may have helped neutralize "the implied threat of technology" that marked Western chemical companies such as Du Pont in the recent war.[77] In semicolonial Egypt the fragility and sexuality associated with nylon stockings also came to symbolize the political weakness and moral decadence of the old regime and the *ifrangi* social and consumption practices of the upper classes.

The Egyptian press had initially welcomed artificial silk thread as a modern product made synthetically and scientifically in the laboratory. The first reports on the technologies of artificial silk referred to its transferability as a technology and documented the chemical processes involved in its production, often comparing the results from the use of different primary materials, such as cotton waste, wood fiber, etc.[78] One article told the story of the process, from wood chip to artificial silk in "four glass jars" in the laboratory.[79] A 1920 article in *al-Nashra al-iqtisadiyya al-misriyya* (the *Egyptian Economic Report*) even noted that the "the Sharduni method," developed in France, used cotton waste dissolved in natron, both products found in Egypt.[80] Since artificial silk represented a textile technology that could make use of Egyptian raw materials, and even be an expanded use for the local cotton crop so promoted by economic nationalists, new interest in the fabrics seemed to challenge the most visible ties of semicolonial dependence.

Consumer interest in the new threads and the cloth they could weave led to substantial imports of rayon fabrics after the early 1930s.[81] British trade officials noted in 1931 that "fine white shirtings are being to some extent replaced by new articles altogether, such as . . . artificial silks."[82] Local plants began weaving rayon textiles from imported thread in the mid-1930s, and by 1937 approximately two thousand looms were in operation.[83] Bank Misr enterprises capitalized on this new consumer interest. The Misr Silk Weaving Company produced several fabrics of imported threads of artificial silk, especially rayon, by 1936, and the cloths retailed at Bank Misr's Egyptian Products Sales Company and local textile chains such as ʿAdès.[84] An Egyptian consumer, in an interview with Harb, praised the high quality of the fabric's weaving, dyeing, and strength, despite its plain appearance.[85] Shortages of rayon yarn required textile mills to resort to weaving cotton during the Second World War, but large-scale production of rayon recommenced afterward.[86] Bank Misr founded a rayon plant in 1946 at Kafr al-Dawwar near its Fine Spinning and Weaving Company, and it became the third-most-capitalized textile firm within a decade.[87] Production at the plant began in 1948, and the "company made rapid progress thereafter, manufacturing rayon and nylon filaments, viscose staple fiber, nylon staple fiber, and transparent fiber."[88] Egyptian-made rayon goods were shipped to Sudan in 1948, 1949, and 1950.[89] In 1954 the company branded its artificial silk thread Misrilon (*misri* is Arabic for "Egyptian"), suggesting its hope to capitalize on the nationalist markets built up around Egyptian cotton in the preceding two decades—or at least pointing to its fear of losing control of them.[90]

Indeed, artificial silk possessed many of the qualities of long-staple cotton fibers that local cotton elites had been promoting in Egypt in the 1930s and 1940s. Artificial fibers could be used to create silky, relatively durable fabrics, and thus a direct competition gradually emerged between artificial silks and some cloth woven from long-staple cotton.[91] A special 1950 issue of the local newspaper *al-Misri* devoted to cotton included a long article detailing the specific technologies used in manufacturing artificial silk. The article explicitly compared the price, quality, durability, and strength of artificial silk fibers with Egyptian long-staple cotton and ominously reported the permanent conversion of many Lancashire factories from weaving only long-staple Egyptian cotton to using artificial silk.[92] Initially a promise to the local economy, artificial silk threads thus emerged as a threat to Egyptian cotton growers by the late 1940s.

SELLING STOCKINGS, SEXUALIZING NYLON

As local production of nylon threads and textiles increased, so did their distribution. Nylon radically altered the women's hosiery market in Egypt after the late 1940s and the communities of consumers associated with it. About half the price of pure natural silk hosiery, artificial silk hosiery carried many of the luxury associations of silk stockings and was more affordable to a larger market of Egyptian women.[93] Although nylon stockings were first sold in the United States in 1940, wartime constraints held up distribution until 1945–1946, when American and European women thronged to stores to purchase them.[94] It took several more years for nylon hose to reach Egyptian consumers in large quantities, and the scarcity of nylon stockings in postwar markets helped transform them "into symbols of luxury."[95] In 1952 imports of stockings made from pure artificial silk and artificial silk blends reached 144,560 dozen pairs. Large quantities were also produced by domestic industry. Owing to a lack of market surveys and the general grouping of nylon hosiery with other artificial silk fabrics in statistical reports, it is difficult to know the size of the market expansion.[96] Nylon stockings came within reach of the budgets of lower-middle-class and middle-class women, who wore nylon hose to work and social events more often than silk stockings, even if they still did not casually purchase nylons. The vast majority of rural women were not consumers of nylon stockings.[97] The postwar mass marketing of women's nylon hosiery differed in significant ways from the promotion of men's socks in the 1930s as a vehicle for knitting various male identities into a national community.

Despite the profusion of stockings in the market and the proliferation of the kinds of consumers able to afford them, women's nylon stockings in the 1940s and 1950s were advertised through unitary, sexualized images of women.

When Chemla and other local department stores listed the variety of brands of nylon stockings available and their prices, the different stockings were not illustrated in the ad copy or linked to particular groups of consumers.[98] Shurbaji's marketing of its luxurious Shehrezade stockings to women in the 1940s and 1950s focused primarily on women's legs. Graphically, these advertisements often represented a single woman, adorned in a very short or raised skirt, seated with pointed toes or reclining, or they showed disembodied legs in much the same poses (see Figure 16).[99] Other manufacturers promoted their stockings in similar ways. The 'Id company advertised its selection of nylon stockings ("the strongest in our market") with a photograph of two sets of women's legs, positioned next to each other and nearly identically attired in short skirts, stockings, and high-heeled pumps; the picture was cropped from the women's skirt hems (at the knee) to their shoes.[100] Such publicity objectified women's bodies as sources of sexual pleasure, emphasizing a generalized femininity uncoupled from the different occupational, generational, regional, or class identities of Egyptian women consumers. It also contrasted sharply with the plurality of men's identities (and the graphic focus on their faces and personalities) marshaled in male sock advertisements a decade earlier.

In satirical commentary in the illustrated press, nylon came to symbolize the fracturing and declension of the nation's unity by the late 1940s, thus inverting the linkage in early 1930s nationalist sock advertising between cotton fabric and national cohesion.[101] Popular criticism of nylon consumption also restricted women to a one-dimensional, sexualized role, almost casting them as reflective mirrors for the collective tribulations of postwar Egypt. In his 1948 short story "Imra't nylun [The Nylon Woman]," 'Ashur 'Ulaysh decried the inequalities of postwar Egyptian society through a contest over an objectified woman. He described the plight of a young lawyer, Ahmad, unemployed because he lacks the social contacts and registration fees needed to apprentice and advance in the profession.[102] Lamenting that the fruit of his educational struggle resulted only in "hunger, vagrancy, and privation," Ahmad watches a chic, beautiful woman say goodbye to her lover departing on the night train. She gazes at herself in a mirror on the wall, "looking attentively at herself in infatuation. . . . She expends every effort to display her beauty." "Like a dog appearing for a bit of meat," he follows her to her sleek car (*sayyara fariha*), "regarding her closely, precisely examining her features, almost devouring her [*yalatihamuha*]. . . . She began to adjust her dress part by part from top to bottom. . . . She wore thin, transparent clothes [*thiyab hafafa shafafa*] that revealed her charms and

Figure 16. Shurbaji's holiday advertising for
women's nylon stockings featured a single,
disembodied pair of long legs. *Al-Musawwar*,
no. 1686 (1 February 1957), 37.

beauty like a full moon." Finally acknowledging him, she waved and laughed at him from her departing car. Suddenly Ahmad "understood everything," and "he began to boil like a cauldron" as he realized, "She wasn't for us. . . . She's for him who can pay the price! Everything for him who owns everything and nothing for him who owns nothing. She was 'nylon,' she herself."[103] The story's illustration depicted Ahmad in a poorly fitting overcoat and trousers and the nylon woman in a short, tight skirt with sheer stockings and very high heels. Mistress of the corrupted upper classes that dominated society, politics, and the economy in this period, the nylon woman signaled the wide corrosive effects of current social inequalities and a system in which privilege or wealth rather than merit or hard work determined social position. The images of reflection (mirror, moon, shiny car, transparent clothing) linking the woman-mistress to nylon underline the idea of nylon as a prism for broader social and political struggles.

Another 1948 satire in *Akhir saʿa* magazine depicted a *baladi* woman named Zulaykha asking for nylon flip-flops (*qabaqib nylun*) at an elegant urban shoe store (see Figure 17).[104] She gazes, her mouth slightly agape and her expression full of wonder, at the rows of fashionable, high-heeled women's pumps and sandals displayed in the glass shop window. Although some expensive models of *qabaqib* (sing. *qubqab*) featured ornamental mother-of-pearl or silver inlay, roughly hewn wooden clogs had long served as utilitarian work shoes for many peasants and manual laborers.[105] The plastic sandal that replaced the common *qubqab* (later called a *shibshib*) gradually spread in local markets after the late 1930s because of, as one local trade official noted, the rubber-soled shoe's "excellent suitability to the climate and its accessibility to the most modest budgets."[106]

In addition to the absurd contrast of shoe styles, the cartoon's humor lies in the naming of the woman customer. Zulaykha, an important character from Qurʾanic sacred history (Joseph's mistress and the wife of his Egyptian master), usually symbolizes female desire and upper-class decadence. By the 1940s, Barbara Stowasser asserts, exegeses of "Joseph and the women" began to cast the story as "a parable with communal rather than just gender-related meaning. For Qutb, the main theme of the story is the struggle between religious righteousness and a corrupt society . . . [whose] representatives were the high-born, spoiled and headstrong Aziz's wife [Zulaykha] and . . . society's aristocracy who spent their days in idleness and materialistic pleasures."[107] As a lover of Joseph—who was Jewish—Zulaykha may also have referred to the increasing

Figure 17. Zulaykha in front of an *ifrangi* shoe store. "I wonder if they sell nylon pattens [*qabaqib nylun*] here?" *Akhir sa'a*, no. 697 (3 March 1948).

politicization of industry during the 1948 conflict in Palestine and the implementation of the 1947 Company Law, both of which, as already described, put increasing pressure on Egyptian Jews in commerce and in other sectors of society, displacing some employees from jobs after 1947 even though large-scale migrations of Jews would wait for another decade. That Zulaykha, associated with the cosmopolitan upper class by name but *baladi* by dress, searched for common, cheap footwear in the vitrine of a fancy shoe store suggests an inversion of social hierarchy anticipated by new nationalist policies. This Zulaykha, like the "Nylon Woman," captured a wider condemnation of monarchical Egypt in which critiques about politics, consumption, and nationalist imaginary intimately intertwined through the language of textiles.

The sale of nylon stockings coincided with a global postwar climate of the 1950s that emphasized a new look and a new femininity for women. The marketing of nylon in Western Europe and North America at the time also tended to objectify women and represent them in a singular mode.[108] Egyptian satirists drew on the image of nylon to critique the West but left the sexualization of women intact in the process. Egypt differed from other nylon markets because the congruence of the cotton and artificial silk markets—their direct competition for the same market niche for silky fabrics—invested nylon with powerful social conflict. The use of nylon as an epithet linked nylon-stocking marketing, to a single, idealized woman consumer, with the older discourse of silkiness as luxury and decadence in other satires of the period. Cartoons and media satire especially used such "habitual images" in their "symbolic repertoire," juxtaposing the old and the new to increase the power of their critique.[109] According to Palmira Brummett, the "effect of a cartoon is dependent both upon its invoking a perceived 'reality' and upon its subsequently breaking the boundaries of that perception."[110] Nylon provided the perfect fodder for such satirical commentary in postwar Egypt.

STORES OF DESIRE AND HUNGER:
SATIRE AND THE AMBIGUITIES OF MASS CONSUMPTION

As the Zulaykha cartoon manifests, political and social satire in the late 1940s hooked textile parables to a depiction of commercial stores as sites that concentrated the anxieties and tensions of mass consumption and the nation's unresolved semicolonial political status. Readers of the popular magazine *Ruz al-yusuf* in 1948 encountered a flurry of satire about the moral dangers of women in commercial space. In January the magazine published a cartoon in which a woman disrobes in a store to get into a bathtub, explaining, "I don't like to buy anything until I try it out," to an uncomfortable salesman.[111] The same month the magazine featured a short story, "Imra' fi shari'a fu'ad [A Woman on Fu'ad Street]," that imagined the moral and social confusion wrought by women's presence in Cairo's commercial downtown. The story traced the discovery of the identity of a woman on Cairo's most chic commercial street. Assuming that she is a naive local shopper—a middle-class girl wearing "simple" clothes and a "stranger in this Western neighborhood"—the narrator watches her startle at the sound of car horns and "glance with amazement" at the glass doors of the street's beautiful stores. He imagines that she is named Sa'diyya, an upwardly mobile girl from a popular quarter of the old city (the "peaceful" Gamaliyya district in Cairo), whose father is a government employee in the tax department and whose mother is preoccupied with arranging her daughter's marriage. The story ends with Sa'diyya entering a prestigious-looking building, which the narrator thinks she believes to be "one of the commercial stores" but is really a nightclub. The narrator's "astonishment is . . . intense" when he finally learns the "true story" from the Nubian porter at the club's door. Improbably, he has guessed her name correctly: "He marveled at his genius that her name was Sa'diyya . . . just as he had imagined." But he is utterly mistaken about her relationship to the downtown commercial district. "Saʿdiyya" is not a disoriented shopper but a dancer in the club's employ, the porter reveals. The story's illustration depicts her wearing a short tight skirt, sheer stockings, high heels, and black gloves.[112] The promiscuous mingling of department stores and nightclubs on Fuʾad Street thus imperils the authentic and simple Egyptian woman, forced to market herself in a commercial geography that welcomes her only as a commodity. A June cartoon (see Figure 18) posed exactly the same problem. Picturing a portly, well-dressed man who eyes a blond, curvaceous runway model inside a store while he attempts to bargain with a worried man in a suit (a store manager or salesman), the cartoon was captioned, "At the fashion show! The *nouveau riche* man asks: And without the dress, what does

في معرض الأزياء ! !
ترى الحرب — ومن غير فستان تساوى كام ! ! !

Figure 18. "At the fashion show! The *nouveau riche* man asks: 'And without the dress, what does she cost?'" *Ruz al-yusuf*, no. 1042 (2 June 1948), 18.

she cost?"[113] Such critiques thus point to anxiety about the postwar polarization of classes intensifying sexual danger in *ifrangi* stores retailing clothes and footwear. Satirical efforts to get to the truth behind the imagined exteriors of commercial space mirrored the tone of 1948's popular street protests.

Stories about shoe stores often criticized the public display of desire enabled by wartime profiteering. "Al-Muntaqima, qissa misriyya [The Avenger, an Egyptian Story]" appeared as a short story in *al-Musawwar* also in 1948.[114] In the story the protagonist, a blond-haired Egyptian woman named Nusa, stopped to "fix her hair in the window of a shoe shop" in downtown Cairo and, instead of seeing her own reflection, spied through the glass the man with whom she had fallen in love, a pharmacist named ʿAlfi. ʿAlfi had told Nusa he would be visiting his family in the country for a week, but he was laughing in a familiar and intimate way with a young woman trying on a pair of high-heeled shoes in the shop; the high heels suggest the relationship between them is sexual. Nusa's expectation of seeing herself mirrored in the shop window but instead finding an amorous rival transforms her love into a desire for vengeance. Although the plot later resolved when Nusa discovered that the other woman was actually ʿAlfi's mother ("she married very young and was only thirteen when [he] was born"), the story suggests the disruptive social potential of consumer desire, the intimacies created by the circulation of commodities, and the danger of commercial shops where men and women mixed freely. Frustrated desire found expression, this story suggested, in vengeful retaliation toward other consumers. Urban commercial space did not mirror individual subjectivity as expected but rather fractured or twisted it in contradictory ways.

Footwear, both shoes and hosiery, particularly symbolized the proliferation of commodities associated with mass consumption in public perception (and satire) in part because of its nature as a commodity. Unlike other goods such as cloth or soap participating in the war-related productive boom, footwear and shoe stores were associated with vast but differentiated quantities of commercial goods. The trope of proliferation centered on the array of styles and fashions of shoes available in stores; the relatively small size of shoes as commodities, which made commercial displays very dense; and the sense of repetition caused by the display and stocking of so many different sizes of the same model of shoe. Conventional depiction focused on the masses of boxes and styles displayed in shoe stores and parodied these huge inventories for their effects on shoe-store customers and employees. In a cartoon from the

Figure 19. Customer and salesclerk at the shoe store. The woman asks, "Can I see the 10,000 shoes that you announced the arrival of?" Shoe stores commonly symbolized the excessive profusion of mass consumer goods. *Al-Musawwar*, no. 1263 (24 December 1948), 55.

December 24, 1948, issue of *al-Musawwar*, for example, a woman customer asks a salesman in a shoe store, "Can I see the 10,000 shoes that you announced the arrival of?" (see Figure 19).[115] Some popular satires explicitly foregrounded the vulnerability and even the loss of individual identity caused by the profusion of commodities in mass consumption. The 1953 *Le progrès égyptien—Almanach* ran a cartoon featuring an angry woman customer standing in her stocking feet on a shoe-store floor littered with shoes. A salesman crawling around on the floor asks her, "Are you certain that you are able to recognize your own shoes, Madame?" (see Figure 20).[116] These cartoons suggest an uneasiness about the potential loss of personal identity caused by exposure to large numbers of shoes—that an individual would become overwhelmed or unrecognizable by proliferating consumption, much as one's own shoes would be misplaced in the profusion of footwear available for sale. In part, this reflected the threat new patterns of consumption posed to existing class relations and the social control of labor. This fear is visible in a cartoon that parodied "the maids of today" by

Etes-vous sûre de pouvoir reconnaître vos propres souliers, Madame !

Figure 20. "Are you certain that you are able to recognize your own shoes, Madame?" Satirical portrayals often linked shoes to identity. *Le progrès égyptien—Almanach,* 1953, 123.

depicting a servant in extremely high-heeled pumps hailing a taxi to take her to the vegetable market.[117]

Bayram al-Tunisi vividly captured the possibilities shoes offered, Cinderella-like, for the lower classes to mirror the consumption and social practices of the upper classes. One of Egypt's most important and versatile writers of the twentieth century, al-Tunisi employed shoes as such a metaphor in his *fawazir ramadan* (Ramadan riddles) written in the late 1940s or early 1950s.[118] Drawing on a complex set of word plays and puns, al-Tunisi formulated modern social criticism through satirical reworkings of genres from the tradition of medieval high Arabic literature (e.g., the *qasida* and the *maqama*) into the new media of film, radio, the popular press, and advertising and into low literary forms such as riddles and colloquial poetry.[119] Broadcast over the radio for several years and remaining "ever-popular," al-Tunisi's Ramadan riddles satirized the daily workings of Egyptian society.[120] His riddle number 81, "The Shoe [*al-hidha'*]" confronts the ambiguities in social relations accompanying the structural, material change in footwear, especially the addition of heels, which led to the pairing of shoes as opposites.

itnayn azwag, azwag itnayn   *fi kul makan, quddam al-ʿayn*

yiftiriqu al-nas, wa-la yiftirqush   *yitʿariku al-nas, wa-la yitʿarkush*

an wahid rah, al-tani warʾaa   *wa-la lahza yaʿish, fi al-dunya bi-laa*

azwag naf'in, lakin masakin   da'iman 'ayishayn, taht al-riglayn
                      'iw'a tihtar wa-taqul dul fayn

Two pairs, pairs of two	Everywhere, in sight
People differ, they don't differ	People fight, they don't fight
If one goes, the other is behind him	Not for a moment does he live in the world without him
Useful pairs, but pitiable	Always underfoot

Beware, you change [them] and say, where are they?[121]

The poem thus employs the tropes of submerged conflict, inescapable coupling, and utilitarian consumption to distinguish footwear as a commodity in a postwar regime of expanded but unequal consumption.

The riddle prominently evokes a theme of mirrored pairings through its play on doublings in word meanings and grammar as well as its structure. A sense of duality ("pairs of two, two pairs") emerges idiomatically from the frequent use of the dual form and the pun on *azwag* (that as an anagram, it can mean the same reversed as both *gawz* and *zawg*).[122] Its poetic structure also reflects the mirrored left-right pairings of shoes through its rhythms, rhymes, and stanza organization.[123] The poem stands out among al-Tunisi's *fawazir* as the only riddle in which the individual lines of verse are divided into pairs of phrases, separated by a comma. Although these pairs do not rhyme with each other, they are often parallels, inverses, or symmetrical mirrors. The image of opposing-yet-wedded groups the riddle uses to describe community conjures the contradictions of social relations under mass consumption: "people differ, they don't differ"; "people fight, they don't fight." "Everywhere in sight," standardized commodities united people in a shared or common style of consumption. At the same time their very ubiquity demanded a narrowing of vision onto the self and its relationship to others around it, producing envy, stratification, and ultimately, differentiation. Allusions to the aspirations and anxieties of social mobility through mass consumption emerge through al-Tunisi's mixing of standard and colloquial Arabic in the poem.[124] The lowly shoe, "always underfoot" yet unable to be left behind, thus captured the tense interlinking of postwar consumption, populist politics, and anticolonialism. Shoes provided a useful metaphor for Egyptian satirists, who could use the theme of mirrored pairing to critique the cultural and political differences rooted in colonialism that by the late 1940s were woven deeply into the fabric of Egypt's daily life, especially in its cities.

AMBIVALENT HEROISM: A SHOE-STORE PARABLE

The ambiguities of postwar consumer politics and a satirical criticism of the linking of desire and the retail of footwear emerged stridently through the yoked tropes of hunger and footwear in the 1950 Egyptian film *al-Batal* (*The Hero*), a comedy directed by Hilmi Rafla and starring Isma'il Yasin as the character named al-Batal.[125] Set in a fashionable shoe store, the film refracted the tensions of interclass romance and the shifting terms of social mobility through the relationships among the storeowner, his family, his employees, and his customers. The film's plot drew on older genres of folktales and morality tales, the naive and inept but honest al-Batal recalling Goha or *sa'idi* characters of popular culture, to construct a comedy of reversals and mirrorings—of employee and owner, marriage and death, gluttony and hunger, spectacle and reality, actor and audience—thematically linked through the image of a pair of shoes (*gawz gazma*). Playing on the different meanings of *gawz* (as "pair" or "husband"), the film depicted the social status proffered in the advertising, display, and consumption of *ifrangi* shoes as hollow, expressed literally as al-Batal's empty stomach. The rush to consume these new status goods, the film argued, could destroy an Egyptian culture based on honesty, sexual morality, and community support.

The film's 1940s Cairo shoe store resembles the family-owned *ifrangi* shops such as Hornstein or Paul Favre that long dotted Egypt's downtown shopping districts. Founded just before the war, *al-Batal*'s shoe store operated as a partnership between a cosmopolitan (possibly Jewish) Egyptian investor, Zakariyya effendi, and a Muslim merchant named Hasan Gildi (his name suggests a more *baladi* past as a leatherworker), who actively managed the business. When Zakariyya disappeared in Europe during the war, Hasan took over the entire concern and ran it as a family business. Wartime patronage and shortages dramatically expanded the business's worth. The store premises are modern in appearance and spatial organization, including a wide showroom furnished with rows of chairs and special footstools for trying on shoes, well-organized shelving for inventory and display, a sumptuous office for Hasan, several storage spaces in the back and below the showroom, and a storefront of tall, plate-glass display windows. Employees wear matching uniforms and caps embroidered with the shop's name. The shop displays *ifrangi*-style shoes, mostly strappy sandals and pumps for women and wing tips for men, and shoes are stored in custom-printed boxes emblazoned with brand names. Although the store does some shoe repair, no real evidence of shoe production is visible in the film.

The film's narrative centers on the bumblings of al-Batal, a gullible and warm-hearted *baladi* sales assistant in the sleek, *ifrangi* shoe shop. Although the orphan al-Batal has been raised since childhood to work in the business, he is unable to carry out the most basic tasks of locating proper shoe sizes, fitting shoes on customers, or wrapping purchases. His mistakes reveal the lines of division and cohesion within the wider society, and his ascension to owner of the store ultimately parodies the program of economic Egyptianization shaping commerce at the time. Halfway through the film, the old partner, Zakariyya, returns unexpectedly to cash out his share of the business. At the same moment, al-Batal discovers that mysteriously he has only seven days left to live. To protect his wartime profit from Zakariyya, Hasan signs over the shop to al-Batal and engages him to his daughter, Sharbat, to keep the business in the family's hands. Hasan also gives al-Batal £E1,000 to spend preparing for his wedding and his funeral—a pairing of opposites that unusually will occur on the same day—and, with this instant wealth, he embarks on a unique journey of consumption, involving a range of *ifrangi* consumer goods, from suit cloth to air conditioners. Once transferred to an unambiguously Egyptian ownership, the company flourishes, and al-Batal emerges as a conscientious and effective manager, overhauling the previously exploitative labor relations in the store. Now solidly middle class and competent, al-Batal, not surprisingly, is "unable" to die, thereby causing all the characters to reevaluate the morality of their actions. The imagined domino effect of social justice that would result from the clarification of ownership in commercial space then fills the narrative space of the rest of the film.

Al-Batal embeds its commentary on the alliance of the local bourgeoisie with foreign capital in the material specificities of footwear. The film opens with a scene that proclaims the ability of shoes as functional objects and shoe stores as an urban space to cohere widely diverse social groups. Store employees gather in the shop's front to promote a shoe sale, drawing in the crowd on the street: single effendi men, upper-middle-class nuclear families, groups of *baladi* girls dressed in peasant garb, rich businessmen, schoolchildren, glamorous movie stars, and elderly ladies. The salesclerks invite the passersby into the store—and viewers into the imaginative space of the film—to "exchange their old shoes for a pair of new ones." In this scene, the film explores the fantastical offers and restrictive realities of shoe consumption. The opening song links footwear to power and sexuality through a variety of popular and colloquial associations. Holding a high-heeled women's sandal, al-Batal entices customers by literally singing the praises of the shoe. Through rhymed couplets, the song weaves conventional advertising phrases such as "brand new, excellent style [*jadid al-lanja, furma azima*]" with social commentary—"look at the belly and snout; each has a mate and will work as a machine-gun." "A great opportunity. . . . Come, buy and get pleasure from a pair, chic and dandy-ish," al-Batal sings. "*I* have shod movie stars." The song's juxtaposition of the coarsely sexual allusions with the trite advertising slogans thus works as a mirrored pairing that lodges the duality of meaning into the single object of the shoe.

This scene introduces shoes as a commodity shared by a diverse group of customers—shared as an item of apparel, but as the song makes clear, consumed for different effects and meanings. As al-Batal enters the store behind the crowd called in off the street, he encounters three groups of women customers: first, three sophisticated, *ifrangi* women, dressed in light-colored, short-sleeve frilly dresses, who demand to see some "chic and pretty" shoes in their sizes and "appropriate" for their social station (the song plays on these double meanings of '*addi*, meaning both "my size" and "appropriate"); next, three lower-class, *baladi* women clad in brightly patterned housedresses covered by long black veils (*milayat*), who want "light-hearted shoes" from the store's selections; and finally an old lady, dressed formally in a black suit and hat, who complains about the "dreadful shape" of her own shoes. Although linked by their need for footwear and their presence in the store, the three groups are at the same time brought into conflict by their different tastes in shoes.

The film takes advantage of the shoe store's commingling of people of different sexes, ages, and classes in a single space, more so than larger stores with separate departments for men's and women's apparel. Men and women try on shoes next to each other, separated only by the arm of a chair, easily able to compare, compete, and flirt with one another. The camera focuses on the postures assumed in selling shoes and the relations of dominance, subservience, and sexuality that these imply; the initial shot into the store, for example, pans across salesmen sitting below their customers on stools, bending low over the stocking feet that they hold in their laps. Love affairs mediated through the eroticization of shoes form a central theme of the film's plot. The link between changing sexual partners and changing shoes was a popular trope in commercial culture and suggests an anxiety that women's purchasing power would invert conventional familial power structures.[126]

Much like the story "The Nylon Woman," the film addresses the consequences of mass consumption by exploring the objectification of people along with the retail of goods—their transformation into "a piece of meat." In part, this reflects the materiality of leather shoes, that they are animal products,[127] and that *gawz kawari'* (sheep's feet) is Egyptian slang for "a pair of pretty legs."[128] This is particularly evident in a series of jokes in *al-Batal* about the two conflicting commercial responsibilities of the husband—"the *gawz*"—in an increasingly fast-paced and depersonalized consumer society. The storeowner, Hasan, has bought a pair of sheep's feet (*gawz kawari'*) to deliver to his wife, who is making soup for lunch. At the same time, he is supervising the delivery of a pair of repaired shoes (*gawz gazma*) to his mistress Tahia, a famous nightclub dancer. He gets confused talking to the two women on the telephone—icon of the new modern yet alienated consumer society—because they each ask for the *gawz* ("pair" or "husband"). The humor lies in this mistaken or crossed identity: how the husband describes each commodity—one traditional and alimentary, the other modern and vestimentary—by the other's characteristics. In one scene, Hasan tells his wife that he will shine and polish the sheep's feet and his mistress that her repaired sandals "are so fatty and good that you will eat the toes after . . . boiling them on the stove for a half an hour . . . [to make] a soup that is a complete treat." In reply, the mistress says, "Are you crazy? I should cook my shoes to make a soup? Do you know who you are talking to? I am Tahia, the famous Arab dancer!" Hasan answers, "You are?! You're talking about a pair of shoes [*gawz gazma*]?" She replies sarcastically by returning from commodities to the language of kinship, "No, I'm talking about your aunt's husband [*gawz khaltik*]." Some store employees then play out the *gawz gazma/gawz kawari'* joke at the expense of al-Batal, who has been given the lowly job of wrapping the dancer's shoes. Opening the shoebox to find the sheep's feet secretly substituted for her shoes, the dancer expresses her public humiliation by hitting al-Batal with the *baladi* cut of meat.[129] Al-Batal's rudeness leads to his verbal and physical punishment. First, Hasan derogatorily calls al-Batal a *shibshib*, a class-inflected epithet in the context of the high-class *ifrangi* shoe store. Al-Batal is next imprisoned in the storage room of the shop, "without anything to eat or drink." In this scene, al-Batal sings about his hunger among all the pairs of fancy shoes in the storeroom, in which a pun is made on the words *gawaz* (meaning "to pair up" but also "to overstep or deceive") and *gawa'* ("to be hungry"). Al-Batal sings, "I'm so hungry, I'm so hungry. My stomach is dry and crying out. I could eat my hand, I'm so hungry." Al-Batal looks into a packing barrel (shaped much as a soup pot) and pulls up a shoe—describing it in the same double terms that the owner Hasan has used in the confused-identity phone calls, although now referring to a single commodity that embodies the mirrored descriptions. "I can't brown it but I will eat it, delicious and seasoned, shined and polished." The scene closes with al-Batal actually eating the shoe. The food association in the slang for "pretty legs" points to the duality and ambiguity of fashion-attired people. Sexualized and objectified, they are captured as commodities for the consumption of others. The bloat of excess consumer goods among the *ifrangi* rich, however, has left the *baladi* poor starved of basic sustenance.

The film thus played on the material fact that shoes came in pairs that, in the case of the heeled *gazma* sold at Hasan's shop, looked the same but were in fact mirror opposites. In this case, the mirroring of commodities—the *baladi* sheep's feet by the more *ifrangi* shoes—points to the increasing imbrication of the dualities of colonialism in the single embodiment of goods or people. The theme of mirrored pairings is central to the film's humor and social critique—linking the series of jokes around the words *gawz* and sheep's meat to a series of discordant pairings: Hasan's wife and his mistress, al-Batal's simultaneous wedding and funeral, the active and the silent business partners, al-Batal's dual roles as incompetent salesman and effective owner, a personalized and a corporate style of trade, and the merchant's household and the store (the plot alternates between these two primary settings). The upwardly mobile main characters display a twinned cultural style that comprises *baladi* and *ifrangi* consumption patterns. Their constant code switching between colloquial Arabic and phrases from European languages highlights the fluidity of urban commercial space. The film's ultimate "restoration" of the shoe store from its partial ownership by "foreign capital" to a single Egyptian proprietor resonates clearly with the critique of *ifrangi* shoe stores as "Jewish capital's mistress" revealed in the Zulaykha cartoon that had appeared just two years earlier and with the wider state-initiated process of Egyptianization already under way in the commercial sector.

REPLAYING ECONOMIC NATIONALISM
THROUGH CLOTH IN THE 1950S

By 1951 world depression and anticolonial political struggle again thrust to the forefront the issue of national consumption and the political tool of boycott. Cotton prices jumped dramatically in 1950–1951 because of international shortages caused by the Korean War, and the entire Egyptian cotton crop was sold at high prices. The resulting profits and foreign currency financed record imports, especially of "luxury items," leading to a massive trade deficit in 1951.[130] In June 1951 Ahmad Husayn denounced Wafdist leader Fu'ad Sirag al-Din— and the "pasha class" he represented—as "immersed in silk."[131] King Faruq's excessive consumption and gambling, including his lavish wedding in May 1951 to Queen Nariman, whom he had met in a gold store, also incensed a broad front of opposition groups.[132] Nineteen months of talks between the Wafd government and the British over Anglo-Egyptian relations ended in October 1951 with the Egyptian abrogation of the 1936 treaty and the 1899 Sudan Condominium Agreement. Many popular groups interpreted treaty abrogation to mean that "the British military presence in Egypt was illegal," and hostilities in the canal zone began in earnest, leading to armed clashes from November 1951 to January 1952, most importantly in the port city of Ismailia.[133]

As part of this renewed and explicit anticolonial protest, the Egyptian Chambers of Commerce threatened in November–December 1951 to launch another boycott of British goods. British textiles played a much-diminished role in the Egyptian market in this period, comprising only about a tenth of all imported cottons and rayons. British officials were concerned, however, that a boycott would jeopardize their sales of woolen goods, which at 1.5 million kilos annually represented more than half of Egypt's wool imports.[134] British paints, pharmaceuticals, welding products, and other goods were on the list of the boycotters, as well as British commercial institutions, including banks, companies, and "all British establishments even if they sell Egyptian goods."[135] The Egyptian Chambers of Commerce "estimated that products of local origin and imported from countries other than Great Britain could replace British merchandise."[136] Boycotters called on the media to halt advertising for British products, on the public to "examine all merchandise carefully and choose local products," and on importers to stop ordering from Great Britain under the threat of "disciplinary measures."[137] British trade agents considered the boycott strongest among small traders.[138] In November and December newspapers published blacklists of British companies and unpatriotic Egyptian companies; popular patrols began to scrutinize and harass merchants and customers in Cairo's downtown district. Members of Ahmad Husayn's Socialist Party barricaded the Rivoli Cinema, and Doria Shafik's Bint al-Nil (Daughter of the Nile) Association blocked the entrance to Barclay's Bank.[139]

Although Bank Misr had suffered financial collapse and a reorganization that ousted Tal'at Harb in 1939, the bourgeois dream of national economic self-sufficiency, anchored in the mechanized production of textiles using locally grown cotton that he had envisioned in the late 1920s, continued to shape mass culture in the early 1950s.[140] By then, however, the success and widespread distribution of local, durable, silky cottons had displaced the earlier binary vision of local canvas and foreign silks, but the pressure of popular politics against colonialism and its handmaiden monarchical regime supplanted it with a new image of internal contradiction: the imbrication of the foreign and the local. In other words, Egyptians and Egyptian goods came to embody in popular satire both sides of the foreign-local dichotomy. The recasting of the earlier binarism became especially visible in a film, *Sayyidat al-qitar* (*The Lady of the Train*), coproduced by one of Bank Misr's companies, Studio Misr, in the tumultuous spring of 1952 and screened that August, just weeks after the end of the monarchy. As Joel Beinin argues, "No element of social realism impinges on [the film's] idyllic" representation of mechanized textile industry, and in particular no evidence of the repressive management of Bank Misr's textile factories.[141] The film's vision of economy and society is not unilaterally triumphant, however. A doubling in the film's casting and in its narrative creates an undertone of ambiguity about the costs of anticolonial struggle against consumer captivity.

The repopularization of the consumption of locally produced cloth as a central action in the national struggle emerged in the film through a rather serpentine plot that starred Layla Murad and 'Imad Hamdi. Although these actors represented the height of commercial cinema, the film was directed by Yusuf Shahin (Youssef Chahine), who would emerge as one of the most durable and important directors of the more artistic public-sector cinema of the 1960s to the 1990s; the film's musical numbers featured lyrics by al-Tunisi. The film accomplished the refiguring of the relationship between *ifrangi* and *baladi* culture as nondichotomous in several registers. On one level, it used the theme of the replaying of events in time or in different generations to situate the early 1950s as the culmination of the national struggle. Events in 1951–1952 did evoke those of a generation earlier: the 1951 boycott recalled those in 1922–1924 and 1931–1932, and the expansion of textile production during and after the deprivation of the Second World War echoed the post-Depression textile expansion of the 1930s. In the film, Murad played a famous singer, named Fikriyya, working in the 1930s and then "replayed" the role of her grown daughter, Nadia, in the second half of the film, set in the late 1940s or early 1950s. In addition to this diachronic relationship, Fikriyya's "death" and "rebirth" as Nadia linked these eras in a particularly corporeal manner, representing the national struggle as a single embodiment of the supposedly antagonistic cultures of consumption that had marked interwar urban Egypt. Murad herself was linked to a doubled identity: born and bred in Egypt in a Levantine Jewish family, Murad had converted to Islam after her marriage to Anwar Wagdi in 1945 and made her conversion public between 1946 and 1948. Although 1948 film magazines depicted her reading the Qur'an and wearing a prayer shawl, she was accused by the press in the summer of 1952 of visiting and contributing funds to Israel. These contradictions about economic nationalism, still incorporating Egypt's cosmopolitan communities but shaped by very different regional and political circumstances from those attending the founding of Bank Misr in 1920, point to a shifting context that defies easy characterization.[142]

Like many nationalist texts, *Sayyidat al-qitar*'s plot centers on the story of a family. As the film opens, Murad's first character, the mother-singer named Fikriyya, is married to an obsessive gambler, Farid. They live an *ifrangi* lifestyle and are wealthy from the earnings from her performances and the profits of a family textile factory, although Farid's gambling in Egypt's Westernized night-clubs threatens the family's stability. After one particularly expensive gambling loss, Fikriyya travels to Aswan—by train, hence the film's title—to raise money to pay the debt. The train crashes, killing hundreds of passengers. Assuming she has also perished, Farid falsely identifies a body as hers to collect on her life insurance and redeem his gambling debts. Fikriyya, however, survives the train wreck through the rescue efforts of several local villagers, so provincial that they do not even recognize her, who nurse her back to health. In effect, Fikriyya does "die" in the crash to her previous Westernized nightclub lifestyle and is "reborn" in the purifying Egyptian countryside under the care of authentic peasants. The film then fast-forwards twenty years. In the second half, Layla Murad "replays" the role of the (new) main character, now her adult daughter, Nadia. Nadia has no idea that her mother is still alive and has been forced to work as a servant under the name Zakiyya for the past two decades. She does not even recognize her when the aged Zakiyya comes to work for Nadia at the family textile firm. The movie climaxes during a charity benefit party that Nadia organizes to support the factory's worker relief fund. Nadia soon discovers that the aging and lecherous Farid, attired by now in tattered and forlorn formal evening dress, has stolen the donated money to fund his gambling. Drunk on alcohol and a flush wallet, Farid falls to his death in a broken elevator shaft, trenchant symbol of the ultimate emptiness and unreliability of the corrupt *ifrangi* lifestyle he leads. Finally rid of the Westernized, parasitic Farid, Nadia recognizes Zakiyya as her mother.

One of the most pivotal elements in the film is the textile factory. Revenue from the venture sustains the family through the ravages of Farid's gambling, and the factory is the site that reunites Nadia and Fikriyya, ultimately symbolizing the completeness and "full personhood" of the nation. The theft of the factory's worker relief fund is the precipitating cause for the ultimate demise of the corrupted and foreignized Farid. Immediately before the film's turning point at the charity benefit, Nadia sings a ballad, "Dur ya mutur [Turn, Motor!]," on the factory floor, where she dances among the looms, spindles, and finishers with men and women workers and customers. The song's lyrics, written by al-Tunisi, reiterate the link made in 1930s popular and mass culture between the rejection of Western fabrics and silks for the national freedom and strength associated with indigenous cloth production:

> Turn, motor, turn!
> Play your role, the greatest role.
> Turn as you like, and wind your thread.
> Don't mind the supervisor and the counter. . . .
> Free Egypt would rather go naked
> Than dress in imported fabric—
> Neither pink silk nor calico. . . .
> Take this from our hands, our brothers:
> Something beautiful,
> Of really strong manufacture. . . .
> Go to hell London and Bristol!
> Turn, motor, turn!
> We are the spindle.
> We are the loom.
> We are the finisher.
> We are the exporters to Marseille and Darfur. . . .
> The age of industry is the age of victory.
> Wear the crown of glory, Egypt!
> Build your skyscrapers seventy stories high.
> Turn, motor, turn![143]

The durability of Egyptian textiles so long proclaimed by nationalist industry leaders such as Tal'at Harb has thus reemerged to represent Egypt's national strength, a quality that merits its independence as a modern nation builder. No longer subservient to British colonialism, the "supervisor and the counter" centered politically in London and economically in textile manufacturing areas such as Bristol, the newly industrialized nation can build its own urban skyscrapers fueled by the ultimate trope of modernity—the motor. As the local textile industry created not only a substitution for British and other textile imports but even a surplus to allow Egypt to export and thus assume colonial power over southern areas of Europe and the Nile Valley, it actually "produced" the Egyptian national community through the instantiation of elements in the production process ("we are the spindle, loom, finisher, exporter"). The song's knitting of national community via textile technology directly echoed hosiery marketing promotions in the middle 1930s. Such a consensus view of a national economic union of complementary parts, a society in which paternalistic or patronage relations managed difference in the nation, rendered class conflict invisible or subsumed to the common national struggle to oust foreigners. The film's critique of gambling corresponded to a broad popular anger at King Faruq's ostentatious nightclubbing and gambling and the campaigns mounted by both the Muslim Brothers and Young Egypt on bars and nightclubs as signs of moral corruption and Western degeneration. Nevertheless, the double casting of Murad—her body representing the Egyptian victims of both generations—points to the corporeal captivity fostered by consumer goods.

By the time the boycotts of the 1930s were replayed during the 1951 boycott, when the country was largely self-sufficient in textiles and the "age of victory" achieved, textile parables like *The Lady of the Train* portrayed the inherent duality embodied in the nation rather than attempting the knitting of multiple identities into a conflict-free community, as hosiery marketing had done in the middle 1930s. Positioning cotton textiles as part of a narrative linked to the durability and duration of the Egyptian national community had created and expanded markets for new types of local goods, especially cotton hosiery in the interwar period, but although these markets promised enfranchisement, it was subverted by the tendency of silkiness to sharpen difference. By contrast, the marketing of nylon stockings in the late 1940s and early 1950s collapsed multiple female identities together and focused on a discourse of pleasure and titillation. Nylon—its transparency, shine, and artificiality—would increasingly symbolize behavior and consumption practices thought to cause moral decay or intensify difference within the national community itself. Dualities emerged even more fully as mirrored pairings in the postwar footwear market.

Like cloth, footwear marked the contentious cultural and political terrain of social relations within the nation.

A popular screen for nationalism, Egyptian cinema reflected the ambiguities of national identity visible in the postwar period, when widespread political protest called into question a heroic vision of the nation as a provider for all its members. If *The Lady of the Train* rather defensively posited the productive space of the textile factory as redemptive for the Egyptian national struggle, the more comedic *The Hero* remained much more ambivalent about the status of retail space. Retail space's tendency to confuse consumer identity, and its increasing association with nightclubs, loomed as a threat in the postwar climate of political and social turmoil. Popular satire such as "The Nylon Woman" or "A Woman on Fu'ad Street" addressed how the problems of gambling and a sexualized urban geography blocked opportunities for hardworking, middle-class Egyptians to advance socially, while other texts, such as "The Avenger" or *The Lady of the Train*, presaged the vengeful retaliation against other residents that would explode in early 1952.

6 THE CAIRO FIRE AND POSTCOLONIAL CONSUMPTION

CAIRO'S *IFRANGI* COMMERCE went up in flames in late January 1952. The great conflagration left scores of people dead, hundreds injured, and tens of thousands without work or home. Despite its great violence, the Cairo Fire has come to symbolize, in the years since, a triumphant national passage, a great moment of reckoning that clarified the ambiguities and inequalities of the postwar years by ripping down the gaudy trappings and cheap mirrors of late colonialism. For some, it was an incident in which ordinary Egyptians reclaimed urban spaces from which they had been previously excluded. For others, it was a clarion call for revolution that would be fulfilled six months later in the bloodless coup that brought the military regime of the Free Officers—and eventually Gamal ʿAbd al-Nasser—to power. "The Cairo Fire was the first sign of the social revolution against the corrupt institutions," Nasser told the Egyptian parliament in 1960, in the midst of widespread nationalizations of the economy. "The Cairo Fire expressed the people's anger, when Egypt was bending beneath the yoke of feudalism, speculation, and capitalism."[1] Indeed, when in May 1954 an Egyptian court amnestied some of those found guilty of looting during the fire, it argued, "The accused had only given material expression to the general feeling."[2]

The struggle to make sense of the Cairo Fire and the changes in social, economic, and political life that followed it has occupied Egyptians and foreigners alike since that Black Saturday in January 1952. The plots of agents operating clandestinely or even openly in the streets, the failures of politicians and government leaders to act, and the telltale signs of premeditation, coordination, and conspiracy have been the subjects of numerous scholarly and popular studies.[3] This chapter does not offer a new answer to the specific question of responsibility or guilt; it is clear that many groups, including the British, the king, the Wafd, the Muslim Brothers, and Ahmad Husayn's Socialist Party, thought they had much to gain from fostering some urban chaos in January 1952. Instead, this chapter provides a rereading of the fire that focuses on the slipperiness of its targets, produced by the colonial politics and urban development of the previous decades: the difficulty of locating precisely the line demarcating the foreign from the local, the themes of shared space and shared attire, the complex material dynamics of place, and ultimately the efforts to police the adulteration and the mixed-up use of commodities. The fire can only be fully understood, I argue, when situated as a product of interwar attempts to configure commercial space and commodities such as textiles as mechanisms to unify the nation. I look at the fire from a variety of sources, including official reports, eyewitness accounts, newspaper coverage, claim reports, published testimony in the trials that followed, and interviews, memoirs, novels, and secondary sources recorded much later. From this recast interpretation of the fire, I turn to the rebuilding of the city, and especially its commercial downtown areas, in the years that followed. As Christine Rosen argues, the "aftermath of great fires" provides historians with a "unique opportunity to see what happened in rapidly growing cities when one of the barriers to environmental redevelopment, the physical durability of structures, was suddenly removed."[4] In colonial contexts or during transitional periods, the rebuilding process has often erased the traces of former regimes of power, rendering urban spaces almost blank canvases to restructure ethnic and class relations.[5] Although city spaces can be leveled by a variety of natural disasters, including floods or earthquakes, fire damage appears as "generally being caused by human actions or inactions, and thus share[s] the moral freight of blame and justification" with forces such as epidemics.[6] Often framed in the language of retribution or purification, urban fires have thus frequently functioned as clarifying processes for the social order of a city.[7]

In the rebuilding of Cairo, new narratives of nation, urban community, and commerce ultimately converged with a series of political events, caught in the shifting context of global decolonization and the Cold War, that would dramatically restructure the social organization of capital and people in Egypt. Throughout the nationalizations and expulsions of the late 1950s, the state would adamantly claim that the downtown areas were the same as before, providing the same types of glamorous goods and services, only increasingly serving a broader audience: the themes of public access to and public ownership of downtown space would progressively mark official storytelling in the late 1950s and early 1960s, just as the stocking of this space and the tenor of the regime's agenda was beginning to focus on change. Providing ordinary Egyptians with the standard of living represented by pre-1952 department stores was a crucial justification for the regime's increasingly aggressive redistributive policies. My focus on space, narratives of commerce, and commodities leads in this chapter to a rather unexpected continuity between pre- and postrevolutionary Egypt, one that challenges a previous scholarly focus on the fire as rupture.[8] Like a large-scale version of the bonfires of *ifrangi* suits in 1932 or Esther Wissa's even earlier proposal to starve the "fois gras" producing goose, the 1952 burning of Cairo's *ifrangi* commercial district was an anticolonial action that revealed the deep lines of contradiction and the stubborn persistence of colonial captivity. Breaking free from consumption's bonds required a painful measure of self-destruction.

"THE FIRE CONSUMED THE HEART OF CAIRO"

On January 26, 1952, angry demonstrators rioted through the Cairo streets radiating from the royal palace at ʿAbdin, where the king, many of his ministers, and the officers of the army and police forces shared a lavish buffet to celebrate the birth of the royal heir. The crowds, composed initially of auxiliary policemen, students from the Azhar and Cairo's secular universities, and workers in the Egyptian State Railways workshops, protested the killing of many Egyptian auxiliary police forces (or the gendarmerie; *buluk al-nizam*) by British troops in the nearby port city of Ismailia in the canal zone the previous day. Although the canal zone had witnessed guerrilla fighting between Egyptian civilians and British troops for several months, the January 25 attack to disarm the gendarmerie had been particularly violent. In addition to the forty or fifty policemen killed, the British attack on the police barracks had wounded another eighty and resulted in the capture of nearly one thousand more troops, including officers and the commander himself.[9] After appealing in vain to the government at ʿAbdin Palace for a response to the British attack, the protestors began to chant slogans against the king, who reportedly authorized his guards to open fire. A detachment of demonstrators would eventually attempt to march to the Soviet Embassy, "to submit the Egyptian people's demands to the Soviet Union representatives" in an effort to bring the pressure of Cold War politics to bear on the crisis, although at the Fuʾad Bridge they too were fired on by police.[10]

Frustrated by the lack of official response to the canal zone killings and probably abetted by members of Husayn's Socialist Party, the Muslim Brothers, and other groups, rioters in Cairo set a total of 217 fires on that Black Saturday.[11] They began with an attack on a famous nightclub, Casino Opera, popularly

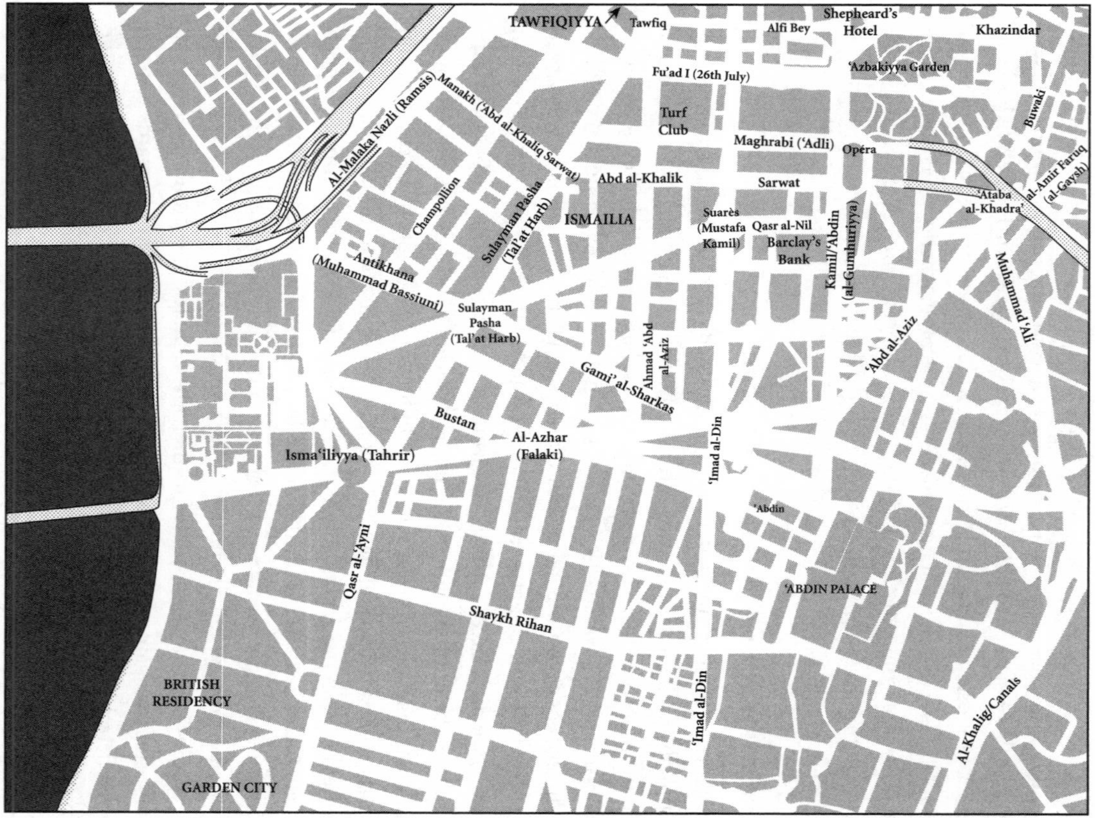

Map 2. Downtown Cairo, 1952

called *sala Badiʿa*. Named after its well-known founder, the Syrian-Egyptian performer Madame Badiʿa al-Masabni, the nightclub had been a popular and profitable haunt of Allied troops in the Second World War; its stars had even performed parodies of Hitler, for which the Allies reportedly secretly paid al-Masabni. By 1952, however, the club was "owned and almost exclusively used by Egyptians."[12] The day of the Cairo Fire, a police officer drinking with a woman dancer on the club's terrace apparently provoked the protestors, who then piled the casino's furniture into a bonfire fueled by paraffin. Legislation had recently tightened regulations on nightclubs, prostitution, and public performances. During the war, nightclubs especially became associated with the debauchery of Allied officers, and the expansion of this area of work for local women became a major concern for the Muslim Brothers and Young Egypt. The state criminalized prostitution in 1949 and in 1951 amended the law on public places to forbid "women who are employed in a public place, [or] those who perform theatrical acts, to sit with the customers of the shop [or] to eat, drink or dance with them."[13]

The sense of combined moral, political, and economic violation caused by the continued British presence in Egypt pushed the crowd down the street from Casino Opera to the cinemas along Fu'ad and Sulayman Pasha Streets. The Rivoli, Metro, Radio, Miami, and Diana Cinemas, screening what the Muslim Brothers considered the "dirty" films of "naked" women imported from the West,[14] were the next string of fires set. At one of the burned cinemas (Cinema Opera), the marquee headlined its showing of the American science-fiction film *When Worlds Collide*, an image picked up by local photographers to capture the cultural and political nature of the conflict.[15] All told, the fires that day in the commercial downtown and out on Pyramids Road in Giza would consume ninety-two bars, seventy-three restaurants and dance halls, sixteen clubs, and forty cinemas.[16] One British official noted, "The gangs attacked most places in the centre of the City where alcoholic drinks and luxury goods were sold, where 'high living' amenities were provided, and where 'Western' entertainment was available, irrespective in all these instances of the nationalities of the owners."[17] At one establishment, when the owner called out to demonstrators to halt their assault because he was Egyptian, the crowd retorted that the shop sold wine.[18]

The crowd did attack official British institutions and establishments that more overtly housed the political and economic power of the British in Egypt. Barclay's Bank and the Turf Club, an all-British, exclusive men's club where the

British ambassador served as president, witnessed some of the most tenacious and severe attacks on their premises and employees or members. The rioters also set fire to Thomas Cook's travel agency; the offices of Shell Oil and the British Overseas Airways Corporation; the British Council and British Institute; British automobile showrooms for Standard, Jaguar, Studebaker, and Ford cars; and the Shell service station.[19] Also hit was Shepheard's Hotel, one of the most prominent sites of European presence and tourism in the country. Shepheard's was destroyed quickly, its big glass-domed ceiling crashing in after only about twenty minutes and its wide terrace and men's Long Bar consumed by flames. Italian opera stars and the king's own mistress were reportedly hotel guests at the time. Clubs associated with the king and the local elites also came under attack, including the Automobile Club, the St. James's Club, and the Cecil Bar, as well as American companies, including the offices of TWA and the Chrysler showroom, and the French Chamber of Commerce, the Michelin Agency, the Peugeot dealer, and several other French businesses.[20] All around the area, thick, black smoke rose from the fire, its blackness intensified by the sacks of sugar and flour from the nearby tearooms (such as Groppi) dumped into the streets and set alight. Even a week later, according to one witness, "in the streets burned automobiles, and piles of charred rubbish and twisted iron still blocked the traffic. The heat of the fires had even lifted and cracked the pavement in certain places."[21]

Although many of the fires set early in the day targeted official and cultural establishments, the trend of the fire changed by late afternoon, when commercial shops came widely under attack. These sites would ultimately account for nearly half of all those burned on January 26. The local correspondent for the London *Times* reported, "Luxury shops were favourite targets, particularly those owned by Jewish or European interests. Goods were removed, and in some cases used as fuel for bonfires in the streets."[22] Fire completely destroyed the five-story Cicurel building, its tall, plate-glass windows shattered, its vast stocks burned, its collapsed upper floors thrust into the street. Perhaps among the burned goods were remnants of the enormous selection of men's and boys' underwear the store had promoted two months earlier and satin ties of natural silk in modern styles, plain or ribbed socks of pure wool, wool sports socks for students, white linen handkerchiefs, or the more expensive Elite brand flannel pajamas or wool dressing gowns with "modern trim."[23] Rioters fired Chemla with gasoline, despite the store owner's pleas for protection to nearby policemen.[24] Its enormous selection of "stockings in all shades," including the Kaiser, Van Raalte, Mojud, and Cameo brands, advertised the previous week, would have burned quickly.[25] At Roberts Hughes Department Store on Qasr al-Nil Street in Mustafa Kamil (ex-Suares) Square, long known as a purveyor of menswear and sports equipment, one British witness saw a group of between twelve and twenty young men, some dressed in galabiyas and others "wearing trousers and shirts," attacking the building.[26] "After they had succeeded in breaking into the shop, they started throwing all the contents into the road. . . . Articles of clothing were thrown into the street and some of them were seized by onlookers who ran away with them. Others were heaped into the road and liquid was poured on them." Shortly thereafter, "a man carrying a flaming torch, who appeared to be in charge of the operation," lit the heaps of oil-soaked clothes in the street and the bundles that had been thrown back in the shop.[27] Although a British company, Roberts Hughes was locally based and did not remit its earnings to the metropole. Several weeks after the fire, the British ambassador in Egypt commented about the store's destruction that "the chief value of such a business is the important, though not measurable, one that it keeps an English name before the public in Cairo."[28] While perhaps not as recognizably English as Roberts Hughes, the destroyed ʿAdès department store on ʿImad al-Din Street would submit the third-largest damages claim of all British properties.[29]

Several blocks away, Orosdi-Back/ʿUmar Effendi Department Store on the corner of Rushdi and ʿAbd al-ʿAziz Streets was also attacked in the early evening of January 26. There, witnesses told of a large group of protestors who approached the building, smashed the front doors, entered the store, and ignited a fire. Muhammad ʿAbd al-Hamid, a law student whose wife was inside the store, was reportedly killed at the scene. Employees inside the building telephoned the store director, René Guyomard, at home in his villa in Giza. Members of the liberation battalions reportedly had demanded that the store's director pay £E1,000 to protect the premises, but Guyomard had refused. At the same time, police and soldiers arrived from the nearby ʿAbdin station and arrested nineteen people at the scene. Along with several unemployed people, those arrested included a newspaper vendor, a tailor, a commission agent, a chicken seller, a worker at the Olympia Cinema, and several domestic servants, government employees, and students, including an intermediate student of commerce. The tailor, who was mute and testified using "hand signals" and sign language, claimed to have come on the scene while heading downtown to buy medicine for a pregnant relative. Firefighters were ultimately able to extinguish the fires to prevent the total destruction of the store.[30] Benzion Department Store at Mustafa Kamil Square, a branch shop that had opened in March 1940, however, was allowed to burn for a considerable time before troops were called in to extinguish the fires.[31]

Specialty stores and smaller boutiques that sold clothing and household goods in the district also suffered extensive damage in the fire. Among them were the furniture stores Pontremoli and Haddad, Jacques nylon hose shop, the Bride shop, Aby's store for handbags, and Fashionable, a store for women's wear. The silver and glassware shop L'Art Contemporain Francais on Qasr al-Nil Street, attacked early in the day, experienced a typical assault. After breaking the vitrine, rioters threw the contents of the shop into the street, lined the inside of the broken shop window with a black cloth heaped with oil-doused rags, and lit the fabric. Many in the crowd attempted to steal the silver piled in the street, but riot leaders took the items and smashed them.[32] Eyewitnesses adamantly claimed that the riot leadership wanted to destroy goods and strongly punished looters; at one department store attack, the organizers threw a looter into the fire where he burned to death.[33] Over and over, witnesses told of huge bonfires fueled by commercial goods lining the streets of the downtown area.

Nevertheless, bystanders widely pillaged commercial merchandise. In the late afternoon, "increasing numbers of poor folk could be seen slipping into the still smoking department stores—Cicurel, Roberts Hughes, Adès. In the doorway of a large Greek grocery shop the salesman cunningly gave out handfuls of piastres and turned away the mob."[34] In a similar way, the department store "Salon Vert saved itself by having its goods thrown into the street. The mob seemed satisfied with the loot."[35] After more than six hundred arrests in the surrounding areas and outside Cairo, especially in poorer areas of the city, considerable quantities of the pillaged merchandise were repossessed in the following days. "Among the articles recovered [were] sewing machines, electrical equipment, bottles of liquor, tobacco, rifles, shotguns, machine guns, ammunition, and daggers. One restaurant [was] found to be fitted out with stolen tables and chairs."[36] A tailor, a salesman, and an electrician were among those apprehended with stolen cloth in the Muski.[37] The screen curtains of the Metro Cinema were pilfered by one of its employees, who was arrested while carrying them at the train station,[38] and according to an American resident in Egypt at the time, "candy bars stolen from Groppi's restaurant [were] being sold in the Mousky bazaar at reduced prices!"[39] The frenzy with which many demonstrators scooped up the merchandise of downtown stores was matched by the shock of residents at the decimation of the giant department-store emporiums. In the local coverage of the fire, the ruined premises of Cicurel department store became one of the most circulated images of the destruction of downtown.[40]

The next day city residents woke up to martial law, a suspended constitution, widespread arrests and interrogations, and a devastated downtown. At least twenty-six people had been killed in the demonstrations, and five hundred more were wounded. Over seven hundred establishments had burned, four hundred buildings lay in total ruin, and the entire downtown business district was pillaged and charred. The cost of the damage would total £E15 million (only one-third of that was British capital in the end).[41] Out of work were some fifteen thousand to thirty thousand employees of "the steady, lower middle class type"—primarily "shop assistants, clerks, book-keepers, waiters and accountants whose principals' business has disappeared."[42] As it was Saturday afternoon and the large stores had closed for the weekend, most shoppers and store employees escaped the riots, but the devastation of the commercial district would scar the area for months. As one Egyptian recalled twenty years later, "The fire consumed the heart of Cairo [*akalat al-nar qalb al-Qahira*]."[43]

FOREIGN OR LOCAL? DISENTANGLING THE GROUND OF COLONIAL POLITICS

The events and people involved in the Cairo Fire constituted a complex imbrication of foreignness and localness. Products of the fluidity of urban commercial space and the morseled and mixed-up styles associated with it that had grown in the interwar years, the physical and social landscapes of the urban downtown were not cleanly partitioned between colonized and colonizer. Hybridized practices constituted by both *ifrangi* and *baladi* influences instead organized space and society into interconnected entanglements. This arrangement challenged demonstrators bent on rooting out the foreign, oppressive elements in the downtown district, frequently rendering the microconflicts of the fire contradictory and contentious navigations.

Perhaps the most prominent person killed in the Cairo Fire, the Scottish economist James I. Craig was linked closely to Egypt's commercial landscape and its role in colonial politics. Eighty-three at his death, Craig was a British official whose fifty-year career in Egypt spanned much of the colonial period and encompassed both world wars; in many ways, it mirrored the changing emphasis of British rule in Egypt. Craig spent most of the first half of his service in Egypt working in the Survey Department, where he published books on Egyptian irrigation. Irrigation works formed a central element of British

efforts to expand Egypt's raw cotton exports, which were offset by the importation of a wide array of finished European goods, most notably textiles, clothing, footwear, and even plate-glass windows.[44] After 1914 much of Craig's work
in Egypt involved financial administration and the compilation of economic
and population statistics, especially the 1927 census and studies on the national
income. He served as financial secretary to the Egyptian Ministry of Finance
from 1928 to 1934, and his most recent position was commissioner for Egyptian
Customs from 1934 to 1947.[45] From increasing exports of agricultural products
to the production of statistics and knowledge in the service of the rationalizing
state to facilitate imports, Craig was involved in many of the processes that led
to the expansion of downtown Cairo as a commercial district.[46] There is no evidence that protestors specifically sought Craig, although postmortem examination revealed bodily injuries that preceded burning. He was killed in the blaze
at the Turf Club, an institution that united important foreign men, including J.
McLeod Boyer, the Canadian trade commissioner, and two senior employees of
the company that sold British accounting machines, all of whom were among
the ten people killed there.[47]

Charles E. Butterworth, who assumed the post of acting Canadian trade
commissioner at Cairo after Boyer's death, had been residing at the Turf Club
at the time of the fire. Butterworth, who tried to rescue Boyer but was caught
by protestors, escaped the fire because an Egyptian stranger hid him in a nearby
building. He reported that "a young Egyptian in western clothes fought his
way through the crowd, grabbed my arm, and yelling and hitting at the mob
dragged me towards the steps of a nearby building which he eventually got me
into, while two other Egyptians held the crowd back. We reached the fourth or
fifth floor where he hid me, and posted a couple of workmen to guard me."[48]
Despite his dramatic rescue, most of his wardrobe and personal possessions did
not survive the Turf Club blaze; his room was "burned badly and thoroughly
looted." Butterworth lost fifty-one pairs of socks, fifteen pairs of underpants,
thirty ties, four scarves, thirty-five shirts, and twenty suits, in addition to various trousers and sports jackets (including a white sharkskin dinner jacket), bed
linens and towels, and seventeen pairs of boots and shoes, including shoes for
golf, tennis, and squash, boots for riding and fishing, patent-leather evening
shoes, crepe sole shoes, slippers, and two pairs each of black, brown, and white
buckskin shoes.[49] His Chevrolet car was also stolen and later recovered in a
damaged condition.[50]

Richard Howard Giles, who had been an assistant commandant of the
police in Cairo in the 1940s and in 1952 worked in "commercial activities"

in Egypt, also lost all of his possessions in the Cairo Fire. According to their lawyer, the Giles family had been "compelled to evacuate their home in great haste owing to the recent riots and incidents in Cairo and, consequential on this evacuation sustained a serious loss in regard to almost the whole of their personal possessions which were deposited in a depository adjoining Shephe[a]rds Hotel. The depository was the property of Thomas Cook Ltd . . . [which] was burnt to the ground during the rioting."[51] Giles lived with his family (wife Joan Mary, née Hart-Cox, and four children) in the posh district of Zamalik. He was a member of the Turf Club and the Gezira Sporting Club and noted that his recreational pursuits included "shooting, golf, cricket, riding."[52] The goods lost included all the household possessions and "the entire wardrobes of Giles Bey, his wife and four children."[53] Enumerated on three single-spaced pages, the Giles family household goods included furniture, china, wedding presents, sports prizes, christening gifts, books, an old Singer sewing machine, and a car; special utensils picked up in the Middle East, such as pottery bowls and vases from Palestine, a copper mug from Mecca, a silver Ethiopian lighter, inlaid boxes, and local carpets; presentation gowns from King Ibn Sa'ud and old police uniforms; and quotidian articles of a growing Anglo-Egyptian family, such as pencil sharpeners, wool blankets, and a baby pram. In Giles's personal wardrobe trunk, he had stored a dinner jacket, a formal suit, brown suit, grey suit, shirts, collars, and socks; another "cabin" was filled with only boots, shoes, and cricket pads. Born in Nicosia, Cyprus, in 1898, Giles had lived in Egypt continuously for the past twenty years and remained on the Egyptian police force until 1946, when it was Egyptianized.[54]

The extensiveness of Butterworth's wardrobe or the Giles family's household possessions, and their ability to classify and record them with state officials, certainly differentiated them from the majority of urban (not to mention rural) Egyptians, although many of the protestors in the Cairo Fire consumed some items similar to those they owned. Photographs of protestors and bystanders and of the defendants and witnesses in the trials that followed show many of them attired in trousers, shoes, jackets, and shirts while others wore galabiyas or turbans; many people also dressed in a mixture of the two styles.[55] Reports described the various outfits in considerable detail, as a code to discern the political organization of the demonstrators. One official noted, for example, "Operations at the Radio Cinema were directed by a man in a grey suit . . . ; at an incident in Kasr el Nil operations were led by a man in a khaki galabieh wearing a turban, and at another in the same road by a man in blue trousers, short shirt sleeves and wearing a green armband. . . . In Sharia Adly Pasha as a whole, most of those taking part in the many attacks were well dressed, wearing European type clothes. . . . At the Americain [*sic*] Bar, there were four or five effendis and 12 men in galabiehs; in Ismailia Midan [home to Qasr al-Nil palace and barracks and later renamed Tahrir] rioters are reported to have been the poorer artisan type, some of whom were dressed in blue overalls."[56] As targets of political protest, then, socks, ties, and shirts were items of both shared attire and symbols of exploitation.

Just as morsels of clothing were consumed across class and ethnic lines, Britons and Europeans were not the only inhabitants of Cairo's downtown business district. The neighborhood encompassed extensive residential housing in addition to its official and business premises. Roughly twelve thousand people were left homeless by the fire.[57] Nelly Hanna argues that the majority of downtown residents, even in the most *ifrangi* neighborhoods, were Egyptians.[58] In 1952 the outspoken Egyptian journalist Fikri Abaza Pasha lived in an eighth-floor apartment in the Immobilia Building at 26 Sharif Pasha Street. Abaza had been elected head of the Journalists' Syndicate in 1944 and had made a name for himself through his strongly anti-British writings and speeches during the 1919 Revolution; he later wrote an Egyptian national anthem. The Immobilia Building housed private residences, travel agents, a pharmacy, many small shops, a large restaurant (the Ermitage), as well as the offices of the firms owned by the 'Abbud group.[59] The building burned during the early afternoon of January 26. In an editorial in *al-Ithnayn* entertainment magazine that appeared only a few days later, Abaza recounted in his elegant and satirical prose the crisis inside the burning building. "At precisely two o'clock, according to my memory, I breathed the suffocating smoke that was so kind to visit me, densely gushing forth from the neighboring residences. My neighbor, who is a cook, became frightened. Then I began to hear the calls for help from all the floors. 'The Fire' leaped into the air from behind the huge glass windows and shattered them, dissolved them, and melted them. Next, the blaze rushed forth into the staircases; the electric lifts were hit." Abaza recalled later the extreme terror of the residents in the building's upper, residential floors during the fire. Fifteen women, dressed only "in their housedresses and even in nightshirts," had come with their children to his apartment to ask for help when the fire first broke out. The residents worried about an explosion because of the large quantity of chemicals in the Imperial Chemist shop on the building's third floor. Abaza managed to exit the building and corralled bystanders into working the heavy hoses that had been abandoned by the firemen. His efforts, combined with those of Muhammad

Naguib Bassiuni, a police officer from the 'Abdin district, helped salvage the upper floors of the building and permit inhabitants to escape.[60]

Even the Rivoli Cinema, which suffered one of the most extended attacks in the fire, was only partially British. In fact, the Rivoli and Odeon Cinemas had been involved in a long-term dispute between a British stockholder (Arthur J. Rank) and Mustafa and Muhamad Gaafar. The Gaafar brothers became co-owners in the mid-1940s and had been contesting British ownership for several years. As part of the dispute and shortly before the fire, the Egyptian government ordered John Stuart Smeedon, the British manager of the Rivoli, to leave Egypt, although he had refused to do so. Smeedon's account of his and his secretary's escape from the burning of the Rivoli featured prominently in British chronicles of the fire. His secretary "although of Egyptian nationality, ha[d] a Swedish mother, and an English education, and [spoke] Arabic with a 'foreign' (non-Egyptian) accent."[61] Although the cinema's Greek employees were able to escape into the street shortly after the building began to burn, Smeedon insisted that the secretary remain in hiding with him. After four hours of evading protestors and looters by taking refuge in small rooms of the burning building, they were finally led to the building next door by fire officials and staff members. The Gaafar brothers would later in the year advertise their ownership of "the three most luxurious" cinema houses in downtown Cairo: the Rivoli, the Opera, and the Radio.[62]

Many commercial premises destroyed by the Cairo Fire were small businesses owned by Cypriots and Maltese, British subjects by virtue of British colonization of Cyprus and Malta but rarely invited into places of colonial power such as the Turf Club. These subjects also sat somewhat uncomfortably between the cultures of consumption and politics ostensibly at war in the fire. Until 1947 their status had been underwritten by the unequal legal system of national privileges, including exemptions from Egyptian taxes and criminal jurisdiction. Nonetheless, they remained an undifferentiated mass to British officials, who did not include their many "small bars and one-man shops" involved in the destruction on the embassy's list of damaged premises. These premises were so small that the British were eventually forced to place their claims in an urgent category because of the owners' destitution. Over forty-three such applications were filed by members of this group. In the end a local lawyer volunteered to represent their claims pro bono and advanced his personal funds toward their court fees.[63] The government of Cyprus and the Maltese community also provided monetary assistance to many of these small traders. British Embassy officials in Cairo noted that "these Cypriots and Maltese, owning or employed in small bars and cafes which formed some of the main targets for attack" were now "deprived . . . of their sole livelihood."[64]

Even though Barclay's Bank had been targeted as a clear instrument of foreign capital, the dead found there did not include any of British nationality but rather two Greek and five Egyptian members of the staff, plus four Egyptians who worked in a canteen on the third floor.[65] Commercial employees and other lower-level workers in the district itself apparently held mixed views about the riots. Kerboeuf argues that 30 percent of the arrested rioters were "skilled workers, craftsmen (shoe repairers, tailors), small shopkeepers, service employees (coffee waiters, sales clerks, tailors, petrol station attendants) or domestic employees (*bawwab* [doorman], *sufragi* [butler], *farrash* [servant])."[66] Their motivations and levels of involvement are difficult to ascertain. British managers reported that they instructed their Egyptian commercial staffs, for their safety in the event of an attack on their premises, to "immediately join with [the rioters] . . . , hail them as compatriots and, to all intents, assist in the ransacking of the office" and then slip away from the district.[67]

Testimonies such as these reveal that an abstract analytic category such as foreign capital—ostensibly the object of protestors—was actually complicated to locate in everyday morseled practice and space. Although demonstrators on January 26 targeted British- and European-owned businesses, many burned premises were owned by locally resident minorities or by Egyptian Muslims, such as Abaza, whose father had been an Azhari *shaykh*. The military court that tried those accused in the events of January 26 would feel the need to publicly declare that all properties, whether owned by foreigners or Egyptians, were equal before the law.[68] For some of the groups probably directly involved in the fire or operating in resistance to the state, such as the Muslim Brothers, Young Egypt, and the communists, members of the upper classes and local residents of diaspora communities such as Greeks and Jews could be easily identified as compradors or agents of foreign capital.[69] Other Egyptians considered this commercial district of downtown Cairo a central part of the national fabric and viewed the fire as not the destruction of a foreign parasite on the national host but an act of self-destruction or self-immolation. Particularly prominent in local depictions of the fire, especially in literary representations of it produced in the decade that followed, was the metaphor of national suicide. Husayn Fawzi, a scientist on the faculty of Alexandria University who would later become rector of the university and in the middle 1950s undersecretary of culture, would label the Cairo Fire "the suicidal act of a people conquered within itself."[70] In the storytelling about suicide, commodities particularly bound Cairenes as captives of colonialism.

In his short 1956 novel *Qissat hubb* (later translated as *City of Love and Ashes*), Yusuf Idris opens the narrative with the Cairo Fire and its effect on the life of the main character, Hamza, who works as a chemist in a silk factory, involved in dyeing clothes.[71] The novel echoes the official view that the fire resulted from an organized plot—"the air filled with the shades of a dark and sinful hand, and the smell of conspiracy mingled with the smell of the gunpowder."[72] Nevertheless, Idris has Hamza mourn the loss of the destroyed city center. "But when he arrived at Cairo Station, [he] saw the thickening columns of smoke livid in the sky, the many blazing buildings appearing dark red in the black of night, the tongues of flame rising from them like the tongues of devils, the incandescent fires, the charred timbers, shops with doors ripped out and contents smashed, all parts of the Cairo he loved hemorrhaging ruins and rubble."[73] Naguib Mahfouz also opened his 1962 novel, *al-Summan wa'l-kharif* (Autumn Quail), with a chapter on the Cairo Fire. In the story the main character, a government official, stumbles into the fire on his return to Cairo from a journey to the canal zone. Even though he has seen the struggle against the British firsthand in the port town of Ismailia, he is shocked by the depth of anger evident in the Cairo protestors. On Ibrahim Street, "any bystander on the sidewalks was seized; petroleum was being poured out, fires were burning, doors were smashed, merchandise was scattered, and streams of water spurted out like a tumult of waves. The mad frenzy was itself without an overseer. It was Cairo revolting, but revolting against itself. It was inflicting on itself the very thing it wanted to inflict on its enemies. It was committing suicide [*inaha tantahiru*]."[74] Mahfouz satirically punctuates the narrative three times with the demonstrators' chant: "Burn! Destroy! Long live the nation [*al-watan*]!"[75] This portrayal of the fire as "suicide" rather than a killing suggests both the broad base of popular connection to this downtown district and the paradoxical nature of the decolonization struggle for local residents—that the protection of the homeland required a certain measure of self-destruction.

Writing roughly during the same time as Mahfouz in the late 1950s and early 1960s, Latifa al-Zayyat also used the Cairo Fire as a catalyst in the plot of her semiautobiographical novel, *al-Bab al-maftuh* (The Open Door).[76] Much like Mahfouz, al-Zayyat portrays the fire as not a simple purge of colonial parasites from the urban fabric but an act of national self-sacrifice. Set between 1946 and 1956, *The Open Door* is a Marxist-nationalist novel that traces the coming of age of a teenage, middle-class girl named Layla growing up in Cairo during the national struggle. The 1952 Cairo Fire finally disenchants Layla of bourgeois marriage and consumer culture, but it is a complicated scene depicting great personal cost. Although she is already deeply committed to the independence movement and the popular conflict in the canal zone leading up to the fire, she is shocked and grieved by the sight of thick, black smoke billowing across the city. The city burns while Layla's cousin, Gamila, tries on her new, expensive wedding dress, made of white satin and chiffon, the fabric bought several weeks before at Cicurel. The narrative in this section is structured around the recurring trope of the whiteness of Gamila's dress, counterposed to the red flames and black smoke of the fire—the very fire that destroys the store that sold her fabric.[77]

The sense of loss and self-destruction wrought by the fire is magnified by the passage's dialogue, in which Layla shifts rapidly from the general political level of the struggle, expressed in the neutral third person, to an immediate, emotional, and possessive first-person identification with the downtown. "The people are burning the city?" Layla asks. "Why? Why are we burning our city?"[78] Spurred by the dislocations that follow the fire, Layla is propelled deeper into the struggle for freedom. Al-Zayyat's rendering of the pain of Layla's personal transformation during the fire underlines, however, the agony and self-destruction of anticolonial protest. Al-Zayyat replays Layla's memory of the fire at the moment of Layla's own engagement party, at which she dresses almost exactly as Gamila, in a white gown made of the same material from Cicurel. Thinking about the emotional death and entrapment she feels awaits her in her upcoming marriage, she returns in her memory to the scene of the fire: "She saw Gamila standing on the roof, on the day of the Cairo Fire, her back to the skies, still as a statue in her white dress, the masses of thick, acrid smoke surrounding her like a frame."[79] The dress circulates and mutates in the novel as a doubled symbol, connecting Gamila's old-regime marriage and Layla's "revolutionary" one and reflecting the persistence of both patriarchy and objectification of women through consumer culture. Gamila's elegant wedding dress was very low cut and glamorous, befitting her husband's wealthy status and *ifrangi* life before the fire. Layla's fiancé, a more middle-class university professor who is emblematic of the post-1956 nation, disapproves of revealing clothes for women. So Layla's wedding dress was "like Gamila's wedding dress, except [Layla's had] a closed bodice and [Gamila's] was low cut. Exactly, though—same cut, same lines, same material."[80] Commodities such as dresses made from department-store fabric bound Egyptians in emotionally complex ways to the downtown areas. As markers of important personal transitions, such commodities helped delineate this urban space as simultaneously a place of affection and oppression. Breaking free from consumer captivity was a complicated process even for ardent nationalists.

REBUILDING THE CITY: REMAKING DOWNTOWN CAIRO THE SAME AS BEFORE

One of the most striking aspects of the Cairo Fire was the speed and ease with which businesses and residents reconstructed the city center. Rebuilding was a massive but not impossible task, in part because the fire had not resulted environmentally from structural weaknesses in the building or the layout of the city.[81] The British ambassador noted ten days following the fire, "In every street that leads away from the centre of town can been seen here and there, sometimes singly, sometimes in groups, the charred remains of offices, shops, cinemas, bars and depots; almost nothing is left but the structure of the buildings. . . . Perhaps the most remarkable feature is that the fires were, in practically all cases, confined to the buildings actually attacked by rioters; the reason was, no doubt, that nearly all buildings that were fired were of reinforced concrete, with very little wood or brick in them."[82] Within the first few weeks businesses opened temporary premises. Chemla created a makeshift shop in March in what had formerly been the Sa'id Store in the Union building across the street from the Rivoli Cinema. The store stocked the temporary showroom with the "latest" notions and other merchandise from local and international factories.[83] Cicurel announced only a week after the fire that the company had moved to an interim office at 9 Fu'ad Street in the premises of the Hornstein shoe store and by July advertised a sale there on salvaged items.[84] Despite its provisional location, Cicurel claimed that the total destruction of the Cairo store forced the company to relieve from service all of its workers and employees by the beginning of March.[85] Other burned stores made similar ad hoc arrangements in less damaged buildings that survived the fire.[86] Stores that suffered less damage, such as Gattegno, advertised that they remained open and posted their hours of operation.[87]

Within the first several months of the fire, the Egyptian state offered loans toward rebuilding establishments, not compensation for damages.[88] Rebuilding credit was most likely available to large, well-connected businesses rather than the smaller shops and bars owned by single proprietors, which in any case could not "possibly incur further debts on top of the heavy losses they have already sustained."[89] Riot insurance had protected only the largest businesses, such as Cicurel.[90] The Free Officers, who took power in July in the midst of the reconstruction negotiations, slowly consolidated the new state during Cairo's rebuilding. Although land reform began in 1952, the regime initially focused on the eradication of British colonial power rather than of foreign capital more generally. It even granted incentives to foreign companies, a political move that facilitated rebuilding the city along its previously existing lines.[91]

Cicurel and Chemla, at least, rebuilt themselves within the year, using the occasion to design even more "modern" store premises.[92] Chemla used part of the old structure of the building that remained standing and opened at the end of December 1952 (see Figure 21). Its original architectural firm executed the new design—its "façade inspired by a rigorous classicism at the same time as a

maquette des architectes EDREI et BALIAN
réalisation de l'ingénieur Chaker ARIDA
cliché des Etablissements OHANNESS

VUE D'ENSEMBLE DES NOUVEAUX « GRANDS MAGASINS CHEMLA »

situés rue Fouad el Awal, — LE CAIRE

Figure 21. Rebuilt premises of Chemla's Fu'ad Street store in Cairo. *L'Egypte nouvelle*, no. 443 (26 December 1952), front cover.

very contemporary modernism"—that provided 1,600 square meters of selling space.[93] One of Cicurel's modernizations was the installation of air conditioning, and its new building had a clean, modernist facade of tall, four-story columns of inset windows rising above the ground-floor display vitrines.[94] Bamco, another shop for women's wear, celebrated its official reopening on October 1, 1952, in new premises on Muhammad Farid Street that also featured "light-colored furniture, contemporary lighting, air conditioning, and smell of new construction."[95]

State officials of the new, revolutionary regime toured Cicurel to mark its grand reopening in November 1952.[96] Local press coverage of the event particularly illustrates the public attitude toward downtown commerce in the aftermath of the fire and regime change. *L'Egypte nouvelle* hailed the store's "resurrection at the end of Fu'ad Street" as "more and better than the sensational opening of the winter 1952 season."[97] It was "a necessity . . . an equilibrium reestablished and thus found again." The article lauded the late Moreno Cicurel as "one of the first to introduce here strict probity as far as commerce is concerned. For him commerce was not the art of conning the customer but very humbly and in all goodness a service rendered to the community [*la collectivité*] and the client, a friend in which he could no more risk losing either the respect nor the confidence that he had worked so hard to gain." The Cicurel sons had continued to apply their father's "magic formula" in this "intimate aspect of the business" and prospered "incredibly." Escorted by Salvator Cicurel, touring officials ʿAbd al-Hadi Ghazali, the governor of Cairo; Muhammad Sabri Maʿmur, the minister of commerce and industry; and Bikbashi Ahmad Anwar, special delegate of President General Muhammad Naguib, posed for photographs in the refurbished interior. Several hours after the tour by the official state delegates, Sagh Fathi Nada of the Tariff Office inspected the store; he searched all of the merchandise counters and certified the clarity of labeling each item's origin and price. The article cited his declaration that, "a business such as this cannot but be in compliance with the law that protects the interests of the public and those of the merchants." The magazine added that the opening was attended by the fashionable *mondain* of the city, who flocked to the streets in front of the reopened store.[98] Such official tours underlined the importance of Cairo's refurbished commerce to Egyptian public culture in the early years of the new regime.[99]

The rebuilding of the downtown, and especially its centerpiece, Fuʿad Street, marked an early effort to delineate a postcolonial urban space in which commerce, with its elegant, imported merchandise, was accessible to a broader group of Egyptians than under the old regime. In this newly conceptualized space, territorial sovereignty took pressure off the old-regime economic-nationalist focus on product nationality; instead focus shifted to the ability of the nation to attract global merchandise. This is especially visible in a January 1954 *al-Musawwar* profile of Fu'ad Street after its refurbishment.[100] The article explicitly detailed the diversity and profusion of commercial activity on the street by enumerating, censuslike, its businesses and institutions, including its 259 stores, of which 30 were "large shops or department stores," 86 cloth merchants, and 35 shoe stores, and compared Fu'ad Street to the major shopping streets in metropolitan capitals: Fifth Avenue in New York, Oxford Street in London, and Rue Royale in Paris. Equal to them in beauty, Fu'ad Street is the "one street in the world that brings together the American Indian and the Czechoslovakian with the Japanese, and the Chinese with the Norwegian, and the Dutch with the Latin American, all of them together. How is that possible? . . . You will meet them in every corner of the street. They exist in the shape of merchandise inside the shops that line the sides of the street." Cosmopolitan in its trade rather than its traders, the rebuilt street now provided the profusion of global goods "to all tastes and all pockets" in Egypt, thanks to the state's investment in the renovation of the downtown district. "The municipality of Cairo bears the cost of renovating Fu'ad Street after the fire, in terms of money, building materials, and labor, [in an amount] sufficient to build a small model city of 40,000 people," according to one of the engineers.

The postcolonial success of the rebuilt downtown, the article contended, also sprang from the commitment of the street's merchants to the public good. "The Egyptian merchants take a great interest in trade not out of greed or avarice, but out of service to the Egyptian economy and to the Egyptian consumer. They are content with a small profit and even bearing loss at certain times." The growing emphasis on the public good of commerce as an economic sacrifice rather than the organization of modern social services, which received praise in the interwar years, coincided with a new historical memory of commerce's urban development. In contrast to earlier dual-city depictions, the article described the bifurcation of domestic commerce as a local process of natural growth, one that occurred in the nineteenth century, long before the British occupation. "The story begins in the Ghuriyya, the original location for the capital's merchants. There began the story of Egypt's commerce more than one thousand years ago. . . . Then the chief merchants [*shahbanda-*

rat al-tujjar ay mashayik al-tijara] split into two groups in the era of Khedive 'Abbas [1848–1854]. Some among them oriented toward Muski Street, or 'the city [*al-madina*]' in the language of the locals, and some of them headed for Fu'ad Street in the downtown, which extends from 'Ataba al-Khadra' Square to Fu'ad Street."[101] Today, however, "all roads of the city lead to Fu'ad Street." The article's photographs and captions featured some of the street's commercial highlights, subtly weaving discourses of nationality into its description of the built topography. It depicted the early and prestigious yet foreign-accented department stores of Cicurel and Chemla as well as the "Egyptian Textile Company, founded by Muhammad Rizq, the first Egyptian to open a store on Fu'ad Street," and "the Shahir Company, one of the street's newest stores," which sold a variety of durable consumer goods, including refrigerators, radios, and furniture.[102] Accounts of the rebuilt downtown do not mention the small shops once owned by Maltese, Greeks, and Cypriots.

A NEW SOCIAL REALISM: COMMERCIAL SPACE
IN MID-1950S CULTURAL TEXTS

The ability of the state and public officials to regulate the health of private consumption among Egyptians marked a new moment of storytelling about commerce and the space of the city evident in several Egyptian films and cartoons in 1954. These films were striking for their focus on actual department-store premises of Cairo's rebuilt downtown and the extensive use of real city streets and urban transportation as their settings. The realistic location helped ground and concretize the new films' portrayal of a paternalistic and helpful state. Kamal al-Shaykh's 1954 film *Haya aw mawt* (*Life or Death*) utilized the search for a dress at a Cairo department store to mark new configurations of urban community in the middle 1950s. The social-realist film was based on a true story and was the first Egyptian movie shot completely on site in the streets of Cairo.[103] The film juxtaposes two shopping excursions gone awry. In the first, the father, Ahmad Ibrahim (played by 'Imad Hamdi) buys for his eight-year-old daughter a new dress from Hannaux, a well-established department store located on what had been Antikhana Street (then Muhammad Bassiuni Street) in downtown Cairo, on the occasion of a religious holiday (see Figure 22). His wistful gaze into the store window at the dress underlines that he has recently lost his job at a firm in the building next door to the department store; as he has not received his severance pay or found a new job, he must hock his wristwatch to purchase the dress. Gazing from the sidewalk into the window display, he visualizes his daughter taking the place of the store's mannequin, adorned in the dress, and resolves to make the sacrifice to purchase it. When later his daughter naively asks for the matching shoes and bag to complete the outfit (her old shoes had completely worn out, leaving her with an exposed nail in one sole), Ahmad feels ashamed of his limited means. Arguing with his wife, who then leaves for her parents' home, he suffers a heart attack. His daughter, Samira, goes to the pharmacy for medicine, thereby initiating the film's second, and much more complicated, shopping excursion.

Finding the local pharmacy closed for the holiday, Samira must navigate across Cairo to a twenty-four-hour pharmacy in 'Ataba Square to fill the prescription. After an arduous trip on foot and by tram from her neighborhood on the edge of the city to the square, she has barely enough money for her purchase. More seriously, the pharmacist realizes, once she has left, that he accidentally mixed the medicine incorrectly, making it lethal rather than revitalizing. As Samira heads home unaware that she carries poison for her father, the pharmacist undertakes a massive search of the city for her, ultimately recruiting ordinary citizens and a contingent of civil servants, including police officers and public radio announcers. In an incisive discussion of the film's civic nostal-

Figure 22. Detail of an advertisement for Hannaux's Cairo store, showing photographs of the front display windows with child-sized mannequins and the second-floor toy department. Pedestrians and a traffic police officer are visible in front of the store. Photographs that depicted stores and goods as they were used in real life in actual city streets became increasingly common in media advertising as well as in film during the 1950s. *Life or Death*'s social realism derived from its willingness to feature Hannaux's actual store premises, window displays, and signage in its footage, a trend that reinforced the documentary style of commercial marketing and a broader cultural emphasis on the concrete postcolonial city. Even after the Cairo Fire, Hannaux continued to be a popular destination for holiday gifts. *Le progrès égyptien—Almanach*, 1953, n.p.

gia in its portrayal of the police of early "Republican officialdom," Joel Gordon notes the film "garnered great success both at home and at international festivals. . . . In *Life or Death* Kamal al-Shaykh captured the civic sensibilities of a generation that saw the nation moving forward. There is nothing particularly 'revolutionary' about the story, except that the police are here not engaged in political activity in the least, nor in crimes that, however universal, needed to be more comfortably set in a royalist, prerevolutionary past."[104]

There is a seriality about consumption in the film, as it opens with the declaration that "when it is the time of the ʿ*id* [Muslim feast holiday], the noise of the city increases and its people head to the streets to go to shops to buy clothes and gifts for their relatives and friends." The camera finds many people shopping the windows and counters of the department stores of the downtown streets.[105] The father's former employer tells his own daughter that he will be buying her a dress, with matching shoes and purse. Samira's trip from pharmacy to pharmacy takes her by a wide array of commercial premises bustling with people preparing for the feast. Ultimately, the importance of state officials to the interception of the adulterated commodity helped signal a new mediator in the relationship between commerce and private consumption: shopping would be dangerous and potentially lethal unless protected and policed by government officials.

The film is fundamentally concerned with the protection of individual identity amidst anxiety about mobility and migration in the vast and complex space of a burgeoning city. At several points in the film, Cairo's population of two and a half million people is mentioned as a deterrent to locating the girl or her ill father, and the problems become almost insurmountable when it is discovered that the family has moved from their old home to a new neighborhood and no one (the doctor; the doorman, or *bawwab*; the small businesses in the street) has their new address. The film opens with shots that pan across the skyline and down the streets of Cairo, while the narrator announces that the bustling life in Cairo never ceases. The police chief despairs of being able to find the father to protect him, wondering how they will locate him among "all the thousands of people named Ahmad Ibrahim" residing in the city; in fact it is only because his name resembles that of an important criminal (Muhammad Ibrahim) wanted by the police that they take up the search at all. Once under way, the hunt depends on technologies and circuits of connection through the city: telephones and police microphones, hospital and pharmaceutical records, tram tickets, radio broadcasts, and the visual circulation of objects (bottles being carried by young girls). Nevertheless, the city emerges in the film as conquerable and knowable: able to be navigated by an eight-year-old girl, the city becomes legible through people, such as helpful police patrols, sympathetic taxi and tram drivers, bystanders who provide directions and temporary escort through the streets, and public officials who can instantly recall all the possible itineraries between ʿAtaba and the girl's neighborhood, listing each street served by various tramlines. Even the department store windows are filmed as they reflect people in the streets in front of them.

Cars, telephones, radios, display windows, and consumption, then, all work to shrink the city and render it a network of relationships rather than an alienating congeries of unconnected communities. The intersection of a focus on mobility in urban space and the ambivalence about consumption—that it is an act that can both link and alienate people; an act that can nourish life and relationships or kill them—makes this film a particularly powerful refiguring of the politics of colonial, urban consumption in the old-regime period. This was not the solitary and specular stroll of the flaneur Baudelaire used to render legible the nineteenth-century Western city. French depictions of the post-Haussmann Paris landscape dwelled on the anonymity offered by wide sidewalks, new forms of transportation, and barriers such as plate glass that emotionally separated city residents despite their increased physical proximity.[106] Samira's purposeful journey, although undertaken alone, only succeeds because of the assistance of a variety of fellow residents, both officials and ordinary dwellers in the city. As the film's title suggests, *Life or Death* points to an urgency to map and navigate the city in the post-1952 political order. Shopping for pharmaceuticals as a spatial practice, one that here is deeply dependent on a series of social interactions with strangers, is a distinctive way to apprehend and thus appropriate the postcolonial city.

The depiction of commercial space strikingly echoes older historical discourses about danger from the adulteration of commodities and their misuse. At one point in the film, the medicine bottle is broken, and a bystander leads Samira to a bar where the medicine-poison is poured into an emptied-out wine bottle. Shortly thereafter on the street, the wine bottle is snatched out of her hand by a drunk, who tries to consume it in the privacy of a car parked in a garage. The mixing of pharmaceuticals, poison, and alcohol as commodities in a series of mislabeled bottles being tracked by dragnets of Cairo police harkens back to actual colonial police campaigns in the 1930s and 1940s. The old-regime police force, headed by British officials until 1946, directly combated the sale of narcotic drugs, such as hashish, opium, and heroin, by pharmacies owned by locally resident foreigners who used their juridical immunity to market the illegal substances.[107] Thomas Russell, the commandant of the Cairo police (and supervisor of Richard Giles), estimated in 1929 that "about half a million Egyptians or one quarter of the male population between the ages of 20 and 30 were addicts."[108] Russell concluded that one response of these groups to the drying up of the narcotics trade was to drink an adulterated form of boiled tea, known as black tea.

> Actually the expression is a misnomer as the blackness is not a characteristic of the actual tea but is caused by the various adulterant matters added to the original tea and by the method of preparation. The basis of this, so-called, black tea is the cheapest imported tea, generally of Japanese origin[;] . . . unscrupulous dealers then add to it large quantities of other substances. . . . The commonest adulterant substances are the leaves of the Sunt Tree, Melokhia leaves, the skins of beans and used tea leaves which are collected from hotels, cafés, ships in harbour, etc., and then dyed and roasted.[109]

The preparation and consumption of black tea became a major public health and police concern in the late 1930s, in part because it challenged a consumption practice that the British saw as central to their cultural self-image, and also in part because it made use of discarded and adulterated consumption waste. Rural officials particularly worried about the consumption of black tea undermining the social control of labor in agriculture. The addiction was reportedly so powerful that peasants cut food from their budgets to spend money on tea, and many began "stealing daily from the crops in the fields where they work so that they can purchase tea."[110] Aziz Abaza Bey, administrative officer in 1938 of the "badly addicted" Fayyum Province, produced a thirty-page report on black tea and its "lamentable effect on the fellaheen."[111] Even when a report by the Egyptian Ministry of Public Health, based on "the results of thorough and careful scientific analysis," concluded that black tea contained levels of tannin and caffeine no higher than infused tea, British and rural officials continued to decry the practice.[112] A decade and a half later, tearooms, that not coincidentally often served as much whisky as tea, were among the highest-profiled targets of the Cairo Fire. The attack on Groppi on Antikhana Street, near Hannaux Department Store and beneath the Greek Club, lasted almost two hours under the eyes of police.[113]

Other cultural texts from the period focused on the complicated task of policing commerce in authentic department-store premises. The 1954 film

Banat Hawwa' (*Daughters of Eve*) was set in a fictionalized, all-women Cairo department store called the Youth and Beauty Department Store, although the opening credits prominently declared that all the fashion creations and models featured in the film had been provided by the actual Chemla department store.[114] A comedy rather than a social-realist drama, several scenes were nevertheless shot in the streets of Cairo, and the numerous scenes on the department store floor included women shopping for lingerie and perfume among modernist glass display cases and well-dressed mannequins and a series of fashion shows at the store. The theme of policing commerce was central to the plot, with karate-skilled saleswomen instructed to chase and capture a thief on the store floor. Much of the film's comedy hinges on the futile attempts of salesclerks to monitor the consumer fantasies and wishful delusions that customers bring into the store. In one scene, a store employee and a customer are confused for mannequins.[115]

In a similar way, a *Ruz al-yusuf* cartoon appearing at roughly the same time set its critique of the monitoring of commercial culture explicitly in the Cicurel Department Store (see Figure 23). The cartoon depicted an *ifrangi* woman customer, scantily dressed in a short skirt, high heels, and a low-cut, sleeveless shirt, trying on a pair of sheer stockings in the women's lingerie department. Behind the counter stood a saleswoman, slightly more modestly dressed than the customer and depicted with blond hair to suggest her cosmopolitan status, and a uniformed male, probably Nubian, assistant or porter. In front of the counter, a turbaned *shaykh* literally drooled over the customer's nylon-attired legs. The caption reads, "Shaykh Matluf at Cicurel. The saleswoman says: 'Sir [*ya sayyidna al-shaykh*], the men's underwear department is on the third floor!'"[116] Appearing in a magazine whose editor, Ihsan 'Abd al-Quddus, supported the regime,[117] the cartoon is a dense cultural text that can be read on many different levels. The explicit naming of the store, its focus on nylon stockings, and the depiction of the moral danger posed by commercial space demonstrate how centrally these issues continued to be connected in this crucial period of economic and political transition. Catalyst of the conflict in the cartoon, the *shaykh* personified the conservative 'ulama', whom the new secular state was attempting to discredit as "forces of reaction."[118] Having successfully crushed the more radical Muslim Brothers in the past several years, Nasser moved to neutralize the mainstream 'ulama' after 1955 when he abolished the shari'a (Islamic law) courts and began the reorganization of al-Azhar University.[119] The blond saleswoman, representing the cosmopolitan salesclerks forced out

Figure 23. Customers received inadequate protection in Cicurel's hosiery department. *Ruz al-yusuf*, no. 1476 (24 September 1956), 19.

of their jobs by the implementation of Egyptianization programs at joint-stock companies such as Cicurel, can only weakly fend off the perverted *shaykh*'s harassment of the woman customer. The caricature of the Nubian porter as a small monkey suggests he too is ineffective as a protector of the sales floor.[120] The linking of the "nylon woman" as symbol of social decadence and the named specificity of the store thus represented a new moment of truth telling in the middle 1950s. The absence of effective monitoring of retail space helped justify the state's entry into commerce.

EVACUATION! POLITICAL AND CULTURAL CLARIFICATION IN THE AFTERMATH OF URBAN RENOVATION

The evacuation agreement to remove British troops from the canal zone, the site of lingering colonial rule in the nation, was signed in October 1954, and the last British troops left Egypt in mid-June 1956. The state and most Egyptians considered this a momentous culmination of the national struggle. Popular celebrations coincided with a strong state propaganda effort to consolidate a new ideological vision for the fully independent state, one that emphasized its modernity, industrial and technological strengths, and nonaligned status in global politics. The state's plans to build a spectacularly high dam at Aswan exemplified the new focus. The regime appointed Fathi Radwan to establish the Ministry of National Guidance in 1956 as part of the effort to articulate and spread the newly emerging philosophy.[121] For individual citizens, the state recycled mandates for a rational and unified consumption order. Playing on the dual meaning of *jala'* as "evacuation" and "clarification," mass cultural texts called for a clarification of the cacophony of local styles to accompany the formal evacuation of British troops from Port Sa'id. In January 1955 *al-Musawwar* magazine published a call for "Our Need for Unity of Dress," one that echoed its earlier campaign in 1937.[122] The article proclaimed that "we want a clarification [*jala'*] of the chaos of Egyptian dress": "In Egypt, there exists a scrapbook [*kashkul*] of popular dress that cannot be described by less than chaos in the clothing of individuals and groups in the villages and cities, and among men and women and in all classes, to the point that in different Egyptian environments tastes differ widely and customs and orientations multiply." The article cited the findings of sociologists that "differences within a group in dress lead to differences in many aspects of its social and national life. Dress is one of the fundamentals of individual and national personality, and it has great influence on the soul [*nafs*]." The Ministry of Social Affairs had recently formed a committee charged with unifying dress, which had studied numerous opinions and suggestions on the subject, including the examples of Turkey and Iran, which both successfully prioritized dress as part of a social reform agenda. "It is necessary for us, as Egypt has entered a post-evacuation era, that the country be concerned about dress reform and abolish the random chaos that currently exists." Photographs of Egyptians in different kinds of dress illustrated the urgency for reform, including a row of six men wearing the variety of sartorial pairings still popular in Egypt: "an eloquent picture of the carnival of dress currently present in Egypt . . . a galabiya with a skullcap, then western [*gharbi*] dress with the tarbush, and galabiya with the turban; galabiya with the tarbush, the galabiya with a hat! and finally the galabiya with a western coat and the Maghrabi tarbush." Unlike the candid shots of street scenes that framed the magazine's 1937 call for sartorial unity, the 1956 version had a static, staged quality, much like Radwan's men in the museum, described in Chapter 1.

The country mounted extensive festivities to mark the British evacuation in June 1956. Urban parades included decorated cars sponsored by companies to promote "Egypt's economic renaissance" that would accompany the final eradication of colonialism.[123] Companies producing cotton clothing, soap, oil, and nylon, in addition to local banks, publishing houses, and insurance companies, used female depictions of liberty (such as Marianne, a French emblem, or the women's demonstrations of 1919) and oversized commercial products to herald the new postcolonial order. The Egyptian Products Sales Company, "participating since the dawn of the renaissance in the path of economic independence," designed a tableau of "the great hero" Ahmad 'Urabi demanding the "people's rights" in front of 'Abdin Palace. Shurbaji's float featured an enormous model of a female leg, cut from the thigh down, toes pointed, and adorned by a nylon stocking.[124] Evacuation festivities included a window display contest among large stores and companies, many of whom depicted "the liberation of Egyptian territory" as a union of the country's cultural duality.[125] One window displayed a "naïve painting" of *feluccas* on the Nile next to "a black and white drawing of a modern street in Cairo." In another, a contemporary Egyptian soldier faced a pharaonic figure against a backdrop with the Pyramids drawn on one side and a silhouette of Cairo on the other. What was judged the "most original window" presented "two women in black cardboard, one wearing a black and red *melaya* and the other a short dress in the colours of the Revolution[, who] are standing harmoniously next to a palm tree."[126] These combinations of *baladi* and *ifrangi* Egypt represented popular support for the revolution's self-view that it had healed the contradictions and doubled identity wrought by colonialism.

Although proclaimed as the end of colonialism in local parades, evacuation was eclipsed in the coming months by Nasser's dramatic nationalization of the Suez Canal and the war and sanctions that followed it. The Egyptian state nationalized British and French interests, and many Jewish businesses, in 1956 following the Suez War, which pitted Egypt against Britain, France, and Israel. Egyptianization intensified after 1956, and an Egyptian law required all foreign commercial companies operating in Egypt to become Egyptian joint-stock companies with a majority of Egyptian capital and management in 1957. The state sequestered Belgian interests in early 1961 and nationalized many companies in June and July 1961—"large- and medium-size concerns of the modern sector as they [were] relatively easy to manage and provide[d] sources of profit for the State and employment for officers and technocrats."[127] Previously restricted to transport and irrigation infrastructure and a few military and petroleum factories, "public ownership of the means of production . . . had extended to all financial institutions, public utilities, and transport (except taxis), and to almost all industrial establishments of significant size, to large construction and haulage firms, department stores, and big hotels" by 1963.[128] The state's Economic Organization (also called the Economic Agency or the Economic Development Organization), established in January 1957, came to control the new government holdings, which gradually included most major firms, even Bank Misr and its subsidiaries. State ownership only slowly altered actual management, however. Generally, "the participation and intervention of the public enterprise (or the Economic Agency) in the various firms under its supervision resembled the intervention of a major shareholder."[129] Firms were subject to the old company laws until 1964, and many public-sector companies continued to run much as they had in the past.[130] The year 1966 saw the first law "promulgated to bring about a total reorganization of public sector firms."[131] Such laws completed a restructuring of commerce already well under way through the events of the 1940s and early 1950s. New Egyptian nationality laws more narrowly defined the requirements for being Egyptian in 1958.[132] Thus, the waves of sequestration and nationalization between 1956 and 1966 altered ownership, and to a lesser extent management, of many firms, although many of the major changes and reorganizations did not occur until well into the 1960s.

As one of the targets of sequestrations that followed the nationalization of the Suez Canal in 1956, many department stores owned by French, British, or Jewish subjects underwent changes of management of varying magnitudes. Orosdi-Back, funded by French capital, was sequestered in early November 1956.[133] Chemla was put under sequestration at the same time, although by the end of the month the special administrator for the stores reported that the "store had opened under a genuine Egyptian administration" and would hold a "special display" of its designer winter clothing on December 2.[134] The state also sequestered Cicurel and ORECO at that time; by the following April, majority ownership passed to the Gabri family, a Muslim merchant family that claimed that its control of the "foreign company" helped fulfill Nasser's program of economic nationalism.[135] It is difficult to know the full impact of sequestration and nationalization on the stores, although many remained open during most of the sequestration. The sequestration administrator advertised the opening of the stores prominently in the local press; on November 19, 1956, for example, "all of the stores" of the Benzion Company reopened.[136] Some sequestered firms continued under the management of former owners, who were paid a salary, although a number reported heavy losses.[137]

The ʿAdès (ʿAdas) company claimed to be "profitable and active and expanding in 1956, [and that it had] suffered grave losses due to the sequestration" that lasted from 1956 to 1960.[138] A chain of department stores in Cairo, Tanta, and Fayyum famous for its textiles, the company had been operated by David ʿAdès and his sons, most of whom held British citizenship, since at least the 1930s.[139] The company by 1956 was "one of the oldest and largest in the soft goods wholesale business in Egypt. . . . It had a subscribed capital of £E920,000, a gross turnover of some £E4 million annually, and a staff of some 350 persons."[140] On November 1, 1956, the firm was sequestered, its senior partner was interned, and "shortly afterwards" the partners in Egypt were expelled from the country. The business came under the purview of a special administrator (*haris khas*) appointed by the state. It remained in sequestration until April 1960. "The partners were unable to return to take over, did not succeed in finding a management team of adequate calibre, and were prevented, by Egyptian regulations, from arranging for an immediate liquidation to prevent further losses being incurred. Their only alternative was to sell."[141] Upon the firm's release from sequestration in 1960, the family attempted to sell the trade of the business (on terms "very unsatisfactory to the proprietors") to the Société des Nouveautés Benzion, a popular, well-established local department store chain, but several ʿAdès partners were resequestered in 1961 before the sale could close.[142] The ʿAdès store was eventually nationalized, but continued to expand in the 1960s into "a national chain . . . [with] a Daoud Addes store in every village," some employees recounted later. It became "a huge warehouse store where they sell everything, from refrigerators on down to pillows. . . . Profit was no longer an issue, and [salesclerks] didn't care if they sold anything. In fact, they [hid] the dresses in cupboards since people [came] to steal."[143]

Once Law 138 of 1961 nationalized even those stores owned by Egyptian subjects, such as Sednaoui or the Gabri-owned Cicurel, the state assigned administration to military officers, and eventually local government factories supplied most of their merchandise. Scholars have often considered nationalization a rupture in the history of Egyptian commerce. According to Samir Raafat, "In July 1961 [when] Egypt's major department stores were nationalized, Mr. Elie Sednaoui, the then-director of S&S Sednaoui et Fils, was given an indefinite leave of absence. An army officer replaced him and the age of drab counters and khaki-coloured co-operatives began."[144] In addition to the owners, who so closely controlled their department stores, many of the cosmopolitan commercial employees ultimately left employment at the stores and eventually the country. The exact timing of this and its effects on the stores awaits further study, however. Anecdotal and oral-history evidence suggests that many of the lower-level "cosmopolitan" employees, many of whom held Egyptian citizenship, left more gradually in the 1960s than studies of company administrators indicate; many continued to work in the stores for some time, bringing a certain continuity to the stores and their marketing and merchandising practices in the era of nationalization, at least until 1966.[145]

SHOPPING IN THE STATE'S NEW RETAIL SECTOR, 1957–1963

The 1956 Suez War and the international economic blockade and domestic sequestrations that followed it changed the international context of trade with Egypt, leading to a steep rise in prices and shortages of imports throughout 1957 and 1958. In this period popular critique blamed greedy merchants for fickle prices and called on the state to make basic goods available to citizens at reasonable and fixed prices. "*Ghala*'," or rising prices, became the new political focus of consumers and politicians alike, its resonance with evacuation (*jala*') poignantly capturing the self-sacrifice that Egypt's bid for complete independence from colonialism entailed. A Women's Committee for the Control of Prices worked in Cairo neighborhoods to monitor and thus standardize all the prices in a single district and to prevent people from purchasing "basic necessities" such as shoes, men's shirts, cloth, butter, sugar, rice, tea, coffee, and medicines on the black market.[146] Department stores and other sequestered businesses continued to purvey stylish clothing and luxury goods to Egyptians although they slightly shifted the social context in which they marketed their merchandise. In contrast to the elegant models of interwar advertising, department-store promotions in the late 1950s frequently depicted satisfied housewives, adorned in aprons and engaged in housework, using merchandise available from the store.[147] The stores continued, however, to emphasize their status as emporiums of vast stocks of high-quality goods. The value of the stores in the new public sector lay in its conquering of their commercial cachet and capturing the revenues that could be drawn from it. A special issue of *al-Ahram* celebrating the Arab nationalism of the United Arab Republic ran an advertisement in 1959 for the by-then Egyptianized department store Cicurel (see Figure 24). The advertisement depicts an elegant woman gazing at an enormous framed portrait of the Cicurel store rendered in complete

isolation from its surrounding commercial district; a double-columned listing
of the categories of merchandise offered in the store lies displaced outside the
portrait's frame and the view of the woman consumer. A trophy for the new
nationalizing economy, Cicurel posed as a testament to the state's power and

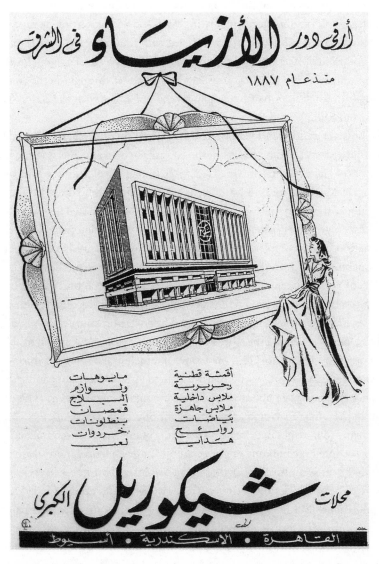

Figure 24. The Egyptianized Cicurel store flattened into a symbol of consumer elegance for the
new regime. *Al-Ahram*, 1959, special issue on the United Arab Republic, 21.

progress, the store's double enframing and one dimensionality starkly pointing to the state's attempt to control, clarify, and make static the store's earlier commercial identity.[148] Such nationalized department stores remained very popular and successful in the 1960s, holding large sales that were attended by many women and lower-middle class shoppers; some of these sales were featured in the local press because of their popularity.[149] By the end of the 1960s, however, the elegant old-regime stores, increasingly stocked with government-produced, cheaply priced goods, could not keep pace with the state's larger retail outlets that purveyed similar merchandise. In 1969, for example, the Egyptian Products Sales Company, with its vast complex of branch stores throughout the country, brought in more than twice the daily revenue of stores such as Cicurel, Hannaux, and Salon Vert.[150]

The state continued to promote the production and sale of local textiles and footwear as building blocks in the country's postcolonial economic independence. The governor of Giza, General ʿUthman Khalil, and the minister of trade, Dr. Muhammad Abu Nasir, were among officials who attended the 1957 opening of the Shurbaji store in Zamalik, which was promoted as a solution to the city's high prices (*ghalaʾ*) and the persistence of "foreign manufacturers in the nation."[151] The press covered the throngs of women's groups that attended the opening week, including the Union of Women of the Republic and the Red Crescent Society, likening them to "a Woman's Demonstration," and reporting on the collective satisfaction with and excitement over the quality of Shurbaji's textiles and especially its nylon stockings. The governor, captured by photographers closely inspecting the stocks of men's underwear and running his hands over women's nylon stockings on a store mannequin, announced during the ceremonies that he would send his own wife to visit the new store and encourage her to proselytize about its products among women citizens. The president of the Union of Women of the Republic offered congratulations to Munir Shurbaji. "Your exhibit is considered the pride of the East. The economist Talʿat Harb anchored the building of our economic independence, and you are completing his mission by constructing Egypt's industrial greatness in its modern history."[152] Shurbaji's productive capacities drew the attention of a wide array of politicians. Delegates of the Chamber of Deputies toured the Shurbaji factory in Imbaba in early January 1958 as part of a series of investigations into the "cornerstones" of the Egyptian economy.[153] A crowd of delegates, including the elderly *shaykh* ʿAbd al-Latif Diraz and the nation's first woman parliamentarian, Rawiya ʿAtiyya, watched closely as Munir Shurbaji stretched a pair of women's nylon stockings to show its durability and sheerness and displayed a summer suit fabric "that competes with its likes from Swiss factories." The "Egyptian housewife's budget will no longer be unbalanced," 'Atiyya proclaimed. "The Egyptian girl will preserve her elegance and grace thanks to what the Shurbaji factories produce by way of nylon clothes, mixed cotton clothes, and nylon stockings. All of them combine good taste, durability, and fair price."[154] Indeed, the reporter concluded that the factory was "a great path that aided us in the victory over colonizing countries with their economic blockade, so that you may lift up your hand to the sky and respond to the call, 'God is great and glory be to Egypt.'"[155] Small-scale, domestic footwear production of famous European styles also expanded in the rebuilt downtown commercial zone in Cairo, and the press heralded such enterprises as nationalist economic responses to the new political reality. The downtown expansion of the Babil Shoe Company, a workshop founded by a young, Upper Egyptian shoemaker and producing knock-offs of women's shoes made by the Swiss firm Bally, drew such praise.[156] Within the next few years, the firm supplied shoes to "most of the large stores in the capital" and began to "conquer international markets."[157] A cooperative nationalist and beneficiary of the economic reforms of the 1940s and 1950s, the company's enterprising owner testified in al-Ahram in 1959 to having lowered his prices by 20 percent in keeping with Nasser's call to reduce the cost of living, and he explicitly linked al-Babil's growth to the Nasserist promotion of the national economy.

Even the physical space of downtown commerce was part of a new imagined geography by the close of the decade, one that had returned to the in-between quarters of the city in the context of postcolonialism and the Cold War. A feature article in al-Ahram in 1959, for example, marveled at the density of commercial activity in the kilometer-long Muski Street: "two hundred million Egyptian pounds and a million people [a month] in a street eight hundred years old; . . . international manufactures and trade with all parts of the world in the richest street in the Middle East."[158] The article positioned Muski Street as not a passageway between two worlds of consumption but instead the nodal point for the conjunction of widely diverse and dense webs of baladi and ifrangi commerce in Cairo. Although parts of the street were like a "river of banknotes" and its wealth comparable to "Gorky Street in Moscow or Wall Street in New York," the Muski also held "the old flea market [suq al-kantu] which houses the trade in cheap notions" and "one of the oldest markets in the world, the Khan al-Khalili market." A center of gravity for the city's commerce, the Muski had preserved its "good reputation" while many local merchants flocked to "the civilization of the mannequin, nylon, and neon lights . . . in the streets of 26th of July [ex-Fu'ad], Muhammad Farid, Sulayman, and Qasr al-Nil." Finally "defeated" thirty years later, these merchants "acknowledged that the Muski was the most firmly established [*rasikh*] pyramid of trade in the world." The article, in a special issue of the newspaper designed to imagine and celebrate the Arab nationalism associated with the newly formed United Arab Republic, was emblematic of the official celebration of the informal urban elasticity that had characterized Cairo for the past fifty years.

The new postcolonial discourse about the public ownership of the private sector, and the upward mobility and aristocratic consumption that it promised, were satirized in a film titled *al-'Ataba' al-khadra'* that appeared in 1959.[159] The film traced the seduction of a *baladi* hotel manager into the underworld of black market corruption and theft. The main characters con salesmen in a series of real businesses in the downtown commercial district, including swindling a jeweler, the Sheffield Silver store, a pharmacy, and the bakery at Groppi. Their ring is based in 'Ataba, and the film opens with a long shot panning the square and following pedestrians, tram cars, and motorized traffic along the streets and around the central plaza. The film climaxes when the hotel manager is duped into purchasing the square itself, an act equivalent to the mythical American fraud of buying the Brooklyn Bridge. Once convinced he is the owner of 'Ataba, with its majestic Tiring Building, wide central park, and lucrative businesses, he begins like a state to administer it: he carefully measures the space, inspects commercial premises, changes the street sign to rename it "'Adila Square, Ltd.," after his wife, and attempts to collect rent from the various municipal services there, including the fire station, post office, and police headquarters. The film's humor lies in the inversion of the current program of claiming public ownership of private companies, as the film's characters privatize the public space of 'Ataba. Its resonance, however, is with the insistent calls for public access to the goods of the city, a sort of democratization of ownership and reframing of the transitional 'Ataba Square as a central point in the city.

The combination of cheap price and modern style of locally produced commodities in the new nationalized economy would have appealed to the family of 'Ismat Ni'man, a government employee in the Electricity Agency who was interviewed about the high cost of living among "the working middle class" in 1957.[160] 'Ismat earned £E28 a month, which he used with difficulty to support his wife and four children between the ages of seven and two, with "a fifth child on the way," living in the Imbaba district of Cairo. They kept meticulous record of their monthly expenses, since they "had to track every millème" to make ends meet. Their major expenses, rent and food, came to nearly £E20. They bought clothing on installment, including the ten pairs of shoes the family required each year and the four dresses of his wife, and paid into a cooperative for major purchases. The tight budget put emotional pressure on the husband, especially about his work clothing that, as a government employee, had to be of "a certain appearance." "You cannot imagine the state of alarm I live in," he told the reporter, "all day in fear of 'the suit' and this 'distinguished' shirt. I fear the moth, the stain, and the tear, so I only wear my 'honored' clothes during very official times of the day." Faced with the difficulty and stress of balancing the household budget, the family called on the government to reduce prices for water, electricity, tram fares, and cinema tickets.

The struggle of lower-level government employees to maintain a middle-class lifestyle on a weak salary became a prominent theme in the popular media during the middle Nasser years.[161] According to Mona Abaza, "Nasserism expanded consumerist appetites for the rising middle classes, which certainly created different markets and circulation of goods."[162] The state's production and distribution of household appliances and *ifrangi* clothing, increasingly sold through its nationalized department stores, were a significant reaction to this trend.[163] Atif Salim's 1963 *Umm al-ʿarusa* (Mother of the Bride), starring ʿImad Hamdi, Tahiya Carioca, and Samira Ahmad, was a film animated by the struggle such government employees faced despite the economic reforms of the first Nasser decade. Much as in his role nearly a decade earlier in *Life or Death*, Hamdi plays a father distressed by his inability to provide the material goods his daughter needs for a socially recognized occasion—a wedding trousseau and furnishings for the new household.[164] He borrows money from a fund he is charged with safeguarding at work to pay for the needed goods. Caught in his fraud, the father is rescued by a friend who has discovered the theft and put his own money in the safe to cover up for the illegal loan—again, a form of communal support and individual self-sacrifice that emerges to provide the new middle-class lifestyle promised by the Revolution.

The middle-class expectations of the family are perhaps most vividly displayed when the groom's family comes to visit. Everyone in the household dons his or her best clothing. The father and eldest son squabble because the son, who has a new suit but no tie, has borrowed the only necktie the father owns. The mother puts on a modest but flattering *ifrangi* dress that just reaches to her knees and a pair of high-heeled pumps. As she struggles to straighten her nylon stockings, she tells her other teenage daughter, "A woman's stockings reflect her status." "What if she doesn't wear any?" the daughter asks. "Then she doesn't have any status," the mother replies. "Then you must buy me some nylons, Mother!" the daughter implores. Once the engagement is made, the daughter and her family set out to purchase the clothing and household furnishings for the new marital home, a project fraught with demands and hostile negotiations about the expectations of what will be purchased (twelve dining chairs, or six?) and who will pay which part of the bill. Even within the bride's family, the levels of tension are high, as the mother pushes for high-quality furnishings while the father attempts to substitute more modest styles and materials to manage the bills. The film follows the father, mother, and bride on an enormous shopping trip that takes them, much as in other recent films, into named Cairo stores to purchase the nuptial goods: the Pontremoli furniture store for the bedroom suite and the dining table, and Gattegno Department Store for cloth, a coffee service, sherbet cups, and even a crystal chandelier. Maison Gattegno was a department store on 'Imad al-Din Street in downtown Cairo selling primarily household furnishings and furniture in *ifrangi* styles, such as dining-room chairs and tables; bedroom sets, including armoires, bed frames, and headboards; and cocktail cabinets. By the 1940s it had diversified into selling a wide range of cloth, women's ready-made clothing, suitcases, hosiery, chandeliers and lighting fixtures, and metal housewares.[165] Gattegno had long specialized in purveying household furnishings for newlyweds. "Going to be married? Read this," a 1940 "Gattegno for Furniture" advertisement proclaimed to brides. "Over the years we have helped hundreds of young married people to start their home furnishing program."[166] In the film, the bride fulfills this advertising call by fully outfitting the new household with products tailored to a middle-class lifestyle. The shopping trip finally ends with the exhausted father slumped in a chair at Gattegno. He pulls off his shoe to rub his aching foot and conspicuously exposes an enormous hole in his own sock.

Trying to make ends meet was of course not an experience new to post-1952 Egyptian society. The struggles of the Egyptian middle classes and especially civil servants to acquire basic necessities had been a driving force of much of the unrest of the 1930s and 1940s. What was new in 1963 was the tone and prominence of the public displays of this struggle. Nasser's revolution had promised that the postcolonial state would ensure a standard of living higher than that experienced by the interwar generation. State efforts to make Egypt's rich commercial spaces accessible to Egyptians of "all tastes and all pockets" ranged from formal sequestration and nationalization to new modes of story-telling about the city and its iconic structures, texts that increasingly featured real streets and real stores. In the new narrative, nylon no longer symbolized artificiality but rather middle-class respectability. Although these strategies reinforced each other, other cultural texts poked fun at these efforts to smooth out the complexities of Egyptian society.

Contrary perhaps to the expectations of many protestors, the Cairo Fire had revealed the deep imbrication of foreign and local aspects of Egyptian society and economy. Its effects on the city were contradictory. While morally freighted, the Cairo Fire did not require an overall reconfiguring of the city's built environment or its building codes, since most of the fires had been con-fined to individual buildings that had been deliberately torched. In the fire's immediate aftermath, the state emphasized the importance of reconstruct-ing the downtown the same as before, although the structure of financing the project through loans rather than direct compensation helped transform the economy along the lines already initiated by Egyptianization programs of the previous half decade. Small Maltese and Cypriot businesses, never possess-ing the same cultural élan of the large department stores and patisserie shops, although perhaps serving an equally wide clientele, could not use loans to rebuild. The department stores' use of the premises of smaller, adjacent firms, such as Hornstein's shoe shop, for temporary locations also suggests the diffi-culty that smaller-scale companies faced in recovering from the damage of the fire and the Egyptianization campaigns that preceded it. Although the fire tar-geted selected parts of the city, its timing, coincident with a growing movement of nationalization, affected Egypt in more drastic ways that recalled the major conflagrations of Salonica (1917) and Izmir (1922), fires that ethnically and socioeconomically remade their entire societies. The urban ecology of Cairo was reimagined in the 1950s to emphasize a new equation of luxury and acces-sibility, to free indigenous businessmen and local consumers from the captivity of colonial commerce. Through this, the city's morseled consumer topography continued to be shaped by nodal points such as Muski Street, ʿAtaba Square, or Fuʾad Street.

CONCLUSION

AN EGYPTIAN EYEWITNESS to the burning of the Casino Badiʿa during the 1952 Cairo Fire reported that the crowd of nearly three thousand Egyptians calmly watched the conflagration "as a spectacle like a film show."[1] The British understood this testimony as proof that the fire had been the conspiratorial work of illegal agents rather than a popular response of the crowd. By contrast, the story reconstructed in this book suggests that the testimony actually reflects the reality of a more complex set of dynamics in urban space, commerce, and film. Interwar and postwar storytelling about the tensions of late colonialism had in fact made extensive use of visual codes lodged in consumption practices and commercial space to explain the contradictory nature of Egyptian development during the past half century. Nylon stockings, *shibshibs*, department-store mannequins, plate-glass windows, trams, and urban sidewalks were often the sites of parables about the effects of colonialism on social relations that played out in short stories, cartoons, novels, photographic collages, and films with wide circulation in Egyptian society. Egyptian cinema in particular had used commercial and spatial practices to construct a more popularized, although not necessarily mass or oppositional, version of nationalist belonging than that which circulated in the more high-cultural writings of intellectuals and in the news columns of the local press. Spectatorship was not an isolated or passive experience, I have argued, but rather a specific, ordinary mode of active engagement with the hybridized culture of the transparent windows of commerce and their mediation of merchandise between merchants and customers, metropolitan producers and local artisans, the public and private realms, and the state and its subjects. The doubling terms through which many postwar cultural texts expressed the deep imbrication of colonial forms into the Egyptian physical and social landscape—the sense that Egyptians were both subjects and objects in the colonial drama—sharpened a sense that anticolonial struggle required self-immolation or some form of collective suicide. The narrative of consumerist politics laid out by *A City Consumed* indicates that watching the 1952 Cairo Fire as a film spectacle represented the connection rather than the alienation of Egyptians to the downtown space of the city.

The book's thesis thus challenges unilateral assessments of commerce and urban space mustered by anticolonial activists to mobilize compatriots in the course of decolonization struggles. Fanon, in a 1961 manifesto on the importance of violence to anticolonial struggle, used the image of "a motionless, Manicheistic world" to attribute the lack of political agency under colonialism to economic captivity. "The immobility to which the native is condemned can only be called into question if the native decides to put an end to the history of colonization—the history of pillage—and to bring into existence the history of the nation—the history of decolonization."[2] Looking back from near the end of Nasser's rule and the Arab defeat of 1967, Anouar Abdel-Malek similarly depicted the Cairo Fire as a false revolution because of the passivity and immobility of local residents in the face of imperial economic exploitation. The city burned, he recalled, "while more than one and a half million persons, the people of Cairo, watched in the streets, chatting or sipping drinks in silence. . . . The people of Cairo stood away from the political scene: they saw no connection between what was put to flames—the modern center of Egypt's capital—and their own destiny. . . . For on that day Cairo was viewed by the Cairenes, and by the Egyptians at large, as no more than the common meeting ground of foreign imperialism and local despotism."[3] Abdel-Malek argued that it was the fifteen years of Nasserist rule after the fire that restored agency and pride to the nation, finally visible when the Egyptian masses rose up to demand that Nasser remain in power despite the crushing military defeat of June 1967. "Gone were the days of passivity. Gone was the feeling of not-belonging. Gone was the lack of identification between a people and its fatherland. The time had finally come for the people of Egypt to come on stage, as fully-fledged actors, and directors-to-be, of its own destiny."[4] The idea that decolonization struggles and the achievement of postcolonial state sovereignty mark a shift from the passive spectatorship of subjects immobilized from the "pillage" of colonialism to that of "fully fledged actors" and "directors of destiny" rests on a discourse of bifurcation that has taken spatial practices of consumption as one of its most vivid manifestations.

This book has instead looked back from the Cairo Fire to chart the creation of a morselized consumer culture that, although spawned in anticolonial politics of contradiction and of self-destruction, was nevertheless a part of the real Egypt of the interwar years. The complex ways urban commercial culture and the commodities it retailed helped materialize community and feelings of belonging in Egypt during the first six decades of the twentieth century challenge easy bifurcations used to construct claims to an authentic national space. In fact, as this book has argued, the Cairo Fire acted much as commercial cinema did as a template to narrate and impose a particular vision of the nation. It was a vision produced in 1930s advertising that depicted cotton as a national unifier, in marketing campaigns for national socks and national stores, and in sexualized images of women's nylon stockings. Like all didactic texts, the fire's message could not be fully implemented in actual practice. It acted as a temporary consolidation of the morseled culture of consumption that developed in the interwar period, launching the restoration of the same city to make it accessible to all citizen-consumers. Thus, the book's linking of the contours of consumer culture across the 1952 dividing line disputes a triumphalist narrative about Nasser's centrality in achieving a postcolonial state.

By the early 1960s, locally made cloth and *ifrangi* footwear had become significant aspects of the Egyptian economy, ordinary people's consumption identities, and new sociopolitical relations. Such locally produced goods mingled with imported items in Egypt's downtown department stores as well as in more *baladi* retail venues, now accessible to a broader range of Egyptian consumers. Many small towns in the Egyptian countryside such as Dayrut, Mit Ghamr, or Shibin al-Kum had become home to a nationalized Bata shoe store and a state-owned branch of the Egyptian Products Sales Company, making a cheap pair of *ifrangi* shoes and a piece of locally produced machine-made cloth increasingly accessible even in provincial areas of the country. As commodities, cloth and shoes had witnessed several shifts in meaning during the past four decades. The ability of silky cloth to bind community—signifying colonial complicity in the 1920s, patriotism in the 1930s, royalist decadence in the 1940s, and hard-won dignity in the 1960s—depended on both the material and the economic relationships among different fabrics in the marketplace. Likewise, the definition of *proper* footwear changed from local, leather slip-ons to more closed and heeled shoes. Political leaders enjoined Egyptians to modernize through the consumption of new footwear, although other elites feared its implications for social control.

While didactic writings offered commodity parables about how consumption should unite the nation, popular consumption operated in more complex registers. Local residents practiced a use of urban space that contradicted a static view of a compartmentalized city. A stylistics of morseling built on the barnacled cultural economies of consumption had taken root in the 1920s and 1930s in city spaces such as the flea market, the premises of local cooperative societies, or Cairo's ʿAtaba Square. Mixed-up dress could be used by the upper classes to signal local connection and authenticity—wearing a tarbush with *ifrangi* suits or a veil with European dresses are two examples. Just as often, however, such morselings of style appealed to poorer Egyptians required to wear *ifrangi* dress to jobs in government offices, upper-class homes, hotels, or commercial premises. Commercial culture frequently translated dualistic identities into single marketing practices, using tools as diverse as bilingual advertising strategies, the cultivation of customers from a range of class and social backgrounds, or local labor to produce "European" goods. While Egyptians could be critical of such morseled styles, they often reworked the official or colonial language of bifurcation into more complex metaphors such as hubs, mirrored pairings, or corporeal embodiment to describe lived practices of space and consumption style. The indeterminacy of interwar styles called forth efforts of clarification, ranging from state-supported retail empires such as the Egyptian Products Sales Company stores to boycotts and urban uprisings. Nevertheless, moments of official clarification never quite took hold on a popular level, perhaps in part because vernacular ways of imagining the nation, in cinema or consumption practices, were at once broader and more nuanced than the dichotomous reactions of colonial collaborator versus loyal traditionalist or of progressive modern versus naive reactionary that nationalists and historians have previously charted as hegemonic for this period. Egyptians as different as Fikri al-Khuli, Fathi Radwan, and Esther Wissa considered consumption a crucial tool in political struggle. A focus on the fluid character of more popular forms of consumption and sociability thus broadens the terrain of the *ifrangi* sphere, thereby challenging a view that Westernization affected only a small elite of parasitical elements and left the majority of Egyptians in possession of an authentic and intact local culture.

Department stores in interwar Egypt dominated the urban spaces they occupied. Brightly lit display windows packed with elegant merchandise were arranged to call out to passersby on the streets, enticing them with bewitching promises of power and influence. Shoppers came to the downtown on different timetables. Upper-class families routinely outfitted their homes and wardrobes with department-store merchandise, whereas members of the middle classes came only for momentous occasions such as the celebration of weddings, births, school matriculation, or a new job. Even poor residents were attracted to the vivid window displays that occupied a space somewhere between the interior and exterior of the store. Downtown shopping districts overlapped with more transitional urban spaces, the *maydan*s and markets in places such as ʿAtaba and Sayyida Zaynab that acted as roundabouts of urban transportation networks and also brought people from different neighborhoods together.

These complex commercial morphologies reflected equally complex trajectories of national belonging. Storeowners and their employees came to Egyptian downtown spaces along many circuits and pathways from different parts of the city, from the countryside, and from various areas of the Mediterranean. Families such as the Cicurels, Sednaouis, Palaccis, or Chemlas defined themselves as Egyptian through an array of social practices, forms of civic participation, and legal mechanisms. Their local roots in old urban neighborhoods modulated the *ifrangi* elegance of their downtown department stores but also pulled in a wide-ranging base of customers that expanded their profitability. Multilingualism and ethnic intermixing dominated the store floors and store shelves of much urban commerce. This cultural mode did not represent the experience of all Egyptians, but it also did not preclude patriotic feelings among its practitioners. Efforts to clarify the ambiguity and freeze the variability in the commercial and national landscape intensified in the 1930s. The development of new national stores established by state-sponsored industrialists emerged in response to the strident boycott rhetoric of the early 1930s and challenged the hegemony of *ifrangi* department stores by offering new definitions of how goods and space could be considered national. Firms such as the Egyptian Products Sales Company called on "citizen consumers" to "only buy what you need from an Egyptian," as the ethnic, religious, and linguistic identities of owners came in the late 1930s and 1940s increasingly to determine "product-nationality."[5] Satirical depictions of Egyptianization in popular films and cartoons set in commercial space continued to disrupt didactic nationalist marketing, however, through the 1950s. Egypt's retail geography, if closely examined for its merchandise, physical space, owners, workers, and shoppers, as this book has done, thus reveals the contingency of definitions of "Egyptian- ness" in the first half of the twentieth century. As Joel Beinin observes, "There can be no unequivocal, transhistorical answer to [the] question [of who is an Egyptian]. Both the question and its answer are historically and socially con- structed cultural categories."[6]

The Egyptian case offers an important case study of the consumerist poli- tics of late colonialism. The axiom that colonial cities are dual cities physically segregated by race and ethnicity rather than by class—that "the consciousness of race, and racial conflict with which it is often associated, is perhaps the major urban manifestation of colonialism"[7]—bears only partially on Egypt's experi- ence of urban space. Although Egypt's cities looked increasingly bifurcated in the early decades of the twentieth century, built forms masked a more complex interweaving created by the mobility of residents. The colonial cities of Egypt thus only partially resembled those of North Africa and other settler colonial societies. Scholars and nationalists have used the model of the dual city in ways that have reinforced the implicit telos of modernization theory long after de- nouncing its politics for perpetuating the hegemony of Western states.[8] Depic- tions of Cairo as two separate communities tend to fold, perhaps unwittingly, temporal and spatial difference into cultural and political frameworks. As Abu- Lughod declared from the perspective of the early 1960s, Cairo's "physical dual- ity was but a manifestation of the cultural cleavage. To the east lay the native city, still essentially pre-industrial in technology, social structure, and way of life; to the west lay the 'colonial' city with its steam-powered techniques, its faster pace and wheeled traffic, and its European identification. To the east lay the labyrinth street pattern . . . to the west were broad straight streets of mac- adam flanked by wide walks. . . . In short, on all critical points the two cities, despite their physical contiguity, were miles apart socially and centuries apart technologically."[9]

The idea that built forms most vividly expressed colonial power must be balanced with attention to the use and meaning of that space. Mixed-up styles and spatial practices could frustrate official efforts, both colonial and national, to order and classify the country, as this book has demonstrated. Colonial cit- ies represent particular topographies of power, formed by the local specificities of and struggles over colonial rule and in turn constraining the expression of those very politics. The study of urban history has oscillated in recent decades between static comparative models and an almost biographical focus on the particularities of individual cities. *A City Consumed* has drawn inspiration from accounts that frame cities as processes rather than things.[10] At the same time, the book's disciplinary roots in history have tilted the lens on process toward the cultural and the narrative, by using a wide range of economic and cultural sources to capture "the spatiality of historical processes."[11] Consumption practices materialized and routinized ideas about the nation and colonial power that otherwise circulated in more abstract and fluid registers or flared up in more drastic actions such as formal protests. In this book, I have argued that the longer and local trajectory of struggles over the emergence and regularization of morselized local styles and uses of space catalyzed important anticolonial political events of the 1950s, such as the Cairo Fire, the Free Officers' coup in July 1952, and the nationalizations after 1956. My history thus underlines the importance of viewing commodity circulation as a spatial practice, one crucial to apprehending urban history and the politics that colonial cities as spaces refracted and fissured. Methodologically, this has meant combining cultural and political-economic approaches to history and broadening the set of cultural and visual sources considered important to nationalist imagining. Commercial objects affected subjectivity more subtly and yet more pervasively than the imagined communities created by nationalist and literary figures in formal politics, literary writings, and mass media.

A history of the spatial politics of consumption demonstrates considerable continuity between old-regime and postcolonial Egypt. The politics of boycotts and the discourse of product nationality in the 1930s made space for the rhetoric and practice of nationalization that would be implemented in the 1950s. Nevertheless, local resistance to the increasing bifurcation of culture required a strong hand of state-driven clarification in Egypt to effect the national socialized economy, much as had happened only a few years earlier in China. "The logic of a movement which insisted that products were 'national' was easily used to undermine the notion that profits derived from selling such goods ought to be 'private.'"[12] Religious politics and the material nature of Egypt's colonial economy politicized consumer culture in ways that differ, however, from the experiences of metropolitan Europe or North America but also from other colonial locations such as Africa, India, and China. The material structure of Egypt's primary agricultural crop, long-staple cotton, made it easier for nationalist elites to reject popular challenges for a social revolution to accompany nationalism in the interwar years. Despite personal and political linkages between Indian and Egyptian patriots, the congruence of the cotton and silk markets

charged shifts to artificial materials such as nylon and rubber with powerful social conflict because they challenged elite political hegemony and social control
of the national workforce. Religious sanction against silkiness inflected new
marketing efforts with a sexual tension that reinforced the exclusion of women
from politics and the public sphere in new ways during the interwar period.

Consumerist politics in the immediate postwar period deeply scored late-
colonial states such as Egypt with fault lines that would take little to shear in
the 1950s. Nevertheless, when the regime in Egypt did finally fracture, many
residents remarked that it was they themselves who were being destroyed in the
process of decolonization. The ubiquitous metaphoric references to national
suicide make sense when located in a longer history of a poetics of protest that
framed colonial consumption as a form of captivity. The intimacy implied by
captivity narratives that highlighted the binding of consumer bodies under colonial politics points us to the importance of corporeality and materiality as
aspects of economic transformation. Captivity narratives should also be recognized as claims for broadening the field of anticolonial protest in ways that
brought women and their provisioning for families to center stage. Nationalist
boycotts created political platforms and concrete experiences for upper-class
women and middle-class youth, both of whom emerged in the interwar years
as significant contenders and players as the new political field unfolded. The
costs of breaking free of the consumer captivity that bound Egyptians to colonial forces in the twentieth century were high, entailing the self-destruction
of a large portion of the urban built environment as well as the physical and
emotional struggles of individuals and institutions forced to cope with new
prescriptions for sartorial consistency and regulation. Put simply, the struggles
that this book has documented reveal the extraordinary depth of colonial intrusion and the diversity and ingenuity of strategies through which urban residents created, accommodated, and challenged that experience. It is a legacy that
continues to shape Egyptian politics and society.

EPILOGUE

FIFTY-NINE YEARS to the day of the Ismailia massacre of Egyptian police forces that sparked the Cairo Fire, another day of rage brought enormous popular protests into Egypt's streets. January 25, 2011, was Egypt's Police Day, a newly minted holiday the state established to shore up the reputation of its contemporary police forces by linking them with the historical milestone of anticolonial struggle.[1] Unlike the popular rage in defense of Egypt's auxiliary police force in 1952, the 2011 protests grew from anger at the police's own oppressive practices that have brutally marked the routine experiences of many Egyptians. The state harshly repressed the peaceful demonstrations of January 25, 2011, leading to four days of fierce street fighting and the protestors' eventual occupation of one of the central downtown squares of Cairo—*maydan* Ismailia, today called Tahrir (Liberation) Square—prominent in the Cairo Fire of 1952. Protestors in 2011 called to overthrow the regime of Nasser's scion, Husni Mubarak. Although happening in a vastly changed global and local context, and overwhelmingly nonviolent, the 2011 protest resembled many aspects of the Cairo Fire. "The whole thing started with the desperate act of self-immolation by a young Tunisian man," one observer notes about the death of Mohamed Bouazizi, an itinerant merchant deeply frustrated by his daily battle with state officials charged with regulating commerce.[2] "His death sparked a wave of rage against poverty, social exclusion, and corruption. Almost overnight, young men and women created spaces in squares, streets, and alleys where we could imagine new Arab countries. . . . In Egypt, Tahrir Square became the epicenter of the people's demands for bread, dignity, and social justice."[3] In 2011 social media and cellular technology received considerable attention as new mechanisms of mobilization, although as one reporter aptly noted less than a week into the protests, "The government . . . could shut down the internet . . . [and] cell phone service. It could force Al Jazeera, which has been providing superb coverage of the events in Egypt, to close its Cairo bureau. It could arrest journalists and seize their equipment. But the streets of Cairo themselves have been the medium that has carried the message of the Egyptian people. So have the streets of Alexandria, Suez, and other Egyptian cities. And the government's efforts to keep people off those streets have failed completely."[4]

Urban streets had persisted in the 1970s as sites of mobilization for popular protest and acts of communal solidarity, ranging in the 1970s from massive funerals for Nasser and the popular singer Umm Kulthum to bread riots opposing President Anwar al-Sadat's elimination of state subsidies on basic goods as a condition of international financial aid during the dismantling of Nasser's public-sector economy. By 2003 Tahrir hosted enormous demonstrations opposing the American-led war in Iraq. The built environment of Tahrir, saturated with symbols of the political, economic, and administrative history of nineteenth- and twentieth-century Egypt, makes it a prime theater for urban politics.[5] Giving its name to the entire downtown district under the old regime, Ismailia Square boasted Khedive Isma'il's nineteenth-century palace, Qasr al-Nil, home to many instruments of the state's authority, including the sovereign, the state treasury, the army, and the council of ministers. After the British occupation in 1882, the palace served as the British military barracks until 1947, nearly adjacent to the wide-gardened residence of the British high commissioner, the locus of colonial power. In the 1950s the state partnered with an international corporation to construct the first Hilton Hotel in Africa on the site of the old barracks. It also opened a massive administrative complex, the Mugamma', a building begun under the old regime in 1950 that would come to symbolize the bloated and obstructionist bureaucracy of the Egyptian state—a new postcolonial governmentality that began to emerge in the first decade of Nasser's rule.[6] To assert its control over the city's public space, the Nasser state renamed fifteen of Cairo's squares and streets in September 1954, and two years later, under the guidance of public works minister 'Abd al-Latif al-Baghdadi, initiated a massive redesign of most of the public squares, including Tahrir, and construction of a public walkway, known as the Corniche, along the Nile's eastern city bank.[7] Huda Sha'rawi's upper-class villa remained on the square until its demolition in the 1970s.[8] Fear of revolution motivated many of the urban reforms of the nineteenth and twentieth centuries, encouraging the state to open small alleyways that could be easily barricaded during insurrections and to create the wide plazas and boulevards that could accommodate army tanks.[9]

The Sadat and Mubarak regimes would continue the state politics of dress and commerce in the decades following Nasser's death in 1970 by provisioning Egyptians, and especially the ever-growing number of impoverished government employees, with proper national dress produced and retailed in state-owned concerns. Andrea Rugh notes, "Starting in 1979, the Ministries of Industry and Supply . . . exerted special efforts to produce large quantities of ready-made 'foreign' clothing: suits, pajamas, shirts, and dresses. . . . As was true of the government subsidized material, the locally produced clothing quickly became identified as products of low cost and often poor quality, to be shunned by those seeking to make a special impression."[10] Mamoun Fandy argues that the postcolonial modernizing state "deliberately promotes Western dress over any other form of dress. Through its own factories, such as the ones at al-Mahallah al-Kubra, the state produces only Western-style polo shirts and Western trousers. . . . Most clothing produced at these factories is also distributed at state-owned outlets such as ['Umar] Effendi [ex-Orosdi-Back]."[11] Retail space and sartorial commodities continue to act as metaphors of social and political power. Much as Naguib Mahfouz's tales of sordid love affairs between customers and shop clerks in the Muski marked storytelling of Egyptian commerce in the first half of the twentieth century, Alaa al Aswany's *The Yacoubian Building* used the decaying built environment of downtown Cairo, and the predations of Syrian-born clothing store managers on young saleswomen, to symbolize disillusionment with the postcolonial regime and the lingering colonial influences in the city.[12] The profusion and diversity of Egyptian shoes continued as an important filmic and literary trope to analyze urban space.[13] The economic imposition of government-produced *ifrangi* dress eventually contributed to new social movements featuring homemade, modest Islamic dress in the 1970s and 1980s.

The final three decades of the twentieth century witnessed a massive restructuring of the Egyptian economy that dismantled Nasser's populist state, which was based in redistributive policies enabled by its control of the economy. Between 1993 and 2006 the government privatized, either fully or partially, 239 state-owned companies, including a number of department stores.[14] At the same time, coalitions of private foundations, cultural elites, and state officials selectively preserved old-regime downtown buildings, including department stores, clearing several lower-class neighborhoods in the "heritization" process.[15] Many Egyptians feared the state would squander public money in privatization deals.[16] The opposition press also greeted the news with announcements that Israelis were returning to Egypt to "buy back" their department stores and would become a fifth column inside the nation.[17] A culmination of postcolonial recasting of the historical memory of the old regime, this argument subsumed Jewish into Israeli identity and disregarded the complexity of Egypt's multiethnic urban societies in which one of the most prominent stores, Sednaoui, was owned by Christians.[18]

By 2011 observers such as Ahmad Shokr again noted that the protests represented the defiance of "the exclusionary logic that had governed . . . urban space" for decades. "In many ways, Tahrir had come to represent the overall decline of public space—people could barely congregate or mingle, let alone protest—under Mubarak's 30-year rule."[19] Although the symbolic center for many observers and participants, Tahrir did not encompass the totality of the 2011 uprising.[20] Widespread labor protests, in the years immediately before the uprising and during the spring and summer of 2011, were pivotal in breaking the barrier of fear between protestors and the security state and in articulating social and political reforms that could constitute an ideological core for transforming the uprisings from a regime overthrow to a revolution. Egyptian textile workers, including massive numbers at the Misr Spinning and Weaving Company at al-Mahalla al-Kubra, struck in 2006–2007 and again through 2011, their activism still carrying strong political symbolism and propelling the momentum of the workers' movement.[21] Among the other labor mobilizations important to giving force to the uprising were successful legal battles to overturn the state's privatization of the old Orosdi-Back ('Umar Effendi) department store.[22]

Economic liberalization had resulted in an enormous proliferation of imported and mass-produced consumer goods in Egyptian urban space since the 1990s, exacerbated by the ascension of the government of businessmen in 2004 under Prime Minister Ahmad Nazif. As Jessica Winegar contends, "The number and variety of mass-produced consumer goods grew at astonishing rates. . . . Soon Egyptians were eating elaborately packaged snacks and fast-food meals made by big companies instead of food made at home or at corner eateries whose takeout meals were usually wrapped in newsprint or other reused paper."[23] An effort to restructure Cairo's waste collection in the hands of European companies in 2000 only increased the sense that Cairenes, now approximately 17 million people, were becoming entombed in discarded merchandise.[24] Many observers attributed the Egyptian military's ambivalence about the protests to its control of assets that amounted to a parallel economy: industries producing goods ranging from bottled water, television sets, washing machines, and food, as well as resorts and childcare centers.[25] That one of the first spontaneous civic projects after the ousting of Mubarak would be to clean up the public space of urban protest—Tahrir Square—testifies to the continuing salience of the deep imbrication of commerce, public space, and political subjectivity, albeit in new ways, in Egypt today. It is impossible to know yet the full impact of Egypt's experience in the 2011 Arab Spring, and such a short epilogue cannot do justice to the complexity of the uprising's causes and political claims. Nevertheless, recent events demonstrate that Egypt's politics of space and the spatiality of politics remain deeply fastened to commerce and consumption, albeit in ways that reflect the historical specificity of new orders of governmentality.

NOTES

Introduction

Portions of this introduction were adapted from Nancy Reynolds, "National Socks and the 'Nylon Woman': Materiality, Gender, and Nationalism in Textile Marketing in Semi-colonial Egypt, 1930–56," *International Journal of Middle East Studies* 43, no. 1 (2011): 49–74. The small portion of reprinted material from this article included here falls under copyright © 2011 Cambridge University Press and has been reprinted by permission. Adapted fragments from this article also appear in Chapters 3, 4, 5, and 6.

1. Jean Lacouture and Simonne Lacouture, *Egypt in Transition*, trans. Francis Scarfe (New York: Criterion Books, 1958), 105–122. I discuss the fire, and my sources for its history, in more detail in Chapter 6.

2. M. T. Audsley, "Report of the British Embassy Committee of Enquiry into the Riots in Cairo on the 26th January 1952," 12, LAB 13/740, NAUK.

3. "Extremists' Role in Riots," *Times* (London), 29 January 1952, 4.

4. Karin Van Nieuwkerk, *"A Trade like Any Other": Female Singers and Dancers in Egypt* (Austin: University of Texas Press, 1995), 48. On the implication of cinemas in urban protest and fires, see also Elizabeth Thompson, "Sex and Cinema in Damascus: The Gendered Politics of Public Space in a Colonial City," in *Middle Eastern Cities 1900–1950*, ed. Hans Chr. Korsholm Nielsen and Jakob Skovgaard-Petersen (Proceedings of the Danish Institute in Damascus I. Aarhus, Denmark: Aarhus University Press, 2001), 89–111.

5. R. T., "La journée du 26 janvier," *Le progrès égyptien—Almanach*, 1953.

6. Eyewitnesses and investigators fixated on rioters' dress as a code to decipher their social class and determine whether there was coordinated middle-class leadership. See Audsley, "Enquiry into the Riots in Cairo," 5, 7–8, LAB 13/740, NAUK. These accounts

corroborate the range of dress among rioters, as do photographs accompanying articles in *al-Ahram*'s coverage of the trials in March 1952 (13 March 1952, 1 and 2; 17 March 1952, 3–4; 18 March 1952, 3 and 7; 23 March, 1952, 3). See also Anne-Claire Kerboeuf, "The Cairo Fire of 26 January 1952 and the Interpretations of History" in *Re-Envisioning Egypt, 1919–1952*, ed. Arthur Goldschmidt, Amy Johnson, and Barak Salmoni (Cairo: American University in Cairo Press, 2005), 194–216.

7. For Husayn's trial, see *al-Ahram*, 13 May 1952, 1. See also "Ma'sah al-Qahira fi 26 yanayir 1952," *al-Ahram*, 12 February 1952, 1–3. Photographs of Ahmad Husayn also appear in Sabri Abu al-Majd, *Sanawat ma qabla al-thawra, 1930–1952* (Cairo: al-Haya' al-Misriyya al-ʿAmma li'l-Kitab, 1987–1989), e.g., vol. 1, photo 74; vol. 2, photo 84.

8. James P. Jankowski, *Egypt's Young Rebels* (Stanford, CA: Hoover Institution Press, 1975), 105–6. For a photograph of the car, see *al-Ahram*, 13 May 1952, 1. Citroën cars were sold in Egypt in 1952 exclusively through V. N. Soussan and Co., which had showrooms located on Nagib al-Rihani Street in Cairo and Safia Zaghlul Street in Alexandria. E. J. Blattner, ed., *Who's Who in Egypt and the Near East, Le mondian égyptien et du Prôche-Orient* (Cairo: Imprimerie Française/Paul Barbey Press, 1952), 354. I have not seen Soussan included in the official lists of establishments damaged in the fire.

9. "Alf sinf wa-sinf," *al-Musawwar*, no. 645, 19 February 1937, 13; for another example, see "Mushkilat libas al-ra's," *al-Musawwar*, no. 75, 19 March 1926, front cover.

10. Finley Acker, "The Streets of Cairo," in *Pen Sketches* (Philadelphia: McLaughlin Bros., 1899), 8–9. This essay was originally printed in the *Philadelphia Inquirer*. See also Douglas Sladen, *Oriental Cairo: The City of the "Arabian Nights"* (London: Hurst and Blackett, 1911), especially the photograph facing p. 281.

11. Disputes about how to be modern—what to emulate from the often politically and militarily dominant West and how to remain true to local cultural and religious affiliations—have formed a significant part of cultural and social conflict in Egypt and the Middle East since the early nineteenth century. See Albert Hourani, *Arabic Thought in the Liberal Age, 1798–1939* (New York: Cambridge University Press, 1962); Leila Ahmed, *Women and Gender in Islam* (New Haven, CT: Yale University Press, 1992); Juan Ricardo Cole, "Feminism, Class, and Islam in Turn-of-the-Century Egypt," *International Journal of Middle East Studies* 13 (1981): 394–407; Elizabeth Thompson, *Colonial Citizens: Republican Rights, Paternal Privilege, and Gender in French Syria and Lebanon* (New York: Columbia University Press, 2000), 127–40; Sibel Bozdogan and Resat Kasaba, eds., *Rethinking Modernity and National Identity in Turkey* (Seattle: University of Washington Press, 1997).

12. Bernard Lewis, *The Emergence of Modern Turkey* (1961; repr., New York: Oxford University Press, 1968), 269, and Bozdogan and Kasaba, *Rethinking Modernity*, 25.

13. Frank Dikötter, *Exotic Commodities: Modern Objects and Everyday Life in China* (New York: Columbia University Press, 2006), 197, 200; Bernard S. Cohn, *Colonialism*

and Its Forms of Knowledge: The British in India (Princeton, NJ: Princeton University Press, 1996), 135, see also 146. This was also true of British perceptions of Africa. See Jeremy Prestholdt, *Domesticating the World: African Consumerism and the Genealogies of Globalization* (Berkeley: University of California Press, 2008), 29, also 161.

14. Yahya Haqqi, "Suq al-kantu," originally published in *al-Masa'* on 6 June 1966, 6; reprinted in Haqqi, *Safahat min tarikh Misr* (Cairo: General Egyptian Book Organization, 1989), 113.

15. Haqqi, *Safahat*, 113–14.

16. See, e.g., Walter Armbrust, *Mass Culture and Modernism in Egypt* (New York: Cambridge University Press, 1996); Lisa Pollard, *Nurturing the Nation* (Berkeley: University of California Press, 2005); Mona Russell, *Creating the New Egyptian Woman: Consumerism, Education, and National Identity, 1863–1922* (New York: Palgrave Macmillan, 2004); Keith Watenpaugh, *Being Modern in the Middle East* (Princeton, NJ: Princeton University Press, 2006).

17. See Jacques Berque, *Egypt: Imperialism and Revolution*, trans. Jean Stewart (London: Faber and Faber, 1972), 477. Mamoun Fandy has sketched a similar picture of contemporary Egyptian styles of dress that are manipulated by local actors of all classes in their struggles against the central, Cairo-based state. "Political Science without Clothes: The Politics of Dress; or, Contesting the Spatiality of the State in Egypt," in *Beyond the Exotic: Women's Histories in Islamic Societies*, ed. by Amira el-Azhary Sonbol (Syracuse, NY: Syracuse University Press, 2005), 381–98.

18. Karl Gerth, "Featured Review of Frank Dikötter, *Exotic Commodities*," *American Historical Review* 113, no. 3 (June 2008): 787. See also Donald Quataert, ed., *Consumption Studies and the History of the Ottoman Empire, 1550–1922: An Introduction* (Albany: State University of New York Press, 2000), 11; and Timothy Burke, *Lifebuoy Men, Lux Women: Commodification, Consumption, and Cleanliness in Modern Zimbabwe* (Durham, NC: Duke University Press, 1996), 7.

19. Karl Gerth, *China Made* (Cambridge, MA: Harvard University Press, 2003), 18–19, 125.

20. Kerboeuf, "Cairo Fire," 194. See also Anne-Claire Kerboeuf, "'La racaille' et les 'intrigants': Etude comparée de deux émeutes," *Egypte/monde arabe* 1–2, nos. 4–5 (2000–2001): 55–80.

21. Derek Hopwood, *Egypt: Politics and Society, 1945–1984*, 2nd ed. (Boston: Allen and Unwin, 1985), 32.

22. P. J. Vatikiotis, *The History of Egypt*, 3rd ed. (Baltimore, MD: Johns Hopkins University Press, 1985), 370; Anouar Abdel-Malek, *Egypt: Military Society. The Army Regime, the Left, and Social Change under Nasser*, trans. Charles Lam Markmann (New York: Vintage Books, 1968).

23. Kerboeuf, "Cairo Fire," 201–2.

24. Frantz Fanon perhaps most famously articulated this about Algeria. See Zeynep Çelik, *Urban Forms and Colonial Confrontations: Algiers under French Rule* (Berkeley: University of California Press, 1997). The radical bifurcation of urban space under apartheid is another latent model. See Janet L. Abu-Lughod, *Rabat: Urban Apartheid in Morocco* (Princeton, NJ: Princeton University Press, 1980); Bill Freund, "The City of Durban: Towards a Structural Analysis of the Economic Growth and Character of a South African City," in *Africa's Urban Past*, ed. David M. Anderson and Richard Rathbone (Portsmouth, NH: Heinemann, 2000), 144–61.

25. Kerboeuf, "Cairo Fire," 195–96. British control of public space was similar in Shanghai; see Leo Ou-Fan Lee, "Shanghai Modern: Reflections on Urban Culture in China in the 1930s," in *Alternative Modernities*, ed. Dilip Parameshwar Gaonkar (Durham, NC: Duke University Press, 2001), 103–4.

26. Janet Abu-Lughod's masterful documentation of Cairo rests on a dual-city model that, although originating in architectural readings of urban space, has come to characterize much thinking about colonial cities; see Abu-Lughod, *Cairo: 1001 Years of the City Victorious* (Princeton, NJ: Princeton University Press, 1971) and "Tale of Two Cities: The Origins of Modern Cairo," *Comparative Studies in Society and History* 7, no. 4 (July 1965): 429–57. Dress often divides these two arenas. See Andrea B. Rugh, *Reveal and Conceal: Dress in Contemporary Egypt* (Syracuse, NY: Syracuse University Press, 1986), 117–18. Fandy, "Political Science without Clothes," 387, questions the "myth of homogeneity" hidden in contemporary bifurcations of dress and culture in Egypt.

27. This perhaps represents Egypt's semicolonial status, in which local actors helped govern society. See Gerth, *China Made*; Hanan Kholoussy, "Monitoring and Medicalising Male Sexuality in Semi-Colonial Egypt," *Gender and History* 22, no. 3 (November 2010): 677–91, esp. 678. Consumption has long formed a topic in studies of the Egyptian economy, usually as one indicator of the overall state of the economy or to determine popular standards of living; these works generally provide useful statistical assessments of the consumption of basic and luxury goods by various classes, although they frequently analyze the variety of items in the market in undifferentiated categories such as textiles or leather footwear. See, e.g., Mahmoud Amin Anis, *A Study of the National Income of Egypt* (Cairo: Société Orientale de Publicité, 1950); Charles Issawi, *Egypt at Mid-Century* (New York: Oxford University Press, 1954); Patrick O'Brien, *The Revolution in Egypt's Economic System* (New York: Oxford University Press, 1966); Donald C. Mead, *Growth and Structural Change in the Egyptian Economy* (Homewood, IL: Richard Irwin, 1967); Bent Hansen, "Income and Consumption in Egypt, 1886/1887 to 1937," *International Journal of Middle East Studies* 10 (1979): 27–47; and Bent Hansen and Girgis A. Marzouk, *Development and Economic Policy in the UAR (Egypt)* (Amsterdam: North Holland Publishing, 1965). Galal Amin, in *Whatever Happened to the Egyptians?* (Cairo: American University in Cairo Press, 2000) and *Whatever Else Happened to the Egyptians?* (Cairo: American University in Cairo Press, 2004), views consumption more as an

index of social health. Historians continue to debate the role of foreign capital in Egypt's economic development and, in particular, its parasitic nature, which created the "lopsided development" of the Egyptian economy in the twentieth century. Charles Issawi, "Egypt since 1800: A Study in Lopsided Development," *Journal of Economic History* 21 (1961): 1–25. See also Robert Tignor, *State, Private Enterprise, and Economic Change in Egypt, 1918–1952* (Princeton, NJ: Princeton University Press, 1984); Robert Tignor, *Egyptian Textiles and British Capital, 1930–1956* (Cairo: American University in Cairo Press, 1989); Eric Davis, *Challenging Colonialism: Bank Misr and Egyptian Industrialization, 1920–1941* (Princeton, NJ: Princeton University Press, 1983); Bent Hansen, "Income and Consumption in Egypt"; Bent Hansen, *Egypt and Turkey: The Political Economy of Poverty, Equity, and Growth* (Washington, DC: Oxford University Press for the World Bank, 1991); Floresca Karanasou, "Egyptianisation: The 1947 Company Law and the Foreign Communities in Egypt" (DPhil diss., Oxford University, 1992); Marius Deeb, "Bank Misr and the Emergence of the Local Bourgeoisie in Egypt," *Middle Eastern Studies* 12, no. 3 (1976): 69–86, esp. 70; Timothy Mitchell, *Rule of Experts: Egypt, Techno-Politics, Modernity* (Berkeley: University of California Press, 2002), 109; Robert Vitalis, "On the Theory and Practice of Compradors: The Role of ʿAbbud Pasha in the Egyptian Political Economy," *International Journal of Middle East Studies* 22, no. 3 (August 1990): 291–315; and Robert Vitalis, *When Capitalists Collide: Business Conflict and the End of Empire in Egypt* (Berkeley: University of California Press, 1995).

28. Michel Foucault, "Of Other Spaces," trans. Jay Miskowiec, *Diacritics* 16, no. 1 (Spring 1986): 23.

29. David Harvey, "The Political Economy of Public Space," in *The Politics of Public Space*, ed. Setha Low and Neil Smith (New York: Routledge, 2006), 17.

30. Will Hanley, "Grieving Cosmopolitanism in Middle East Studies," *History Compass* 6, no. 5 (2008): 1346.

31. Benedict Anderson, *Imagined Communities: Reflections on the Origin and Spread of Nationalism* (London: Verso, 1991). John D. Kelly and Martha Kaplan, in *Represented Communities: Fiji and World Decolonization* (Chicago: University of Chicago Press, 2001), revise Anderson's classic model of nationalism by attending to relatively coercive juridical and representational structures.

32. Leora Auslander, "Beyond Words," *American Historical Review* 110, no. 4 (October 2005): 1015–45.

33. On the cultural influence of the middle class, or *effendiyya*, especially their control of the Arabic-language press, in this period, see Israel Gershoni and James Jankowski, *Egypt, Islam and the Arabs: The Search for Egyptian Nationhood, 1900–1930* (New York: Oxford University Press, 1986); Israel Gershoni and James Jankowski, *Redefining the Egyptian Nation, 1930–1945* (New York: Cambridge University Press, 1995); Relli Shechter, "Press Advertising in Egypt: Business Realities and Local Meaning, 1882–1956," *Arab Studies Journal* 10, no. 2, and 11, no. 1 (Fall 2002/Spring 2003): 48–50; Hanan Kholoussy,

For Better, For Worse: The Marriage Crisis That Made Modern Egypt (Stanford, CA: Stanford University Press, 2010), 2; Lucie Ryzova, "Egyptianizing Modernity through the 'New *Effendiya*': Social and Cultural Constructions of the Middle Class in Egypt under the Monarchy," in *Re-Envisioning Egypt, 1919–1952*, ed. Arthur Goldschmidt, Amy Johnson, and Barak Salmoni (New York: American University in Cairo Press, 2005), 124–63.

34. Marshall Berman, *All That Is Solid Melts into Air: The Experience of Modernity* (New York: Penguin Books, 1988), 136. See also Harvey, *Paris, Capital of Modernity* (New York: Routledge, 2003); Perry Anderson, "Modernity and Revolution," *New Left Review*, no. 144 (1984): 96–113; Marshall Berman, "Signs in the Street: A Response to Perry Anderson," *New Left Review*, no. 144 (1984): 114–23; Marshall Berman, "Why Modernism Still Matters," in *Modernity and Identity*, ed. Scott Lash and Jonathan Friedman (Malden, MA: Wiley-Blackwell, 1992), 33–58; Walter Benjamin, "Paris, Capital of the Nineteenth Century," in *Reflections*, ed. Peter Demetz, trans. Edmund Jephcott (New York: Harcourt Brace Jovanovich, 1978), 146–62. On the dandy and the flaneur, see Berman, *All That Is Solid*, and Harvey, *Paris, Capital of Modernity*; on women in new cities, see Joanne Meyerowitz, *Women Adrift: Independent Wage Earners in Chicago, 1880–1930* (Chicago: University of Chicago Press, 1991); Judith Walkowitz, *City of Dreadful Delight* (Chicago: University of Chicago Press, 1992).

35. Susan Porter Benson, *Counter Cultures: Saleswomen, Managers, and Customers in American Department Stores, 1890–1940* (Urbana: University of Illinois Press, 1986). Emile Zola, whose 1883 novel *Au bonheur des dames* was based on the Bon Marché and the Louvre department stores in Paris, put forth the image of department store as church. The literature on Euro-American department stores and commerce is extensive; as a field these studies have shifted from more celebratory accounts of individual firms, merchandising and managerial revolutions, and the liberation of women through shopping to more critical and ambivalent narratives about the effects of consumerism and shopping as leisure activity on class relations and ideological formation. See, e.g., Michael B. Miller, *The Bon Marché: Bourgeois Culture and the Department Store, 1869–1920* (Princeton, NJ: Princeton University Press, 1981); Phillip Nord, *Politics of Resentment* (1986; repr., New Brunswick, NJ: Transaction, 2005); Erika Diane Rappaport, *Shopping for Pleasure: Women in the Making of London's West End* (Princeton, NJ: Princeton University Press, 2000); Geoffrey Crossick and Serge Jaumain, *Cathedrals of Consumption: The European Department Store, 1850–1939* (Brookfield, VT: Ashgate, 1999); Rosalind H. Williams, *Dream Worlds: Mass Consumption in Late Nineteenth-Century France* (Berkeley: University of California Press, 1982); Gail Reekie, *Temptations: Sex, Selling, and the Department Store* (St. Leonards, Australia: Allen and Unwin, 1993); Mary Louise Roberts, "Gender, Consumption, and Commodity Culture," *American Historical Review* 103, no. 3 (June 1998): 817–44. See also William R. Leach, "Transformations in a Culture of Consumption: Women and Department Stores, 1890–1925," *Journal of Amer-*

ican History 71, no. 2 (September 1984): 319–42, and William R. Leach, *Land of Desire: Merchants, Power, and the Rise of a New American Culture* (New York: Vintage, 1994).

36. Claire Walsh, "Newness of the Department Store: A View from the Eighteenth Century," in *Cathedrals of Consumption,* ed. Geoffrey Crossick and Serge Jaumain (Brookfield, VT: Ashgate, 1999), 46.

37. On "the spatial turn," see Barney Warf and Santa Arias, "Introduction: The Reinsertion of Space into the Social Sciences and Humanities," in *The Spatial Turn: Interdisciplinary Perspectives,* ed. Barney Warf and Santa Arias (New York: Routledge, 2009), 1. Examples of recent studies include Rappaport, *Shopping for Pleasure*; Lise Shapiro Sanders, *Consuming Fantasies: Labor, Leisure, and the London Shopgirl, 1880–1920* (Columbus: Ohio State University Press, 2006); Lisa Tiersten, *Marianne in the Market: Envisioning Consumer Society in Fin-de-Siècle France* (Berkeley: University of California Press, 2001); Irene Guenther, *Nazi Chic?* (New York: Berg, 2004); Gerth, *China Made*; Matthew Daunton and Martin Hilton, eds., *The Politics of Consumption: Material Culture and Citizenship in Europe and America* (New York: Berg, 2001).

38. Although some scholars examined the global marketing of European objects or the shaping of metropolitan consumption by colonial anxieties, they used primarily prescriptive sources and implicitly attributed considerable power to European cultures to influence colonial economies directly. See, e.g., Thomas Richards, *The Commodity Culture of Victorian Britain* (London: Verso, 1990); Anne McClintock, *Imperial Leather* (New York: Routledge, 1995).

39. Burke, *Lifebuoy Men,* 3; Prestholdt, *Domesticating the World,* 8. See also Karen Tranberg Hansen, *Salalua: The World of Secondhand Clothing and Zambia* (Chicago: University of Chicago Press, 2000); Jean Allman, ed., *Fashioning Africa* (Bloomington: Indiana University Press, 2004); Beshara Doumani, *Rediscovering Palestine: Merchants and Peasants in Jabal Nablus, 1700–1900* (Berkeley: University of California Press, 1995); Thompson, *Colonial Citizens*; Quataert, *Consumption Studies*; Haris Exertzoglou, "The Cultural Uses of Consumption: Negotiating Class, Gender, and Nation in the Ottoman Urban Centers during the Nineteenth Century," *International Journal of Middle East Studies* 35 (2003): 77–101.

40. Several multivalent histories of important individual local commodities, such as cotton, textiles, tobacco, and wheat, demonstrate how goods act as windows and catalysts to larger social and political processes in Egypt. See Roger Owen, *Cotton and the Egyptian Economy, 1820–1914* (London: Oxford University Press, 1969); Tignor, *Egyptian Textiles*; Mitchell, *Rule of Experts,* chap. 8 on wheat and sugarcane; Shechter, *Smoking, Culture, and Economy in the Middle East: The Egyptian Tobacco Market 1850–2000* (New York: I. B. Tauris, 2006). Russell, *Creating the New Egyptian Woman,* examines consumer commodities in her discussion of advertising and prescriptions about new roles for women in an earlier period. Several early modern studies have attempted to quantify material culture in the Middle East but have also charted the effects of shifts in Ottoman

tax policies and trade with Europe to create specific and flexible regional economies. See also Pollard, *Nurturing the Nation*; Relli Shechter, ed., *Transitions in Domestic Consumption and Family Life in the Modern Middle East* (New York: Palgrave Macmillan, 2003); Mona Abaza, *Changing Consumer Cultures of Modern Egypt* (Leiden, Netherlands: Brill, 2006); Uri M. Kupferschmidt, *The Orosdi-Back Saga* (Istanbul: Ottoman Bank Archives and Research Centre, 2007); and Uri M. Kupferschmidt, "Who Needed Department Stores in Egypt? From Orosdi-Back to Omar Effendi," *Middle Eastern Studies* 43, no. 2 (March 2007): 175–92.

41. Leor Halevi, "Christian Impurity versus Economic Necessity: A Fifteenth-Century Fatwa on European Paper," *Speculum* 83, no. 4 (October 2008): 917–45; Gregory Starrett, "The Political Economy of Religious Commodities in Cairo," *American Anthropologist* 97, no. 1 (March 1995): 51–68; Charles Hirschkind, *The Ethical Soundscape* (New York: Columbia University Press, 2006); Yael Navaro-Yashin, "The Market for Identities: Secularism, Islamism, Commodities," in *Fragments of Culture: The Everyday of Modern Turkey*, ed. Deniz Kandiyoti and Ayse Saktanber (New Brunswick, NJ: Rutgers University Press, 2002), 221–53; Arang Keshavarzian, *Bazaar and State in Iran* (Cambridge: Cambridge University Press, 2007); Annika Rabo, *A Shop of One's Own: Independence and Reputation among Traders in Aleppo* (London: I. B. Tauris, 2005); Toufoul Abou-Hodeib, "Taste and Class in Late Ottoman Beirut," *International Journal of Middle East Studies* 43, no. 3 (August 2011): 475–92.

42. Frederick Cooper, *Colonialism in Question* (Berkeley: University of California Press, 2005), 146. See also Timothy Mitchell, "The Stage of Modernity," in *Questions of Modernity*, ed. Timothy Mitchell (Minneapolis: University of Minnesota Press, 2000), 26; Prestholdt, *Domesticating the World*, 89; Paul Rabinow, *French Modern: Norms and Forms of the Social Environment* (1989; repr., Chicago: University of Chicago Press, 1995).

43. The lack of definition for tradition actually often enhances this role of foil, as the inchoateness of the past or the backward renders the distance traveled by the modern ever more impressive. For a useful overview of the persistence of modernization theory in Middle Eastern history, see Zachary Lockman, *Contending Visions of the Middle East* (New York: Cambridge University Press, 2004). Talal Asad argues for a perspective on tradition that posits it as "a dimension of social life and not a stage of social development." "Modern Power and the Reconfiguration of Religious Traditions: An Interview with Talal Asad," by Saba Mahmood, *Stanford Humanities Review* 5, no. 1 (1995): 2.

44. Timothy Mitchell, *Colonising Egypt* (Berkeley: University of California Press, 1988), ix.

45. Partha Chatterjee, *The Politics of the Governed* (New York: Columbia University Press, 2004); Anderson, *Imagined Communities*. See also David Scott, "Colonial Governmentality," in *Anthropologies of Modernity: Foucault, Governmentality, and Life Politics*, ed. Jonathan Xavier Inda (Oxford: Blackwell, 2005), 23–49; James Scott, *Seeing like a State* (New Haven, CT: Yale University Press, 1998); James Ferguson, *The Anti-Politics*

Machine (Minneapolis: University of Minnesota Press, 1994); Omnia El Shakry, *The Great Social Laboratory: Subjects of Knowledge in Colonial and Postcolonial Egypt* (Stanford, CA: Stanford University Press, 2007); Ilana Feldman, *Governing Gaza* (Durham, NC: Duke University Press, 2008); Aradhana Sharma and Akhil Gupta, *Anthropology of the State* (Malden, MA: Blackwell, 2006). *Governmentality* is, of course, Foucault's term. See G. Burchell, C. Gordon, and P. Miller, eds., *The Foucault Effect: Studies in Governmentality* (Chicago: University of Chicago Press, 1991).

46. Chatterjee, *Politics of the Governed*, 36.

47. David Ludden, "India's Development Regime," in *Colonialism and Culture*, ed. Nicholas B. Dirks (Ann Arbor: University of Michigan Press, 1992), 262.

48. Daunton and Hilton, *Politics of Consumption*, 11. See also Meg Jacobs, *Pocketbook Politics: Economic Citizenship in Twentieth-Century America* (Princeton, NJ: Princeton University Press, 2005).

49. See Quataert, *Consumption Studies*, 11.

50. Mitchell, *Rule of Experts*, 111.

51. Luise White, "Cars Out of Place: Vampires, Technology, and Labor in East and Central Africa," in *Tensions of Empire: Colonial Cultures in a Bourgeois World*, ed. Ann Laura Stoler and Frederick Cooper (Berkeley: University of California Press, 1997), 438. See Ann Laura Stoler, *Carnal Knowledge and Imperial Power: Race and the Intimate in Colonial Rule* (2002; repr., Berkeley: University of California Press, 2010), 7. See also Palmira Brummett's analysis of the work of satire in the Ottoman press in *Image and Imperialism in the Ottoman Revolutionary Press, 1908–1911* (Albany: State University of New York Press, 2000).

52. Fandy, "Political Science without Clothes," 396, 390.

53. I refer to the literature on colonial cities in various places in the book. Two important collections include Robert Ross and Gerard J. Telkamp, *Colonial Cities* (Boston: Martinus Nijhoff, 1985); and Nezar AlSayyad, ed., *Forms of Dominance: On the Architecture and Urbanism of the Colonial Enterprise* (Brookfield, VT: Avebury, 1992).

54. The Indian case was complex and had been followed for years in Egypt. See Noor-Aiman Iftikhar Khan, "The Enemy of My Enemy: Indian Influences on Egyptian Nationalism, 1907–1930" (PhD diss., University of Chicago, 2006). The early 1930s witnessed a new spate of comparisons. See "The Meeting of the Wafd and the Present Political Situation," *al-Ahram*, 2 March 1931, FO 141/770/515, NAUK; confidential note from Keown-Boyd to Commercial Secretary, 4 May 1932, FO 141/711/465, NAUK; H. Clayton Hartley, "Some Aspects of the Prospective Establishment of Textile Factories in Egypt," *EC*, no. 110 (July 1928): 599; back-cover cartoon of *Ruz al-yusuf*, no. 332, 2 July 1934. On the Indian campaign, see C. A. Bayly, "The Origins of Swadeshi (Home Industry): Cloth and Indian Society, 1700–1930," in *The Social Life of Things: Commodities in Cultural Perspective*, ed. Arjun Appadurai (New York: Cambridge University Press, 1986), 285–321; Lisa Trivedi, *Clothing Gandhi's Nation: Homespun and Modern India* (Bloomington:

Indiana University Press, 2007). China had a similar national-products campaign in the 1920s; see Gerth, *China Made*. The United States provides another obvious example: see, e.g., Michael Zakim, "Sartorial Ideologies: From Homespun to Ready-Made," *American Historical Review* 106, no. 5 (December 2001): 1553–86.

55. Sandria B. Freitag, "Visions of the Nation: Theorizing the Nexus between Creation, Consumption, and Participation in the Public Sphere," in *Pleasure and the Nation*, ed. Rachel Dwyer and Christopher Pinney (New Delhi: Oxford University Press, 2001), 35; Trivedi, *Clothing Gandhi's Nation*, xvii. See also Gerth, *China Made*, for the importance of a "nationalistic visuality" as a means to spread a new consumer culture.

56. Çelik, *Urban Forms*; Gwendolyn Wright, *The Politics of Design in French Colonial Urbanism* (Chicago: University of Chicago Press, 1991); David Prochaska, *Making Algeria French: Colonialism in Bône, 1870–1920* (New York: Cambridge University Press, 1990).

57. On the legal differences created by the capitulation treaties, which protected foreigners, see Jasper Yeates Brinton, *The Mixed Courts of Egypt*, rev. ed. (New Haven, CT: Yale University Press, 1968); Elizabeth Shlala, "Mediterranean Migration, Cosmopolitanism, and the Law: A History of the Italian Community of Nineteenth-Century Alexandria, Egypt" (PhD diss., Georgetown University, 2009).

58. Pauline Turner Strong, *Captive Selves, Captivating Others: The Politics and Poetics of Colonial American Captivity Narratives* (Boulder, CO: Westview, 1999), 1. See also Susan L. Carruthers, *Cold War Captives* (Berkeley: University of California Press, 2009). The Mediterranean has a long, indigenous history of captivity politics: see Gillian Weiss, "Barbary Captivity and the French Idea of Freedom," *French Historical Studies* 28, no. 2 (Spring 2005): 231–64. Invoking a captivity narrative allowed individuals "to represent an entire nation in its conflict with another culture; the public concern over their captivity was part of a larger story about national identity, foreign policy, and racial constructs." Melani McAlister, *Epic Encounters: Culture, Media, and U.S. Interests in the Middle East since 1945*, rev. ed. (Berkeley: University of California Press, 2005), 199.

59. McAlister, *Epic Encounters*, 199–200.

60. Prakash, *After Colonialism*, 3, 8.

61. Anthony D. King, "Colonial Cities: Global Pivots of Change," in *Colonial Cities*, ed. Robert Ross and Gerard J. Telkamp (Boston: Martinus Nijhoff, 1985), 15; Prochaska, *Making Algeria French*, 20.

62. Abdel-Malek, *Egypt*, 37.

63. Bernard Lewis, *What Went Wrong? Western Impact and Middle Eastern Response* (London: Phoenix, 2002).

64. Jean Baudrillard, *The System of Objects*, trans. James Benedict (New York: Verso, 1996); Prestholdt, *Domesticating the World*, 96. See also Arjun Appadurai's notion of a "regime of value," *The Social Life of Things: Commodities in Cultural Perspective* (New York: Cambridge University Press, 1986), 4, and on taste and habitus, Pierre Bourdieu's *Distinction*, trans. Richard Nice (Cambridge, MA: Harvard University Press, 1984),

and *The Logic of Practice*, trans. Richard Nice (Stanford, CA: Stanford University Press, 1990).

65. See Shechter, "Press Advertising" and "Reading Advertisements in a Colonial/Development Context," *Journal of Social History* 39, no. 2 (Winter 2005): 483–503; and Russell, *Creating the New Egyptian Woman*.

66. Armbrust, "The Golden Age before the Golden Age," in *Mass Mediations*, ed. Walter Armbrust (Berkeley: University of California Press, 2000), 312. See also Martin Stokes, "Listening to Abd al-Halim Hafiz," in *Global Soundtracks*, ed. Mark Slobin (Middletown, CT: Wesleyan University Press, 2008), 309–33.

67. On "cultural capital," see Bourdieu, *Logic of Practice*, 124–25, and "Forms of Capital," 243–48.

68. Magdi Wahba, "East and West: Cairo Memories," *Encounter* 62, no. 5 (May 1984): 74–79.

69. Abu-Lughod, *Cairo*, 191, discusses *baladi*: "This virtually untranslatable term, an adjective derived from the noun for community (country, city, town, village), now connoted native in contrast to Westernized; folk as contrasted with sophisticated; untutored and low class as opposed to refined; traditional as contrasted with modern."

Chapter 1

Portions of this chapter were adapted from Nancy Reynolds, "*Sharikat al-Bayt al-Misri*: Domesticating Commerce in Egypt, 1931–1956," *Arab Studies Journal* 7, no. 2, and 8, no. 1 (Fall 1999/Spring 2000): 74–99. The small portion of reprinted material from this article included here has been reprinted by permission. Adapted fragments from this article also appear in Chapters 2, 5, and 6.

1. "Le scandale de la société des tramways," *EN*, no. 14 (1 October 1922), 223–24.

2. Joel Beinin and Zachary Lockman also note that tram ridership was 30 percent higher in 1918 than it had been before the war. *Workers on the Nile: Nationalism, Communism, Islam, and the Egyptian Working Class, 1882–1954* (Princeton, NJ: Princeton University Press, 1987), 91. The previous November, another article also complained of dangerous overcrowding and the interminable waiting caused by full trams. See *al-Lata'if al-musawwara* 7, no. 354 (21 November 1921), 4.

3. Beinin and Lockman, *Workers on the Nile*, 57–66, 91–95, 113–20.

4. Raymond, *Cairo*, trans. Willard Wood (Cambridge, MA: Harvard University Press, 2000), 324.

5. For population figures, see Janet Abu-Lughod, *Cairo: 1001 Years of the City Victorious* (Princeton, NJ: Princeton University Press, 1971), 121–24. The tram's fare in 1918 was 5 millèmes for second class and 10 millèmes for first class; trams left ʿAtaba for ʿAbbasiyya every four minutes and ran alternately via Fuʾad, Canal, or Clot Bey Streets. See SOP, *1918 Egyptian Directory*, 20. On the frequency of trams and the reduction in travel time around the city they enabled, see Abu-Lughod, *Cairo*, 132–38.

6. Gwendolyn Wright, *The Politics of Design in French Colonial Urbanism* (Chicago: University of Chicago Press, 1991); Zeynep Çelik, *Urban Forms and Colonial Confrontations: Algiers under French Rule* (Berkeley: University of California Press, 1997).

7. Wright, *Politics of Design*. French building in Damascus created a similar duality between the newer and older parts of the city. See Elizabeth Thompson, *Colonial Citizens: Republican Rights, Paternal Privilege, and Gender in French Syria and Lebanon* (New York: Columbia University Press, 2000), 177.

8. Çelik, *Urban Forms*, 5.

9. Frantz Fanon, *The Wretched of the Earth*, trans. Constance Farrington (New York: Grove Weidenfeld, 1963), 38.

10. Ibid., 39. See also Çelik, *Urban Forms*; Gwendolyn Wright, "Boulevard Muhammad V," in *Streets: Critical Perspectives on Public Space*, ed. Zeynep Çelik, Diane Favro, and Richard Ingersoll (Berkeley: University of California Press, 1994), 225–34; Janet Abu-Lughod, *Rabat: Urban Apartheid in Morocco* (Princeton, NJ: Princeton University Press, 1980).

11. Khaled Fahmy, "An Olfactory Tale of Two Cities: Cairo in the Nineteenth Century," in *Historians in Cairo*, ed. Jill Edwards (New York: American University in Cairo Press, 2002), 165. See also Heba Farouk Ahmed, "Nineteenth-Century Cairo: A Dual City?," in *Making Cairo Medieval*, ed. Nezar AlSayyad, Irene A. Bierman, and Nasser Rabbat (New York: Lexington Books, 2005), 143–72; Khaled Fahmy, "Modernizing Cairo: A Revisionist Narrative," in *Making Cairo Medieval*, ed. Nezar AlSayyad, Irene A. Bierman, and Nasser Rabbat (New York: Lexington Books, 2005), 173–99. The uncritical replication of the colonial "dual city" model has been pervasive among historians. See, for example, Abu-Lughod, *Cairo*, 208, and "Tale of Two Cities: The Origins of Modern Cairo," *Comparative Studies in Society and History* 7, no. 4 (July 1965): 429–57; Nadav Safran, *Egypt in Search of Political Community: An Analysis of the Intellectual and Political Evolution of Egypt, 1804–1952* (Cambridge, MA: Harvard University Press, 1961), 35; Raymond, *Cairo*, 309, 317; and Jacques Berque and Mustafa al-Shakaa, "La Gamaliya depuis un siècle," *Colloque international sur l'histoire du Caire* (Cairo: General Egyptian Book Organization, 1969), 68.

12. Magdi Wahba, "East and West: Cairo Memories," *Encounter* 62, no. 5 (May 1984): 74.

13. Fanon, *Wretched of the Earth*, 38.

14. Roger Owen, *Cotton and the Egyptian Economy, 1820–1914* (London: Oxford University Press, 1969).

15. Robert Tignor, *Egyptian Textiles and British Capital, 1930–1956* (Cairo: American University in Cairo Press, 1989), 8–17; Sidney H. Wells, "L'industrie du tissage en Egypte," *EC*, 4 November 1910, 578–84, and 5 January 1911, 52–73; Roger Owen, *The Middle East in the World Economy, 1800–1914* (New York: Methuen, 1981), 94.

16. Fahmy ("Modernizing Cairo") has argued that the rebuilding of Cairo preceded and was more complex than a result of Isma'il's 1867 visit to Paris.

17. P. J. Vatikiotis, *The History of Egypt*, 3rd ed. (Baltimore, MD: Johns Hopkins University Press, 1985), 173.

18. Ibid., 174.

19. Enid Hill, "The Golden Anniversary of Egypt's National Courts," in *Historians in Cairo*, ed. Jill Edwards (New York: American University in Cairo Press, 2002), 203–22; Nathan J. Brown, "The Precarious Life and Slow Death of the Mixed Courts of Egypt," *International Journal of Middle East Studies* 25, no. 1 (February 1993): 33–52. The British reduced taxes as part of their dismantling of state services, such as education. See John T. Chalcraft, *The Striking Cabbies of Cairo and Other Stories: Crafts and Guilds in Egypt, 1863–1914* (Albany: State University of New York Press, 2004), 128, 147; Jasper Yeates Brinton, *The Mixed Courts of Egypt*, rev. ed. (New Haven, CT: Yale University Press, 1968), 177–79. Although the regime of Capitulations was abolished by the Montreux Convention in 1937, foreign judicial officials continued to participate in trying foreigners until 1949. An income tax was first instituted in 1937 as well.

20. Vatikiotis, *Egypt*, 173. On the effects on the labor market, see also Chalcraft, *Striking Cabbies*, 128; Beinin and Lockman, *Workers on the Nile*, 184.

21. Robert Mabro, "Alexandria, 1860–1960," in *Alexandria, Real and Imagined*, ed. Anthony Hirst and Michael Silk (Burlington, VT: Ashgate, 2004), 254.

22. See Brinton, *Mixed Courts*; Elizabeth Shlala, "Mediterranean Migration, Cosmopolitanism, and the Law: A History of the Italian Community of Nineteenth-Century Alexandria, Egypt" (PhD diss., Georgetown University, 2009).

23. Chalcraft, *Striking Cabbies*, 127.

24. Timothy Mitchell, *Rule of Experts: Egypt, Techno-Politics, Modernity* (Berkeley: University of California Press, 2002), 95–98.

25. Mitchell, *Rule of Experts*, 111.

26. Malak Zaalouk, *Power, Class, and Foreign Capital in Egypt* (London: Zed, 1989), 2; Robert Vitalis, *When Capitalists Collide: Business Conflict and the End of Empire in Egypt* (Berkeley: University of California Press, 1995).

27. Often, these were preserved as parallel institutions. See, e.g., Brown, "Shariʿa and State in the Modern Muslim Middle East," *International Journal of Middle East Studies* 29 (1997): 359–76.

28. Beinin and Lockman, "1919: Labor Upsurge and National Revolution," in *The Modern Middle East*, 2nd ed., ed. Albert Hourani, Philip S. Khoury, and Mary C. Wilson (New York: I. B. Tauris, 2005), 395–428.

29. Ellis Goldberg, "Peasants in Revolt—Egypt 1919," *International Journal of Middle East Studies* 24 (1992): 261–80, esp. 262.

30. Abu-Lughod, *Cairo*, 120–21; Daniel Panzac, "The Population of Egypt in the Nineteenth Century," *Asian and African Studies* 21 (1987): 11–32.

31. Abu-Lughod, *Cairo*, 121. Panzac, "Population of Egypt," 15, cites 6 percent in 1897.

32. Robert Ilbert, *Alexandrie, 1830–1930*, 2 vols. (Cairo: Institut Français d'Archéologie Orientale, 1996), 758. The total population growth in Alexandria was from about 8,000 people in 1798 to 573,063 in 1927.

33. Karl Baedeker, *Egypt and the Sudan: Handbook for Travellers*, 8th ed. (New York: Scribner's, 1929), 36, 189, 183, and 203.

34. Abu-Lughod, *Cairo*, 118–31. The physical expansion of the city limits at various times also accounted for some of the increase in Cairo's population in this period; Abu-Lughod argues, however, that most population growth resulted from in-migration and natural increase.

35. Ilbert, *Alexandrie*, 759.

36. Tignor, *State*, tables A1 and A2.

37. Michael J. Reimer, *Colonial Bridgehead: Government and Society in Alexandria, 1807–1882* (Boulder, CO: Westview, 1997), 97.

38. Ibid., 102–3.

39. Ibid., 102.

40. Ibid., 127.

41. Ibid.; Ilbert, *Alexandrie*, 205.

42. Ilbert, *Alexandrie*, 209. The British also controlled public spaces in Shanghai with the same mechanisms. See Leo Ou-Fan Lee, "Shanghai Modern: Reflections on Urban Culture in China in the 1930s," in *Alternative Modernities*, ed. Dilip Parameshwar Gaonkar (Durham, NC: Duke University Press, 2001), 103–4.

43. Baedeker, *Egypt and the Sudan*, 11. On the urban development of Alexandria, see also Will Hanley, "Foreignness and Localness in Alexandria, 1880–1914" (PhD diss., Princeton University, 2007).

44. See Fahmy, "Modernizing Cairo," for an account of the development that preceded the 1867 building. His article effectively challenges the Paris-as-model argument and the dominant role usually accorded to ʿAli Mubarak.

45. Jean-Luc Arnaud, *Le Caire: Mise en place d'une ville moderne, 1867–1907* (Arles, France: Sindbad, 1998), 77–79, 109–16.

46. Ibid., 80. On the limitations of Arnaud's study, see Fahmy, "Modernizing Cairo," 178–79.

47. Nelly Hanna, "The Urban History of Cairo around 1900," in *Historians in Cairo: Essays in Honor of George Scanlon*, ed. Jill Edwards (New York: American University in Cairo Press, 2002), 198.

48. Ibid. See also Ilbert, *Alexandrie*, 209; Sami Zubaida, "Cosmopolitanism and the Middle East," in *Cosmopolitanism, Identity, and Authenticity in the Middle East*, ed. Roel Meijer (New York: RoutledgeCurzon, 2003), 26.

49. Sladen, *Oriental Cairo: The City of the "Arabian Nights"* (London: Hurst and Blackett, 1911); Hanna "Urban History of Cairo," 200.

50. Fahmy, "Olfactory Tale," 181.

51. See also Yahya Haqqi, "'Arabi wa-ifrangi" (1966), in *Safahat min tarikh Misr* (Cairo: General Egyptian Book Organization, 1989), 100.

52. See Abu-Lughod, *Cairo*, and Fahmy, "Olfactory Tale" and "Modernizing Cairo." There was at the same time an effort to preserve the old city as medieval. See Nairy Hampikian, "Medievalization of the Old City as an Ingredient of Cairo's Modernization: Case Study of Bab Zuwayla," in *Making Cairo Medieval*, ed. Nezar AlSayyad, Irene A. Bierman, and Nasser Rabbat (New York: Lexington Books, 2005), 201–34; Paula Sanders, *Creating Medieval Cairo* (New York: American University in Cairo Press, 2008); AlSayyad, Bierman, and Rabbat, *Making Cairo Medieval*.

53. An enormous literature on the Islamic city developed in the 1960s and 1970s as part of a Weberian project to understand the stymied economic development and decline of the Middle East (its "inability" to transform to capitalism). See Janet Abu-Lughod, "The Islamic City—Historic Myth, Islamic Essence, and Contemporary Relevance," *International Journal of Middle East Studies* 19 (1987): 155–76; Magda Baraka, *The Egyptian Upper Class between Revolutions* (Oxford: Ithaca Press, 1998), chap. 3.

54. Muhammad Shirabli has argued that perhaps the most important trait of the Islamic market is the relationship between the street, the shop, and the customer. "Al-Suq: Qalb al-madina al-islamiyya," *al-Hilal* 96 (August 1989): 75. See also Walter M. Weiss and Kurt-Michael Westermann, *The Bazaar: Markets and Merchants of the Islamic World* (New York: Thames and Hudson, 1998).

55. Jeremiah Lynch, *Egyptian Sketches* (London: Edward Arnold, 1890), 38–39. See also Sladen, *Oriental Cairo*, 11, where he divides Cairo into two sections: "Europeanised Cairo" and "Oriental Cairo."

56. M. D. du Buttafoco, *Géographie générale de l'Egypte* (Cairo, 1880), 45, cited in Ilbert, *Alexandrie* 1:196–97. My translation.

57. Baedeker, *Egypt and the Sudan*, 183. Tanta was another provincial city to gain a European quarter in the nineteenth century; see Timothy Mitchell, *Colonising Egypt* (Berkeley: University of California Press, 1988), 67.

58. Sladen, *Oriental Cairo*, 68–70 (for the entire description of Muski Street). Mitchell, *Colonising Egypt*, addresses the desire for "perspective" and visual order as a hallmark of Orientalism and what he calls its drive toward "enframing." The citational nature of these Orientalist depictions is quite remarkable. For two earlier versions, see E. A. Reynolds-Ball, *Cairo of To-day: A Practical Guide to Cairo and its Environs*, 2nd ed. (London: Adam and Charles Black, 1899), 74; Florence Groff, *Guide to Cairo and Environs* (Cairo: Lavados, 1893), 19.

59. Sladen, *Cairo*, 68.

60. Translated by Roger Allen as *A Period of Time: A Study and Translation of Hadith 'Isa Ibn Hisham by Muhammad al-Muwaylihi* (Reading, MA: Ithaca Press, 1992). Naguib Mahfouz, in his Cairo Trilogy, also relied on a disparity between the two parts of Cairo to highlight the cultural, social, and political struggles of his characters in the period

between the 1910s and the 1930s. See, e.g., *Palace of Desire*, trans. William Maynard
Hutchins, Lorne M. Kenny, and Olive E. Kenny (New York: Anchor Books, 1991), 140.

61. Abu-Lughod, *Cairo*, 191. She calls ʿAtaba "the transitional belt" of Cairo.

62. Ibid., 209. See also Arnold Wright and H. A. Cartwright, *Twentieth-Century
Impressions of Egypt: Its History, People, Commerce, Industries, and Resources* (London:
Lloyd's Greater Britain Publishing, 1909), 337.

63. Sladen, *Oriental Cairo*, 64.

64. Abu-Lughod, *Cairo*, 138.

65. Muhammad Sayyid Kilani, *Tram al-Qahira* (Cairo: Dar al-Farjani, 1968), 13,
40–44. See also Abu-Lughod, *Cairo*, 132–39; Raymond, *Cairo*, 324. Abu-Lughod notes
that the tramways were essentially completed by 1917 (see 140).

66. See also Samir Raafat, "The House of Cicurel," *Ahram Weekly*, 15 December 1994.

67. Kilani, *Tram*, 20–22.

68. Mulock, *Egypt, May 1928*, 31; Raymond, *Cairo*, 324 and 320. Cairo's population at
this time was more than a million people. Traffic problems became rampant in the postwar period. See "Tajriba al-murur fi ittijah wahid," *al-Misri*, 5 January 1948; and Kamal
Ismaʿil, "10,000 haditha murur," *al-Musawwar*, no. 1240 (16 July 1948), 24–25.

69. Wright and Cartwright, *Twentieth-Century Impressions*, 337.

70. Ibid.

71. These sellers of notions in Bayn al-Nahdayn Street contracted an agreement
among themselves, written in Arabic, to adhere to similar business practices in 1905.
Signed by at least eight merchants, several of whom had recognizably Muslim names,
the petition is enclosed in letter from Anastassiuf and Cavessa to Butrus Ghali, Cairo,
2 January 1910, MW: Sharikat wa-Jamʿiyyat, 3J; DWQ. SOP, *1918 Egyptian Directory*,
1476–78, lists five sellers of notions (*mercerie, al-kurdawat*) on Bayn al-Nahdayn: Kirillos
Choucri; Mahmud Muhammad Skenderani; Rafla Guergues; Toussié, Dwek and ʿAdès;
and J. Pérèz.

72. Wright and Cartwright, *Twentieth-Century Impressions*, 337.

73. Ibid., 340.

74. Ibid., 342. In 1909 only 546 water hydrants serviced the entire city. The Muski fire
reportedly resulted in £E14,000 of damages. In 1908 the city's fires totaled 261 with an
estimated property loss of £E17,500. Ibid. See also Sladen, *Oriental Cairo*, 67.

75. On the telephone service and the automatic exchange at ʿAtaba, see "al-Tilifun:
Nizamuhu wa-taqaddumuhu fi Misr," *Misr al-haditha al-musawwara*, no. 7 (April–May
1927): 3–9.

76. Cited in Yunan Labib Rizq, "'Al-Ahram': A *Diwan* of Contemporary Life," no.
109, *al-Ahram Weekly*, 30 November–6 December 1995, 13.

77. Rizq, "*Al-Ahram.*" On the cultural significance of these covered market spaces,
see Robert Ilbert, "L'invention du marché: Alexandrie, 1850–1920," in *Les villes dans
l'Empire Ottoman: Activités et sociétés*, vol. 2, ed. Daniel Panzac (Paris: CNRS Editions,

1994), 357–76; Pascal Garret, "Les 'Marchés modernes' en Egypte," *Lettre d'information de l'observatoire urbain du Caire contemporain* (Centre d'Études et de Documentation Économiques [CEDEJ]) 41–42 (September 1995): 20–29.

78. Garret, "Marchés modernes," 21–22.

79. Wright and Cartwright, *Twentieth-Century Impressions*, 337.

80. Unless otherwise noted, these references to services and businesses located in ʿAtaba have been gleaned from the various listings (by trade) in SOP, *1918 Egyptian Directory*.

81. Bars and cafés in SOP, *1918 Egyptian directory*, 1206–8.

82. Shirabli, "al-Suq," 75.

83. Wright and Cartwright, *Twentieth-Century Impressions*, 336–37. See also Sladen, *Oriental Cairo*, 66. See also *al-Lataʾif al-musawwara*, no. 349 (17 October 1921), 9.

84. Wright and Cartwright, *Twentieth-Century Impressions*, 337.

85. Samir Raafat, "Adopt a Monument: How about the Tiring Department Store on Ataba Square?" *Egyptian Mail*, 22 February 1997, 3; Kilani, *Tram*, 40; Russell, *Creating the New Egyptian Woman: Consumerism, Education, and National Identity, 1863–1922* (New York: Palgrave Macmillan, 2004), 72.

86. Wright and Cartwright, *Twentieth-Century Impressions*, 372. The description of Stein's store in 1909 is drawn from the description and the accompanying full page of photographs on 372–74. On urban electrification, see Kilani, *Tram*, 30.

87. Stein's sold primarily for cash, although the store did report £E5,000 worth of sales on credit in 1916. War Trade Department of Egypt, "Report on Policy Adopted in Restraint and Liquidation of Enemy Trade (Confidential), June 1917" (Cairo: Government Press, 1917), 17–18, 79, le Caire-Ambassade, 602/547, CADN. This represented only a small fraction of their overall sales; their cash transactions in the same period amounted to £E223,000. According to these British estimates, Stein's did a much larger business than any of the other "German and Austrian" stores in ʿAtaba and the Muski.

88. Stein's, Tiring, Salamander, and Mayer were all Austrian stores in Egypt with head offices in Vienna (although Stein's also had at least some affiliation with Britain) by the First World War. War Trade Department of Egypt, "Report, June 1917," 17–18, 79, le Caire-Ambassade, 602/547, CADN; letter no. 13, Consul to Defrance, Cairo, 20 February 1915, and enclosed "Note sur le commerce allemand en Egypte," February 1915, le Caire-Ambassade 602/546, CADN; and Uri Kupferschmidt, *The Orosdi-Back Saga* (Istanbul: Ottoman Bank Archives and Research Centre, 2007), 18, 54.

89. SOP, *1918 Egyptian Directory*; Wright and Cartwright, *Twentieth-Century Impressions*; al-Mawardi advertisement, *al-Ahram*, 15 June 1925, 2.

90. *Fihris sharikat al-taʿawun al-manzali li-muwazzafiy al-hukuma*, September 1926, ʿAbdin: Maliyya: Bunuk wa-Sharikat, no. 264 (1909–1949), DWQ. This cooperative society had existed since at least 1923, when it published a luxurious Ramadan fasting calendar (ʾimsakiyya) bound in white satin. See "ʾImsakiyya ramadan al-muʿazim,"

al-Akhbar, 23 April 1923, 3. Many cooperative societies developed during the inflationary period brought on by the First World War and dealt "in foodstuffs, all household commodities, and clothing . . . and their total membership [stood] at 60,499, their profits being devoted to running expenses, bonuses on members' shares, and the cheapening of such articles as cannot otherwise be sold except at a loss." E. Homan Mulock, for UK Department of Overseas Trade, *Report on the Economic and Financial Situation of Egypt, March 1921* (London: HMSO, 1921), 29–30. See also A. N. Cumberbatch for UK Board of Trade, *Egypt: Economic and Commercial Conditions in Egypt, October 1951* (London: HMSO, 1952), 90.

91. On the *effendiyya*, see Lucie Ryzova, "Egyptianizing Modernity through the 'New *Effendiya*': Social and Cultural Constructions of the Middle Class in Egypt under the Monarchy," in *Re-Envisioning Egypt, 1919–1952*, ed. Arthur Goldschmidt, Amy Johnson, and Barak Salmoni (New York: American University in Cairo Press, 2005), 124–63.

92. *Fihris sharikat al-taʿawun al-manzali li-muwazzafiy al-hukuma*, ʿAbdin: Maliyya: Bunuk wa-Sharikat, no. 264 (1909–1949), DWQ.

93. Wright and Cartwright, *Twentieth-Century Impressions*, 337.

94. Rizq, "*Al-Ahram*."

95. Wright and Cartwright, *Twentieth-Century Impressions*, 462–64.

96. Abu-Lughod, *Cairo*, 110.

97. Ibid., 110.

98. Ibid., 134.

99. Fathi Radwan, *Khatt al-ʿataba: Hayat tifli misri* (Cairo: Dar al-Maʿarif, 1973), 28, 110, 92. Wahba discusses the mobility of employees similar to Radwan's father in "East and West," 74–75.

100. Ibid., 112, 120, 15–16. On Radwan, see also James P. Jankowski, *Egypt's Young Rebels* (Stanford, CA: Hoover Institution Press, 1975), 9–11.

101. Radwan, *Khatt al-ʿataba*, 56. According to Kilani (*Tram*, 13), the Suares and other companies for omnibuses actually were formed in 1899, three years after the start of the trams; they were very slow and designed for short distances.

102. Radwan later made a film of Mustafa Kamil. See Joel Gordon, "Film, Fame, and Public Memory: Egyptian Biopics from *Mustafa Kamil* to *Nasser 56*," *International Journal of Middle East Studies* 31 (1999): 65. It is worth noting that Kamil did not distinguish as clearly as Radwan between Egyptian Jews and Muslims or Christians.

103. Radwan, *Khatt al-ʿataba*, 56.

104. Ibid., 57.

105. Radwan, *Khatt al-ʿataba*, 57.

106. Ibid., 58.

107. Ibid.

108. Ibid., 59–60; see also 61–62.

109. Beshara Doumani, *Rediscovering Palestine: Merchants and Peasants in Jabal Nablus, 1700–1900* (Berkeley: University of California Press, 1995), 69.

110. Abdel Aziz El Sherbini and Ahmed Fouad Sherif, "Marketing Problems in an Underdeveloped Country—Egypt," *EC* 47, no. 285 (July 1956): 29–30.

111. Wahba, "East and West," 74.

112. See Mitchell, *Colonising Egypt*; and Timothy Mitchell, "Stage of Modernity," in *Questions of Modernity*, ed. Timothy Mitchell (Minneapolis: University of Minnesota Press, 2000), 26.

113. Sherbini and Sherif, "Marketing Problems," 30. See also Hanna, "Urban History of Cairo," 193.

114. "Al-Mamarr al-tijari . . . mamarr al-ighra'," *al-Musawwar*, no. 1233 (28 May 1948), 26.

115. Ibid.

116. "Shar'ia fu'ad," *al-Musawwar*, no. 1529 (29 January 1954), 52.

117. Al-Maliji was interviewed for his memories of "generations" of important students who had bought sweets from him over the years. "Min dhikrayat 'Amm 'Uthman," *al-Musawwar*, no. 657 (14 May 1937), 26.

118. See *al-Balagh*, 23 November 1947.

119. On these stationers, see their petition to Edward Gray, Cairo, 3 June 1914, in FO 371/1967, TNA. In addition to "poor," the salesmen claimed to be physically disabled ("blind, lame, diseased") with an average capital of only £E2 and daily earnings of about 5 piastres (one shilling); the group included four Muslims, a Christian, and a Jew.

120. "Shakwa" from 'Abd al-Maqsud Khalaf Hasan, president of *niqabat al-ba'a al-mutajawwilin*, to King Faruq, 17 October 1944, 'Abdin, box 26, DWQ. See also "Port Sa'id's Street Hawkers: Stricter Regulations," *Egyptian Gazette*, 21 June 1912, 3.

121. Another textile store that emphasized its ability to unite "religious and national" identities was the clothing and notions store of Hafiz and Muhammad Farnawani located in 'Ataba in the 1930s. See *Ruz al-yusuf* articles, no. 333 (9 July 1934), 53; no. 334 (16 July 1934), 35; no. 335 (23 July 1934), 33; and advertisements for the company in *Ruz al-yusuf*, no. 303 (4 December 1933), 16; *al-Ahram*, 1 May 1934, 10; *al-Ahram*, 8 October 1935, 10. "Ijtima'a dini wa-watani," *Ruz al-yusuf*, no. 339 (20 August 1934), 47, notes the store's sponsorship of the *mawlid* (birthday) of Husayn in 1934. On the recent growth of Islamist department stores in Turkey, see Yael Navaro-Yashin, "The Market for Identities: Secularism, Islamism, Commodities," in *Fragments of Culture: The Everyday of Modern Turkey*, ed. Deniz Kandiyoti and Ayse Saktanber (New Brunswick, NJ: Rutgers University Press, 2002), 234–47.

122. Ahmad Mahmud Ahmad 'Awf and Khayri Mahfuz Ahmad, interviews by author, Cairo, 23 March 1996 and 7 August 1997.

123. See advertisements in *Ruz al-yusuf*, no. 196 (16 November 1931), 17, and no. 212 (7 March 1932), 14.

124. Sladen, *Oriental Cairo*, 134, 106. Sladen reports that, although the market smelled strongly of old clothes, "the tout ensemble was really not so very unlike a sale of costumes at a Kensington shop" (134). Cairo had other secondhand markets. See, for example, articles in *al-Musawwar*: no. 1253 (15 October 1948), 30–31, and no. 1316 (30 December 1949), 18–19.

125. Sladen, *Oriental Cairo*, 106.

126. Yahya Haqqi, "Suq al-kantu" (1966), in *Safahat min tarikh Misr* (Cairo: General Egyptian Book Organization, 1989), 113–14. For a similar description of the seductive and duplicitous dialogue of merchants at the *suq al-kantu*, see Victor Marotti, "Bazar de vente," *EN*, no. 128 (6 December 1924), 11. On the importance of used clothing in creating consumer demand for ready-made clothes and launching the industrial revolution in England, see Beverly Lemire, "Consumerism in Preindustrial and Early Industrial England: The Trade in Secondhand Clothes," *Journal of British Studies* 27, no. 1 (January 1988): 1–24; and Margaret Spufford, *The Great Reclothing of Rural England* (London: Hambledon Press, 1984). On used clothing trades in Africa, see Karen Tranberg Hansen, *Salaula: The World of Secondhand Clothing and Zambia* (Chicago: University of Chicago Press, 2000).

127. Haqqi, "Suq al-kantu," 113.

128. Commercial Counselor to M. le Delegué Général du Centre National du Commerce Extérieur à Paris, Cairo, 7 May 1947, "a/s: Débouchés offerts par l'Egypte au créations de la haute-couture parisienne," le Caire-Ambassade, 602/248, CADN.

129. Commercial Counselor to Lanvin, Confidential letter no. 2306, Cairo, 1 August 1946, le Caire-Ambassade, 602/248, CADN.

130. Commercial Counselor to M. le Delegué Général du Centre National du Commerce Extérieur à Paris, Cairo, 7 May 1947, le Caire-Ambassade, 602/248, CADN.

131. Ibid.

132. Ibid.

133. Commercial Counselor to Lanvin, Confidential letter no. 2306, Cairo, 1 August 1946, le Caire-Ambassade, 602/248, CADN. I have not seen evidence of official charges and cannot attest to the truth of the commercial counselor's claim.

134. Hers was supposedly a nationalist project since most Egyptian couture owners were Levantines. Inji Aflatun, *Mudhakkirat* (Cairo: Dar Su'ad al-Sabah, 1993), 13.

135. Ibid.

136. "Mudat al-sayyf fi hathi al-'am," *al-Musawwar*, special summer issue, 17 June 1935, 18–19. This article dates the opening of her boutique to March 1935. Aflatun, *Mudhakkirat*, states 1936.

137. Baraka, *Egyptian Upper Class*, 168; see also Abaza, *Changing Consumer Cultures of Modern Egypt* (Leiden, Netherlands: Brill, 2006), 124–25.

Chapter 2

Portions of this chapter were adapted from Nancy Reynolds, "Salesclerks, Sexual Danger, and National Identity in Egypt, 1920s–1950s," *Journal of Women's History* 23, no. 3

(Fall 2011). The small portion of reprinted material from this article included here falls under copyright © 2011 *Journal of Women's History* and has been reprinted by permission of the Johns Hopkins University Press. Adapted fragments from this article also appear in Chapter 6.

1. Janet Abu-Lughod, *Cairo: 1001 Years of the City Victorious* (Princeton, NJ: Princeton University Press, 1971), 185.

2. See Timothy Mitchell, *Colonising Egypt* (Berkeley: University of California Press, 1988), 11.

3. L. Benoit, "Croquis Egyptiens," *EN*, no. 59 (11 August 1923), 8. For a similar fascination with the temptations of this new commercial culture, see "'Itfaddali ya hanim," *al-Lata'if al-musawwara* 7, no. 356 (5 December 1921), 12; "Shari'a 'imad al-din," *al-Muqattam*, 17 February 1922, 3; "La paille et la poutre," *EN*, no. 26 (24 December 1922), 14; "Les Achats," *EN*, no. 26 (24 December 1922), 16.

4. Although originating as an institution in the Euro-American context, department stores of a similar variant emerged rather organically and contemporaneously in the Middle East, shaped by broad changes in systems of production and distribution in the world economy after the 1850s. The department store organized space, labor, and retail practices in novel ways and on an unprecedented scale. It combined diverse lines of trade, sold for cash on fixed prices, and made more autonomous the relationship between retailer and customer, allowing free entry with no obligation to buy, thus rendering shopping at once more rational and more leisurely. See Phillip Nord, *Politics of Resentment* (1986; repr., New Brunswick: Transaction, 2005), 65; Michael B. Miller, *The Bon Marché: Bourgeois Culture and the Department Store, 1869–1920* (Princeton, NJ: Princeton University Press, 1981), 27, 54; Erika Diane Rappaport, *Shopping for Pleasure: Women in the Making of London's West End* (Princeton, NJ: Princeton University Press, 2000); Geoffrey Crossick and Serge Jaumain, *Cathedrals of Consumption: The European Department Store, 1850–1939* (Brookfield, VT: Ashgate, 1999); William R. Leach, "Transformations in a Culture of Consumption: Women and Department Stores, 1890–1925," *Journal of American History* 71, no. 2 (September 1984): 319–42; Susan Porter Benson, *Counter Cultures: Saleswomen, Managers, and Customers in American Department Stores, 1890–1940* (Urbana: University of Illinois Press, 1986); and Gail Reekie, *Temptations: Sex, Selling, and the Department Store* (St. Leonards, Australia: Allen and Unwin, 1993). Outside the metropole and in areas without a nearby industrial base, however, department stores incorporated more variety and cultural specificity into these practices. Egyptian stores were generally smaller than their counterparts in Europe and the United States. See Kerrie L. MacPherson, ed., *Asian Department Stores* (Honolulu: University of Hawaii Press, 1998); Amy E. Randall, "Legitimizing Soviet Trade: Gender and the Feminization of the Retail Workforce in the Soviet 1930s," *Journal of Social History* 37, no. 4 (Summer 2004): 965–90; and Ara Wilson, *Intimate Economies of Bangkok* (Berkeley: University of California Press, 2004), 29–67.

5. Bulaq Street was renamed Fu'ad Street in the early 1920s and today is called 26th July Street. I have used Fu'ad throughout to simplify the narrative.

6. Morums advertisement, *al-Ahram*, 11 June 1925, 6. See also *Egyptian Gazette*, 12 June 1925, and *al-Ahram*, 6 June 1925, 7.

7. Shohet interview, OHD 35:1, 20 November 1964, 47.

8. "Hawla al-tasfiya al-kubra fi mahallat ikhwan shimla," *Ruz al-yusuf*, no. 347 (15 October 1934), 48.

9. Orosdi-Back advertisement, *Ruz al-yusuf*, no. 247 (7 November 1932), 18.

10. Cicurel advertisement, *La femme nouvelle*, March 1949. See also Benzion advertisement in the *Egyptian Gazette*, 22 September 1934. Importing could be tricky business for the stores, however. Shipments were often delayed, transportation was unreliable, and merchandise was held up in customs. See letter from Cohen for Chemla Frères to President of the French Chamber of Commerce in Cairo, dated Cairo, 8 May 1919, in Afrique, 1918–1929, Egypte 85–86, MAEP; letter from the director of Orosdi-Back to Defrance, Cairo, 23 August 1917, le Caire-Ambassade, 602/547, CADN; and Chalons customs fraud case, *Egyptian Gazette*, 12, 21, 25 May and 3, 5 June 1912. In the absence of actual buying records, most of which were destroyed by fire or renovation, the precise amounts of department-store merchandise that were imported and locally produced remain unknown. Despite their extensive publicity about imports, Egyptian department stores procured much of their merchandise from local producers. Donald Quataert notes that in Istanbul home-sewn garments were sold in local department stores at the turn of the century. *Manufacturing and Technology Transfer in the Ottoman Empire 1800–1914* (Istanbul: Isis Press, 1992), 24.

11. René Péron, *La Fin des vitrines: Des temples de la consommation aux usines à vendre* (Cachan, France: Editions de l'Ens-Cachan, 1993), 16.

12. Naguib Mahfouz, *Midaq Alley*, trans. Trevor Le Gassick (Washington, DC: Three Continents Press, 1977), 34.

13. Ibid., 40–41. Mahfouz explicitly sexualizes the encounter between the customer and the salesman.

14. *Rex vs. John Hayes for obtaining goods under false pretenses and larceny*, HBM Supreme Court dossier no. 95 of 1920, FO 841/195, NAUK. The Cairo Davies Bryan store, which sold British-made goods at fixed prices, had moved in 1910 to the St. David's Buildings on the corner of Manakh and ʿImad al-Din Streets in the Ismailia section of Cairo. See advertisement in the *Egyptian Gazette*, 2 January 1911; SOP, *1918 Egyptian Directory*; Arnold Wright and H. A. Cartwright, *Twentieth-Century Impressions of Egypt: Its History, People, Commerce, Industries, and Resources* (London: Lloyd's Greater Britain Publishing, 1909), 372, 468; and Samir Raafat, "Davies Bryan & Co.," *Egyptian Mail*, 27 May 1995. In the 1910s the company also had a store location in Khartoum, Sudan, with which Hayes may have been familiar.

15. See employees' testimony and store receipts in *Rex vs. John Hayes*, FO 841/195, NAUK.

16. Ibid.

17. In this case, although Hayes initially stole all these goods from the store, much of the merchandise was eventually recovered, and Hayes was sent to prison in Malta for six months of hard labor. For another case in which the company took a British captain to court to settle a large outstanding debt, see *Davies Bryan vs. J. H. Hadow*, case 15 of 1911, folder 10, FO 847/46, NAUK.

18. Plate glass was primarily a European import through the 1960s in Egypt, even though Muhammad Yasin's National Glassworks had opened a sheet-glass factory by 1951. See A. N. Cumberbatch for UK Board of Trade, *Egypt: Economic and Commercial Conditions in Egypt, October 1951* (London: HMSO, 1952), 66; Board of Trade, *Report of the United Kingdom Trade Mission 1955*, 34; United Arab Republic, *Twelve Years of Industrial Development*, 250.

19. Huda Shaarawi, *Harem Years: The Memoirs of an Egyptian Feminist, 1879–1924*, trans. Margot Badran (New York: Feminist Press of the City University of New York, 1987), 68–69.

20. Ibid., 68–69. In the memoir, this episode plays a metaphoric role in the establishment of Shaʿrawi's liberation from what she considers the patriarchal confines imposed by her class position.

21. Cited in Jacques Berque, *Egypt: Imperialism and Revolution*, trans. Jean Stewart (London: Faber and Faber, 1972), 349. On Muhammad Taymur (1891–1921), see Roger Allen, *The Arabic Literary Heritage* (New York: Cambridge University Press, 1998), 298, 330. The play *al-Hawiya* was written just before his death. See Julie Scott Meisami and Paul Starkey, *Encyclopedia of Arabic Literature*, vol. 2 (New York: Routledge, 1998), 762–63.

22. See *al-Lataʾif al-musawwara* 9, no. 430 (7 May 1923), 5, 8–9; "Cairo corso," *Egyptian Gazette*, 25 April 1923, 6; and various articles in *EN*, including "Nice au Caire," no. 41 (7 April 1923), 13; back-cover advertisement, no. 43 (21 April 1923); "Le corso carnavalesque," no. 44 (28 April 1923), 15–16. Corsos were also held in 1924 and 1929.

23. "Le corso fleuri," *La bourse égyptienne*, Alexandria edition, 24 April 1923, 3.

24. Mukhtar had sculpted a small-scale version of *Nahdat misr* after the 1919 Revolution, and in 1920 it won a French prize. Its photographic reproduction in the local press popularized it before the monumental statue was installed in 1928 in front of the Cairo train station. Beth Baron, *Egypt as a Woman* (Berkeley: University of California Press, 2005), 67–68.

25. *EN*, "Le corso carnavalesque," 15–16.

26. "Le corso fleuri," 3.

27. Orosdi-Back list of employees in letter from Leon Orosdi to Defrance, dated Manchester, 4 November 1914, le Caire-Ambassade, 602/546, CADN. On Sednaoui, see Jurji Zaydan, *Tarajim mashahir al-sharq* (Beirut: Dar Maktabat al-Haya, 1970), 1:409–19. The International Association of Commercial Employees of Cairo claimed in 1910 to represent five thousand employees in one thousand shops (Anastassiuf and Cavessa to Butrus Ghali, Cairo, 2 January 1910, MW: Sharikat wa-Jamaʿiyyat, 3J; DWQ). The

numbers remained roughly the same in the 1940s and 1950s. In 1952 only 1.75 percent of retail establishments employed more than fifteen workers per store, but this small number of stores engaged a full quarter of the nation's commercial workforce. See Ahmed Hussein and M. A. Badry, "A Statistical Report on Commercial Workers and the Effect of the Minimum Wage Scheme on Their Wages," EC 44, no. 271 (January 1953): 3; Abdel Aziz El Sherbini and Ahmed Fouad Sherif, "Marketing Problems in an Underdeveloped Country—Egypt," EC 47, no. 285 (July 1956): 29; and the three industrial and commercial censuses of 1927, 1937, and 1947 (which do not report their findings consistently). In 1947 Cicurel employed over 700 people, of which half were salesclerks, and 392 employees worked inside Sednaoui's stores (of which 254, or almost 65 percent, were salesclerks). See MS records, DWQ, Cairo: Cicurel, MS 75, 1947 lists; Sednaoui, MS 76, 1947 and 1949 lists and supporting biographical data.

28. Wright and Cartwright, *Twentieth-Century Impressions*, 372, 468; Samir Raafat, "Davies Bryan & Co.," *Egyptian Mail*, 27 May 1995.

29. On the Louvre and Bon Marché, see advertisements, *EN*, 1 January 1924, special issue.

30. *Al-Ahram*, 30 September 1901; Report by French commercial consul at Port Said, "Mouvement commercial de Port-Said en 1908," in NS, Egypte 118, no. 1:1908–1909, MAEP; Grandguillot to Ministre du Commerce et de l'Industrie in Paris, Alexandria, 22 April 1932, "a/s La crise et les grands magasins," in MAE, Afrique, 1918–1940, Egypte 108, MAEP.

31. See the *Egyptian Gazette*, 8 and 13 June 1925 and 28 March 1925. Miller, in *The Bon Marché*, mentions in passing the existence of branch stores in Algeria and Abyssinia but not Cairo.

32. L. D., "La fête du XIV juillet," *EN*, no. 55 (14 July 1923), 4.

33. *L'egyptienne* 3, no. 24, March 1927, inside back cover. The school was known as the Ecole de Poterie et de Céramique de Rod al-Farag. See also *L'egyptienne* 2, no. 16 (1 May 1926), no page number.

34. Grandguillot to Ministre du Commerce et de l'Industrie in Paris, Alexandria, 22 April 1932, "a/s La crise et les grands magasins," in MAE, Afrique, 1918–1940, Egypte 108, MAEP; Boeglin to Ministre du Commerce et de l'Industrie in Paris, Alexandria, 31 January 1936, "a/s Suppression des succursales des grands magasins," le Caire-Ambassade, 602/248, CADN.

35. See probate of Edward Davies Bryan in 1929, FO 841/298, NAUK.

36. Store architect Garo Balian designed several commercial buildings and the Egyptian University in Cairo in addition to Ottoman government buildings and monuments. See Wright and Cartwright, *Twentieth-Century Impressions*, 362. On the 1920 store fire, see *Times* (London), 21 October 1920, 9.

37. Cicurel's winter 1924–1925 catalog (Paris: Léon Ullman), in author's possession.

38. Wright and Cartwright, *Twentieth-Century Impressions*, 377, and Joel Beinin, *The Dispersion of Egyptian Jewry* (Berkeley: University of California Press, 1998), 47–49. On the Cicurel family, see also Gudrun Krämer, *The Jews in Modern Egypt, 1914–1952* (Seattle: University of Washington Press, 1989), 44–45; Maurice Mizrahi, *L'Egypte et ses juifs: Le temps révolu* (Lausanne, Switzerland: Imprimerie Avenir, 1977), 64–65; Nabil ʿAbd al-Hamid Sayyid Ahmad, *al-Hayat al-iqtisadiyya waʾl-ʿijtimaʿiyya liʾl-yahud fi Misr, 1947–1956* (Cairo: Maktabat Madbuli, 1991), 38–40; Samir Raafat, "The House of Cicurel," *al-Ahram Weekly*, 15 December 1994.

39. Shohet interview, OHD 35, no. 1 (20 November 1964), 46–47.

40. Solomon (b. 1881) died in 1927, and Yusuf became the senior partner until his death sometime during the Second World War (probably 1939), at which time the youngest brother, Salvator, took over the business until the family sold it in 1956. In 1927 Yusuf returned to Egypt to negotiate a buyout of Morums Oriental Stores; see "Another Murder in Cairo," *Egyptian Gazette*, 5 March 1927. The Cicurel firm was converted into an Egyptian limited stock company in February 1938, although it remained a family business. Clement Levy, *The Stock Exchange Year-Book of Egypt, 1941* (Cairo: Stock Exchange Year-Book of Egypt), 613–14. On store branches, see 1947 employee lists in Cicurel file, MS 75, DWQ; Cicurel advertisement, *La femme nouvelle*, March 1949.

41. "Masraʿ sulmun shikuril," *Al-Ahram*, 7 March 1927, 1.

42. List of board members, Cairo, 20 January 1948, doc. 2, folder 1, MS 75, DWQ.

43. "Lauriers," *EN*, no. 115 (21 June 1946), 2. He reportedly paid his numerous employees their salaries during three separate reconstructions of the store. See Mizrahi, *L'Egypte et ses juifs*, 65. In addition to reconstructions in 1920 and 1952, the store was also rebuilt in 1948.

44. Maurice Mizrahi, "The Role of Jews in Economic Development," in *The Jews of Egypt: A Mediterranean Society in Modern Times*, ed. Shimon Shamir (Boulder, CO: Westview, 1987), 86.

45. Mizrahi, *L'Egypte et ses juifs*, 64; Beinin, *Dispersion*, 47; Mizrahi, "Role of Jews," 86. See also "Lauriers," 2.

46. Cicurel advertisement, *La femme nouvelle*, March 1949.

47. This description of the interior of the early Chemla store was recalled by one of the Chemla granddaughters many years later. See Shohet interviews 35, no. 1 (20 November and 10 December 1964), OHD, 40–42. On the Chemla stores, see also Ahmad, *al-Hayat al-iqtisadiyya*, 38–41; and Krämer, *Jews in Modern Egypt*, 44.

48. Chemla catalog for December 1928, in author's possession.

49. Shohet interview 35, no. 1, OHD; "Hawla al-tasfiya al-kubra fi mahallat ikhwan shimla," *Ruz al-yusuf*, no. 347 (15 October 1934), 48. In 1946 the company was reorganized under new ownership (Ovadia Salem and Alfred Cohen). See "Fi ʿalam al-sharikat," *al-Balagh*, 18 May 1946.

50. Abu-Lughod, *Cairo*, 162; Samir W. Raafat, "Sednaoui," *Cairo Times*, 29 May–11 June 1997. On the histories and construction of the important French department stores, see Bernard Marrey, *Les grands magasins des origines à 1939* (Paris: Picard, 1979).

51. MS 76 file, DWQ, and Zaydan, *Tarajim mashahir al-sharq*, 409–19. See also Floresca Karanasou, "Egyptianisation: The 1947 Company Law and the Foreign Communities in Egypt" (DPhil diss., Oxford University, 1992), 270–85 (and esp. 270–73); Donald Reid, "Syrian Christians, the Rags-to-Riches Story, and Free Enterprise," *International Journal of Middle East Studies* 1 (1970): 358–67; Thomas Philipp, *The Syrians in Egypt, 1725–1975* (Stuttgart: Franz Steiner Verlag, 1985), 80, 93, 121, 122, 138; and Raafat, "Sednaoui," 21.

52. Zaydan, *Tarajim mashahir*, 415.

53. Zaydan gives the date as 1879, but all other sources indicate 1878.

54. In January 1907 the company was converted into an English limited liability company, and it remained a foreign company through the 1940s. Salim died in 1908, and Samʿan controlled the family firm until his death in 1936. At that time, Samʿan's son Yusuf took over the management of the company, which he still controlled in the late 1940s. Yusuf held Egyptian nationality. See information sheet dated 20 January 1948, folder 1, doc. no. 45, MS 76, DWQ. In 1939 the company was capitalized at £E209,625, but by 1947 the total amount of paid-up capital had expanded to £E645,000. Levy, *Stock Exchange Year-Book 1939*, 586; Elie I. Politi, ed., *Annuaire des sociétés égyptiennes par actions 1947* (Alexandria: Imprimerie Procaccia), 327–28.

55. MS 76, DWQ.

56. In the middle 1940s, Orosdi-Back's Egyptian branches used local buyers—Zaki Benzakein (who held Egyptian nationality) and Pandelis Demitriadis (a Greek)—who traveled to Manchester and France to purchase goods. See telegram from Lescuyer to Diplofrance, Paris, no. 145, Cairo, 22 February 1946, le Caire-Ambassade, 602/249, CADN. See also Colette Rossant, *Memories of a Lost Egypt: A Memoir with Recipes* (New York: Clarkson Potter, 1999), 19, on the use of buying agents for Palacci stores.

57. The business was founded in 1855 in Istanbul by two families (the Orosdis and the Backs) of Jewish, Austro-Hungarian descent. The first store in Istanbul was located in the Galata neighborhood and took its name from a previous building on its site: the ʿUmar Effendi khan. The company was registered in Paris in 1888. Uri M. Kupferschmidt, "Who Needed Department Stores in Egypt? From Orosdi-Back to Omar Effendi," *Middle Eastern Studies* 43, no. 2 (March 2007): 175–92, and *The Orosdi-Back Saga* (Istanbul: Ottoman Bank Archives and Research Centre, 2007); Samir Saul, *La France et l'Egypte de 1882 à 1914: Intérêts économiques et implications politiques* (Paris: Comité pour l'Histoire Économique et Financière de la France, 1997), 170–74; Samir Raafat, "Our Magyars: The Hungarians of Egypt," *Egyptian Mail*, 13 April 1996, 3; Léon Orosdi to Defrance, Paris, 1 May 1915, le Caire-Ambassade 602/546, CADN.

58. Wright and Cartwright, *Twentieth-Century Impressions*, 368. Annual turnover ranged from £150,000 to £180,000 (sterling) in the 1900s.

59. See advertisement in *Kashkul*, no. 259 (30 April 1926), 2. See also advertisement in *al-Ahram*, 12 June 1925, 3.

60. Rossant, *Memories of a Lost Egypt*, 32. She notes that the oldest Palacci sons (including her grandfather Vita) continued to marry Ladino-speaking Jewish women from Istanbul into the middle twentieth century.

61. Ibid., 41.

62. Favre's shop was the exclusive agent for the Unic brand of French shoes from Rômans (Drome), as well as shoes imported from Paris, Lyon, and Blois in the 1920s. Grandguillot to Ministre du Commerce et l'Industrie à Paris, Alexandria, 3 November 1922, le Caire-Ambassade 602/254, CADN. See also Consul at Port-Said to Bonnefoy, Port-Said, 12 January 1911, NS, Egypte 119, MAEP; *Bulletin mensuel de la chambre de commerce française d'Alexandrie* 14, no. 147 (January 1905): 44; See also *al-Dalil al-ʿamm 1927* (Cairo: al-Muqtataf/Muqtatam Press, 1927), 1110.

63. Wright and Cartwright, *Twentieth-Century Impressions*, 377.

64. *Al-Ahram*, 7 March 1896. See also *al-Ahram*, 29 September 1898; *al-Ahram*, 24 August 1901; *al-Ahram*, 6 January 1902.

65. Letter no. 92, Consul de France au Caire to Defrance, Cairo, 22 May 1917, le Caire-Ambassade 602/547, CADN. V. Debono was listed as a member of the Alexandria branch of the British Chamber of Commerce in Egypt in January 1905. See British Chamber of Commerce in Egypt, *Monthly Journal*, no. 16 (January 1905): 26. Matton was listed as an active member in the French Chamber of Commerce of Alexandria in 1912; *Bulletin mensuel de la chambre de commerce française d'Alexandrie* 21, no. 231 (January 1912): 35. Like Hornstein and Juster, Matton and Debono were listed on the monthly closing agreement in 1905: "Contrat," Cairo, 3 December 1905, copy attached to letter from Anastassiuf and Cavessa to Butrus Ghali, Cairo, 2 January 1910, MW: Sharikat wa-Jamaʿiyyat, 3J, DWQ.

66. By 1917 the company was wholly owned by Vincent Debono and his son Paul. See letter no. 92, Consul de France au Caire to Defrance, Cairo, 22 May 1917, le Caire Ambassade 602/547, CADN; SOP, *1918 Egyptian Directory*, 309, 420. The firm apparently closed after the store fire in 1926, as no mention of the shops appears in any of the directories after 1927 that I examined.

67. *George Debono vs. Francesco Azzopardi*, HBM Supreme Court at Cairo, 1927, FO 841/262, NAUK.

68. Magdi Wahba, "East and West: Cairo Memories." *Encounter* 62, no. 5 (May 1984): 74. See also E. Homan Mulock, *Report on the Economic and Financial Situation of Egypt, May 1928* (London: HMSO, 1928), 8. Krämer links Cicurel, Sednaoui, and Chemla as "striking[ly] parallel" stories of "rags to riches" in the development of commerce in

Egypt, and particularly department stores; Krämer, *Jews in Modern Egypt*, 45. See also Reid, "Syrian Christians."

69. Marius Schemeil, *Le Caire: Sa vie, son histoire, son peuple* (Cairo: Dar al-Maaref, 1949), 397.

70. Ibid., 396.

71. For an overview of the ideologies of Egyptian nationalism in the first half of the twentieth century, see Israel Gershoni and James Jankowski, *Egypt, Islam, and the Arabs: The Search for Egyptian Nationhood, 1900–1930* (New York: Oxford University Press, 1986), and *Redefining the Egyptian Nation, 1930–1945* (New York: Cambridge University Press, 1995).

72. Scholars have noted that Mediterranean migrations tended to be crisscrossing and temporary, in part because of the closed nature of the Mediterranean Basin. Peregrine Horden and Nicholas Purcell, "The Mediterranean and 'the New Thalassology,'" *American Historical Review* 111, no. 3 (June 2006): 733–37.

73. Beinin, *Dispersion*, 47.

74. Ibid., 44.

75. Ibid., 48.

76. Wahba, "East and West," 76. Wahba is careful to distinguish the nature of Cairo's cosmopolitanism from that of Alexandria or even of some of the large cities of the Delta.

77. Ibid., 76–77. It is noteworthy that Wahba does not account for Cairo's large population of Karaite Jews.

78. Ibid., 74.

79. "Un joli catalogue," *EN*, no. 126 (22 November 1924), 7. Cicurel's spring 1925 catalog was also acclaimed by the magazine as "exquisite" and a "work of art." See *EN*, no. 145 (4 April 1925), 107.

80. "La bonne publicité," *EN*, no. 125 (15 November 1924), 7–8. The local Bon Marché's summer 1925 catalog also was designed by Bréval and included a complete history of the Paris-based house as well as numerous photographs. See *EN*, no. 146 (11 April 1925), 33.

81. Cicurel's winter 1924–1925 catalog, printed by Léon Ullmann, Paris. Cicurel also had an illustrated summer catalog for 1924 printed in Paris (see *EN*, no. 90 [15 March 1924], 164) and one for winter 1923 (see *EN*, no. 73 [17 November 1923], 310). Cicurel's toy and gift catalog for 1930 and 1931 was less sumptuous (perhaps reflecting the economics of the depression years) as it was only in a single color, but it was still bilingual French and Arabic. A twenty-page Chemla sale catalog from December 1928 was also bilingual Arabic and French, although less lavish in its paper quality and the reproduction of the images and texts than the Cicurel catalogs of 1924–1925 and even 1930–1931.

82. *Al-Ahram*, 7 March 1896. See also *al-Ahram*, 29 September 1898; *al-Ahram*, 24 August 1901; *al-Ahram*, 6 January 1902. Bangkok stores used similar strategies. See Wilson, *Intimate Economies*, 46.

83. Ann Stoler uses the slightly more general term "cultural competencies" about a different topic in *Carnal Knowledge and Imperial Power: Race and the Intimate in Colonial Rule* (2002; repr., Berkeley: University of California Press, 2010), 84.

84. French consul to Mme. Cruppi, Cairo, 14 April 1921, le Caire-Ambassade 602/245, CADN. See also Lefevre-Pontalis to Millerand, Cairo, 15 February 1920, le Caire-Ambassade 602/245, CADN, and the classified ads in *EN*.

85. Jacques d'Aumale, *Voix de l'Orient* (Montreal: 1945), 75, quoted in Kupferschmidt, *Orosdi-Back Saga*, 45. See also Robert Ilbert, Ilios Yannakakis, and Jacques Hassoun, *Alexandria, 1860–1960* (1992; repr., Alexandria, Egypt: Harpocrates, 1997), 110.

86. "Taqrir al-taftish," 10 July 1950, and 1949 employee lists, Cicurel, MS 75, DWQ.

87. Walter Armbrust, *Mass Culture and Modernism*, chap. 3 (New York: Cambridge University Press, 1996).

88. List of employees and their nationality, enclosed in letter from Leon Orosdi to Defrance, Manchester, 4 November 1914, le Caire-Amabassade, 602/546, CADN. This list did not specify type of employment, except for the "domestiques" and directors.

89. "Local subjects" is often a confusing term in this period, as Egyptian citizenship did not exist in 1914. Before that, Egyptians would have been considered Ottoman subjects, as would have others born outside Egypt but still within the boundaries of the Ottoman Empire, whether or not they had moved to Egypt. That this document distinguished between "local subjects" and "Ottomans" suggests to me, however, that in this case "local subject" did refer more specifically to those born or domiciled for some time in Egypt.

90. Not all people in the employee list were classified by nationality. List of employees and their nationality, enclosed in letter from Leon Orosdi to Defrance, Manchester, 4 November 1914, le Caire-Amabassade, 602/546, CADN.

91. The Greeks tended to move into rural areas or provincial cities in Egypt more than other groups of migrants. See Alexander Kitroeff, *The Greeks in Egypt, 1919–1937: Ethnicity and Class* (London: Ithaca Press, 1989).

92. See 1947 employee lists for Cicurel, MS 75, DWQ. Data on employee ethnicity comes from company investigations by Egyptian officials in the Department of Corporations (*maslahat al-sharikat*; MS) to monitor the mandatory Egyptianization of capital, administration, and staffs of joint-stock companies registered in Egypt. Although companies were not always honest in their disclosures, the nature of the MS monitoring appears to have fairly quickly encouraged compliance. See Liliane S. Dammond with Yvette M. Raby, *The Lost World of the Egyptian Jews: First-Person Accounts from Egypt's Jewish Community in the Twentieth Century* (New York: iUniverse, 2007), 195. Since many of the employee lists include dates of hire, the files can be read backward to glimpse salesclerk ethnicity in the 1910s, 1920s, and 1930s. It is difficult to compare accurately the Cicurel employees to those at Sednaoui, Chemla, and other stores because the Cicurel employee lists for 1947 do not include specific nationality of the foreign

employees (they are merely listed as foreign). See also Karanasou, "Egyptianisation," on the MS.

93. See, e.g., case of Qadriyya al-Qattan, Chemla employee lists and notes doc. pp. 53, 204–5, MS 73, DWQ.

94. See employee lists for 1947, Chemla, MS 73, DWQ. At least two department heads were Chemla family members: Albert Sabban and Leon Shohet. For the identities of the cousins, see Shohet interview 35, no. 1.

95. See employee lists and supporting biographical data for the 1947 employee lists and the 1949 employee lists in Sednaoui's file, MS 76, DWQ. This is one of the few entire departments that can be reconstructed from the archives.

96. See Joel Beinin and Zachary Lockman, *Workers on the Nile: Nationalism, Communism, Islam, and the Egyptian Working Class, 1882–1954* (Princeton, NJ: Princeton University Press, 1987), 111. See also "L'agitation travailliste: Les employés de commerce et d'industrie," *La bourse égyptienne* (Alexandria ed.), 22 August 1919, 2; "Un nouveau syndicat," *La bourse égyptienne* (Alexandria ed.), 27 August 1919, 2; "L'agitation travailliste: Dans un magasin de notre ville," *La bourse égyptienne* (Alexandria ed.), 17 September 1919.

97. See "Un délit d'opinion," *EN*, no. 91 (22 March 1924), 8; Goldenberg, "Employeurs and employés," *EN* 2, no. 80 (5 January 1924), 2. Goldenberg was arrested and jailed for his activism in March 1924.

98. *EN*, no. 75 (1 December 1923), 8; *EN*, no. 150 (9 May 1925), 591.

99. Beinin and Lockman, *Workers on the Nile*, 328–29; see also 333–49.

100. Mona Abaza, *Changing Consumer Cultures of Modern Egypt* (Leiden, Netherlands: Brill, 2006), 77–79; Magda Baraka, *The Egyptian Upper Class between Revolutions* (Oxford: Ithaca Press, 1998); Mona Russell, *Creating the New Egyptian Woman: Consumerism, Education, and National Identity, 1863–1922* (New York: Palgrave Macmillan, 2004), 56.

101. Morums advertisement, *al-Ahram*, 11 June 1925, 6; *al-Lataʾif al-musawwara* 7, no. 365 (5 December 1921), 12; Latifa al-Zayyat, *The Open Door*, trans. Marilyn Booth (New York: American University in Cairo Press, 2000), 110–12. The 1939 Egyptian film *Resolution* (*al-ʿAzima*) featured a series of scenes in a Cairo department store as its climax. A group of women from a lower-middle-class neighborhood entice a new bride to the department store, where she unexpectedly finds her husband working as a lowly wrapper. On the tensions of the film's representation of lower-class life, see Armbrust, *Mass Culture*, 100.

102. Mary Louise Roberts, "Gender, Consumption, and Commodity Culture," *American Historical Review* 103, no. 3 (June 1998): 817–44. She writes on page 841, for example, that we must discard "a definition of power as simply the 'power of the purse'—the economic ability to make consumer decisions and purchases. . . . By broadening our notion of the power operative in commodities . . . we can explore a fuller range of ways

that they shaped subjectivity and experience. Nor should we confine our explorations to the literal act of consumption."

103. See probate files in Micallef Affair 1936, FO 841/551, NAUK.

104. On the near absence of market analysis done by businesses in Egypt, see Sherbini and Sherif, "Marketing Problems," 69–70.

105. Roger Owen, *The Middle East in the World Economy, 1800–1914* (New York: Methuen, 1981), 219. See also *La publicité à l'étranger: Comment la faire? Egypte* (Paris: Publications de l'Office National du Commerce Extérieur, January 1914), 4, le Caire-Amabssade 602/256, CADN. On the consumption patterns of the upper classes in this period, see Baraka, *Egyptian Upper Class.*

106. R. M. Turner, *Economic Conditions in Egypt, July 1931* (London: HMSO, 1931), 42–43.

107. BOT, *Report of the United Kingdom Trade Mission 1955*, 51.

108. Ibid. Sherbini and Sherif ("Marketing Problems," 32) also estimate that middle-class families, mostly business, commercial, and government employees, formed the "basis" of customers for Egyptian department stores.

109. The Egyptian Clothing and Equipment Co., which managed the shop Au Carnavale de Venise, had at least four commission agents on its staff in 1947. "Taqrir taftish," 28 September 1949, 89, Egyptian Clothing and Equipment Co., MS 164, DWQ; inspector's report, dated 1 March 1950, 110, Egyptian Clothing and Equipment Co., MS 164, DWQ. See also *Juifs d'Egypte: Images et textes*, 2nd ed. (Paris: Editions du Scribe, 1984), 202–3. Some commission agents probably acted as brokers importing goods into Egypt from foreign factories. See the advertisement by an "Egyptian commission agent" in *al-Muqattam*, 5 March 1922, 3.

110. Kahanoff interview, 11 June 1965, p. 25 of transcript, OHD; Raafat, "Sednaoui," 21.

111. *Morgenstern vs. Christoforou*, dossier 34/1928, in FO 841/272, NAUK.

112. Sednaoui advertisement, *EN*, no. 56 (10 September 1943), 12.

113. See advertisement for Cicurel in *EN*, no. 624 (28 September 1956). See also *al-Balagh* on 16 September 1947.

114. M. de Chabrol, "Essai sur les moeurs des habitans modernes de l'Egypte," in *La description de l'Egypte*, vol. 14, (Paris: Imprimerie Impériale, 1809), 506.

115. Fikri al-Khuli recounts shopping for the ʿid in his memoirs of the 1920s. He and other villagers bought food, cloth handkerchiefs, shoes, and especially children's clothing to mark the holiday. See al-Khuli, *al-Rihla*, vol. 1 (Cairo: Dar al-Ghad, 1987–1992), 40–41. See also Ibrahim Abdel Meguid, *No One Sleeps in Alexandria*, trans. Farouk Abdel Wahab (Cairo: American University in Cairo Press, 1999), 98, 102.

116. Complaints about merchants engaging in price gouging and other "corrupt" practices also existed around the increased demand for goods at holidays. See, for example, "Kaifa qada al-kathirun hadha al-ʿid?," *al-Liwaʾ*, 15 December 1910, 1.

117. Chemla Brothers advertisement, *al-Liwa'*, 17 September 1910, 7. See also Cicurel advertisement, *al-Ahram*, 12 February 1933, 13; Sednaoui advertisement, *al-Musawwar*, no. 1240 (16 July 1948), 35; Gattengo's *'id* sale listing, *al-Balagh*, 3 July 1951.

118. R. M. Turner, for UK Department of Overseas Trade, *The Economic and Financial Situation in Egypt, June 1929* (London: HMSO, 1929), 27.

119. Al-Mawardi advertisement, *al-Ahram*, 15 June 1925, 2; see also Sednaoui advertisement, *al-Musawwar*, no. 1252 (8 October 1948), 36.

120. See, for example, Cicurel advertisement in *al-Ahram*, 26 March 1927; Sednaoui advertisement in *al-Ahram*, 15 April 1935. In January 1924 Chemla announced a sale of toys and other gifts for the Orthodox New Year. See *EN*, 1 January 1924, special issue.

121. "Rapport sur les services des compagnies de navigation françaises entre la France et l'Egypte," pt. 2, 2, attached to letter, Cairo, 23 October 1929, in Afrique, 1918–1929, Egypte 64, MAEP. Italics in original.

122. See, for example, Chemla's advertisement for Passover in *EN*, no. 146 (11 April 1925), 441.

123. Letter from Anastassiuf and Cavessa to Butrus Ghali, Cairo, 2 January 1910, MW: Sharikat wa-Jam'iyyat, 3J; DWQ. In the early 1950s, legislation to regulate the working hours of commercial employees required unpaid overtime during Ramadan and before the *'id al-'adha*, Catholic and Orthodox Christmases, Gregorian New Year, and regional *mawlids*. See the text of Bylaw of 15 May 1951 for "*heures de travail*," *La gazette fiscale, commerciale et industrielle*, ed. Zaki Hassan (Alexandria), 1, nos. 11–12 (July–August 1951), 438.

124. Sherbini and Sherif, "Marketing Problems," 27.

125. Chemla advertisement ("Pour vous aussi, messieurs"), *EN*, no. 78 (22 December 1923), 14. See also Raafat, "Sednaoui," 21.

126. See Judith Tucker, *Women in Nineteenth-Century Egypt* (New York: Cambridge University Press, 1985), 82; Shaarawi, *Harem Years*, 48; Edward Lane, *Manners and Customs of the Modern Egyptians* (1836, 1895; repr., London: East-West Publications, 1989), 161.

127. Examples of advertisements aimed at men include Cicurel advertisements for overcoats, suits, and headgear in *al-Ahram*, 4 January 1935, 7, and *Ruz al-yusuf*, no. 374 (22 April 1935), 34; Cicurel advertisement for men's suits in *Ruz al-yusuf*, no. 367 (4 March 1935), 19; and Sednaoui advertisement in *al-Ahram*, 3 December 1937, for men's robes and overcoats. For the companionate family, see advertisements for the Egyptian Products Sales Co. store, *al-Ahram*, 1 November 1938, 10; and for al-Tarabishi dry-goods store, *al-Balagh*, 21 August 1946. In al-Zayyat's *The Open Door*, the Cicurel sale in which Gamila purchases her trousseau is attended by a "crush" of shoppers that included Gamila's brother; "a man in a gray suit [and] . . . his wife, who was setting a hat with a large feather in it on her head" and buying English cloth on sale; and groups of women customers, some even dressed in black gowns (*thiyab suda'a*) usually associated with

more conservative families from the old city (110–12). And see Latifa al-Zayyat, *al-Bab al-Maftuh* (1960; Cairo: al-Hayat al-Misriyya al-ʿAmma liʾl-Kitab, 1989), 103.

128. Russell, *Creating the New Egyptian Woman*, 84. See also Relli Shechter, *Transitions in Domestic Consumption and Family Life in the Modern Middle East* (New York: Palgrave Macmillan, 2003).

129. Russell, *Creating the New Egyptian Woman*, 37. See also Lisa Pollard, *Nurturing the Nation* (Berkeley: University of California Press, 2005); Shaarawi, *Harem Years*; Margo Badran, *Feminists, Islam, and Nation* (Princeton, NJ: Princeton University Press, 1995); and Beth Baron, *The Women's Awakening in Egypt: Culture, Society, and the Press* (New Haven, CT: Yale University Press, 1994), and "The Making and Breaking of Marital Bonds in Modern Egypt," in *Women in Middle Eastern History*, ed. Nikki R. Keddie and Beth Baron (New Haven, CT: Yale University Press, 1991), 275–91.

130. Shaarawi, *Harem Years*, 68–69.

131. Wright and Cartwright, *Twentieth-Century Impressions*, 372.

132. See advertisement "Morums et la mode," *EN*, no. 55 (14 July 1923), inside cover; Russell, *Creating the New Egyptian Woman*, 66.

133. See Miller, *Bon Marché*, 183.

134. Phillip Nord, *The Politics of Resentment* (1986; repr., New Brunswick: Transaction, 2005); Rappaport, *Shopping*; Lise Shapiro Sanders, *Consuming Fantasies: Labor, Leisure, and the London Shopgirl, 1880–1920* (Columbus: Ohio State University Press, 2006); Lisa Tiersten, *Marianne in the Market: Envisioning Consumer Society in Fin-de-Siècle France* (Berkeley: University of California Press, 2001).

Chapter 3

1. Letter from Esther F. Wissa (signed "Isis, a Daughter of Egypt") Cairo, 20 December 1924, listed as document 23, FO 141/511/5/14083, NAUK. Wissa's letter was written in English from the Continental Hotel in Cairo. That she incorrectly spells the French word for "liver" (*foie*), substituting the similar-sounding *fois*, meaning "time," points to her English education and the broad influence of French culture. This file contains several letters from her to the British of a similar tone; she continued to write to the British in the 1930s. On Wissa, see H. Wissa, *Assiout: The Saga of an Egyptian Family* (Sussex, UK: Book Guild, 1994), which reprints many of her letters to the British, although not the one cited here. Upper-class women in Mandate Palestine also wrote similar appeals to the British. See Ellen Fleischmann, *The Nation and Its "New" Women: The Palestinian Women's Movement, 1920–1948* (Berkeley: University of California Press, 2003).

2. Wissa letter, Cairo, 20 December 1924, document 23, FO 141/511/5/14083, NAUK.

3. Captivity images were popular in locally produced depictions of Egyptians under colonial rule. These texts included important sculptures, paintings, and cartoons, and many of them used the image of women to represent captive Egypt. This was especially

true of discourse associated with Mustafa Kamil. See Beth Baron, *Egypt as a Woman* (Berkeley: University of California Press, 2005), 62, 65, 72.

4. The Andersonian imagined community privileges the novels and newspapers of print capitalism as sites for the production of nationalism. Benedict Anderson, *Imagined Communities: Reflections on the Origin and Spread of Nationalism* (London: Verso, 1991). On the development of nationalism in Egyptian print capitalism, see Israel Gershoni and James Jankowski, *Egypt, Islam and the Arabs: The Search for Egyptian Nationhood, 1900–1930* (New York: Oxford University Press, 1986), and Israel Gershoni and James Jankowski, *Redefining the Egyptian Nation, 1930–1945* (New York: Cambridge University Press, 1995).

5. Some British Foreign Office officials noted that she was "cracked on the subject of the Jews," although others admired that she "gives High Commissioners her views on the political situation" and felt that she was generally "sane, and a good, charitable woman." See "Political Situation, views of Saadist Women's Committee" folders in FO 141/593/150 and FO 141/705/595, NAUK.

6. Wissa, *Assiout*, 240.

7. Ibid. See Baron, *Egypt*, 174–77.

8. Wissa, *Assiout*, 173, 179.

9. Baron, *Egypt*, 175.

10. Wissa, *Assiout*, 75–76. Tawfiq al-Hakim describes such a river salvage in *Yawmiyat na'ib fi'l-aryaf* (Cairo: Maktabat Misr, 1988), 57.

11. On the variety of styles of galabiya in Egypt, see Mamoun Fandy, "Political Science without Clothes: The Politics of Dress; or, Contesting the Spatiality of the State in Egypt," in *Beyond the Exotic: Women's Histories in Islamic Societies*, ed. by Amira el-Azhary Sonbol (Syracuse, NY: Syracuse University Press, 2005), 381–98; and Andrea B. Rugh, *Reveal and Conceal: Dress in Contemporary Egypt* (Syracuse, NY: Syracuse University Press, 1986).

12. V. Shearer, "Report on the Weaving Industry in Assiout," *EC* 1 (1910): 184–85.

13. Wissa, *Assiout*, contains numerous photographs of her. It is very possible she would have worn galabiya more privately at home.

14. In contrast to a labor boycott, a consumer or commercial boycott has been defined as "an attempt by one or more parties to achieve certain objectives by urging individual consumers to refrain from making selected purchases in the marketplace." Monroe Friedman, *Consumer Boycotts: Effecting Change through the Marketplace and the Media* (New York: Routledge, 1999), 4.

15. Karl Gerth, *China Made* (Cambridge, MA: Harvard University Press, 2003); C. A. Bayly, "The Origins of Swadeshi (Home Industry): Cloth and Indian Society, 1700–1930," in *The Social Life of Things: Commodities in Cultural Perspective*, ed. Arjun Appadurai (New York: Cambridge University Press, 1986), 285–321; Emma Tarlo, *Clothing Matters: Dress and Identity in India* (Chicago: University of Chicago Press, 1996); Manu Goswami, *Producing India: From Colonial Economy to National Space* (Chicago: University

of Chicago Press, 2004). On boycotts in South Africa in 1917, see A. Adu Boahen, *Africa under Colonial Domination, 1880–1935* (Berkeley: University of California Press, 1990), 290; and in colonial Gabon, see Jeremy Rich, *A Workman Is Worthy of His Meat: Food and Colonialism in the Gabon Estuary* (Lincoln: University of Nebraska Press, 2007). *Boycott* was coined in 1880 in Ireland during struggles between Irish peasants and British landowners. See Friedman, *Consumer Boycotts*, 5–8.

16. Breen, *The Marketplace of Revolution: How Consumer Politics Shaped American Independence* (New York: Oxford University Press, 2004), 20. See also Michael Zakim, "Sartorial Ideologies: From Homespun to Ready-Made," *American Historical Review* 106, no. 5 (December 2001): 1553–86.

17. Breen, *Marketplace of Revolution*, xvi.

18. James Scott, *Weapons of the Weak: Everyday Forms of Peasant Resistance* (New Haven, CT: Yale University Press, 1985), 248–55; Breen, *Marketplace of Revolution*; Lawrence B. Glickman, *Buying Power: A History of Consumer Activism in America* (Chicago: University of Chicago Press, 2009), 14, 18–19, 25. Glickman investigates American boycotts of slave-produced goods; similar boycotts of sugar occurred in Great Britain in the 1790s. See also Glickman, "'Buy for the Sake of the Slave': Abolition and the Origins of American Consumer Activism," *American Quarterly* 56, no. 4 (December 2004): 889–912. On the European boycotts in the 1930s against Nazi Jewish policies, the 1974–1984 boycott of Nestlé for infant formula sales in third-world countries, and African American boycotts in the U.S. civil rights struggle, see Michele Micheletti, *Political Virtue and Shopping* (New York: Palgrave Macmillan, 2003), and Friedman, *Consumer Boycotts*. On contemporary boycotts of American goods in Egypt, see Taline Djerdjerian, "Political Consumerism and the Boycott of American Goods in Egypt," in *Cairo Contested*, ed. Diane Singerman (Cairo: American University in Cairo Press, 2009), 393–413.

19. See Glickman, "'Buy for the Sake of the Slave.'" Glickman charts change from the eighteenth to twentieth centuries in American consumer politics as a result of changing ideas of political economy, and especially the acceptance of Adam Smith's theories of the economy. When the American changes are compared to boycotts in other parts of the world, however, the difference between eighteenth and nineteenth century U.S. boycotts seems to align more with colonial versus noncolonial dynamics and the importance of creating a nation-state through consumption in the colonial contexts.

20. Glickman, *Buying Power*, 14. By contrast, nineteenth-century American abolitionist boycotts of slave-made goods invested the act of purchasing (rather than use or nonuse of a good) with moral power.

21. Breen, *Marketplace of Revolution*, 19–20, xvi. See also Daniel Boorstin's notion of "consumption communities," in *The Americans: The Democratic Experience* (New York: Random House, 1973), 89–90.

22. Glickman, "'Buy for the Sake of the Slave,'" 893. On the morality of the marketplace in consumerist politics, see also Matthew Hilton and Martin Daunton, "Material

Politics," in *The Politics of Consumption: Material Culture and Citizenship in Europe and America*, ed. Martin Daunton and Matthew Hilton (New York: Berg, 2001), 14–18.

23. Glickman, *Buying Power*, 23–24.

24. Lizabeth Cohen, *A Consumer's Republic: The Politics of Mass Consumption in Postwar America* (New York: Vintage Books, 2003).

25. Meg Jacobs, *Pocketbook Politics: Economic Citizenship in Twentieth-Century America* (Princeton, NJ: Princeton University Press, 2005); Glickman, *Buying Power*, 14.

26. Gerth, *China Made*, 118.

27. Ibid., 125. Supported by an elaborate regional institutional structure, the Chinese movement incorporated a range of social classes and both men and women consumers.

28. Ibid., 4.

29. Ibid., 120.

30. Ibid., 25.

31. Palmira Brummett, *Image and Imperialism in the Ottoman Revolutionary Press, 1908–1911* (Albany: State University of New York Press, 2000), 175–76; Uri M. Kupferschmidt, *The Orosdi-Back Saga* (Istanbul: Ottoman Bank Archives and Research Centre, 2007), 32–33; Michelle U. Campos, *Ottoman Brothers: Muslims, Christians, and Jews in Early Twentieth-Century Palestine* (Stanford, CA: Stanford University Press, 2011), 100–109. The Ottomans also participated in an important Greek boycott in 1910 (Kupferschmidt, *Orosdi-Back Saga*, 32–33).

32. See, e.g., Mark LeVine, *Overthrowing Geography: Jaffa, Tel Aviv, and the Struggle for Palestine, 1880–1948* (Berkeley: University of California Press, 2005); Micheletti, *Political Virtue and Shopping*, 64–65.

33. Lisa Trivedi, *Clothing Gandhi's Nation: Homespun and Modern India* (Bloomington: Indiana University Press, 2007); Lajpat Rai, *Young India: The Nationalist Movement* (New York: B. W. Huebsch, 1917), 163–80.

34. Noor-Aiman Iftikhar Khan, "The Enemy of My Enemy: Indian Influences on Egyptian Nationalism, 1907–1930" (PhD diss., University of Chicago, 2006).

35. Ibid., 179.

36. Marilyn Booth, *May Her Likes Be Multiplied: Biography and Gender Politics in Egypt* (Berkeley: University of California Press, 2001), 42–43, 140; Margo Badran, *Feminists, Islam, and Nation* (Princeton, NJ: Princeton University Press, 1995), 103–4.

37. Khan, "The Enemy of My Enemy," 1–3, 181–84.

38. Subhas Chandra Bose, *Swadeshi and Boycott* (Calcutta, 1931), cited in Micheletti, *Political Virtue and Shopping*, 41–42. See Micheletti for a discussion of private and public virtue in consumerist politics.

39. See Baron, *Egypt as a Woman*, 107.

40. Telegram from Hoda Charaoui to Lloyd George et al., Cairo, 21 January 1922, doc. no. 2, FO 141/511/14083, NAUK. See telegram no. 28, Allenby to [Curzon?], Cairo, 23 January 1922, FO 371/7730, NAUK. Signatories included Hamad el-Basel, Wissa Wasif,

Aly Maher, George Khayat, Wasif Ghali, Morcos Hanna, Elwi el Gazzar, and Murad el Shareii, prominent Wafdist leaders. See also Juan Ricardo Cole, "Feminism, Class, and Islam in Turn-of-the-Century Egypt," *International Journal of Middle East Studies* 13 (1981): 394–407; "Ihtijaj al-sayyidat," *Misr*, 24 January 1922; "Ijtimaʿa al-sayyidat al-misriyyat," *al-Ahram*, 23 January 1922, 2; "al-Muqataʿa fiʾl-ʿasima," and "Ijtimaʿa al-sayyidat al-misriyyat," *Misr*, 25 January 1922, on the boycott and its resolutions. See also "Ephémérides," *EN*, no. 124 (8 November 1924), 298.

41. Oath cited in Badran, *Feminists, Islam, and Nation*, 83, and Russell, *Creating the New Egyptian Woman*, 90.

42. In March 1924 there were 31,000 telephones in Egypt, with many new services recently opened in the provinces. "The telephone," according to the British annual report, "is becoming more and more a necessity of provincial life in Egypt, both for commercial and private affairs. . . . [It] is increasingly used by harem women, who gossip on it frequently and at prodigious length." Allenby to MacDonald, "Egypt Annual Report, 1923," 23 July 1924, 45, FO 371/10060, NAUK. See also "al-Tilifun," *Misr al-haditha al-musawwara*, no. 7 (April–May 1927): 3–9.

43. Grace Thompson Seton, *A Woman Tenderfoot in Egypt* (New York: Dodd, Mead, 1923), 29.

44. Ibid., 29–30.

45. Ibid., 30–31.

46. Eric Davis, *Challenging Colonialism: Bank Misr and Egyptian Industrialization, 1920–1941* (Princeton, NJ: Princeton University Press, 1983), 116–17. See also "al-Nahda al-misriyya fi tawrha al-jadid," *al-Ahram*, 3 January 1922, 1.

47. Hawwaʾ Idris, "My Cousin Hoda Shaʿarawy: Synopsis of Her Struggle for the Country and for Women," unpublished and undated manuscript in the personal papers and clippings collection of Hawwaʾ Idris, deposited at the Rare Book Library of the American University in Cairo.

48. *Al-Ahram*, 23 January 1922, 2. Zifta was a regional center for hand weaving of cloth.

49. See translation of letter of 5 April 1922 from Mme. Saad Zaghlul to her husband, in Minister of Interior to Furness, 6 April 1922, doc. 13, FO 141/511/14089, NAUK.

50. "Aswaq jadida," *Misr*, 31 January 1922, 2. Samnud had witnessed strong protests for the boycott the week before. See "Ihtijaj al-sayyidat," *Misr*, 24 January 1922.

51. "Al-Muqataʿa fiʾl-buhayra," *al-Akhbar*, 17 January 1922, 3. See also "al-Muqataʿa fiʾl-aqalim," *al-Akhbar*, 12 January 1922, 2; and "Hawla al-muqataʿa," *al-Akhbar*, 12 January 1922, 2.

52. "Feuille d'information commerciales—Egypte, no. 13," dated 27 January 1922, le Caire-Ambassade, 602/246, CADN.

53. *Al-Akhbar*, 29 January 1922, 3.

54. *Al-Ahram*, 20 March 1922, 4.

55. "Qarar al-wafd al-misri fi'l-muqawama al-salabiyya," *al-Muqattam*, 24 January 1922, 2.

56. Ibid.

57. Muhammad Ghali Fawda, "Ma hila al-tujjar," *al-Muqattam*, 31 January 1922, 1.

58. See al-Mawardi advertisement, *al-Muqattam*, 26 February 1922, 3.

59. Husayn al-Halabi, "Ta'sis jam'iyya li-nashr al-bada'i al-wataniyya," *al-Akhbar*, 16 January 1922, 2.

60. Ibid.

61. "Hajat Misr ila al-sina'," *Misr*, 26 January 1922.

62. Mustafa Muhammad al-Ray'a, "al-Nasij al-watani," *Misr*, 15 February 1922, 3.

63. Ibid.

64. Badran, *Feminists, Islam, and Nation*, 87; Baron, *Egypt as a Woman*, 173.

65. Telegram from Sha'rawi to Allenby, Cairo, 10 November 1924, doc. 19 in FO 141/511/14083, NAUK.

66. Ibid.

67. Baron, *Egypt as a Woman*, 176.

68. E. Homan Mulock, *Report on the Economic and Financial Situation of Egypt, April 1923* (London: HMSO, 1923), 48; G. H. Selous and L. B. S. Larkins, for UK Department of Overseas Trade, *Economic Conditions in Egypt, July 1933* (London: HMSO, 1933), 101.

69. Malak Badrawi, *Isma'il Sidqi* (Richmond, UK: Curzon, 1996), 83, 75.

70. Baron, *Egypt as a Woman*, 176.

71. Loraine to Secretary of State, 18 June 1931, FO 141/770, NAUK.

72. E.g., *Ruz al-yusuf*, no. 202 (28 December 1931), 8. I discuss the commercial response later.

73. On the 1912 Agricultural Fair at Giza, see "Agricultural Show: Great Display at Giza," *Egyptian Gazette*, 13 February 1912.

74. See Bordereau d'envoi, 20 April 1931, including Grandguillot to Ministre du Commerce et de l'Industrie, Cairo, 20 March 1931, "a/s Egypte: Exposition agricole et industrielle," Afrique, 1930–1940, Egypte 107, MAEP.

75. Boycott proclamations, the Egyptian press, and the British noted her presence there. See FO 141/770, NAUK.

76. Confidential letter from Keown-Boyd, Cairo, 3 March 1931, FO 141/770, NAUK.

77. See 'Abd al-Rahman al-Rafi'i, *Fi a'qab al-thawra al-misriyya*, 3rd ed. (Cairo: Dar al-Ma'arif, 1987), 2:340–41. Naguib Mahfouz also characterizes the "boycott of foreign goods" to be one of the three primary concerns of Egyptian university students in the early 1930s; *al-Qahira al-jadida* (Cairo: Dar Misr li'l-Tiba'a, 1945), 15.

78. Gershoni and Jankowski, *Egypt, Islam and the Arabs* and *Redefining the Egyptian Nation*.

79. Residency Minute, 16 June 1931, FO 141/770, NAUK.

80. Residency Minute, 11 March 1931, FO 141/770, NAUK.

81. Ibid.

82. Draft Residency memo, "Boycott, British Goods," 7 March 1931, FO 141/770, NAUK.

83. "Committee of the Young Wafdist Volunteers for the Purpose of Encouraging Egyptian Manufactured Goods," a notice appearing in *al-Fallah*, 3 March 1931, and *al-Dia*, 3 March 1931, translated and enclosed in Keown-Boyd to Oriental Secretary, Cairo, 3 March 1931, FO 141/770/515, NAUK.

84. Ibid.

85. "Formation of a committee for encouraging native manufactured goods," a notice appearing in *al-Fallah*, 3 March 1931, and *al-Dia*, 3 March 1931, translated and enclosed in Keown-Boyd to Oriental Secretary, Cairo, 3 March 1931, FO 141/770/515, NAUK.

86. Keown-Boyd to Smart, Cairo, 1 May 1932, FO 141/711/465, NAUK. At the same time, the Wafd reportedly drew up a list of commission agents handling the importation of British goods. See Turner, Residency Minute, 10 March 1932, FO 141/711/465, NAUK.

87. Keown-Boyd to Smart, Cairo, 1 May 1932, FO 141/711/465, NAUK. See also translation (4 May 1932) of secret ministerial report obtained by Keown-Boyd, FO 141/711/465, NAUK. Although the British called them "rare and unconvincing bonfires of allegedly English clothing" (see draft letter by Loraine, Cairo, 28 May 1932, FO 141/711/465, NAUK), the constant surveillance and reporting of these activities suggest that the British did take them seriously. Certainly they received considerable attention in the local Arabic press (the FO reports cite coverage in *al-Balagh, Jihad, Kawkab al-sharq, al-Ahram, al-Fallah,* and other periodicals).

88. *Ruz al-yusuf,* no. 221 (9 May 1932), 11.

89. *Ruz al-yusuf* was pro-Wafd and strongly nationalist at this time. The call to buy local products extended beyond textiles and products from the Bank Misr conglomerate to include textiles from al-Shurbaji and the Piastre Plan tarbush factory, among other companies.

90. *Ruz al-yusuf,* no. 221 (9 May 1932), 5.

91. Al-Rafiʿi, *Aʿqab al-thawra,* 2:341.

92. Taha Saʿd ʿUthman, interview by author, Cairo, 23 July 1997.

93. See al-Rafiʿi, *Aʿqab al-thawra,* 2:340–41.

94. See G. H. Selous, for UK Department of Overseas Trade, *Economic Conditions in Egypt, July 1935* (London: HMSO, 1935), 52; G. H. Selous, *Report on Economic and Commercial Conditions in Egypt, May 1937* (London: HMSO, 1937), 104–5. See also Robert Tignor, *State, Private Enterprise, and Economic Change in Egypt, 1918–1952* (Princeton, NJ: Princeton University Press, 1984), 135–36.

95. Tignor, *State,* 127.

96. In addition to James P. Jankowski, *Egypt's Young Rebels* (Stanford, CA: Hoover Institution Press, 1975), 11–12, I have also relied for the history of the Piastre Plan on

al-Rafiʿi, *Aʿqab al-thawra*, 2:341–42. See also Gershoni and Jankowski, *Redefining the Egyptian Nation*, 21.

97. Jankowski, *Egypt's Young Rebels*, 11. See also al-Rafiʿi, *Aʿqab al-thawra*, 2:341.

98. Subscription drives continued yearly through 1937, although their success was gradually reduced. See Jankowski, *Egypt's Young Rebels*, 12. On the outcome of the 1935 drive, see "Shabab nahid!," *Ruz al-yusuf*, no. 371 (1 April 1935), 30; "al-Tarbush wa'l-talaba," *al-Musawwar*, no. 546 (29 March 1935), 20.

99. "Al-Burnayta wa'l-tarbush," *al-Musawwar*, no. 43 (7 August 1925), 6.

100. President of the Egyptian Medical Association, "al-Tarbush am al-burnayta," *al-Muqtatif* 69, no. 2 (August 1926): 141.

101. Al-Rafiʿi, *Aʿqab al-thawra*, 2:342. See tarbush advertisement for the "*al-qirsh* factory for *tarabish* and wool spinning" in *al-Ahram*, 28 October 1951. On the fate of the factory, see also Ibrahim el-Mouelhy, "Le tarbouche et son histoire," *Le progrès égyptien—Almanach*, 1953, 68; Jankowski, *Egypt's Young Rebels*, 12; and al-Rafiʿi, *Aʿqab al-thawra*, 2:342.

102. See al-Rafiʿi, *Aʿqab al-thawra*, 2:342.

103. See *Ruz al-yusuf*, no. 329 (11 June 1934), 52; "Fi ʿalam al-sinaʿ," *Ruz al-yusuf*, no. 328 (4 June 1934), 34; advertisement, *al-Ahram*, 29 October 1938, 6.

104. H. Clayton Hartley, "Some Aspects of the Prospective Establishment of Textile Factories in Egypt," *EC*, no. 110 (July 1928): 599. This belief was widely shared. See also Pierre Arminjon, *La situation économique et financière de l'Egypte* (Paris: Librarie Générale du Droit, 1911), 207; al-Rafiʿi, *Aʿqab al-thawra*, 2:308; and André Eman, *Industrie du coton en Egypte: Etude d'économie politique* (Cairo: Imprimerie de l'Institut Français d'Archéologie Orientale, 1943), 1.

105. Mulock, *Egypt, April 1923*, 35, 48.

106. Ibid., 48; Selous and Larkins, *Egypt, July 1933*, 101. It is difficult to estimate average individual consumption of cloth in this period. During the Second World War, cloth rations of seven meters annually per person were considered too meager. Mahmoud Anis, in his deconstruction of Egyptian cost-of-living indexes, cites the government's basic list of clothing consumption for 1914 and 1939. This included two grades of calico fabric, a castor collar, a flannel handkerchief, natural and artificial silk (only in 1939), and poplin for shirting, as well as ready-made clothes, *tarabish*, shoes, and stockings. See Mahmoud Amin Anis, *A Study of the National Income of Egypt* (Cairo: SOP, 1950), 881–82.

107. Robert Tignor, *Egyptian Textiles and British Capital, 1930–1956* (Cairo: American University in Cairo Press, 1989), 8–17; Sidney H. Wells, "L'Industrie du tissage," *EC*, 4 November 1910, 578–84, and 5 January 1911, 52–73; Roger Owen, *The Middle East in the World Economy, 1800–1914* (New York: Methuen, 1981), 94. The number of weavers in Egypt increased 40 percent between 1897 and 1907, rising to 45,456 people (men, women, and children), or about 29 percent of the working class, in 1907. M. Lefeuvre-

Meaulle, "L'Egypte: Rapport de M. Lefeuvre-Meaulle, attaché commercial en Orient," 50, enclosed in Lefeuvre-Meaulle à Selves, Paris, 28 July 1911, NS, Egypte 118, MAEP. Owen in *Middle East,* 240, gives similar numbers.

108. M. el Darwish, "Where Egyptian Cotton Scores: A Wide Variety of Uses," *Manchester Guardian Commercial,* special issue on Egypt, 19 March 1931, 35.

109. See N. Seddon-Brown, "The Effect of the Quality of Cotton upon Costs of Production and the Quality of Cloth," in *Official Report of the International Cotton Congress Held in Egypt, 1927,* ed. IFMCSMA (Manchester, UK: Taylor Garnett Evans, n.d.), 148.

110. Moritz Schanz, *Cotton in Egypt and the Anglo-Egyptian Sudan, submitted to the 9th International Cotton Congress* (1913; repr., Greenville, CA: Dyer Press, 2007), 103, 100.

111. IFMCSMA, *Cotton Congress,* 49.

112. Ibid.

113. K. Vera Tranter, "The Wearer's Point of View: Garments of Egyptian Cotton," *Manchester Guardian Commercial,* special issue on Egypt, 25 March 1933, 31.

114. See Grandguillot, "Note sur les éléments d'une propagande à faire en France ou en Europe en faveur des cotons égyptiens," Cairo, 15 April 1931, Afrique, 1918–1940, Egypte 108, MAEP.

115. Naguib Mahfouz depicts the switch in dress from *ifrangi* suit (*badla*) to a galabiya at home in his 1946 novel *Khan al-khalili* (1946; repr., Cairo: Dar Misr li'l-Taba'iyya, n.d.), 12. See also Lefeuvre-Meaulle, "L'Egypte," 54–55, NS, Egypte 118, MAEP.

116. In his memoirs, Fikri al-Khuli describes a variety of different qualities and types of fabric for use in galabiyas. See e.g., *al-Rihla* (Cairo: Dar al-Ghad, 1987–1992), 1:65, 2:10, 1:111, 1:140, 1:200.

117. W. V. Shearer, "Report on the Weaving Industry in Assiout," *EC* 1 (1910): 184–85. See also Norman L. Ablett, "Notes on the Industries of Assiut made during June–July 1909," *EC* (1910): 330; Lefeuvre-Meaulle, "L'Egypte," 51, NS, Egypte 118, MAEP.

118. Wells, "Industrie du tissage," 60. See also Lefeuvre-Meaulle, "L'Egypte," 51, NS, Egypte 118, MAEP, on Qalyubiyya.

119. R. M. Turner and L. B. S. Larkins, for UK Department of Overseas Trade, *Economic Conditions July 1931* (London: HMSO, 1931), 48.

120. See appendixes 5a and 5b in E. Homan Mulock, *Report on the Economic and Financial Situation of Egypt, June 1925* (London: HMSO, 1925), 46–47.

121. Schanz, *Cotton in Egypt,* 98. See also Eman, *Industrie du coton,* 82–83. It is difficult to trace exactly the raw cottons for these imported yarns, as their origin is not recorded in the trade statistics.

122. Schanz, *Cotton in Egypt,* 99.

123. On the local cotton varieties, see appendix 2, IFMCSMA, *Cotton Congress,* esp. 191–93.

124. Owen, *Cotton,* 310 and 300–301; see also Eman, *Industrie du coton,* 82.

125. Eman, *Industrie du coton,* 146–47; Tignor, *Egyptian Textiles,* 46–47.

126. Davis, *Challenging Colonialism*; Tignor, *State*. Tignor and Davis assess differently the role of economic as opposed to other forms of nationalism.

127. Interview with *al-Ahram*, 31 July 1935, reprinted in Muhammad Talʿat Harb, *Majmuʿ at khutub Muhammad Talʿ at Harb basha* (Cairo: Imprimerie Misr, 1957/n.d.), 3:161.

128. Davis, *Challenging Colonialism*, 3; Joel Beinin, *Workers and Peasants in the Modern Middle East* (New York: Cambridge University Press, 2001), 102–3.

129. Davis, *Challenging Colonialism*, 134–35, 129.

130. Beinin, *Workers and Peasants*, 103.

131. Davis, *Challenging Colonialism*, 136. Davis defines *qintar* as "a weight measurement, particularly as used to refer to the weight of cotton; equal to 44.93 kg" (224).

132. Tignor, *Egyptian Textiles*, 11–17.

133. On the Filature, see Tignor, *Egyptian Textiles*, and also Floresca Karanasou, "Egyptianisation: The 1947 Company Law and the Foreign Communities in Egypt" (DPhil diss., Oxford University, 1992), chap. 6.

134. See Davis, *Challenging Colonialism*, chap. 6; and Tignor, *State*.

135. R. M. Turner, for UK Department of Overseas Trade, *The Economic and Financial Situation in Egypt, June 1929* (London: HMSO, 1929), 28. See also E. Homan Mulock, *Report on the Economic and Financial Situation of Egypt, May 1927* (London: HMSO, 1927), 28–29.

136. L. H. C. Tippett, *A Portrait of the Lancashire Textile Industry* (New York: Oxford University Press, 1969), 38–39; Turner and Larkins, *Egypt, July 1931*, 48.

137. Turner, *Egypt, June 1929*, 30–31.

138. Turner and Larkins, *Egypt, July 1931*, 48.

139. Eman, *Industrie du coton*, 93. See also 138; he was probably citing a report by the Misr Spinning and Weaving Company, 31 December 1938.

140. E. Homan Mulock, *Report on the Economic and Financial Situation of Egypt, May 1928* (London: HMSO, 1928), 38; Turner, *Egypt, June 1929*, 31. See also E. D. Papasian, *L'Egypte: Economique et financière, 1922–1923* (Cairo: Imprimerie Misr, 1923), 87; Turner and Larkins, *Egypt, July 1931*, 48.

141. Selous and Larkins, *Egypt, July 1933*, 58.

142. Selous, *Egypt, May 1937*, 57. See also Selous, *Egypt, July 1935*, 51; and Pettit to Ministre des Finances et Affaires Economiques à Paris, Cairo, 23 September 1948, 7–8, le Caire-Ambassade 602/250/3806, CADN.

143. Hand-loomed cloth production, although never as fully destroyed as colonial powers depicted, nevertheless suffered under the onslaught of British imports during the protectorate and, unlike in Syria, did not become known for creating complex weaves that could be produced only by hand. Wells, "Industrie du tissage"; Dominique Chevallier, "Un example de résistance technique de l'artisantat syrien aux XIXe et XXe siècles: Les tissues ikatés d'Alep et de Damas," *Syria: Revue d'art oriental et d'archeologie* 39 (1962): 300–24.

144. *Ruz al-yusuf,* no. 202 (28 December 1931), 8.

145. *Ruz al-yusuf,* no. 221 (9 May 1932), 15.

146. *Ruz al-yusuf,* no. 224 (30 May 1932), 25.

147. *Ruz al-yusuf,* no. 222 (16 May 1932), 15.

148. "Sa'a fi mahall al-muntajat al-misriyya," *Ruz al-yusuf,* no. 226 (13 June 1932), 21.

149. Ibid.

150. Ibid. The store probably closed sometime in the middle 1930s.

151. *Al-Muqattam,* 4 April 1940, 2; *al-Misri,* 1 November 1951, 3. It was perhaps owned by a Muhammad Rizq until his death in mid-1957, when Muhammad ʿAbd al-ʿAziz ʿAtiyya and sons assumed the administration. See advertisements in *Ruz al-yusuf,* no. 1513 (10 June 1957), 38; *al-Musawwar,* no. 1727 (15 November 1957), 41.

152. *Al-Musawwar,* no. 1240 (16 July 1948), 33; *Ruz al-yusuf,* no. 1238 (3 March 1952), 31.

153. In his study of Bank Misr, Davis pays scant attention to the retail company. See Davis, *Challenging Colonialism,* 135, 187.

154. Morums moved from ʿAtaba to Fu'ad Street in June 1925. See Morums advertisement in the *Egyptian Gazette,* 12 June 1925; see also Percival to Wiggin, 31 December 1925, FO 141/747/8861, NAUK; and Bouzon, "Rapport," Alexandria, 16 December 1918, Afrique, 1918–1940, Egypte 63, MAEP.

155. "Fi dar al-sharika al-jadida," *al-Ahram,* 4 January 1933, 7.

156. Advertisement in *Ruz al-yusuf,* no. 264 (6 March 1933), 21.

157. *Ruz al-yusuf,* no. 316 (12 March 1934), 27. See also *Ruz al-yusuf,* no. 291 (11 September 1933), 14. By the 1940s and 1950s, the company offered a wide selection of products in at least nine departments, including silks, notions, cottons, shoes, men's woolens, ready-to-wear, gifts, household appliances, and furniture. See advertisement in *Ruz al-yusuf,* no. 1290 (2 March 1953), 37.

158. *Ruz al-yusuf,* no. 316 (12 March 1934), 27.

159. *Al-Ahram,* 25 February 1933, 5. Such characteristics also marked clothing as Chinese in this period. Gerth, *China Made,* 120.

160. *Al-Ahram,* 25 February 1933, 5; see also *Ruz al-yusuf,* no. 263 (27 February 1933), 33.

161. Lisa Pollard, *Nurturing the Nation* (Berkeley: University of California Press, 2005); Partha Chatterjee, *The Nation and Its Fragments* (Princeton, NJ: Princeton University Press, 1993).

162. Information on branch openings is taken from an undated (probably April 1954) list of branch stores, doc. pp. 87–91 of folder no. 2, MS 74, DWQ.

163. *Ruz al-yusuf,* no. 291 (11 September 1933), 14, and no. 327 (28 May 1934), 34. On al-Sayufi, see Arnold Wright and H. A. Cartwright, *Twentieth-Century Impressions of Egypt: Its History, People, Commerce, Industries, and Resources* (London: Lloyd's Greater Britain Publishing, 1909), 375; *Ruz al-yusuf,* no. 205 (18 January 1932), 31, and advertisements from February 1932 to February 1933.

164. MS records indicate that some branch stores were owned by individuals, companies, or estates; the Eastern Company owned the Disuq shop, opened in early 1949. Roughly fourteen out of the thirty-eight branches listed in 1954 belonged to an independent owner. No explication of this was given in the company's memo. See undated list of branch stores, doc. pp. 87–91 of folder no. 2, MS 74, DWQ.

165. Davis, *Challenging Colonialism*, 187.

166. See employee lists for 1947 and 1948, in MS 74, DWQ. Despite its repeated professions to be "100 percent Egyptian," the company was continually inspected by the MS, and eventually a handful of non-Egyptian employees (primarily Sudanese and Palestinian, but mostly Muslim) was identified. See, for example, doc. 187: 1955 list of nine "foreign employees."

167. Unless otherwise noted, all the information here on the Tanta opening, including the quotations from speeches, is from "Yawm Tanta al-mashud," *al-Ahram*, 13 February 1937. The paper had announced the opening on 11 February in an advertisement from the company, which proclaimed that it was the fourteenth branch of the store to open. See advertisement, *al-Ahram*, 11 February 1937, 7.

168. On Khayri, see Walter Armbrust, "The Golden Age before the Golden Age," in *Mass Mediations*, ed. Walter Armbrust (Berkeley: University of California Press, 2000), 296.

169. *Al-Ahram*, 13 February 1937. State support for the company continued into the 1950s. On the opening of the Giza branch in 1956, see "Farʿ sharika baiʿ al-masnuʿat al-misriyya al-jadid biʾl-Giza," *Ruz al-yusuf*, no. 1489 (24 December 1956), 20.

170. Tignor, *State*, 61.

171. Al-Rafiʿi, *Aʿqab al-thawra*, 2:208–9, 284.

172. Selous, *Egypt, May 1937*, 7.

173. Ibid.

174. Badran, *Feminists, Islam, and Nation*, 83–84; Huda Shaarawi, *Harem Years: The Memoirs of an Egyptian Feminist, 1879–1924*, trans. Margot Badran (New York: Feminist Press of the City University of New York, 1987), 125–26; Mona Russell, *Creating the New Egyptian Woman: Consumerism, Education, and National Identity, 1863–1922* (New York: Palgrave Macmillan, 2004), 89–92.

Chapter 4

1. Al-Khuli, *al-Rihla* (Cairo: Dar al-Ghad, 1987–1992), 1:52. Al-Khuli composed his memoir in colloquial Arabic while he was imprisoned in the late 1950s and early 1960s for labor activism. Textile workers did not typically write memoirs. Joel Beinin has argued, however, for the authenticity of al-Khuli's text because it does not follow the accepted ideological canon of communist memoirs. See Joel Beinin, *Workers and Peasants in the Modern Middle East* (New York: Cambridge University Press, 2001), chap. 4 and esp. p. 104. For another example of silk as a consumer goal for peasants, see M. Lefeuvre-

Meaulle, "L'Egypte: Rapport de M. Lefeuvre-Meaulle, attaché commercial en Orient," 60, enclosed in Lefeuvre-Meaulle à Selves, Paris, 28 July 1911, NS, Egypte 118, MAEP.

2. See al-Khuli, *al-Rihla*, 2:48, 56. Al-Khuli reports that he initially wrote his memoir to counter other Egyptian communists who argued that the Bank Misr textile factories at Mahalla, where al-Khuli worked, promoted the welfare of Egyptian workers because they were owned by Egyptian industrialists. See Beinin, *Workers and Peasants*, 100.

3. The 1918 *Rapport* of the Egyptian Commission on Commerce and Industry particularly illustrated the importance of mechanization for Egypt's bourgeoisie.

4. For a useful definition of mass consumption in France, see Rosalind H. Williams, *Dream Worlds: Mass Consumption in Late Nineteenth-Century France* (Berkeley: University of California Press, 1982), 3. Williams highlights "a radical division between the activities of production and of consumption, the prevalence of standardized merchandise sold in large volume, the ceaseless introduction of new products, widespread reliance on money and credit, and ubiquitous publicity. . . . The merchandise itself is by no means available to all, but the *vision* of a seemingly unlimited profusion of commodities is available, is, indeed, nearly unavoidable." Mass consumption on this model probably did not characterize Egyptian society until the 1970s and 1980s. See Saad Eddin Ibrahim, *The New Arab Social Order: A Study of the Social Impact of Oil Wealth* (Boulder, CO: Westview, 1982); Malcolm Kerr and El Sayed Yassin, eds., *Rich and Poor States in the Middle East: Egypt and the New Arab Order* (Boulder, CO: Westview, 1982); and Relli Shechter, "The Cultural Economy of Development: Economic Nationalism, Hidden Economy and the Emergence of Mass Consumer Society during Sadat's Infitah," *Middle Eastern Studies* 44, no. 4 (2008): 571–83.

5. Very few historians have discussed footwear production and consumption. Philippe Perrot puts it perhaps most succinctly: "Nothing appears less serious than a pair of underpants or more laughable than a necktie or socks." *Fashioning the Bourgeoisie*, trans. Richard Bienvenu (Princeton, NJ: Princeton University Press, 1994), 3. Brief descriptions on shoes and hosiery in the Middle East exist in Jennifer Scarce, *Women's Costume of the Near and Middle East* (London: Unwin Hyman, 1987); Nancy Micklewright, "Women's Dress Nineteenth-Century Istanbul: Mirror of a Changing Society" (PhD diss., University of Pennsylvania, 1986); Yedida Kalfon Stillman, *Arab Dress from the Dawn of Islam to Modern Times: A Short History*, ed. Norman Stillman (Boston: Brill, 2003); Nancy Lindisfarne-Tapper and Bruce Ingham, eds., *Languages of Dress in the Middle East* (London: Curzon, 1997); Charlotte Jirousek, "Transition to Mass Fashion System Dress in the Later Ottoman Empire," in *Consumption Studies and the History of the Ottoman Empire, 1550–1922*, ed. Donald Quataert (Albany: State University of New York, 2000), 201–41; Samer S. Shehata, "Plastic Sandals, Tea and Time: Shop Floor Politics and Culture in Egypt" (PhD diss., Princeton University, 2000).

6. Edward Lane, *Manners and Customs of the Modern Egyptians* (1836, 1895; repr., London: East-West Publications, 1989), 40.

7. M. de Chabrol, "Essai sur les moeurs des habitans modernes de l'Egypte," in *La description de l'Egypte*, vol. 14 (Paris: Imprimerie Impériale, 1809), 413; see also M. Jomard, "Description abrégée de la ville et de la citadelle du Kaire," in *La description de l'Egypte*, vol. 14 (Paris: Imprimerie Impériale, 1809), 706.

8. De Chabrol, "Essai," 415. See also Lane, *Manners and Customs*, 52.

9. De Chabrol, "Essai," 510.

10. Lane, *Manners and Customs*, 40. See also Rachel Arié, "Notes sur le costume en Egypte dans la première moitié du xixe siècle," *Extrait de la revue des études islamiques* 2 (1968): 207 and 210, who cites Clot Bey and other European accounts about the use of "double shoes" among nineteenth-century Egyptians of the upper classes and the lack of knitted socks or stockings.

11. Lane, *Manners and Customs*, 42, see also 56–57 on women's footwear.

12. John Bowring, *Report on Egypt and Candia* (London: Clowes for HMSO, 1840), 51–52. On the army and its role in the reform and modernization of Egypt, see Khaled Fahmy, *All the Pasha's Men: Mehmed Ali, His Army, and the Making of Modern Egypt* (New York: Cambridge University Press, 1997), esp. 143–44, 186, and 222 on shoes.

13. Fahmy, *All the Pasha's Men*, frontispiece and 312.

14. Ibid., 144, 222.

15. Mickelwright, "Women's Dress."

16. R. Turner Wilcox, *The Mode in Footwear* (New York: Scribner's, 1948), 90.

17. Lefeuvre-Meaulle, "L'Egypte," NS, Egypte 118, MAEP. See also Uri M. Kupferschmidt, "Who Needed Department Stores in Egypt? From Orosdi-Back to Omar Effendi," *Middle Eastern Studies* 43, no. 2 (March 2007): 182. As stockings were a new sartorial item, popular advice manuals explained how to care for feet confined in fitted shoes and in stockings to prevent harm to the feet and "an offensive smell." See ʿAli Fikri, *Adab al-fatah*, 3rd ed. (Cairo: al-Liwaʾ, 1901), 38.

18. E. Homan Mulock, *Report on the Economic and Financial Situation of Egypt, May 1927* (London: HMSO, 1927), 31.

19. "Chaussures," in Rapport commercial 1911, enclosed in de Longchamps to Poincaré, Cairo, 9 May 1912, NS, Egypte 118:3, MAEP.

20. On shoe polish see Ministère du Commerce, Office Commercial d'Egypte, "Monographie: Cirages pour chaussures" in Bordereau d'envoi no. 21, Alexandria, 24 December 1921, le Caire-Ambassade 602/245, CADN; El-Hanafi El-Sayed Fahmy, "Survey of Industry in Egypt," *Egypt News Bulletin*, July 1950, 12. On shoe blacks, see *Industrial and Commercial Census* reports (1927, 1937, 1947); Douglas Sladen, *Oriental Cairo: The City of the "Arabian Nights,"* (London: Hurst and Blackett, 1911), 15, 64–65.

21. "Egyptian Industries," February–March 1931, 72, BT60/29/2, NAUK. See also Robert Tignor, *State, Private Enterprise, and Economic Change in Egypt, 1918–1952* (Princeton, NJ: Princeton University Press, 1984), 101.

22. Baron E. de Gaiffier d'Hestroy, *Egypte: Situation economique, financière et commerciale en 1907* (Brussels: Piquart, 1908), 48–49.

23. Ibid., 49.

24. Ibid., 48–49; E. Homan Mulock, *Report on the Economic and Financial Situation of Egypt, June 1926* (London: HMSO, 1926), 15.

25. See, for example, "Fashions in London," *Egyptian Gazette*, 21 July 1913, 5; "Azya' al-rabiʿa," *al-Balagh al-usbuʿi*, 11 March 1927, 34; "Azya' al-rabiʿa," *al-Balagh al-usbuʿi*, 18 March 1927, 35; "Azya' al-rabiʿa," *al-Siyasa al-ʾusbuʿiyya* 2, no. 59 (23 April 1927); "Fi ʿalam al-azya,'" *al-Balagh al-usbuʿi*, 20 March 1929, 30–31.

26. "Li yad al-sayyida wa-li-rigliha," *Misr al-haditha al-musawwara*, no. 3 (25 December 1927), 34.

27. See, for example, the illustrations of "Ziyy sharqi hadith" accompanying the article on "Azya' al-sayyidat," *Majallat al-maraʾ al-misriyya* 6, no. 8 (15 October 1925): 436–38. See also the fashions by "Chic Oriental" in "Ahdath al-azya'" in *Misr al-haditha al-musawwara*, no. 4 (25 January 1928), 28.

28. See, e.g., *al-Musawwar*, no. 75 (19 March 1926), front cover.

29. *Al-Liwaʾ*, 17 September 1910, 7.

30. *Al-Ahram*, 19 March 1927.

31. The Louis XV heel was a curved heel, but very high; the Cuban heel was a more moderate, commonsense height. See Wilcox, *Mode*, 154.

32. Chemla catalog, for 17 December 1928, 15. The Richelieu was a men's oxford or wing-tip shoe known in Arabic as the "*jazma nisf jild*."

33. Cicurel catalog for winter 1924–1925 (Paris: Imprimerie Léon Ullman, n.d.), 37–41.

34. *Al-Nashra al-iqtisadiyya al-misriyya*, no. 18 (24 October 1920).

35. "Where We Get the Silk for Our Jumpers and Frocks," *Egyptian Gazette*, 3 June 1925; *al-Musawwar*, no. 686 (3 December 1937), 19.

36. *Al-Musawwar*, no. 686 (3 December 1937), 19.

37. See Sednaoui advertisement for Van Raalte stockings in *Ruz al-yusuf*, no. 304 (11 December 1933), 38; *Egyptian Gazette*, 5 October 1934, 6. See also *Egyptian Gazette*, 2 November 1934, 6; 5 October 1934, 6; and 19 October 1934, 6; and *al-Musawwar*, no. 686 (3 December 1937), 19; *al-Musawwar*, no. 559 (28 June 1935), 29. Although some other luxury goods were advertised without prices, this was most pronounced with silk stockings.

38. G. de R., "Bas de soie, bas de fil," *EN*, no. 9 (22 May 1942), 18.

39. Advertisement in *Ruz al-yusuf*, no. 306 (25 December 1933), 50; see also Mona Russell, *Creating the New Egyptian Woman: Consumerism, Education, and National Identity, 1863–1922* (New York: Palgrave Macmillan, 2004), 64.

40. Russell, *Creating the New Egyptian Woman*, 62.

41. On the era's marketing to Egyptian women, see Mona Russell, "Marketing the Modern Egyptian Girl: Whitewashing Soap and Clothes from the Late Nineteenth Century to 1936," *Journal of Middle East Women's Studies* 6, no. 3 (Fall 2010): 19–57.

42. Russell, *Creating the New Egyptian Woman*, 61.

43. Relli Shechter, "Reading Advertisements in a Colonial/Development Context," *Journal of Social History* 39, no. 2 (Winter 2005): 486.

44. See Relli Shechter, "Press Advertising in Egypt: Business Realities and Local Meaning, 1882–1956," *Arab Studies Journal* 10, no. 2, and 11, no. 1 (Fall 2002/Spring 2003): 44–66, and Shechter, "Reading Advertisements." On visual literacy, see Beth Baron, *Egypt as a Woman* (Berkeley: University of California Press, 2005). On pre-1922 advertising, see Russell, *Creating the New Egyptian Woman*, 61–78; Beth Baron, *The Women's Awakening: Culture, Society, and the Press* (New Haven, CT: Yale University Press, 1994), esp. 69, 94.

45. Shechter, "Press Advertising," 49. This was still a small fraction of the Egyptian population, which stood at roughly nineteen million in 1947.

46. Shechter, "Reading Advertisements," 485. He discusses the correlated expansion of readership on 485–86. See also Palmira Brummett, *Image and Imperialism in the Ottoman Revolutionary Press, 1908–1911* (Albany: State University of New York Press, 2000).

47. Shechter, "Press Advertising," 51.

48. Lucie Ryzova, "'I Am a Whore but I Will Be a Good Mother': On the Production and Consumption of the Female Body in Modern Egypt," *Arab Studies Journal* 12, no. 2, and 13, no. 1 (Fall 2004/Spring 2005): 104; on the scrapbooks, see 101–5.

49. On this change of shape of the tarbush from the nineteenth to twentieth centuries, see Samir Raafat, "The Tarbouche: The Turko-Egyptian Hat Incident of October 29, 1932," *Egyptian Gazette*, 26 October 1996. In 1921 it was worn about fourteen centimeters tall. "Monographie du tarbouche," Alexandria, 10 December 1921, le Caire-Ambassade 602/245, CADN.

50. Ibid. *Al-Ahram* advertised that a "*khawaga*" from Mansura was looking for a "white *tarbush*" in 1908. See "al-Tarbush al-abyad," *al-Ahram*, 3 November 1908; Arié, "Notes sur le costume," 204–6.

51. F. Moore Gordon, "Notes on the Weaving Industry at Mehalla-Kebir (October 13, 1909)," *EC* (1910): 335.

52. R. M. Turner and L. B. S. Larkins, for UK Department of Overseas Trade, *Economic Conditions July 1931* (London: HMSO, 1931), 48.

53. G. H. Selous and L. B. S. Larkins, for UK Department of Overseas Trade, *Economic Conditions in Egypt, July 1933* (London: HMSO, 1933), 60.

54. See 'Adès advertisement in *Ruz al-yusuf*, no. 371, 1 April 1935, 19. See also 'Adès advertisement in *al-Ahram*, 4 May 1935, 11.

55. See *al-Ahram*, 1 May 1934, 10. These fabrics were shown made up into European-style dresses for women, rather than galabiyas, or robes, although this clothing style may reflect more on the perceived readership of the newspaper advertisements than the actual use of fabrics.

56. See, e.g., Naguib Mahfouz, *Khan al-khalili* (1946; repr., Cairo: Dar Misr li'l-Taba'iyya, n.d.), 40.

57. Ibid., 12.

58. He mentions that he washed his galabiya on his day off. Al-Khuli, *Al-Rihla*, 1:65; see also 2:10.

59. Andrea B. Rugh, *Reveal and Conceal: Dress in Contemporary Egypt* (Syracuse, NY: Syracuse University Press, 1986), 8.

60. Shechter, "Press Advertising," 53–54.

61. Moritz Schanz, *Cotton in Egypt and the Anglo-Egyptian Sudan, submitted to the 9th International Cotton Congress* (1913; repr., Greenville, CA: Dyer Press, 2007), 103. See also N. Seddon-Brown, "The Effect of the Quality of Cotton upon Costs of Production and the Quality of Cloth," in *Official Report of the International Cotton Congress Held in Egypt, 1927*, ed. IFMCSMA (Manchester, UK: Taylor Garnett Evans, n.d.), 148, 149; M. el Darwish, "Where Egyptian Cotton Scores: A Wide Variety of Uses," *Manchester Guardian Commercial*, special issue on Egypt, 19 March 1931, 35.

62. ʿAli Mubarak described, for example, the chief Maliki mufti in such terms in the 1880s. See Indira Falk Gesink, "'Chaos on the Earth': Subjective Truths versus Communal Unity in Islamic Law and the Rise of Militant Islam," *American Historical Review* 108, no. 3 (June 2003): 722.

63. Hasan Al-Banna, *Five Tracts of Hasan al-Banna*, trans. Charles Wendell (Berkeley: University of California, 1978), e.g., 19, 83, 86, 124. James Grehan argues that religious elites accepted silk blends more easily in eighteenth-century Damascus even though many Islamic jurists considered silk "morally dubious." *Everyday Life and Consumer Culture in 18th-Century Damascus* (Seattle: University of Washington Press, 2007), 214.

64. Sayyid Qutb, *al-ʿAdala al-ijtimʿiyya fi'l-islam* (1953; repr., Beirut: Dar al-Shuruq, 1975), 145. See also Qutb, *Social Justice in Islam*, trans. John B. Hardie with Hamid Algar (New York: Islamic Publications International, 2000), 160. On silk as a distraction from the worship of God, see also Bayly, "The Origins of Swadeshi (Home Industry): Cloth and Indian Society, 1700–1930," in *The Social Life of Things: Commodities in Cultural Perspective*, ed. Arjun Appadurai (New York: Cambridge University Press, 1986), 290.

65. Qutb, *al-ʿAdala al-ijtimʿiyya*, 138–46, esp. 143–44.

66. "Des baigneuses sur les étoffes imprimées," *La bourse égyptienne* (Alexandria ed.), 14 December 1937, 3. Mary Rowlatt reports that she saw "a small girl of about five dressed in a flannelette dress, the pattern on it being bathing belles, each beauty in her bathing dress covered about a foot of material, so that only three or four of them were on the dress at all." Rowlatt, *A Family in Egypt* (London: Robert Hale, 1956), 151. Parliamentarians also debated "the indecency of short dresses" in 1927. See Jacques Berque, *Egypt: Imperialism and Revolution*, trans. Jean Stewart (London: Faber and Faber, 1972), 477n3.

67. "Des baigneuses sur les étoffes imprimées," *La bourse égyptienne* (Alexandria ed.), 14 December 1937, 3.

68. "Vague de Pudeur: des baigneuses sur des étoffes imprimées," *La bourse égyptienne* (Alexandria ed.), 24 December 1937, 3. Shaykh Abu al-ʿAyun was notorious

for his campaigns against women's bathing suits. He was the secretary-general of the Azhar when he was killed in an accident on the Metro in 1951. See *Le progres égyptien— Almanach,* 1953, unnumbered page.

69. Lefeuvre-Meaulle, "L'Egypte," 60, NS, Egypte 118, MAEP.

70. Al-Khuli, *al-Rihla,* 1:46.

71. Ibid., 172. He makes at least four references to this on 174–77.

72. Interview with Harb in *Misr,* 19 December 1936, reprinted in Harb, *Majmuʿat khutub Muhammad Talʿat Harb basha* (Cairo: Imprimerie Misr, 1957/n.d.), 3:173. See also statement to the press by Harb in May 1938, Harb, *Majmuʿat khutub,* 3:138.

73. Robert Tignor, *Egyptian Textiles and British Capital, 1930–1956* (Cairo: American University in Cairo Press, 1989), 25.

74. Tignor, *State,* 129.

75. Eman, *L'industrie du coton en Egypte: Etude d'économie politique* (Cairo: Imprimerie de l'Institut Français d'Archéologie Orientale, 1943), 145.

76. Roger Owen, *Cotton and the Egyptian Economy, 1820–1914* (London: Oxford University Press, 1969), 301.

77. See, e.g., al-Nahhas advertisement, *Ruz al-yusuf,* no. 221 (9 May 1932), 15; Misr Silk Weaving Company advertisement, *Ruz al-yusuf,* no. 290 (4 September 1933), 27.

78. For example, see advertisements in *Ruz al-yusuf,* no. 306 (25 December 1933), 50, and no. 303 (4 December 1933), 49.

79. Advertisement in *Ruz al-yusuf,* no. 307 (1 January 1934), 47.

80. Statement to the press by Harb in May 1938, Harb, *Majmuʿat khutub,* 3:141; see also 3:138.

81. Interview with Harb in *Misr,* 19 December 1936, and press statement in May 1938 reprinted in Harb, *Majmuʿat khutub,* 3:173 and 3:141; see also 3:138.

82. Fédération Egyptienne de l'Industrie, *Foreign Trade of Egypt* (Cairo: SOP, 1955), 221–26. Many of the trademarks had been in use for a number of years. See *Ruz al-yusuf,* no. 248 (14 November 1932), 32; and *La femme nouvelle,* March 1949.

83. *Ruz al-yusuf,* no. 349 (29 October 1934), 27.

84. See, for example, the following advertisements for Holeproof Hosiery: *al-Musawwar,* no. 50 (25 September 1925), 11; *al-Musawwar,* no. 51 (2 October 1925), 14; *al-Musawwar,* no. 85 (28 May 1926), 11; *Misr al-haditha al-musawwara,* no. 4 (25 January 1928), 33; and *Misr al-haditha al-musawwara,* no. 5 (February 1928), 81. Holeproof Hosiery was listed along with other British brand-name products as advertisers in the Egyptian press in Mulock, *Egypt, June 1926.*

85. *Misr al-haditha al-musawwara,* January 1928, 33; *Al-Lataʾif al-musawwara,* 22 November 1926, 15.

86. *Al-Lataʾif al-musawwara* 10, no. 469 (4 February 1924): 17.

87. Cicurel catalog for winter 1924–1925 (Paris: Imprimerie Léon Ullman, n.d.), 66.

88. Egyptian Clothing Company ad, *al-Ahram*, 1 February 1931, 13.

89. These hosiery plants grew directly out of Egyptian nationalist-industrialist desires to expand production using domestic cotton without competing with the large mechanized weaving plants already established, such as Filature and Bank Misr's company. Tignor, *Egyptian Textiles*, 58.

90. See "Qism al-triku," *al-Ahram*, 5 October 1935. Fifty-eight women took the exam in fall 1935. The names of the four most outstanding knitters from the class included at least three Muslims.

91. Thomas Philipp, *The Syrians in Egypt, 1725–1975* (Stuttgart: Franz Steiner Verlag, 1985), 140. These included the "Shurbaji, Qabbani, Mardini, Halbuni, Abu ʿAuf, and Kasm families."

92. Eman, *Industrie du coton*, 115.

93. G. H. Selous, *Report on Economic and Commercial Conditions in Egypt, May 1937* (London: HMSO, 1937), 105.

94. Tignor, *Egyptian Textiles*, 58.

95. Cited in Tignor, *Egyptian Textiles*, 56. See also Eman, *Industrie du coton*, 115; Selous, *Egypt, May 1937*, 66, 105; and C. Empson, for UK Department of Overseas Trade, *Report on Economic and Commercial Conditions in Egypt, June 1939* (London: HMSO, 1939), 27. Trade records inconsistently report imports, making it difficult to estimate actual consumption of hosiery. Imports in the late 1930s amounted to between 400,000 to 500,000 dozen pairs. See Jean Schatz, "Le commerce extérieur de l'Egypte pendant les deux guerres mondiales," *EC*, nos. 232–233 (1946): 172–73 (annexed tables).

96. "Note sur le marché de la bonneterie en Egypte," April 1954, 3–4, le Caire-Ambassade 602/253, CADN.

97. See "Masaniʿ al-Shurbaji bi-Imbaba," *al-Ahram*, special issue 1950, 34; and "al-Mudhakkira," n.d., in "Bunuk: 1945–49," ʿAbdin, Maliyya, no. 264: Bunuk wa-Sharikat, 1909–1949, DWQ. These two documents offer conflicting dates for the establishment of these factories. Nearly £E300,000 was transferred from factories outside Egypt to the Shurbaji Brothers in Egypt through various accounts in the Ottoman Bank and Bank Misr in 1941 and 1942.

98. "Al-Mudhakkira." Several industrial concerns connected to Bank Misr (including the textile factories at Mahalla, the silk weaving company, and the National Glass Factory) received industrial loans in the same period.

99. *EN*, no. 161 (16 May 1947), 387; and Levy, *Stock Exchange Year-Book of Egypt, 1957*, 714–15.

100. See "Ziyara li-masnaʿ al-Shurbaji," *Ruz al-yusuf*, no. 328 (4 June 1934), 26; "Masaniʿ al-Shurbaji liʾl-shurabat: Hisn min husunina al-iqtisadiyya al-misriyya," *Ruz al-yusuf*, no. 347 (15 October 1934), 28; "Al-Ustadh Subhi al-Shurbaji," *Ruz al-yusuf*, no. 347 (15 October 1934), 14; "Masnaʿ jawarib Shurbaji," *Ruz al-yusuf*, no. 358 (31 December 1934), 35; and "Sinaʿat al-jawarib fi Misr," *al-Musawwar*, no. 572 (27 September 1935), 2.

This could also be because the local press was predominantly owned and run by Syrians resident in Egypt.

101. "Sinaʿt al-jawarib fi Misr," *al-Musawwar*, no. 572 (27 September 1935), 2.

102. Ibid.

103. Ibid.

104. "Ziyara li-masnaʿ al-Shurbaji," *Ruz al-yusuf*, no. 328 (4 June 1934), 26. The hosiery factory used thread from the spinning and weaving factories of Bank Misr, except for the very finest grades, which it imported from abroad. The war exacerbated supply shortages, however. See Subhi Shurbaji to the Egyptian Finance Minister, Alexandria, 10 April 1942, in ʿAbdin, Maliyya, no. 264: Bunuk wa-Sharikat, 1909–1949, DWQ.

105. "Sinaʿat al-jawarib fi Misr," *al-Musawwar*, no. 572 (27 September 1935), 2; "Ziyara li-masnaʿ al-Shurbaji," *Ruz al-yusuf*, no. 328 (4 June 1934), 26.

106. "Masaniʿ al-Shurbaji bi-Imbaba," *al-ʿImara*, nos. 3–4 (1940): 204–5.

107. "Masaniʿ al-Shurbaji liʾl-shurabat," *Ruz al-yusuf*, no. 347 (15 October 1934), 28; "Masnaʿ jawarib Shurbaji," *Ruz al-yusuf*, no. 358 (31 December 1934), 35.

108. File on "Sharikat masaniʿ Shurbaji liʾl-ghazl waʾl-nasj waʾl-triku," MS 51, DWQ. A 1950 profile on the company estimated a workforce of two thousand. It noted that the factory provided a mosque for the use of the workers, thereby emphasizing a particular definition of the workforce as "Egyptian." See "Masaniʿ al-Shurbaji bi-Imbaba," *al-Ahram*, special issue 1950, 34. "Workers" and "employees" were different categories used by MS officials in setting Egyptianization quotas. Essentially, employees' job duties included reading and writing and workers' did not.

109. Joel Beinin and Zachary Lockman, *Workers on the Nile: Nationalism, Communism, Islam, and the Egyptian Working Class, 1882–1954* (Princeton, NJ: Princeton University Press, 1987), 434 and 392; and FO 371/102931, NAUK.

110. "Masnaʿ jawarib Shurbaji," *Ruz al-yusuf*, no. 358 (31 December 1934), 35; "Sinaʿat al-jawarib fi Misr," *al-Musawwar*, no. 572 (27 September 1935), 2. See also advertisement in *Ruz al-yusuf*, no. 307 (1 January 1934), 27.

111. Cigarette marketing also linked men from different classes. See Relli Shechter, *Smoking, Culture, and Economy in the Middle East: The Egyptian Tobacco Market, 1850–2000* (New York: I. B. Tauris, 2006).

112. *Ruz al-yusuf*, no. 258 (23 January 1933), 37.

113. *Ruz al-yusuf*, no. 343 (17 September 1934), 18. See also "Sinaʿat al-jawarib fi Misr," *al-Musawwar*, no. 572 (27 September 1935), 2.

114. "Masnaʿ jawarib Shurbaji," *Ruz al-yusuf*, no. 358 (31 December 1934), 35.

115. Shurbaji advertisement in *Ruz al-yusuf*, no. 307 (1 January 1934), 27.

116. "Masnaʿ jawarib Shurbaji," *Ruz al-yusuf*, no. 358 (31 December 1934), 35.

117. "Masaniʿ al-Shurbaji liʾl-shurrabat!" *Ruz al-yusuf*, no. 347 (15 October 1934), 28.

118. "Ziyara li-masnaʿ al-Shurbaji," *Ruz al-yusuf*, no. 328 (4 June 1934), 26.

119. The monopoly character of the interwar press, described earlier, helps explain why so many of Shurbaji's sock advertisements circulated in *Ruz al-yusuf* and *al-Musawwar*.

120. *Ruz al-yusuf*, no. 301 (20 November 1933), 29; another ad depicted the same three people dressing: *Ruz al-yusuf*, no. 307 (1 January 1934), 26.

121. *Al-Musawwar*, no. 534 (4 January 1935); see also *al-Balagh*, 10 October 1942. See also NuNu Brothers advertisements in *al-Ithnayn*: no. 680 (23 June 1947), 29; no. 685 (28 July 1947), 31; no. 662 (17 February 1947), 28.

122. On literary and political nationalist discourse, see Israel Gershoni and James Jankowski, *Egypt, Islam and the Arabs: The Search for Egyptian Nationhood, 1900–1930* (New York: Oxford University Press, 1986), and Israel Gershoni and James Jankowski, *Redefining the Egyptian Nation, 1930–1945* (New York: Cambridge University Press, 1995).

123. Alfred Dennis, "Economic Conditions and American Trade Possibilities in Egypt," *Commerce Reports*, no. 30 (5 February 1921), Washington, DC, 714, in Afrique, 1918–1940, Egypte 63, MAEP.

124. Engravings of upper-class dining rooms in the eighteenth or early nineteenth century in Egypt consistently portray Egyptians seated cross-legged on couches, their shoes left by the edge of the room's rug. See Lane, *Manners*, 154, 150, 147. See also Ahmad Amin, *Qamus al-ʿadat waʾl-taqalid waʾl-taʿbir al-misriyya* (Cairo: Lajnat al-Taʾlif waʾl-Tarjama waʾl-Nashr, 1953), fig. 2.

125. Lane, *Manners*, 90. See also his engravings, 81 and 87.

126. "Egypt's Boot and Shoe Trade," *British Chamber of Commerce of Egypt's Monthly Journal*, no. 24 (September 1905), 2.

127. D'Hestroy, *Egypte*, 48–49; "Egypt's Boot and Shoe Trade," *British Chamber of Commerce of Egypt's Monthly Journal*, no. 24 (September 1905), 2. See also "Chaussures," in "Rapport commercial 1911," enclosed de Longchamps to Poincaré, Cairo, 9 May 1912, NS, Egypte 118:3, MAEP.

128. "Egypt's Boot and Shoe Trade," *The British Chamber of Commerce of Egypt's Monthly Journal*, no. 24 (September 1905), 3.

129. Ministère du Commerce, Office Commercial d'Egypt, "Monographie: Cirages pour chaussures," Bordereau d'envoi no. 21, Alexandria, 24 December 1921, le Caire-Ambassade 602/245, CADN.

130. Chemla catalog for 17 December 1928 sale, 15.

131. Cicurel catalog for winter 1924–1925, 37–40.

132. Bata advertisement, *al-Ahram*, 5 February 1931, 10.

133. Andrea Rugh, in a study of Egyptian dress in the late 1970s and early 1980s, also found a common use of European and especially French terms. See Rugh, *Reveal and Conceal*, 26, 18, 172.

134. Department of Commerce and Industry, *Katalug al-maʿrad al-daʾim* (Cairo, n.d.), 15, 16. The Department of Commerce and Industry's "permanent Exhibition

representative of some home industries" was inaugurated by King Fu'ad on 30 December 1920. See Ministry of Finance, *Almanac for the Year 1931*, 303. Some of this terminology was adapted from British terminology. See Wilcox, *Mode*, 105–6, 134. The formal and collective term for shoes, *al-hidha'* (pl. *al-ahdhiyya*), comes from a root connoting opposites. In modern Egyptian Arabic, it means "leather sandals" and carries rural associations linked to shoeing a horse. Martin Hinds and el-Said Badawi, *A Dictionary of Egyptian Arabic* (Beirut: Librarie du Liban, 1986), 196; see also Edward Lane, *Arabic-English Lexicon*, bk. 1, part 2 (1862; repr., New York: Ungar, 1956), 537. Today, the word *sarma* connotes old shoes (Hinds and Badawi, *Dictionary*, 502).

135. On the Mamluk and Ottoman shoe markets in Cairo, see André Raymond and G. Wiet, *Les Marchés du Caire: Traduction annoté du texte de Maqrizi* (Cairo: Institut Français d'Archéologie Orientale du Caire, 1979), 230, 236; and see 251, 255, 257; André Raymond, *Artisans et commerçants au Caire au XVIIIe siècle* (Damascus, Syria: Institut Français de Damas, 1973), 1:328–29; and Gabriel Baer, *Egyptian Guilds in Modern Times* (Jerusalem: Israel Oriental Society, 1964). Hinds and Badawi, *Dictionary*, 502, suggest that *sarma* was "probably" derived from the Persian word *charm*. See also Lane's *Lexicon*, bk. 1, part 4, 1684. *Bulgha* and *khuff* appear to be more directly etymologically connected to Arabic. See Hinds and Badawi, *Dictionary*, 100, 258; J. M. Cowan, ed., *The Hans Wehr Dictionary of Modern Written Arabic*, 3rd ed. (Ithaca, NY: Spoken Language Services, 1976), 74, 249; Lane, *Lexicon*, bk. 1, part 2, 770.

136. IC Census, 1927.

137. The 1868 census already used the term *jazmajiyya* for "shoemakers making shoes in European styles," according to John T. Chalcraft, *The Striking Cabbies of Cairo and Other Stories: Crafts and Guilds in Egypt, 1863–1914* (Albany: State University of New York Press, 2004), 58, 114. On the development of separate guilds for shoemakers of European and local shoes, see Chalcraft, *Striking Cabbies*, and Juan Ricardo Cole, *Colonialism and Revolution in the Middle East: Social and Cultural Origins of Egypt's 'Urabi Movement* (Princeton, NJ: Princeton University Press, 1993), 185–86. According to Maria Golia, the "word 'shoes' (*shooz*) recently entered the ranks [of foreign niceties in Egypt], replacing the Arabic *gazma* when it comes up in conversation, '*gazma*' being a popularly employed insult directed towards someone perceived as obstinate or stupid." *Cairo* (London: Reaktion Books, 2004), 146.

138. On *gazma*, see Hinds and Badawi, *Dictionary*, 159–60, where they list the term as a derivation from the Turkish *çizme*, meaning a knee-high boot.

139. Hinds and Badawi, *Dictionary*, 449, describe *shibshib*s as "pair of backless slippers, (loosely) pair of backless light shoes."

140. Neither is listed in Cowan's *Hans Wehr Dictionary* or *al-Munjid* (Beirut: Dar al-Mashriq, 1994).

141. "Foreign-yet-familiar" comes from Walter Armbrust, *Mass Culture and Modernism in Egypt* (New York: Cambridge University Press, 1996); and Afsaneh Najmabadi,

"Hazards of Modernity and Morality: Women, State, and Ideology in Contemporary Iran," in *Women, Islam, and the State*, ed. Deniz Kandioyti (Philadelphia: Temple University Press, 1991), 48–76.

142. On the *effendiyya*, see Lucie Ryzova, "Egyptianizing Modernity through the 'New *Effendiya*': Social and Cultural Constructions of the Middle Class in Egypt under the Monarchy," in *Re-Envisioning Egypt, 1919–1952*, ed. Arthur Goldschmidt, Amy Johnson, and Barak Salmoni (New York: American University in Cairo Press, 2005), 124–63.

143. *Fihris sharikat al-taʿawun al-manzali li-muwazzafiy al-hukuma* (Cairo: Dar al-Kutub al-Misriyya biʾl-Qahira, 1926), ʿAbdin, Maliyya, no. 264: Bunuk wa-Sharikat, 1909–1949, DWQ.

144. Ibid.

145. "Egypt's Boot and Shoe Trade," 2.

146. For these import figures, see 1908–1909 commercial report, NS, Egypte 118:1, MAEP; and Egyptian Customs Administration, *Annual Statement of Foreign Trade*, 1914, 1915, 1916, 1919, 1921, 1928. Some volumes contain figures for multiple years.

147. Mouktar Abdel Kerim el-Bannani to Ambassadeur de France au Caire, Cairo, 9 August 1926, le Caire-Ambassade 602/427, CADN.

148. See IC Census, 1927, 38–39.

149. Census reporting often relied on self-reporting through written forms. Many smaller or informal workplaces likely did not return forms. Also, many Egyptians did not report census information to the state out of a fear of increased taxation or other penalties.

150. See IC Census, 1937.

151. Commission du Commerce et de l'Industrie, *Rapport*, 73.

152. Department of Overseas Trade, "Memorandum on the Market for Leather Footwear in Egypt," *Report of the United Kingdom Trade Mission to Egypt*, February–March 1931, 61.

153. Selous, *Egypt, May 1937*, 102.

154. Ministry of Finance, *Almanac for the Year 1934*, 208. On the dominance of the British in these government contracts for uniform boots, see "Egypt's Boot and Shoe Trade" (1905); and Department of Overseas Trade, "Leather Footwear in Egypt," 61. Between 1929 and 1935 the UK's share of the market decreased from 27 percent to 7.6 percent. Selous, *Egypt, May 1937*, 101–2.

155. Ahmad Saoui, "Mashruʿ," presented to the Ministry of Commerce and Industry, Egypt, August 1936 (partial copy of the project's report, in Arabic), le Caire-Ambassade, 602/248, CADN.

156. Ibid. "Parcelized" structures of manufacturing, rather than mass-production methods, were also characteristic of France. See Whitney Walton, *France at the Crystal Palace: Bourgeois Taste and Artisan Manufacture in the Nineteenth Century* (Berkeley: University of California Press, 1992), 4.

157. Saoui, "Mashru'," le Caire-Ambassade, 602/248, CADN.

158. Department of Overseas Trade, "Leather Footwear in Egypt," 61.

159. Ibid.; Abdel Aziz El Sherbini and Ahmed Fouad Sherif, "Marketing Problems in an Underdeveloped Country—Egypt," *EC* 47, no. 285 (July 1956): 33.

160. Bata in England employed a similar strategy. BOT, *Boots and Shoes*, 38. See also Tomas Bata, *Knowledge in Action* (Washington, DC: IOS Press, 1991). The book contains several photographs of Tomas Bata examining shoes and local shoe production in the Middle East (e.g., 180 and 192).

161. Clement Levy, comp., *The Stock Exchange Year-Book of Egypt, 1943* (Cairo: Stock Exchange Year-Book of Egypt), 672; Bata ad, *al-Ahram*, 5 February 1931, 10.

162. Bata ad, *al-Ahram*, 20 January 1933, 10.

163. See Levy, *Stock Exchange Year-Book, 1943*, 672, and Bata, *Knowledge*.

164. "Al-Ahdhiyya al-misriyya taghazu al-'aswaq al-'alamiyya," *al-Ahram*, 1950 (special issue titled "Tatawwur Misr fi 75 sana, 1876–1950"), 38. See also A. N. Cumberbatch, for UK Board of Trade, *Egypt: Economic and Commercial Conditions in Egypt, October 1951* (London: HMSO, 1952), 67.

165. Many members of the Bata family appear to have acquired non-Czechoslovakian citizenship by the 1940s and 1950s. See stock exchange yearbooks from this period, Clement Levy, comp., *The Stock Exchange Year-Book of Egypt* (Cairo: Stock Exchange Year-Book of Egypt), and Nabil 'Abd al-Hamid Sayyid Ahmad, *al-Nashat al-itqisadi li'l-ajanib wa-atharuhu fi'l-mujtama' al-misri min sanat 1922 ila sanat 1952* (Cairo: al-Haya' al-Misriyya al-'Amma li'l-Kitab, 1982), 214.

166. See also Bata advertisement, *Le progres égyptien—Almanach*, 1953, 213.

167. "Al-Ahdhiyya al-misriyya," *al-Ahram*, 1950 (special issue titled "Tatawwur Misr fi 75 sana, 1876–1950"), 38. Such promotional efforts should not, of course, hide what was undoubtedly an oppressive and exploitative culture on the shop floor.

168. Ibid. See Société Orientale de Publicité, *The Egyptian Directory, L'Annuaire Egyptien, al-Dalil al-Misri* (Cairo: SOP Press, 1944), 229–31.

169. "Al-Ahdhiyya al-misriyya," *al-Ahram*, 1950 (special issue titled "Tatawwur Misr fi 75 sana, 1876–1950"), 38; Bata, *Knowledge*, 94.

170. "Al-Ahdhiyya al-misriyya," *al-Ahram*, 1950 (special issue titled "Tatawwur Misr fi 75 sana, 1876–1950"), 38.

171. Ibid.

172. Ibid.

173. Al-Khuli, *al-Rihla*, 1:121.

174. It is likely that the prevalent use of *qabaqib* would have provided an easy way to dock worker pay. Shehata describes wearing open-toed sandals as "*the* sign that one is a worker" in the 1990s. Shehata, "Plastic Sandals, Tea and Time," 30.

175. Al-Khuli, *al-Rihla*, 1:123. Al-Kuli had two different kinds of shoes in his wardrobe (al-Khuli, *al-Rihla*, 2:48). Although the memoir does not specify what style of shoes

al-Khuli meant by *"gazma"* (and it is quite possible that he invoked the word anachronistically when composing his memoir thirty years later after the word's usage had become more common), the late 1920s did witness the acceleration of shoe consumption and the availability of new styles of ready-made, closed shoes (such as *gazma*) in popular markets. His region of the Delta, in particular, was at the forefront of provincial production of these new styles. Industrial Census, Table 1, IC Census, 1927.

176. See Beinin and Lockman, *Workers on the Nile.*

177. In 1940 Egyptian public health officials estimated that 75 percent of Egyptians were afflicted with bilharzia. See Nancy Elizabeth Gallagher, *Egypt's Other Wars: Epidemics and the Politics of Public Health* (Syracuse, NY: Syracuse University Press, 1990), 15. In the 1940s the Egyptian government undertook a "barefoot campaign" to shod peasants as protection from bilharzia. See Nathan J. Brown, *Peasant Politics* (New Haven, CT: Yale University Press, 1990), 76. On the factory, see Campbell to FO, 28 February 1950, "Monthly Economic Report for January 1950," FO 371/80399, NAUK.

178. Cromer is famous for such declarations. See House of Commons, "Report by H.M. Agent and Consul General," 1905, 572.

179. Berque, *Egypt,* 477.

Chapter 5

1. "Kaifa taʿuniyna bi-qadamiyyiki," *Biladi,* no. 39 (10 August 1945), 28–29.

2. Chamber of Deputies, 22 May 1933, 1341, cited in Magda Baraka, *The Egyptian Upper Class between Revolutions* (Oxford: Ithaca Press, 1998), 267.

3. Chamber of Deputies, 9 June 1937, 1197, cited in Baraka, *Egyptian Upper Class,* 267–68.

4. A. N. Cumberbatch, for UK Board of Trade, *Egypt: Economic and Commercial Conditions in Egypt, October 1951* (London: HMSO, 1952), 67.

5. J. de la Taille to Ministre des Finances et Affaires Etrangères à Paris, Cairo, March 1948, "a/s Egypte: Limitation des bénéfices sur certaines marchandises," le Caire-Ambassade 602/249, CADN. That same year, an article complaining of the high expenses involved in raising a child also listed among children's needs two pairs of shoes: "Tifl sana 1948," *al-Musawwar,* no. 1224 (26 March 1948), 18–19.

6. Commercial reports rarely break out nylon from overall hosiery production. See appended *statistique* on imports and 3–4, "Note sur le marché de la bonneterie en Egypte," April 1954; "Masaniʿ al-Shurbaji bi-Imbaba," *al-Ahram,* special issue 1950, 34.

7. Frantz Fanon, *The Wretched of the Earth,* trans. Constance Farrington (New York: Grove Weidenfeld, 1963), 39.

8. Walter Armbrust, "The Golden Age before the Golden Age," in *Mass Mediations,* ed. Walter Armbrust (Berkeley: University of California Press, 2000), 312.

9. Ibid., 312, 304. This cinema was largely disparaged by Egyptian intellectuals of the 1960s and later.

10. By comparison, local industry produced 192 films from its start in 1923 through 1944. Recognizing the power of film, the Nasserist state would fund the vast expansion of cinema under the public sector in the 1960s. See Layane Chawaf and Ali Abou Chadi, "Répertoire des films," in *Egypte: 100 ans de cinema*, ed. Magda Wassef (Paris: Editions Plume, 1995), 286–315; Armbrust, "Golden Age," 301.

11. Gyan Prakash, ed., *After Colonialism* (Princeton, NJ: Princeton University Press, 1995), 3.

12. Artemis Cooper, *Cairo in the War, 1939–1945* (London: Hamish Hamilton, 1989), 4. According to the census reports, Cairo's population in 1937 stood at 1.3 million and in 1947 at 2 million people. The borders of the city saw only a limited expansion in these years, so that the population growth in this decade was about 5 percent. Janet L. Abu-Lughod, *Cairo: 1001 Years of the City Victorious* (Princeton, NJ: Princeton University Press, 1971), 129.

13. Joel Beinin and Zachary Lockman, *Workers on the Nile: Nationalism, Communism, Islam, and the Egyptian Working Class, 1882–1954* (Princeton, NJ: Princeton University Press, 1987), 237.

14. See, for example, J. W. Taylor, for UK Board of Trade, *Egypt: Economic and Commercial Conditions in Egypt, November 1947* (London: HMSO, 1948).

15. P. J. Vatikiotis, *The History of Egypt*, 3rd ed. (Baltimore, MD: Johns Hopkins University Press, 1985), 343–71; see also Israel Gershoni and James Jankowski, *Confronting Fascism in Egypt* (Stanford, CA: Stanford University Press, 2010).

16. Vatikiotis, *Egypt*, 349–50.

17. Jacques Berque, *Egypt: Imperialism and Revolution*, trans. Jean Stewart (London: Faber and Faber, 1972), 583.

18. Ibid., 584.

19. On dating the start of the Cold War, see Odd Arne Westad, *The Global Cold War* (New York: Cambridge University Press, 2007); Susan L. Carruthers, *Cold War Captives* (Berkeley: University of California Press, 2009).

20. Westad, *Global Cold War*, 89.

21. John Ruedy, *Modern Algeria* (Bloomington: Indiana University Press, 1992), 144–55.

22. Floresca Karanasou, "Egyptianisation: The 1947 Company Law and the Foreign Communities in Egypt" (DPhil diss., Oxford University, 1992), 60.

23. A photograph of the bombed windows of Cicurel on Fu'ad Street ("its merchandise thrown into the sidewalk and street from the force of the blast") and several other shops, including ORECO, appeared in *al-Musawwar*, no. 1241 (23 July 1948), 16. On the bombings, see correspondence from the British embassy in Cairo to the FO, 30 July–2 August 1948, in FO 371/69260, NAUK; Seigfried Landshut, *Jewish Communities in the Muslim Countries of the Middle East: A Survey for the American-Jewish Committee and the Anglo-Jewish Association* (London: Jewish Chronicle, 1950), 37–39; Gudrun

Krämer, *The Jews in Modern Egypt, 1914–1952* (Seattle: University of Washington Press, 1989), 213–15; and Joel Beinin, *The Dispersion of Egyptian Jewry* (Berkeley: University of California Press, 1998), 48–49 and 66–70.

24. Speaight, "Note for Conversation with the Minister for Foreign Affairs about the Attacks on Jews and Europeans," 20 July 1948, FO 141/1309, NAUK.

25. Memorandum, 22 July 1948, FO 141/1309, NAUK. There are suggestions in this and in Kashaby to Campbell, FO 141/1309, NAUK that the Egyptian government encouraged these actions to divert popular anger from the government.

26. Confidential note from Speaight, 2 August 1948, FO 141/1309, NAUK.

27. Aide Memoire, 20 July 194, FO 141/1309, NAUK.

28. Ibid.

29. Confidential note from Speaight, 2 August 1948, FO 141/1309, NAUK.

30. Marrack to Sansom, 21 July 1948, FO 141/1309, NAUK.

31. Minute by J. W. Taylor, 28 July 1948, FO 141/1309, NAUK. The merchants also discussed riot insurance.

32. Ibid.

33. Israel Gershoni and James Jankowski, *Egypt, Islam and the Arabs: The Search for Egyptian Nationhood, 1900–1930* (New York: Oxford University Press, 1986), and Israel Gershoni and James Jankowski, *Redefining the Egyptian Nation, 1930–1945* (New York: Cambridge University Press, 1995). Their work spawned a debate about the diffusion of Egyptian nationalism. See Gershoni, "The Evolution of National Culture in Modern Egypt: Intellectual Formation and Social Diffusion, 1892–1945," *Poetics Today* 13 (1992): 325–50; Charles D. Smith, "Imagined Identities, Imagined Nationalisms: Print Culture and Egyptian Nationalism in Light of Recent Scholarship," *International Journal of Middle East Studies* 29, no. 4 (November 1997): 607–22; Gershoni and Jankowski, "Print Culture, Social Change, and the Process of Redefining Imagined Communities in Egypt; Response to the Review by Charles D. Smith of *Redefining the Egyptian Nation*," *International Journal of Middle East Studies* 31, no. 1 (February 1999): 81–94; Smith, "'Cultural Constructs' and Other Fantasies: Imagined Narratives in Imagined Communities; Surrejoinder to Gershoni and Jankowski's 'Print Culture, Social Change, and the Process of Redefining Imagined Communities in Egypt,'" *International Journal of Middle East Studies* 31, no. 1 (February 1999): 95–102; Jankowski and Gershoni, eds. *Rethinking Nationalism in the Arab Middle East* (New York: Columbia University Press, 1997); Joel Beinin, "Egypt: Society and Economy, 1923–1952," in *The Cambridge History of Egypt*, ed. M. W. Daly (New York: Cambridge University Press, 1998), 2:309–33.

34. Karanasou, "Egyptianisation," 32.

35. Ibid., 54, 70; see also Krämer, *Jews in Modern Egypt*, 206.

36. The formal name of the new department changed over time. See Karanasou, "Egyptianisation," 98–99. Although the law came into force on November 4, 1947, the Egyptian parliament began to debate legal provisions to Egyptianize the capital,

administration, and staffs of locally registered joint-stock companies in 1941, and the draft law was refined and radicalized over the next six years. Law 26 of 1954 replaced the 1947 law but essentially retained the structure of the process and the quotas. Other laws in the late 1940s and 1950s Egyptianized a variety of sectors of society, including professions such as stockbrokers, accountants, and auditors, in addition to restricting landowning by non-Egyptians. Laws in the 1910s and 1920s had mandated varying levels of national capital and employees, although without real enforcement provisions. See Karanasou, 73–75. Law 138 of 1947 mandated that all joint-stock companies registered as Egyptian had to achieve a quota of Egyptians among their employees (75 percent who receive 65 percent of the total salaries), workers (90 percent who receive 80 percent of the wages), and stockholders and capital (51 percent), as well as members of the board (40 percent) within three years starting 4 November 1947. The MS defined employees as those who had to write in their jobs, as opposed to workers, who did not.

37. Stores that deposited compliance records in the MS archive paid a substantial proportion of salesclerk salaries as commission. Commissions included sales percentages and bonuses and varied from company to company. See Lefevre-Pontalis to Millerand, Cairo, 15 February 1920, "a/s Marché du travail en Egypte"; and French consul to Millerand, Cairo, 28 February 1920, "a/s Marché du travail en Egypte," le Caire-Ambassade, 602/245, CADN; and letter, Cairo, 15 April 1949, doc. 112, Egyptian Products Sales Co., MS 74, DWQ.

38. MS department store records reveal high turnover among junior employees during the investigations, and a certain continuity of employment among senior salesclerks and department heads who did not hold Egyptian nationality. See also Karansou, "Egyptianisation," esp. 40, 330, and interview with Henriette Zeitoui Hallak in Liliane S. Dammond with Yvette M. Raby, *The Lost World of the Egyptian Jews: First-Person Accounts from Egypt's Jewish Community in the Twentieth Century* (New York: iUniverse, 2007), 195. Hallak's father had worked as an underwear salesman and a salesclerk at Orosdi-Back before opening a small store in the Muski on the eve of the Second World War.

39. On Sednaoui, see Karansou, "Egyptianisation," 282. For Chemla, see MS inspection report dated 15 January 1952, doc. 230-32, MS 73, DWQ.

40. Cited in Karanasou, "Egyptianisation," 102–3.

41. Ibid., 103–4.

42. Krämer, *Jews in Modern Egypt*, 32–34.

43. See esp. Karanasou, "Egyptianisation."

44. On the Greeks, see Karanasou, "Egyptianisation"; Alexander Kitroeff, *The Greeks in Egypt, 1919–1937: Ethnicity and Class* (London: Ithaca Press, 1989); and Stratis Tsirkas, *Drifting Cities*, trans. Kay Cicellis (Athens: Kedros, 1995). On the Italian community, see Elizabeth Shlala, "Mediterranean Migration, Cosmopolitanism, and the Law: A History of the Italian Community of Nineteenth-Century Alexandria, Egypt" (PhD diss., Georgetown University, 2009).

45. Vatikiotis, *Egypt*, 320–21.

46. Ahmed Abdalla, *The Student Movement and National Politics in Egypt* (London: al-Saqi Books, 1985).

47. James P. Jankowski, *Egypt's Young Rebels* (Stanford, CA: Hoover Institution Press, 1975), 78, 69.

48. Beinin and Lockman, *Workers on the Nile*, 351–62; Joel Beinin, *Was the Red Flag Flying There?* (Berkeley: University of California Press, 1990); Vatikiotis, *Egypt*, 341.

49. Beinin and Lockman, *Workers on the Nile*, 360.

50. Ibid., 361.

51. Hasan Al-Banna, *Five Tracts of Hasan al-Banna*, trans. Charles Wendell (Berkeley: University of California, 1978), 127–29.

52. Al-Banna, "Toward the Light" (probably 1947), in *Five Tracts of Hasan al-Banna*, 127–28.

53. Cited in Brynjar Lia, *The Society of the Muslim Brothers in Egypt* (Reading, MA: Ithaca Press, 1998), 199.

54. Sayyid Qutb, *Social Justice in Islam*, trans. John B. Hardie with Hamid Algar (New York: Islamic Publications International, 2000), 77.

55. Lia, *Society of the Muslim Brothers*, 154.

56. Richard P. Mitchell, *The Society of the Muslim Brothers* (1969; repr., New York: Oxford University Press, 1993), 277, see 274–77; see also Beinin and Lockman, *Workers on the Nile*, 374–75. Although it is highly likely that ties, scarves, and other items were made of silk, the Brothers' economic institutions were designed to promote the national economy and better the situation of the "poverty-stricken masses" (Mitchell, *Society of the Muslim Brothers*, 272), which suggests they produced affordable, modest cotton textiles.

57. Gershoni and Jankowski, *Confronting Fascism*, 235.

58. Ibid., 240.

59. Jankowski, *Egypt's Young Rebels*, 86–87.

60. Ibid., 30–33, 92–93.

61. Gershoni and Jankowski, *Confronting Fascism*, 265.

62. Jankowski, *Egypt's Young Rebels*, 38.

63. Ahmad Husayn, *Jaridat Misr al-fatah* (November 1938), cited in Jankowski, *Young Egypt*, 38.

64. Gershoni and Jankowski, *Confronting Fascism*, 255. See also Jankowski, *Young Egypt*, 39.

65. Quoted from the party program as published in 1933 in the journal *al-Sarkhah*, quoted in Jankowski, *Egypt's Young Rebels*, 69.

66. Jankowski, *Egypt's Young Rebels*, 107.

67. Ibid., 114.

68. Elie I. Politi, ed., *Annuaire des sociétés égyptiennes par actions, 1955* (Cairo: Imprimerie Procaccia, 1932; Alexandria, 1942, 1947, 1955); for Société el-Beit el-Masri, see 361.

69. See, for example, advertisement in *al-Musawwar*, no. 1257 (12 November 1948), 43; or *al-Musawwar*, no. 1252 (8 October 1948), 33; or *al-Ahram*, 23 April 1951, 6.

70. *Al-Musawwar*, no. 1243 (6 August 1948), 41.

71. Advertisement in *al-Musawwar*, no. 1252 (8 October 1948), 33.

72. *Al-Musawwar*, no. 1241 (23 July 1948), 34. This was precisely during widespread bombing of non-Muslim stores; indeed the Cicurel bombing was covered only a few pages away in the same issue.

73. Subhi Shurbaji to the Egyptian finance minister, Alexandria, 10 April 1942, in ʿAbdin, Maliyya, no. 264: Bunuk wa-Sharikat, 1909–1949, DWQ. See also Robert Tignor, *Egyptian Textiles and British Capital, 1930–1956* (Cairo: American University in Cairo Press, 1989), 58. Despite Shurbaji's claims, there is no evidence that existing fibers were necessarily deficient or inadequate.

74. Subhi Shurbaji to the Egyptian finance minister, Alexandria, 10 April 1942, in ʿAbdin, Maliyya, no. 264: Bunuk wa-Sharikat, 1909–1949, DWQ.

75. In 1952 imports of stockings made from pure artificial silk and artificial-silk blends reached 144,560 dozen pairs. "Note sur le marché de la bonneterie en Egypte," April 1954, 4, le Caire-Ambassade 602/253, CADN.

76. See "Masaniʿ al-Shurbaji bi-Imbaba," *al-Ahram*, special issue 1950, 34. It is not surprising that the United States monopolized production of nylon, since the fiber had been invented there. In October 1938 Dupont announced the invention of nylon, and in 1939 the first nylon stockings were displayed at the New York World's Fair. See Susannah Handley, *Nylon* (Baltimore, MD: Johns Hopkins University Press, 1999), 2–6.

77. Handley, *Nylon*, 51.

78. On primary materials, see L. H. C. Tippett, A *Portrait of the Lancashire Textile Industry* (New York: Oxford University Press, 1969), 29–34. Later synthetics would use coal and oil as the basis of their fibers.

79. "The Story of Artificial Silk Told in Four Glass Jars," *Egyptian Gazette*, 14 April 1925.

80. "Al-Harir al-sinaʿi," *al-Nashra al-iqtisadiyya al-misriyya*, no. 12 (12 September 1920), 466.

81. G. H. Selous, *Report on Economic and Commercial Conditions in Egypt, May 1937* (London: HMSO, 1937), 76–77.

82. R. M. Turner and L. B. S. Larkins, for UK Department of Overseas Trade, *Economic Conditions in Egypt, July 1931* (London: HMSO, 1931), 48.

83. Selous, *Egypt, May 1937*, 116. Important mills included the Usines Textiles al-Kahira, with 350 looms weaving rayon in 1937, and the Misr Silk Weaving Company, with 400 looms working rayon and silk. Selous estimated that there were thirty-four "concerns" weaving rayon in Egypt, from as small as 5 looms to 400. See also C. Empson, for UK Department of Overseas Trade, *Report on Economic and Commercial Conditions in Egypt, June 1939* (London: HMSO, 1939), 45.

84. Interview with Harb in *Misr*, 19 December 1936, reprinted in Muhammad Tal'at Harb, *Majmu'at khutub Muhammad Tal'at Harb basha* (Cairo: Imprimerie Misr, 1957/n.d.), 3:173.

85. Ibid.

86. Cumberbatch, *Egypt, October 1951*, 59.

87. Tignor, *Egyptian Textiles*, 55–56. See also Eric Davis, *Challenging Colonialism: Bank Misr and Egyptian Industrialization, 1920–1941* (Princeton, NJ: Princeton University Press, 1983), 144.

88. Tignor, *Egyptian Textiles*, 56.

89. Cumberbatch, *Egypt, October 1951*, 59.

90. Politi, *Annuaire des sociétés, 1955*, 415.

91. IFMCSMA, *Official Report of the International Cotton Congress Held in Egypt, 1927* (Manchester: Taylor Garnett Evans, n.d.), 38. "Hayah kulaha nylun," *al-Ithnayn*, no. 678, 9 June 1947, 10.

92. "Al-Tawsi'a fi'l-istikhdam al-khuyut al-sina'iyya," *al-Misri*, special issue on cotton, 1950, 71.

93. Jean Schatz, "Le commerce extérieur de l'Egypte pendant les deux guerres mondiales," *EC* nos. 228/229 (1945): 796 (tables); "Note sur le marché de la bonneterie en Egypte," 4.

94. Handley, *Nylon*, 48–50. In several U.S. cities tens of thousands of women lined up to purchase nylon hose; these were called the nylon riots.

95. Ibid., 50.

96. Appended *statistique* on imports and pp. 3–4, "Note sur le marché de la bonneterie en Egypte"; "Masani' al-Shurbaji bi-Imbaba," *al-Ahram*, special issue 1950, 34.

97. Anecdotal evidence suggests that even for middle-class and upper-middle-class women, nylon stockings were a splurge item in the 1950s. See "Shurrabi . . . Shurrabi!" *Hawwa al-jadida*, special issue, 1 May 1955, 67; Shurbaji store advertising in *al-Musawwar* in winter 1957–1958.

98. Chemla advertisement, *'Akhir lahza*, no. 74 (31 May 1950), 2.

99. See, for example, *al-Musawwar*, no. 1258 (19 November 1948), 39; *al-Musawwar*, no. 1260 (3 December 1948), 39; *al-Musawwar*, no. 1686 (1 February 1957), 37. See also advertisements for Shurbaji, *al-Ahram*, July 1959 (special issue), 71; Gabri Store, *al-Ahram*, 22 November 1951, 2, and *Bint al-nil*, December 1954, 80; Bata stockings (silk and artificial silk), *al-Ithnayn*, no. 562 (19 March 1945), 22; Kayser nylons, *Images*, no. 170 (9 February 1952); 14; Cameo nylons, *Hawwa al-jadida*, no. 11 (1 November 1955), 70.

100. *Al-Ahram*, 20 November 1951, 1.

101. On the social unrest in the 1940s, see, e.g., Abdalla, *Student Movement*; Beinin and Lockman, *Workers on the Nile*.

102. ʿAshur ʿUlaysh, "Imraʾt nylun," *Ruz al-yusuf*, no. 1026 (11 February 1948), 33–34. See also graphics of "al-Tawsiʿa fi al-istikhdam al-khuyut al-sinaʿiyya," *al-Misri*, special issue on cotton, 1950, 71.

103. ʿUlaysh, "Imraʾt nylun."

104. *Akhir saʿa*, no. 697 (3 March 1948).

105. Edward Lane, *Manners and Customs of the Modern Egyptians* (1836, 1895; repr., London: East-West Publications, 1989), 52; Fikri al-Khuli, *al-Rihla* (Cairo: Dar al-Ghad, 1987–1992), 1:121; *Biladi*, no. 39 (10 August 1945), 16; "Alf sinf wa-sinf," *al-Musawwar*, no. 645 (19 February 1937), 13. See also Samer S. Shehata, "Plastic Sandals, Tea and Time: Shop Floor Politics and Culture in Egypt" (PhD diss., Princeton University, 2000).

106. I. Levi, "Le commerce extérieur et l'industrialisation de l'Egypte," *EC* 30, nos. 186–187 (1939): 625.

107. Barbara Freyer Stowasser, *Women in the Qurʾan, Traditions, and Interpretation* (New York: Oxford University Press, 1994), 54–55, see also 50.

108. Handley, *Nylon*, 28, 40–43.

109. Palmira Brummett, *Image and Imperialism in the Ottoman Revolutionary Press, 1908–1911* (Albany: State University of New York Press, 2000), 19–20.

110. Ibid., 18.

111. *Ruz al-yusuf*, no. 1024 (28 January 1948), 19.

112. Muhammad Husayn, "Imraʾ fi shariʿa fuʾad," *Ruz al-yusuf*, no. 1023 (21 January 1948), 34.

113. *Ruz al-yusuf*, no. 1042 (2 June 1948), 18.

114. Sufi ʿAbd Allah, "al-Muntaqima, qissa misriya," *al-Musawwar*, no. 1259 (26 November 1948), 36–37.

115. *Al-Musawwar*, no. 1263 (24 December 1948), 55. For similar themes, see *al-Ithnayn*, no. 656 (6 January 1947), 21; *al-Musawwar*, no. 1244 (13 August 1948), 7.

116. *Le progrès égyptien—Almanach*, 1953, 123.

117. *Ruz al-yusuf*, no. 1030 (10 March 1948), 17.

118. The foot and consequently the shoe are eroticized in numerous cultural traditions. Whereas many works on the erotic nature of feet tend to generalize about behavior across cultures by positing an essentialized psychological need or desire, other works argue for a more culturally specific sexual economy linked to feet. See Inea Bushnaq, ed. and trans., *Arab Folktales* (New York: Pantheon, 1986); William A. Rossi, *The Sex Life of the Foot and Shoe* (New York: Dutton, 1976), esp. 159–61, where he attributes the origins of Cinderella to a seventeenth-century BCE Egyptian tale.

119. See Marilyn Booth, *Bayram al-Tunisi's Egypt: Social Criticism and Narrative Strategies* (Exeter, UK: Ithaca Press, 1990), esp. 128, on the *fawazir*. See also Walter Armbrust, *Mass Culture and Modernism in Egypt* (New York: Cambridge University Press, 1996), 55–58.

120. Booth, *Bayram al-Tunisi's Egypt*, 128; see also 127 and 131.

121. Bayram Al-Tunisi, *Ashʿar Bayram al-Tunisi* (Cairo: Maktabat Madbuli, 1985), 322.

122. Word play and especially puns are important tools of humor in Arabic literature and popular culture; see Pierre Cachia, *Popular Narrative Ballads of Modern Egypt* (Oxford: Clarendon Press, 1989), 34.

123. Drawing on the traditional style of the *qasida*, al-Tunisi visually pairs two-verse segments on the same line and then links them through final rhymes, which are further repeated and connected between lines one and two and lines seven and eight, in effect binding the poem in a reflective structure. On the *qasida*, see Salma Khadra Jayyusi, "Introduction," in *Modern Arabic Poetry: An Anthology*, ed. Salma Khadra Jayyusi (New York: Columbia University Press, 1987), esp. 8–13. See Booth, *Bayram al-Tunisi's Egypt*, on how Bayram plays with and modifies "traditional" forms in his poetry, although she does not include the *fawazir* in this discussion.

124. On his use of an educated colloquial more generally, see Booth, *Bayram al-Tunisi's Egypt*, 388–404. See also Armbrust, *Mass Culture*, 37–62.

125. Yasin was a popular actor for burlesque roles. He made seventeen films in 1950, out of a total Egyptian production of forty-eight for the year. Anwar Wagdi wrote *al-Batal*'s script.

126. Al-Batal portrays his relationship to Sharbat in this way in the film. For a cartoon on exactly this subject, see *Ruz al-yusuf*, no. 1022 (14 January 1948), 21.

127. The local tanning industry was subject to similar ambiguities and depictions. See Sirri al-Din, "al-Dhahab . . . taht aqdam ʿal-muwasha,'" *Ruz al-yusuf*, no. 1067 (24 November 1948), 26.

128. Al-Tunisi, for example, used such a pun in his riddle (number 44) "al-Shurrab [The Sock]": "Two individuals, comrades with us in the streets; Filling them at all times, a pair of pretty legs / sheep's feet [*gawz kawariʿ*]" (*Ashʿar*, 313).

129. The joke repeats itself in another confused telephone conversation about meat between al-Batal and the owner's daughter, Sharbat. When Sharbat telephones the store to speak to her father, al-Batal answers the phone in an unprofessional manner. She asks, "Is this the shoe store?" Al-Batal replies, "No, it is the *kabab* and *kufta* [kabob and meat patty] store."

130. Keith Wheelock, *Nasser's New Egypt* (New York: Praeger, 1960), 149–50; Vatikiotis, *Egypt*, 391.

131. Ahmad Husayn in *al-Shaʿb al-jadid*, 4 June 1951, cited in Joel Gordon, *Nasser's Blessed Movement: Egypt's Free Officers and the July Revolution* (1992; repr., Cairo: American University in Cairo Press, 1996), 27–28.

132. Samir Faraj, *Nariman: Akhir malikat Misr* (Cairo: Ahram Publishing, 1992).

133. Vatikiotis, *Egypt*, 368. On this political situation, see, for example, Gordon, *Nasser's Blessed Movement*, 25–26; Vatikiotis, *Egypt*, 368–70. See also Berque, *Egypte*, 692–704.

134. Confidential Cairo telegram no. 1217, Cumberbatch to Couldrey, 15 December 1951, FO 371/90172, NAUK. See also Cumberbatch to BOT, Cairo, 17 December 1951, in FO 371/90172, NAUK; Cumberbatch, *Egypt, October 1951*, 97–101; Tippett, *Portrait*, 16.

135. See "Revue de la Presse," enclosed in Bordereau d'envoi no. 1756DE, Ambassade to MAE Paris, dated Cairo, 29 December 1951, le Caire-Ambassade, 602/251, CADN.

136. Ibid.

137. Ibid.

138. Confidential Cairo telegram no. 1217, Cumberbatch to Couldrey, 15 December 1951, FO 371/90172, NAUK.

139. Anne-Claire Kerboeuf, "The Cairo Fire of 26 January 1952 and the Interpretations of History," in *Re-Envisioning Egypt, 1919–1952*, ed. Arthur Goldschmidt, Amy Johnson, and Barak Salmoni (Cairo: American University in Cairo Press, 2005), 197–98.

140. Davis, *Challenging Colonialism*; Robert Tignor, *State, Private Enterprise, and Economic Change in Egypt, 1918–1952* (Princeton, NJ: Princeton University Press, 1984), 162–74.

141. Joel Beinin, *Workers and Peasants in the Modern Middle East* (New York: Cambridge University Press, 2001), 109–10.

142. On Murad and "the politics of ethnoreligious identity" in Egyptian popular and mass culture, see Beinin, *Dispersion*, 83–85; Armbrust, "Golden Age," 299. Murad became increasingly ostracized from Egyptian public life after 1952. She abruptly retired in 1955, although she remained in Cairo until her death and continued to be popular among Egyptians, including Nasser.

143. Lyrics by Bayram al-Tunisi, sung by Layla Murad, from *Sayyidat al-qitar*.

Chapter 6

1. Cited in Anne-Claire Kerboeuf, "The Cairo Fire of 26 January 1952 and the Interpretations of History," in *Re-Envisioning Egypt, 1919–1952*, ed. Arthur Goldschmidt, Amy Johnson, and Barak Salmoni (Cairo: American University in Cairo Press, 2005), 201.

2. Cited in Jean Lacouture and Simonne Lacouture, *Egypt in Transition*, trans. Francis Scarfe (New York: Criterion Books, 1958), 122.

3. For an excellent discussion of the fire and the attribution of responsibility in Egyptian history and historiography, see Kerboeuf, "Cairo Fire." She convincingly argues that "many . . . specialists could not bear the idea of the Egyptian people burning their own capital" and so have offered conspiracy theories, often grounded in close readings of archives and accounts, about the collusion among various forces (usually the palace or the British in alliance with political players such as the Socialist Party, the Muslim Brothers, the communists, the Free Officers, or the Wafd); see esp. 199–202. Other important sources on the fire include Jamal al-Sharqawi, *Hariq al-Qahira* (Cairo: Dar al-Thaqafa al-Jadida, 1976); anonymous, "Ma'sah al-Qahira fi 26 yanayir 1952," *al-Ahram*, 12 February 1952, 1–3; R. T., "La journée du 26 janvier," *Le progrès égyptien—Almanach*, 1953;

Lacouture and Lacouture, *Egypt in Transition*, 105–22; Anouar Abdel-Malek, *Egypt: Military Society. The Army Regime, the Left, and Social Change under Nasser*, trans. Charles Lam Markmann (New York: Vintage Books, 1968), vii–xiii, 16–17, 34–38; and Austin L. Moore, *Farewell, Farouk* (Chicago: Scholars' Press, 1954), 31–42. See also Afaf Lutfi al-Sayyid Marsot, *A Short History of Modern Egypt* (New York: Cambridge University Press, 1986), 104–6; Joel Gordon, *Nasser's Blessed Movement: Egypt's Free Officers and the July Revolution* (1992; repr., Cairo: American University in Cairo Press, 1996), 26–27; Gudrun Krämer, *The Jews in Modern Egypt, 1914–1952* (Seattle: University of Washington Press, 1989), 219–21; Max Rodenbeck, *Cairo: The City Victorious* (New York: Knopf, 1999), 155–57; Artemis Cooper, *Cairo in the War, 1939–1945* (London: Hamish Hamilton, 1989), 330–36; Trevor Mostyn, *Egypt's Belle Epoque: Cairo and the Age of the Hedonists* (1989; repr., New York: I. B. Tauris, 2007), 167–71; and Muhammad Anis, *Hariq al-Qahira* (Beirut: al-Mu'assasa al-'Arabiyya li'l-Dirasat wa'l-Nashr, 1972).

4. Christine Rosen, *The Limits of Power: Great Fires and the Process of City Growth in America* (New York: Cambridge University Press, 1986), 89. See also Karen Sawislak, *Smoldering City: Chicagoans and the Great Fire, 1871–1874* (Chicago: University of Chicago Press, 1995).

5. Mark Mazower, *Salonica, City of Ghosts: Christians, Muslims and Jews, 1430–1950* (New York: Knopf, 2005), 298–310. See also Zeynep Çelik, *The Remaking of Istanbul* (Berkeley: University of California Press, 1986), 49–81; and Daniel Goffman, "Izmir: From Village to Colonial Port City," in *The Ottoman City between East and West*, ed. Edhem Eldem, Daniel Goffman, and Bruce Masters (New York: Cambridge University Press, 1999), 79–134.

6. Alan Smart, *The Shek Kip Mei Myth: Squatters, Fires, and Colonial Rule in Hong Kong, 1950–1963* (Hong Kong: Hong Kong University Press, 2006), 4.

7. Carl Smith, *Urban Disorder and the Shape of Belief*, 2nd ed. (Chicago: University of Chicago Press, 2007), 35–38.

8. Derek Hopwood, *Egypt: Politics and Society, 1945–1984*, 2nd ed. (Boston: Allen and Unwin, 1985), 32; P. J. Vatikiotis, *The History of Egypt*, 3rd ed. (Baltimore, MD: Johns Hopkins University Press, 1985), 370; Abdel-Malek, *Egypt*.

9. Sources cite contradictory numbers for the casualties on January 25; the British official count was thirty-six and the Egyptian eighty. See Lacouture and Lacouture, *Egypt in Transition*, 107.

10. Lacouture and Lacouture, *Egypt in Transition*, 115.

11. For good discussions of the involvement of different political groups, see Lacouture and Lacouture, *Egypt in Transition*, and Kerboeuf, "Cairo Fire." Ahmad Husayn of the Socialist Party (formerly Young Egypt) was accused and tried for instigating the fires, although the case against him was dismissed once the Free Officers came to power the following summer. Several Free Officers, including Anwar Sadat and probably also Nasser, had previously been members of Young Egypt. Nasser blamed the communists

for the fire in 1956. See Lacouture and Lacouture, *Egypt in Transition*, 119. Historians who have studied the fire in some detail generally agree, however, that the British Intelligence Service played some role in it. See Kerboeuf, "Cairo Fire," 207–8, and al-Sharqawi, *Hariq al-Qahira.* That urban unrest in Alexandria did not lead to fire and looting has been attributed to the actions of its mayor, who closed and secured the city early on January 26. See Moore, *Farewell, Farouk*, 34.

12. M. T. Audsley, "Report of the British Embassy Committee of Enquiry into the Riots in Cairo on the 26th January 1952," 5, LAB 13/740, NAUK. See also Roberta L. Dougherty, "Badiʿa al-Masabni, Artiste and Modernist," in *Mass Mediations*, ed. Walter Armbrust (Berkeley: University of California Press, 2000), 243–68. On the Casino Opera and al-Masabni, see also Arthur Goldschmidt, *Biographical Dictionary of Modern Egypt* (Boulder, CO: Lynne Rienner, 2000), 125–26; Karin Van Nieuwkerk, *"A Trade like Any Other": Female Singers and Dancers in Egypt* (Austin: University of Texas Press, 1995), 46–48; Samir W. Raafat, *Cairo: The Glory Years* (Alexandria: Harpocrates, 2003), 240–44, and *L'Indicateur Touristique d'Egypte/Tourists' Egyptian Companion*, 1952–1953 (Cairo: A. Karama, 1952), 88. Accounts differ as to whether Masabni actually owned the Casino Opera at this time.

13. Van Nieuwkerk, *"A Trade like Any Other,"* 48.

14. Richard P. Mitchell, *The Society of the Muslim Brothers* (1969; repr., New York: Oxford University Press, 1993), 223.

15. The photograph was carried in *al-Ahram*. See also Jacques Berque, *Egypt: Imperialism and Revolution*, trans. Jean Stewart (London: Faber and Faber, 1972), plate 28. The film, produced by Paramount Pictures in August 1951, recounted the struggle against a star on a collision course with the earth.

16. These were the numbers reported by the government. "Responsibility for January 26: Detailed report of inquiry by Prosecutor-General," *Egyptian Mail*, 8 March 1952. See also confidential report from Stevenson to Eden, "Damage to British Interests in Cairo in the Riots of 26th January, 1952," Cairo, 5 February 1952, FO 371/96957/JE1123/1, NAUK; and Moore, *Farewell, Farouk*, 37.

17. Audsley, "Enquiry into the Riots in Cairo," 7.

18. This occurred at the Doll Cabaret situated near Groppi's on ʿAdli Pasha Street, where a former employee and another man who worked in a nearby doctor's clinic led the attack. *Al-Ahram*, 17 March 1952, 3.

19. The British car dealerships included Universal Motor Company, E.A.S.T. Company, Anglo-Egyptian Motors (Ford agents for Cairo), British Egyptian Automobile Corp., and Cairo Motor Company. See appendix A, Stevenson to Eden, "Damage to British Interests."

20. See Audsley, "Enquiry into the Riots in Cairo," and secret telegram from Stevenson to FO, 27 January 1952, FO 141/1474, NAUK.

21. Moore, *Farewell, Farouk*, 33.

22. "Extremists' Role in Riots," *Times* (London), 29 January 1952, 4.

23. Cicurel advertisement, *al-Ahram*, 11 November 1951, 6.

24. Audsley, "Enquiry into the Riots in Cairo," 10, 15. Managed by Ovadia Mercado Salem, a local Jewish businessman and a naturalized Egyptian, Chemla in 1952 was owned by Joseph Aquilina, a Maltese British subject. See E. J. Blattner, ed., *Who's Who in Egypt and the Near East* (Cairo: Paul Barbey Press, 1943), 443; Blattner, *Who's Who in Egypt, 1952*, 575; Raafat, *Cairo*, 172, 178–79. On Aquilina, see Blattner, *Who's Who in Egypt, 1948*, 149; and letter 27 February 1952, in FO 371/97024/JE1481/19, NAUK.

25. Advertisement, *EN*, 3rd series, no. 394, 18 January 1952, back cover.

26. "Statement by Mr. Eric Titterington," appendix F, 54, of Audsley, "Enquiry into the Riots in Cairo." In 1940 the store offered a range of men's wear, shoes, silver and gifts, toys and games, and sports goods. See advertisements in the *Egyptian Gazette*, 9 March 1940, 22 November 1937, and 24 March 1925; *al-Ahram*, 13 January 1935, 4.

27. "Statement by Mr. Eric Titterington," appendix F, 54, of Audsley, "Enquiry into the Riots in Cairo."

28. Stevenson to Eden, "Damage to British Interests." The British Chambers of Commerce put the case of "prestige" even more bluntly. "The disappearance of British influence, both economic and cultural, with its many educational, medical and other institutions, will not be long in following that of the commercial community." "Memorandum on Anglo-Egyptian Trade by the British Chambers of Commerce in Egypt," p. 3, in Cumberbatch to Allen, Cairo, 19 January 1953, FO 371/102788, NAUK.

29. The ʿAdès claim was for £E216,000; the firm estimated its monthly loss of business to be £E30,000. The Roberts Hughes claim totaled £E55,544, with an estimated monthly loss of business of only £E2,608. The two largest claims were for British Overseas Airways Corp. (BOAC) and one of the car dealerships. See "Claims for Damage Sustained in Riots of Saturday January 26th 1952," Enclosure 1 to Cairo dispatch no. 62 (Consular), 31 March 1952, FO 371/97025, NAUK.

30. Trial testimony on the Orosdi-Back/ʿUmar Effendi case, *al-Ahram*, 13 March 1952, 1, 2, 3. The newspaper minutely transcribed the testimony, as it was the first day of the trials for the events of 26 January. Guyomard took the stand and testified in French, and the court's lead judge reportedly translated. On Guyomard, see Blattner, *Who's Who in Egypt, 1952*, 374. The court ruled that fourteen of those arrested were bystanders. The remaining five received various terms of imprisonment with hard labor. The mute tailor, Ahmad Shalabi al-Sayyid, was sentenced to seven years of hard labor. *Al-Ahram*, 17 March 1952, 3–4.

31. See the press summaries of the Egyptian prosecutor's report enclosed in FO 371/96957, NAUK. On the store opening, see the *Egyptian Gazette*, 22 March 1940, 2. Benzion was known among Egyptian department stores for its many local branches (*Egyptian Gazette*, 22 September 1934, 2). By 1956 the store had twenty-one branches in Egypt. *Ruz al-yusuf*, no. 1477 (1 October 1956), 45. Even though the Cairo store sold

a wide array of cloth, clothing, and housewares, the company promoted its stocks of cheap "popular cloth" in the trying postwar years. See advertisements in *al-Balagh*, on 17 September 1945 and 2 February 1946.

32. Audsley, "Enquiry into the Riots in Cairo," 9, 11.

33. Ibid., 11. See also "Extremists' Role in Riots," *Times* (London), 29 January 1952, 4.

34. Lacouture and Lacouture, *Egypt in Transition*, 112.

35. Moore, *Farewell, Farouk*, 37.

36. Moore, *Farewell, Farouk*, 37. On a Fulbright grant, Moore was a lecturer in history at Farouk I University in Alexandria from September 1951 to July 1952. Ten gunsmiths were destroyed in the fire.

37. Trial of the looters is covered (relatively briefly) in *al-Ahram*, 3 April 1952, 3. Some of those arrested testified that they found goods in the street, others stole goods inside stores, and yet others declared that the "police thrust goods into their hands." Those arrested also included three shoemakers, a shirt maker, two tailors, a salesman, a fruit seller, a chicken merchant, a musician, several government employees, workers, and students.

38. Kerboeuf, "Cairo Fire," 203.

39. Moore, *Farewell, Farouk*, 33.

40. See "Ma'sah al-Qahira fi 26 yanayir 1952," *al-Ahram*, 12 February 1952, 1–3; photograph in *Le progrès égyptien—Almanach*, 1953, 42. See also Rodenbeck, *Cairo*, 155–57; Cooper, *Cairo in the War*, 330–36; Mostyn, *Egypt's Belle Epoque*, 167–71; Anis, *Hariq al-Qahira*. Cicurel was also frequently singled out for mention by local observers. See, e.g., Hopwood, *Tales of Empire*, 112. Many of the attacks on the department stores occurred after the army arrived in the late afternoon in central Cairo: Chemla, Orosdi-Back, and Benzion were targeted at this time, probably because the army moved in first to protect political sites such as foreign consulates.

41. Vatikiotis, *Egypt*, 370, notes that 750 establishments were destroyed. Newspaper accounts at the time put the figure at "about 700." Included were 8 motorcar showrooms, 13 hotels, 30 commercial offices, and 117 offices and flats. "Responsibility for January 26," *Egyptian Mail*, 8 March 1952. See also Stevenson to Eden, "Damage to British Interests." Nezar AlSayyad gives a much higher number of dead in *Cairo: Histories of a City* (Cambridge, MA: Belknap Press, 2011), 228.

42. Stevenson to Eden, "Damage to British Interests."

43. Al-Sharqawi, *Hariq al-Qahira*, 6. The phrases "qalb al-madina" or "qalb al-qahira" commonly refer to the center of the city or of Cairo. However, I have translated it here in its literal meaning as "heart" because of the broader context of the passage and al-Sharqawi's use of the verb "to eat or consume" (*akala*).

44. Roger Owen calls this the "cotton terms of trade." *The Middle East in the World Economy, 1800–1914* (New York: Methuen, 1981), 219.

45. Craig is best known for the survey of the Nile he prepared with William Will-cocks, *Egyptian Irrigation*, 2 vols. (London: Spon, 1913), and inventing a map projection of Mecca so Muslims could pray in its direction from anywhere in the world.

46. See James I. Craig, "Notes on the National Income of Egypt," *EC*, no. 66 (1924): 1–9; "Mr. J.I. Craig, Obituary," *Times* (London), 30 January 1952, 8; Blattner, *Who's Who in Egypt, 1948*, 209.

47. Both Craig and Boyer were wounded by the attackers but apparently died by asphyxiation. See "Ambassador's Arrival," *Times* (London), 2 May 1952, 5; Hopwood, *Tales of Empire*, 111; "Wearing Apparel etc. on the Person of Mr. J.M. Boyer at the time of his death at the Turf Club, Cairo, on January 26, 1952," 7 March 1952, FO 371/97025/ JE1481, NAUK. On the employees of the British Tabulating Machine Co., Thibaut and Waldmeyer, see FO 371/97025, NAUK.

48. Audsley, "Enquiry into the Riots in Cairo," 19. This report detailed several incidents in which Egyptians protected Europeans and other subjects. Butterworth was assistant trade commissioner for Canada at the time of the fire. On his attempt to rescue Boyer, see Stevenson to Bowker, 18 February 1952, FO 371/96940/JE 1062/2, NAUK.

49. "C.E. Butterworth: List of Personal Effects Lost at the Turf Club, Cairo, on January 26, 1952, Showing Depreciated Values," and "Wearing Apparel," FO 371/97025/JE1481, NAUK. On the way goods and memory are used to construct loss claims, see Leora Auslander, "Beyond Words," *American Historical Review* 110, no. 4 (October 2005): 1015–45.

50. See claim in FO 371/97025/JE1481, NAUK.

51. Letter from his lawyers, Rubinstein, Nash to the FO, 5 February 1952, FO 371/97024/JE 1481/5, NAUK.

52. See Blattner, *Who's Who in Egypt, 1948*, 267; and "Statement of Loss Sustained by Miralai R.H. Giles Bey OBE and His Family Arising Out of the Cairo Riots," 25 February 1952, FO 371/97024/JE 1481/18, NAUK.

53. "Statement of Loss."

54. See Blattner, *Who's Who in Egypt, 1948*, 267; FO 371/97024/JE1481/5, NAUK. The Egyptianization of the police force occurred at roughly the same time as the Egyptianization of commerce. In 1946 Thomas Russell retired as head of the Cairo police and was replaced by the first Egyptian commandant, launching a reorganization of the police service. See Peter Mansfield, *The British in Egypt* (New York: Holt, Rinehart and Winston, 1971), 266; and Sir Thomas Russell, *Egyptian Service, 1902–1946* (London: John Murray, 1949).

55. See the photographs accompanying articles in *al-Ahram*'s coverage of the trials in March 1952 (i.e., 13 March 1952, 1 and 2; 17 March 1952, 3–4; 18 March 1952, 3 and 7; 23 March 1952, 3); see also "Ma'sah al-Qahira fi 26 yanayir 1952," *al-Ahram*, 12 February 1952, 1–3. Audsley, "Enquiry into the Riots in Cairo," 5, 7–8. These accounts corroborate the range of dress among rioters. See also Kerboeuf, "Cairo Fire," 210, and Kerboeuf, "La

'racaille' et les 'intrigants': Etude comparée de deux émeutes," *Egypte/monde arabe* 1–2, nos. 4–5 (2000–2001): 69.

56. Audsley, "Enquiry into the Riots in Cairo," 7–8.

57. Lacouture and Lacouture, *Egypt in Transition*, 116.

58. Hanna, "The Urban History of Cairo around 1900," in *Historians in Cairo: Essays in Honor of George Scanlon*, ed. Jill Edwards (New York: American University in Cairo Press, 2002), 193.

59. *L'Indicateur touristique d'Egypte*, 124. On ʿAbbud Pasha, see Robert Vitalis, *When Capitalists Collide: Business Conflict and the End of Empire in Egypt* (Berkeley: University of California Press, 1995); he mentions the Immobilia Building on 217.

60. Quoted material from Fikri Abaza Basha, "Shaiʾ yujanninu," *al-Ithnayn*, no. 921 (4 February 1952), 8–9; see also the transcription of his interview in March 1975 with Jamal al-Sharqawi, in al-Sharqawi, *Hariq al-Qahira*, 745–48; "Responsibility for January 26," *Egyptian Mail*, 8 March 1952, in FO 371/97025/JE 1481, NAUK; and Hopwood, *Tales of Empire*, 111.

61. On the Rivoli Cinema, see FO 371/97035, NAUK; Rank claimed to be the majority owner, with a 51 percent interest in the company. For Smeedon's account of the fire, see Audsley, "Enquiry into the Riots in Cairo," 51–52.

62. *L'Indicateur touristique d'Egypte*, 84–85.

63. See March Progress Report, 6 in FO 371/97025; FO 371/97026/ JE 1481/56, NAUK; Stevenson to FO, Cairo, 27 February 1952, FO 371/97024/ JE 1481/19, NAUK. The lawyer, Mr. W. R. Fanner of Perrott, Fanner, and Sims Marshall, died in May, before the claims were settled. His law offices had also been destroyed by the fire. Hopwood, *Tales of Empire*, 111.

64. Letter number 32, 27 February 1952, FO 371/97024, NAUK. The downtown Maltese Club was also destroyed in the Cairo Fire. Audsley, "Enquiry into the Riots in Cairo."

65. Audsley, "Enquiry into the Riots in Cairo," 21.

66. Kerboeuf, "Cairo Fire," 203.

67. Statement of Mr. Hambrook, manager of Marconi Radio Telegraph Cairo branch, in Audsley, "Enquiry into the Riots in Cairo," 49. Stevenson (to Eden, 5 February 1952, FO 371/96957/ JE 1123/1, NAUK) also commented on the "remarkable loyalty" of "many local staffs both during the riots . . . and afterwards."

68. *Al-Ahram*, 18 March 1952, 3, 7.

69. For a local communist perspective on the fire, see *Bulletin d'études et d'information sur l'Egypte et le Soudan*, no. 13 (February 1952): 2–4. The *Bulletin* was edited by the Democratic Movement for National Liberation.

70. Husayn Fawzi, *Sindbad misri* (1961), cited in Abdel-Malek, *Egypt*, 393. On Fawzi's significance, see Abdel-Malek, *Egypt*, 308–16. Writing in *La bourse égyptienne* in June 1952, Ibrahim Farhi likened the fire to the American Indian potlatch, in which "it is their own wealth that the [Indians] are intent on destroying. The more they destroy,

the greater their prestige. . . . They disfigure themselves, burn themselves, set fire to their houses. After the ritual, they place themselves in the care of a doctor, who treats their wounds." Hamada al-Nahl used the concept of "collective suicide" in an article in *al-Ahram* on 18 June 1956. Both are cited in Lacouture and Lacouture, *Egypt in Transition*, 121–22.

71. Idris, *City of Love and Ashes*, trans. R. Neil Hewison (Cairo: American University in Cairo Press, 1999), 3. *Qissat hubb* appeared in 1956. The Cairo Fire serves as the pivot of the novel, as it ushers in a regime of martial law that changes the course of Hamza's life.

72. Idris, *City of Love and Ashes*, 15. After 1955 Idris became "one of the warmest defenders" of Nasser's regime. P. M. Kurpershoek, *The Short Stories of Yusuf Idris* (Leiden, Netherlands: Brill, 1981), 29.

73. Idris, *City of Love and Ashes*, 15.

74. Mahfouz, *al-Summan wa'l-kharif* (1962; repr., Cairo: Maktabat Misr, n.d.), 6. See also Mahfouz, *Autumn Quail*, trans. Roger Allen with John Rodenbeck (New York: Anchor Books, 1985), 18.

75. Mahfouz, *Autumn Quail*, 20.

76. Al-Zayyat, *The Open Door*, trans. Marilyn Booth (New York: American University in Cairo Press, 2000).

77. These three bands of color—white, red, and black—probably alluded to the new Egyptian national flag, just released in 1958 while al-Zayyat wrote her novel. While in the flag the white symbolizes the bloodless coup of July 1952, al-Zayyat substitutes the virginal bride as sacrificial victim, bringing gender and violence to the center of the story of national liberation.

78. Al-Zayyat, *al-Bab al-maftuh*, 146. See also Al-Zayyat, *The Open Door*, 152.

79. Al-Zayyat, *The Open Door*, 263.

80. Ibid., 262.

81. See Rosen, *Limits of Power*, 89.

82. Stevenson to Eden, "Damage to British Interests." He added that "had the riots taken place on 27th January when there was a stiff breeze, this fact [that most buildings were built of concrete] could hardly have saved the rest of the business quarter from destruction."

83. See photograph of shoppers in the temporary store and caption in *al-Ahram*, 28 March 1952.

84. *EN*, 3rd series, no. 397, (1 February 1952), 74, 76; *al-Ahram*, 5 February 1952, 4; on the sale, see *EN*, 3rd series, no. 421 (18 July 1952), back cover.

85. Company to MS, 30 January 1952, 122 folder 3, MS 75, DWQ. The fire also destroyed all of the company's records: see letter dated 24 March 1953, folder 3, MS 75, DWQ.

86. Bamco and Vanity Shop transferred their winter sales to the Belmode store at 6 Fu'ad Street, where managers and personnel of all three shops worked together. *EN*, 3rd series, no. 399, (15 February 1952), 117.

87. *Al-Ahram*, 5 February 1952, 4.

88. Confidential Memo from Stevenson to FO, 14 March 1952, FO 37197024/JE 1481/24, NAUK; "Shar'ia fu'ad: shari'a al-mal wa'l-jamal wa-'shahbandarat' al-tujjar!" *al-Musawwar*, no. 1529 (29 January 1954), 32. The Egyptian government authorized £E5 million in loans; the British noted that the smallest businesses, including the tiny bars and shops owned by Cypriots and Maltese, could not afford to rebuild on a loan.

89. British Embassy to FO, 27 February 1952, FO 371/97024/JE1481/19, NAUK. See also Murray Graham, "Progress Report," 6 March 1952, FO 371/97025/JE1481/25, NAUK. The Egyptian claims committee announced that "only commercial claims for loss of business property and buildings" would be considered for assistance. See British Embassy to FO, 13 May 1952, FO 371/97026/JE 1481/56, NAUK.

90. Stevenson to Eden, "Damage to British Interests."

91. See Gordon, *Nasser's Blessed Movement*; Malak Zaalouk, *Power, Class and Foreign Capital in Egypt* (London: Zed, 1989), 25.

92. See Cicurel advertisements, *EN*, 3rd series, no. 436 (7 November 1952), back cover; *EN*, 3rd series, no. 452 (27 February 1953), back cover.

93. See front cover and article pp. 604–5 in *EN*, 3rd series, no. 443 (26 December 1952). On the architectural firm, see Arnold Wright and H. A. Cartwright, *Twentieth-Century Impressions of Egypt: Its History, People, Commerce, Industries, and Resources* (London: Lloyd's Greater Britain Publishing, 1909), 362; Blattner, *Who's Who in Egypt, 1952*, 316.

94. Gilbert Sedbon, "Cairo, City of Minarets and Skyscrapers, Vast 'Face-Lifting' Operation," *Egypt Travel Magazine*, special issue, 1954, 40.

95. Vilma, ""Notre couverture," *EN*, 3rd series, no. 433 (10 October 1952), 403–4. Bamco had a woman director, M. Elka Palombo. The store opened a new branch in Heliopolis in September 1956. See *Ruz al-yusuf*, no. 1476 (24 September 1956), 41.

96. Puck, "L'Actualité par l'image," *EN*, 3rd series, no. 437 (14 November 1952), 499. The full restocking of all the store's departments—its "total reopening"—did not occur until 9 February 1953. *Ruz al-yusuf*, no. 1287 (9 February 1953), 35; *EN*, 3rd series, no. 449 (6 February 1953), back cover. Cicurel was owned by the same family the entire time. See also Joel Beinin, *The Dispersion of Egyptian Jewry* (Berkeley: University of California Press, 1998), 48–49.

97. "Actualité par l'image," *EN*, 3rd series, no. 437 (14 November 1952), 499. See also Beinin, *Dispersion of Egyptian Jewry*, 48–49, on the relationship of Cicurel to the Free Officers.

98. Puck, "L'Actualité par l'image," *EN*, 3rd series, no. 437 (14 November 1952), 499.

99. The sub-governor of Cairo, 'Abd-al Fattah al-Bindari, attended the Bamco reopening in October 1952. *EN*, 3rd series, no. 433 (10 October 1952), 403–4.

100. "Shar'ia fu'ad," *al-Musawwar*, no. 1529 (29 January 1954), 32.

101. Ibid.

102. Ibid. Chemla, for example, was described as "bring[ing] together an imposing [*fakhama*] building and a beautiful selection of goods"; *fakhama* conveys a sense of a foreign dignitary, as in "His Excellency." On Shahir, see advertisements in *al-Musawwar*, no. 1687 (8 February 1957), 3; no. 1691 (8 March 1957), 3; no. 1698 (26 April 1957), 3; and no. 1721 (5 October 1957), 3.

103. Joel Gordon, *Revolutionary Melodrama: Popular Film and Civic Identity in Nasser's Egypt* (Chicago: Middle East Documentation Center, 2002), 255; Magda Wassef, ed., *Egypte: Cent ans de cinéma* (Paris: Institut du Monde Arabe, 1995), 253. The film also starred Yusuf Wahbi, Madiha Yusri, and Husayn Riyad. I have benefitted from Joel Gordon's excellent analysis of the film, especially of its genre and setting.

104. Gordon, *Revolutionary Melodrama*, 259.

105. Hannaux advertised a great white sale in early February 1954, in which it purveyed a wide array of children's clothing, including smocked dresses and pajamas. Hannaux catalog, "Grande semaine de blanc," 1–8 February 1954 (Alexandria: Ventura, 1954); in author's possession.

106. See Marshall Berman, *All That Is Solid Melts into Air: The Experience of Modernity* (New York: Penguin Books, 1988); and David Harvey, *Paris, Capital of Modernity* (New York: Routledge, 2003). Harvey argues that Balzac's flaneur is by contrast, "purposeful and active rather than motiveless and merely drifting" (56), and that in this way "Balzac simultaneously confronts and represents the city as a fetish object" (57). Leo Ou-Fan Lee argues that the Chinese writers preferred to explore the city with others and be recognized rather than anonymous. See "Shanghai Modern: Reflections on Urban Culture in China in the 1930s," in *Alternative Modernities*, ed. Dilip Parameshwar Gaonkar (Durham, NC: Duke University Press, 2001), 111.

107. Russell, *Egyptian Service*, esp. chaps. 18–22; Mansfield, *British in Egypt*, 266. See also Douglas Sladen, *Oriental Cairo: The City of the "Arabian Nights,"* (London: Hurst and Blackett, 1911), 68.

108. Mansfield, *British in Egypt*, 266.

109. CNIB, *Annual Report, 1938*, 92.

110. Ibid., 98.

111. CNIB, *Annual Report, 1939*, 104. After Russell announced black tea to be "a plague" in 1934, the state raised customs on tea, which reportedly encouraged its adulteration. The International Tea Bureau subsequently undertook an intensive publicity campaign to alter local preparation of tea and thus increase demand for "pure" tea. The bureau sponsored "propaganda wagons" that worked through the villages "to teach the fellahin the proper way to make a palatable non-injurious tea," although local officials did not find any actual changed practice as a result. (CNIB, *Annual Report, 1938*, 96–97). See letter from C. J. Harper, International Tea Bureau, Cairo, to Commercial Counselor, British Embassy, Cairo, 30 January 1937, enclosed with report by Somiers Cock, "Tea Trade in Egypt," 5 March 1937, FO 371/20897, NAUK. On tea drinking in contemporary

Egypt, see Samer S. Shehata, "Plastic Sandals, Tea and Time: Shop Floor Politics and Culture in Egypt" (PhD diss., Princeton University, 2000).

112. CNIB, *Annual Report, 1939*, 104.

113. Audsley, "Enquiry into the Riots in Cairo," 55. On the Swiss-owned Groppi, see Raafat, *Cairo*, 22–25. Liquor bottles were among the most common items smashed in the streets during the fire. See Audsley, "Enquiry into the Riots in Cairo," 48; Lacouture and Lacouture, *Egypt in Transition*, 111. The trial for the attack on Groppi is covered in *al-Ahram*, 17 March 1952, 3 and 4.

114. The film was produced by Studio Misr and directed by Niyazi Mustafa.

115. On commodification's effect on the line between people and things, see Igor Kopytoff, "The Cultural Biography of Things: Commoditization as Process," in *The Social Life of Things*, ed., Arjun Appadurai (New York: Cambridge University Press, 1986), 64–65, 83–90.

116. *Ruz al-yusuf*, no. 1476 (24 September 1956), 19. The text appears to be misprinted as "shaykh manluf."

117. Gordon, *Nasser's Blessed Movement*, 196.

118. Based on Molière's character Tartuff, Shaykh Matluf was a popular caricature of the provincial religious cleric. Corrupt, hypocritical, and lewd, with a beaklike nose and enormous turban, he was a lustful sexual predator hiding behind his religious garb. Carol Bardenstein, "The Role of the Target-System in Theatrical Adaptation: Jalal's Egyptian-Arabic Adaptation of *Tartuffe*," in *The Play Out of Context*, ed. Hanna Scolnicov and Peter Holland (New York: Cambridge University Press, 1989), 146–62; Berque, *Egypt*, 475. It is also possible that the name alluded to Shaykh Hasanayn Makhluf, a conservative religious scholar who served as state mufti in 1946–1950 and again 1952–1954. In 1952 Makhluf issued a fatwa against women's suffrage, probably in response to the actions of Durya al-Shafiq's organization Bint al-Nil (Daughter of the Nile). See Jakob Skovgaard-Petersen, *Defining Islam for the Egyptian State: Muftis and Fatwas of the Dar al-Ifta* (New York: Brill, 1997), 170–80. Women had just voted for the first time in July 1956.

119. September 1956 itself witnessed intense negotiations with the Muslim Brotherhood for official support of the Nasser regime.

120. Nubian doormen had long been considered fixtures of downtown buildings in Cairo. On Egyptian attitudes toward black Africans, see Eve M. Troutt Powell, *A Different Shade of Colonialism: Egypt, Great Britain, and the Mastery of the Sudan* (Berkeley: University of California Press, 2003).

121. Khaled Adham, "Making or Shaking the State: Urban Boundaries of State Control and Popular Appropriation in Sayyida Zaynab Model Park," in *Cairo Contested*, ed. Diane Singerman (New York: American University in Cairo Press, 2009), 42–43. The new ministry would become the Ministry of Culture in 1958.

122. N. A. "Hajatna illa tawhid al-azya'," *al-Musawwar*, 31 January 1955, 100–101. The earlier call was "Alf sinf wa-sinf," *al-Musawwar*, no. 645 (19 February 1937), 13.

123. *Al-Musawwar*, no. 1655 (29 June 1956), 31–38.

124. Ibid., 32.

125. Wilna Salinas, "Window Dressing in Alexandria," *Egypt Travel Magazine*, no. 25 (August 1956), 36–37.

126. Ibid.

127. Robert Mabro, *The Egyptian Economy, 1952–1972* (Oxford: Clarendon Press, 1974), 130. Belgian interests were nationalized in reaction to Belgian complicity in Patrice Lumumba's assassination in Congo in January 1961; his family went into exile in Egypt. By October and November 1961, businesses and personal property of nearly seven hundred families of the old elite (many of them of "Levantine origin") were also confiscated.

128. Mabro, *Egyptian Economy*, 124–25. See also Zaalouk, *Power, Class and Foreign Capital*, 17–45. The Czechoslovakian Bata Co. was also nationalized in this period.

129. Zaalouk, *Power, Class and Foreign Capital*, 38.

130. Ibid., 40. Economists differ as to the specific timing of the deep effects of nationalization. According to Mourad M. Wahba, "The period 1958–1961 represents a period of transition from a society where the state had begun to operate as an economic agent, where the dominant ideology was etatist, but where the actual role of the state in the economy was minor. After 1961, the Egyptian economy can be seen as wholly etatist." *The Role of the State in the Egyptian Economy, 1945–1981* (Reading, UK: Ithaca Press, 1994), 81–82.

131. Zaalouk, *Power, Class and Foreign Capital*, 38. According to Mona Abaza the most significant changes in consumer culture and standards of living occurred after 1961. *Changing Consumer Cultures of Modern Egypt* (Leiden, Netherlands: Brill, 2006), 141.

132. Michael M. Laskier, *The Jews of Egypt, 1920–1970* (New York: New York University Press, 1992), 257, 264. The regime left private gender relations essentially intact, however. See Mervet Hatem, "The Enduring Alliance of Nationalism and Patriarchy in Muslim Personal Status Laws," *Feminist Issues*, Spring 1986, 19–43.

133. See announcements in *al-Ahram*: 21 November 1956, 3; 23 November 1956, 2; 25 November 1956, 6. The store remained open during sequestration.

134. *Al-Ahram*, 22 November 1956, 5; *al-Ahram*, 27 November 1956, 1. The store held large sales that year through October. See, for example, its advertisements in *EN*: no. 591 (10 February 1956), 98; no. 606 (13 April 1956), 258; no. 607 (1 June 1956), 367; no. 612 (6 July 1956), 9; no. 621 (7 September 1956), 155; no. 625 (5 October 1956), 207.

135. The state representative announced that the stores would be open to the public during sequestration: *al-Ahram*, 21 November 1956, 3; 22 November 1956, 3. The new board was installed on 15 April 1957, and included Hasanayn Mubarak al-Gabri as the delegated administrator, in addition to at least four other members of the Gabri family. All were listed as Egyptian citizens. See letter from Hasanayn Mubarak al-Gabri to MS, 7 May 1957 (p. 150), folder 5, MS 75. The Gabri owners often wrote in florid nationalist

terms to MS inspectors about the new ownership of the company. See, e.g., telegram from Ibrahim and Hasanayn al-Gabri to MS, 22 March 1957, folder 5, MS 75. On the Gabri sale, see also Joel Beinin, "Egypt: Society and Economy, 1923–1952," in *The Cambridge History of Egypt*, ed. M. W. Daly (New York: Cambridge University Press, 1998), 2:331–32. Hasanayn and Ibrahim Gabri are listed as Cairo merchants in Blattner, *Who's Who in Egypt, 1954*, 353.

136. *Al-Ahram*, 19 November 1956, 2. On the Orosdi-Back store, see *al-Ahram*, 21 November 1956, 3; 23 November 1956, 2; 25 November 1956, 6; for Cicurel, see *al-Ahram*, 21 November 1956, 3; 22 November 1956, 3.

137. Claudia Douek Roden recalled that her uncle, Musa Douek, continued to run his wholesale cloth business throughout sequestration well into the 1960s. Liliane S. Dammond with Yvette M. Raby, *The Lost World of the Egyptian Jews: First-Person Accounts from Egypt's Jewish Community in the Twentieth Century* (New York: iUniverse, 2007), 251–52.

138. They estimated that when the firm was released from sequestration in 1960 "losses were being incurred (£E 25,000 in the first three months of 1960 alone)." "David Ades and Son," FO 950/733, NAUK.

139. ʿAdès was founded in 1899 by the brothers Nessim and David ʿAdès. On the store in the 1930s, see advertisement in *al-Ahram*, 4 April 1935. On the nationality of the family members, see probate of Nessim Habib ʿAdès, dossier 17 of 1926, FO 841/244, NAUK; "David Ades and Son," FO 950/733, NAUK.

140. "David Ades and Son," FO 950/733, NAUK. The store on the corner of Alfi Bey and ʿImad al-Din Streets in downtown Cairo was bombed in July 1948. Little damage was done to the store itself, other than a large hole in the ceiling, damage to the parcels delivery counter, and broken windows. A barber and the building's doorman were injured, as well as a Jewish employee of the store. See Emery to Jenkins, secret memo, "Bomb Outrage at David Ades Store," 29 July 1948 in FO 371/69260; and "Ades Bomb— More Alarm than Damage," *Egyptian Gazette*, 29 July 1948. In 1956 David's son Emile served as the senior partner.

141. "David Ades and Son," FO 950/732, NAUK.

142. Ibid. David H. ʿAdès and Norman N. ʿAdès were resequestered in 1961 and remained under sequestration in 1964. In March 1964 Proclamation no. 297 of 1964 placed Emile David ʿAdès under sequestration, which also included his wife and all his children.

143. This was reported to Claudia Douek Roden, the daughter of a textile merchant in Cairo's Muski Street in the interwar years and friend of the ʿAdès family, who visited the David ʿAdès store after it was nationalized and recounted it later in an interview. Dammond with Raby, *Lost World of the Egyptian Jews*, 252.

144. Raafat, *Cairo*, 58.

145. This is based on my conversations with department store managers and employees in Cairo and Alexandria in the middle 1990s. See also the accounts in Dammond with Raby, *Lost World of the Egyptian Jews*.

146. "Al-Ghala'," *al-Musawwar*, no. 1684 (18 January 1957), 24–26 and 40. The Women's Committee blamed the "greed" of the city's retail merchants for the rise in prices. Others interviewed for the article blamed the government, import shortages, and consumers.

147. See, for example, Benzion advertisement in *al-Musawwar*, no. 1737 (24 January 1958), 34.

148. For a critique of the state's ability to flatten the complexity of Egyptian society, see cartoon in *Ruz al-yusuf*, no. 1568 (30 June 1958), 4.

149. Abaza, *Changing Consumer Cultures*, 120.

150. A *Ruz al-yusuf* article reported in 1969 the following rough daily sales revenues: the Egyptian Products Sales Co., £E60,000; Salon Vert, £E30,000; Cicurel and Hannaux, £E25,000 each. Madiha, *Ruz al-yusuf*, no. 2133 (17 February 1969), 44, cited in Abaza, *Changing Consumer Cultures*, 120.

151. Marzuq Hilal, "Ahya' al-Qahira fi diyafa al-zamalik; rigal wa-nisa' yahtafun: La ghala' ba'd al-yawm wa-la sina'a ajnabiyya bayn al-qawm," *al-Musawwar*, no. 1730 (6 December 1957), 22–23.

152. Ibid.

153. "Nuwab al-sha'b ma' abtalna alladhina hatamu al-hisar al-iqtisadi," *al-Musawwar*, no. 1735 (10 January 1958), 35.

154. Ibid. 'Atiyya was originally from Giza. Goldschmidt, *Biographical Dictionary of Modern Egypt*, 26.

155. "Nuwab al-sha'b," *al-Musawwar*, no. 1735 (10 January 1958), 35.

156. After an apprenticeship in a "large shoe factory," the owner, 'Abduh 'Abu al-'Aynayn, opened his first workshop on 'Imad al-Din Street with £E250 in 1950. In 1955 it expanded into a new workshop on 'Adli Street, next to Gattegno's department store. By 1959 the company's revenues totaled roughly £E49,000. "Muntajat masani' ahdhiyyat Babil," *al-Ahram*, July 1959, special issue on the United Arab Republic, 140.

157. Ibid. Its owner traveled in 1959 to international expositions in New York, Chicago, Canada, and Italy, in addition to sponsoring international training for company managers and technicians, traveling to open new markets in the Middle East and Africa, and consulting to an Indian shoemaker. The company used German and Italian machinery and German lasts (from the Fagus company) in its production.

158. "200 malyun ginaih wa-malyun shakhs fi shar'ia 'umruhu 800 sana," *al-Ahram*, special issue on the United Arab Republic, July 1959, 128.

159. The film was directed by Fatin 'Abd al-Wahab and starred Sabah, Ahmad Mazhar, and Isma'il Yasin.

160. Lutfi Radwan, "Hazm al-ghala'," *al-Musawwar*, no. 1722 (11 October 1957), 12–15.

161. Another film set in the household of a civil servant that appeared in this era was Henri Barakat's *Fi baytina rajl* (A Man in Our House) starring Omar Sharif and released in 1961. On middle-class representations of modernity in film and other popular cultural texts, see Walter Armbrust, *Mass Culture and Modernism in Egypt* (New York: Cambridge University Press, 1996).

162. Abaza, *Changing Consumer Cultures*, 141.

163. Ibid., 114–115; Abdel-Malek, *Egypt*, xvii. See Shahir company advertisements in *al-Musawwar*, no. 1687 (8 February 1957), 3; no. 1691 (8 March 1957), 3; no. 1698 (26 April 1957), 3; and no. 1721 (5 October 1957), 3.

164. On the predilection of Egyptian films to situate themselves in "an intricate architecture of references designed to evoke . . . Egypt's own [film] tradition," see Armbrust, "The Golden Age before the Golden Age," in *Mass Mediations*, ed. Walter Armbrust (Berkeley: University of California Press, 2000), 312.

165. See advertisements in *EN*, no. 105 (12 April 1946), 11; *al-Balagh*, 11 May 1947 and 3 July 1951; and *Ruz al-yusuf*, no. 1496 (11 February 1957), 35. The company's advertisements from the 1930s primarily focus on furniture. See, for example, advertisements in *al-Ahram*, 8 February 1937, 9 and 13 November 1938, 10; and *Egyptian Gazette*, 17 January 1940. The last advertisement focused specifically on furnishing homes for newlyweds. Founded in 1917 by members of the Gattegno family, the company by 1946 also manufactured aluminum and household wares, bronze, and electric fittings. Silvio Gattegno remained the acting partner in 1952. *Egyptian Trade Index, 1952* (Alexandria: Middle East Publishing, 1952, 1956–57), 231–32.

166. *Egyptian Gazette*, 17 January 1940.

Conclusion

1. M. T. Audsley, "Report of the British Embassy Committee of Enquiry into the Riots in Cairo on the 26th January 1952," 5, LAB 13/740, NAUK.

2. Frantz Fanon, *The Wretched of the Earth*, trans. Constance Farrington (New York: Grove Weidenfeld, 1963), 51.

3. Anouar Abdel-Malek, *Egypt: Military Society. The Army Regime, the Left, and Social Change under Nasser*, trans. Charles Lam Markmann (New York: Vintage Books, 1968), vii–viii.

4. Ibid., x.

5. Karl Gerth, *China Made* (Cambridge, MA: Harvard University Press, 2003), 125.

6. Beinin, *The Dispersion of Egyptian Jewry* (Berkeley: University of California Press, 1998), 21.

7. Anthony D. King, "Colonial Cities: Global Pivots of Change," in *Colonial Cities*, ed. Robert Ross and Gerard J. Telkamp (Boston: Martinus Nijhoff, 1985), 15.

8. On modernization theory, see Zachary Lockman, ed., *Contending Visions of the Middle East* (New York: Cambridge University Press, 2004).

9. Janet L. Abu-Lughod, *Cairo: 1001 Years of the City Victorious* (Princeton, NJ: Princeton University Press, 1971), 98. On the uses of space versus time to imagine cities, see Gyan Prakash, "The Urban Turn," in *Sarai Reader 2002: The Cities of Everyday Life*, ed. Ravi S. Vasudevan, Ravi Sundaram, Jeebesh Bagchi, Monica Narula, Shuddhabrata Sengupta, and Geert Lovink (Delhi, India: New Media Initiative, 2002), 5.

10. Edhem Eldem, Daniel Goffman, and Bruce Masters, *The Ottoman City between East and West* (New York: Cambridge University Press, 1999), 13.

11. Prakash, "Urban Turn," 5.

12. Gerth, *China Made*, 25.

Epilogue

1. Mona El-Ghobashy, "The Praxis of the Egyptian Revolution," *Middle East Report* 258 (Spring 2011): 5.

2. Nefissa Naguib, "Basic Ethnography at the Barricades," *International Journal of Middle East Studies* 43, no. 3 (August 2011): 383. See Laryssa Chomiak and John P. Entelis, "The Making of North Africa's Intifadas," *Middle East Report* 259 (Summer 2011): 8–15, on the longer history of active opposition in Tunisia.

3. Naguib, "Basic Ethnography at the Barricades."

4. Sarah Goodyear, "In Egypt, You Can Switch Off the Internet but Not the Streets," The City Is the Message, 31 January 2011, http://www.grist.org/article/2011-01-31-the-egyptian-government-has-been-able-to-shut-down-the-internet-/.

5. On the evolution of Tahrir Square, see Samir W. Raafat, *Cairo: The Glory Years* (Alexandria: Harpocrates, 2003), 15–17; Nezar AlSayyad, *Cairo: Histories of a City* (Cambridge, MA: Belknap Press, 2011), 242–45; Jessica Winegar, *Creative Reckonings: The Politics of Art and Culture in Contemporary Egypt* (Stanford, CA: Stanford University Press, 2006), xv–xvii.

6. AlSayyad, *Cairo*, 243.

7. Raafat, *Cairo*, 17; AlSayyad, *Cairo*, 242.

8. Raafat, *Cairo*, 16.

9. Eric Hobsbawm, "Cities and Insurrections," in *Revolutionaries* (1973; repr., New York: New Press, 2001), 261–78. It is interesting to note Hobsbawm's prediction that cities cease to become riotous when their populations grow over a million inhabitants, because at that point "sheer size . . . reduces the city to an administrative abstraction, and a conglomerate of separate communities or districts" (270). Cairo's population stood at 1.5 million people in 1952 and 17 million in 2011.

10. Andrea B. Rugh, *Reveal and Conceal: Dress in Contemporary Egypt* (Syracuse, NY: Syracuse University Press, 1986), 128–29.

11. Mamoun Fandy, "Political Science without Clothes: The Politics of Dress; or, Contesting the Spatiality of the State in Egypt," in *Beyond the Exotic: Women's Histories in Islamic Societies*, ed. Amira el-Azhary Sonbol (Syracuse, NY: Syracuse University Press, 2005), 393.

12. Alaa Al Aswany, *The Yacoubian Building*, trans. Humphrey Davies (2004; repr. New York: Harper Perennial, 2006), 32–34, 43–48.

13. See Iqbal Barakah, "The Shoes (a short story)," trans. Mohammad Khazali, in *Women and the Family in the Middle East*, ed. Elizabeth Warnock Fernea (Austin: University of Texas Press, 1985), 289–92; Yusuf Shahin's 1991 film, *Cairo as Seen by Chahine*; and Nur Elmessiri, "Cairo: Nur Elmessiri Reviews Youssef Chahine's *Cairo as Seen by Chahine*," *Middle East Report 202* (Winter 1996): 31–32.

14. Omar S. Dahi, "Understanding the Political Economy of the Arab Revolts," *Middle East Report 259* (Summer 2011): 5. Sherine Abdel-Razek, "What's in Store for Omar Effendi?" *al-Ahram Weekly*, 768, 10–16 November 2005; Karim El-Sayed, "Egypt's Last Effendi: On the Government Efforts to Privatize Department Stores," *Economic and Business History Research Center Chronicles* 1, no. 4 (April–June 2006): 22–24.

15. Galila El Kadi and Dalia ElKerdany, "Belle-époque Cairo: The Politics of Refurbishing the Downtown Business District," in *Cairo Cosmopolitan*, ed. Diane Singerman and Paul Amar (New York: American University in Cairo Press, 2006), 345–71.

16. Alaa Al Aswany, *On the State of Egypt: What Made the Revolution Inevitable*, trans. Jonathan Wright (New York: Vintage Books, 2011), 104.

17. Local newspapers feverishly covered the initial announcements that the stores, including also Cicurel, Sednaoui, and Rivoli, would be reprivatized in February 1996. See, e.g., "al-Yahud qadamun," *al-Sha'b*, 27 February 1996, 8; *al-Akhbar*, 28 February 1996, 1; *al-Ahram*, 1 March 1996, 1; *al-Ahali* no. 755, 6 March 1996, 1.

18. The majority of department store owners did not go to Israel when they left Egypt but emigrated to Europe or North America. Most of the Cicurel family members went to France and Switzerland after they left Egypt. Salvator died in Lausanne in 1976 at age 83. Maurice Mizrahi, *L'Egypte et ses juifs: Le temps revolu* (Lausanne, Switzerland: Imprimerie Avenir, 1977). See Joel Beinin, *The Dispersion of Egyptian Jewry* (Berkeley: University of California Press, 1998).

19. Shokr, "The 18 Days of Tahrir," *Middle East Report 258* (Spring 2011): 15.

20. Hesham Sallam, "Striking Back at Egyptian Workers," *Middle East Report 259* (Summer 2011): 25.

21. Joel Beinin, "A Workers' Social Movement on the Margin of the Global Neoliberal Order, Egypt, 2004–2009," in *Social Movement, Mobilization, and Contestation in the Middle East and North Africa*, ed. Joel Beinin and Frédéric Vairel (Stanford, CA: Stanford University Press, 2011), 192–93; Beinin, "Egypt at the Tipping Point?," 31 January 2011, http://mideast.foreignpolicy.com/posts/2011/01/31/egypt_at_the_tipping_point. See also Sallam, "Striking Back."

22. Sallam, "Striking Back," 22.

23. Jessica Winegar, "Taking Out the Trash: Youth Clean Up after Mubarak," *Middle East Report* 259 (Summer 2011): 33.

24. Ibid. See also David Sims, *Understanding Cairo* (New York: American University in Cairo Press, 2010), 106.

25. David D. Kirkpatrick, "Egyptians Say Military Fights Open Economy," *New York Times*, 18 February 2011, 1.

BIBLIOGRAPHY

Archival Collections

The American University in Cairo: Rare Books and Special Collections, Cairo
    Private papers of Hawwa' Ahmad Idris
Centre des Archives Diplomatiques, Nantes (CADN), France
    Le Caire—Ambassade, Série des 602
Dar al-Watha'iq al-Qawmiyya (DWQ; Egyptian National Archives), Cairo
    'Abdin
        Iltimasat
        Majlis al-Wuzara'
        Maliyya
    Majlis al-Wuzara' (MW; Council of Ministers)
        Al-Fatra Ba'da 1923
        Maliyya
        Sharikat wa-Jam'iyyat
    Maslahat al-Sharikat (MS; Department of Corporations)
Ministère des Affaires Étrangères de France, Quai d'Orsay, Paris (MAEP)
    Afrique, 1918–1940:
        Afrique, 1918–1929, Egypte
        Afrique, 1930–1940, Egypte
        Egypte
    Nouvelle Série (NS): Egypte
National Archives of the United Kingdom, Kew (NAUK)
    Board of Trade (BOT) 11, 59, 60
    Foreign Office (FO)
        141 (Confidential Prints)

371 (General Correspondence, Political, Egypt)

407, 950 (General Correspondence, Claims)

841 (Consular Court records, Cairo)

Oral History Department (OHD), Institute of Contemporary Jewry, Hebrew University, Jerusalem. Series 35:

1. Shohet, Yvonne (née Chemla). 20 November and 10 and 16 December 1964

6. Kahanoff, Jacqueline (née Shohet), 21 January and 11 June 1965

Magazines and Newspapers

Al-Ahram

Al-Ahram Weekly

Al-Akhbar

Akhir lahza

Akhir saʿa

Al-Balagh

Al-Balagh al-usbuʿi

Biladi

Bint al-nil

La bourse égyptienne (Alexandria)

British Chamber of Commerce of Egypt's Monthly Journal

Bulletin de la Chambre de commerce égyptienne d'Alexandrie

Bulletin mensuel de la Chambre de commerce égyptienne (Cairo)

Bulletin mensuel de la Chambre de commerce française d'Alexandrie

Cairo Times

Egypt Cultural Bulletin

Egypt News

Egypt News Bulletin

Egypt Travel Magazine

L'Egypte contemporaine (*EC*)

L'Egypte nouvelle (*EN*)

Egyptian Gazette

Egyptian Mail

L'egyptienne

La femme nouvelle

La gazette fiscale, commerciale et industrielle (Alexandria)

Hawwaʾ

Images (Cairo)

Al-ʿImara

Al-Ithnayn
Al-Kashkul
Kawkab al-sharq
Al-Lataʾif al-musawwara
Le lien
Al-Liwaʿ
Majallat ghurfat al-qahira
Majallat al-marʾa al-misriyya
Manchester Guardian
Manchester Guardian Commercial
Misr
Misr al-haditha al-musawwara
Al-Misri
Al-Muqattam
Al-Muqtataf
Al-Musawwar
Al-Nashra al-iqtisadiyya al-misriyya
Le progrès égyptien—Almanach (1953, 1954, 1955)
Ruz al-yusuf
Al-Siyasa
Times (London)

Government Publications

Board of Trade (UK; BOT). *Boots and Shoes.* London: HMSO, 1946.
———. *Report of the British Goodwill Trade Mission to Egypt, November–December 1945.* London: HMSO, 1946.
———. *Report of the United Kingdom Trade Mission to Egypt, the Sudan, and Ethiopia, February 1955.* London: HMSO, 1955.
Central Narcotics Intelligence Bureau (Egypt; CNIB). *Annual Report for the Year 1934.* Cairo: Government Press, Bulaq, 1935.
———. *Annual Report for the Year 1938.* Cairo: Government Press, Bulaq, 1939.
———. *Annual Report for the Year 1939.* Cairo: Government Press, Bulaq, 1940.
Commission du Commerce et de l'Industrie (Egypt). *Rapport.* Cairo: Government Press, 1918.
Department of Commerce and Industry (Egypt). *Katalug al-maʿrad al-daʾim liʾl-masnuʿat al-misriyya.* Cairo, n.d.
Department of Overseas Trade (UK). *Report of the United Kingdom Trade Mission to Egypt, February–March 1931.* London: HMSO, 1931.

————. *Reports on the Economic and Financial Situation of Egypt*, 1919–1939, 1947, 1951 (compiled by various agents and listed by author in "Other Sources"). London: HMSO, 1920–1939, 1948, 1952.

Direction Générale des Douanes Egyptiennes (Egypt). *Le commerce extérieur de l'Egypte pendant l'année 1914; 1915; 1916*. Alexandria, 1915–1917.

House of Commons (UK). "Report by H.M. Agent and Consul General on the Finances, Administration, and Condition of Egypt and the Sudan" (1905), *Sessional Papers*, vol. 137 (1906).

Ministère de la Justice (Egypt). *Table de recueil des lois, décrets and rescrits royaux*, 1947, 1949, 1951. Cairo, 1948, 1952, 1953.

Ministry of Finance (Egypt). *Almanac*, 1931. Cairo: Government Press, 1931.

————. *Almanac*, 1934. Cairo: Government Press, 1934.

————. *Industrial and Commercial Census 1927*. Cairo, 1931.

————. *Industrial and Commercial Census 1937*. Cairo, 1942.

————. *Industrial and Commercial Census 1947*. Cairo, 1955.

————. *Statistics of Wages and Working Hours in Egypt 1950*. Cairo, 1952.

Ministry of Finance, Customs Administration. *Annual Statement of the Foreign Trade of Egypt*, 1918, 1919, 1921, 1920–1924. Cairo, 1920, 1922, 1925.

Ministry of Finance, Statistical Department. *Annual Statement of the Foreign Trade*, 1928, 1932, 1935, 1938, 1939, 1944, 1946–1947. Cairo, 1930, 1934, 1936–1937, 1940, n.d., 1946, 1950.

————. *Annual Statement of the Foreign Trade of Egypt during 1922–1926*. Cairo, 1927.

Ministry of Finance and Economy (Egypt), Statistical Department. *Annual Statement of Foreign Trade, 1950–51, 1952*. Cairo, 1953, 1954.

Nizarat al-Maliyya (Egypt). *Al-Ihsaʾ al-sanawi al-ʿamm, 1910, 1913*. Cairo, 1911, 1913.

United Arab Republic. *Twelve Years of Industrial Development, 1952–1964*. Cairo, 1964.

Wizarat al-Maliyya (Egypt). *Ihsaʾ al-muwazzafin waʾl-mustakhdamin biʾl-hukuma waʾl-haiʾat al-ʿamma, 1945, 1948, 1951, 1952*. Cairo, 1947, 1951, 1953, 1955.

Wizarat al-Maliyya waʾl-Iqtisad (Egypt). *Al-Taʿdad al-ʿamr liʾl-sukkan, 1947*. Cairo, 1953.

Films

ʿAtabaʾ al-khadraʾ ('Ataba Square). 1959. Directed by Fatin ʿAbd al-Wahab, starring Sabah, Ahmad Mazhar, and Ismaʿil Yasin.

Al-ʿAzima (Resolution). 1939. Directed by Kamal Salim, starring Husayn Sidqi and Fatima Rushdi. Cairo: Gamal al-Laythi.

Banat Hawwaʾ (Daughters of Eve). 1954. Directed by Niyazi Mustafa, starring Muhammad Fawzi, Madiha Yusri, and Shadiyya. Produced by Studio Misr.

Al-Batal (The Hero). 1950. Directed by Hilmi Rafla, starring Ismaʿil Yasin, Tahiya Carioca, Zaynat Sidqi, Shadiyya, and Muhammad Kamal al-Masri. Produced by United Films/Anwar Wagdi. Cairo: Gamal al-Laythi.

Cairo as Seen by Chahine. 1991. Directed by Yusuf Shahin.

Fi baytina rajl (A Man in Our House). 1961. Directed by Henri Barakat, starring Omar Sharif, Zubayda Sarwat, and Hasan Yusuf.

Haya aw mawt (Life or Death). 1954. Directed by Kamal al-Shaykh, starring ʿImad Hamdi, Madiha Yusri, and Yusuf Wahbi.

Sayyidat al-qitar (The Lady of the Train). 1952. Directed by Yusuf Shahin, starring Layla Murad, ʿImad Hamdi, and Yahya Shahin. Produced by Aflam ʿAbduh Nasr/Studio Misr. Cairo: Gamal al-Laythi.

Umm al-ʿarusa (Mother of the Bride). 1963. Directed by Atif Salim, starring ʿImad Hamdi, Tahiya Carioca, and Samira Ahmad. Distributed by Arab Film.

Other Sources

Abaza, Mona. *Changing Consumer Cultures of Modern Egypt.* Leiden, Netherlands: Brill, 2006.

Abdalla, Ahmed. *The Student Movement and National Politics in Egypt.* London: al-Saqi Books, 1985.

Abdel-Malek, Anouar. *Egypt: Military Society. The Army Regime, the Left, and Social Change under Nasser.* Translated by Charles Lam Markmann. New York: Vintage Books, 1968.

Abdel Meguid, Ibrahim. *No One Sleeps in Alexandria.* Translated by Farouk Abdel Wahab. Cairo: American University in Cairo Press, 1999.

Abou-Hodeib, Toufoul. "Taste and Class in Late Ottoman Beirut." *International Journal of Middle East Studies* 43, no. 3 (August 2011): 475–92.

Abu-Lughod, Janet L. *Cairo: 1001 Years of the City Victorious.* Princeton, NJ: Princeton University Press, 1971.

———. "The Islamic City—Historic Myth, Islamic Essence, and Contemporary Relevance." *International Journal of Middle East Studies* 19 (1987): 155–76.

———. *Rabat: Urban Apartheid in Morocco.* Princeton, NJ: Princeton University Press, 1980.

———. "Tale of Two Cities: The Origins of Modern Cairo." *Comparative Studies in Society and History* 7, no. 4 (July 1965): 429–57.

Abu al-Majd, Sabri. *Sanawat ma qabla al-thawra, 1930–1952.* 3 vols. Cairo: al-Hayaʾ al-Misriyya al-ʿAmma liʾ l-Kitab, 1987–1989.

Acker, Finley. "The Streets of Cairo." In *Pen Sketches.* Philadelphia: McLaughlin Bros., 1899.

Adham, Khaled. "Making or Shaking the State: Urban Boundaries of State Control and Popular Appropriation in Sayyida Zaynab Model Park." In *Cairo Contested*, edited by Diane Singerman, 41–62. New York: American University in Cairo Press, 2009.

Aflatun, Inji. *Mudhakkirat.* Cairo: Dar Suʿad al-Sabah, 1993.

Ahmad, Nabil ʿAbd al-Hamid Sayyid. *Al-Hayat al-iqtisadiyya waʾl-ʿijtimaʿiyya liʾl-yahud fi Misr, 1947–1956.* Cairo: Maktabat Madbuli, 1991.

———. *Al-Nashat al-itqisadi liʾl-ajanib wa-atharuhu fi al-mujtamaʿ al-misri min sanat 1922 ila sanat 1952.* Cairo: al-Hayaʾ al-Misriyya al-ʿAmma liʾl-Kitab, 1982.

Ahmed, Heba Farouk. "Nineteenth-Century Cairo: A Dual City?" In *Making Cairo Medieval,* edited by Nezar AlSayyad, Irene A. Bierman, and Nasser Rabbat, 143–72. New York: Lexington Books, 2005.

Ahmed, Leila. *Women and Gender in Islam.* New Haven, CT: Yale University Press, 1992.

Allen, Roger. *The Arabic Literary Heritage.* New York: Cambridge University Press, 1998.

———. *A Period of Time: A Study and Translation of Hadith ʿIsa Ibn Hisham by Muhammad al-Muwaylihi.* Reading, MA: Ithaca Press, 1992.

Allman, Jean, ed. *Fashioning Africa.* Bloomington: Indiana University Press, 2004.

AlSayyad, Nezar. *Cairo: Histories of a City.* Cambridge, MA: Belknap Press of Harvard University Press, 2011.

———, ed. *Forms of Dominance: On the Architecture and Urbanism of the Colonial Enterprise.* Brookfield, VT: Avebury, 1992.

Amin, Ahmad. *Qamus al-ʿadat waʾl-taqalid waʾl-taʿbir al-misriyya.* Cairo: Lajnat al-Taʾlif waʾl-Tarjama waʾl-Nashr, 1953.

Amin, Galal. *Whatever Else Happened to the Egyptians?* Cairo: American University in Cairo Press, 2004.

———. *Whatever Happened to the Egyptians?* Cairo: American University in Cairo Press, 2000.

Anderson, Benedict. *Imagined Communities: Reflections on the Origin and Spread of Nationalism.* London: Verso, 1991.

Anderson, Perry. "Modernity and Revolution." *New Left Review,* no. 144 (1984): 96–113.

Anis, Mahmoud Amin. *A Study of the National Income of Egypt.* Cairo: SOP, 1950.

Anis, Muhammad. *Hariq al-Qahira.* Beirut: al-Muʾassasa al-ʿArabiyya liʾl-Dirasat waʾl-Nashr, 1972.

Appadurai, Arjun, ed. *The Social Life of Things: Commodities in Cultural Perspective.* New York: Cambridge University Press, 1986.

Arié, Rachel. "Notes sur le costume en Egypte dans la première moitié du xixe siècle." *Extrait de la revue des études islamiques* 26 (1968): 201–13.

Armbrust, Walter. "The Golden Age before the Golden Age." In *Mass Mediations,* edited by Walter Armbrust. Berkeley: University of California Press, 2000.

———. *Mass Culture and Modernism in Egypt.* New York: Cambridge University Press, 1996.

———, ed. *Mass Mediations.* Berkeley: University of California Press, 2000.

Arminjon, Pierre. *La situation économique et financière de l'Egypte.* Paris: Librarie Générale du Droit, 1911.

Arnaud, Jean-Luc. *Le Caire: Mise en place d'une ville moderne, 1867–1907*. Arles, France: Sindbad, 1998.

Asad, Talal. "Modern Power and the Reconfiguration of Religious Traditions: An Interview with Talal Asad." By Saba Mahmood. *Stanford Humanities Review* 5, no. 1 (1995): 1–16.

Al Aswany, Alaa. *On the State of Egypt: What Made the Revolution Inevitable*. Translated by Jonathan Wright. New York: Vintage Books, 2011.

———. *The Yacoubian Building*. Translated by Humphrey Davies. 2004. Reprint, New York: Harper Perennial, 2006.

Auslander, Leora. "Beyond Words." *American Historical Review* 110, no. 4 (October 2005): 1015–45.

Badran, Margo. *Feminists, Islam, and Nation*. Princeton, NJ: Princeton University Press, 1995.

Badrawi, Malak. *Isma'il Sidqi*. Richmond, UK: Curzon, 1996.

Baedeker, Karl. *Egypt and the Sudan: Handbook for Travellers*. 8th ed. New York: Scribner's, 1929.

Baer, Gabriel. *Egyptian Guilds in Modern Times*. Jerusalem: Israel Oriental Society, 1964.

Al-Banna, Hasan. *Five Tracts of Hasan al-Banna'*. Translated by Charles Wendell. Berkeley: University of California, 1978.

Baraka, Magda. *The Egyptian Upper Class between Revolutions*. Oxford: Ithaca Press, 1998.

Barakah, Iqbal. "The Shoes (a short story)." Translated by Mohammad Khazali. In *Women and the Family in the Middle East*, edited by Elizabeth Warnock Fernea, 289–92. Austin: University of Texas Press, 1985.

Bardenstein, Carol. "The Role of the Target-System in Theatrical Adaptation: Jalal's Egyptian-Arabic Adaptation of *Tartuffe*." In *The Play Out of Context*, edited by Hanna Scolnicov and Peter Holland, 146–62. New York: Cambridge University Press, 1989.

Baron, Beth. *Egypt as a Woman*. Berkeley: University of California Press, 2005.

———. "The Making and Breaking of Marital Bonds in Modern Egypt." In *Women in Middle Eastern History*, edited by Nikki R. Keddie and Beth Baron, 275–91. New Haven, CT: Yale University Press, 1991.

———. *The Women's Awakening in Egypt: Culture, Society, and the Press*. New Haven, CT: Yale University Press, 1994.

Barthes, Roland. *The Fashion System*. Translated by Matthew Ward and Richard Howard. Berkeley: University of California Press, 1990.

Bata, Tomas. *Knowledge in Action*. Washington, DC: IOS Press, 1991.

Baudrillard, Jean. *The System of Objects*. Translated by James Benedict. New York: Verso, 1996.

Bayly, C. A. "The Origins of Swadeshi (Home Industry): Cloth and Indian Society, 1700–1930." In *The Social Life of Things: Commodities in Cultural Perspective*, edited by Arjun Appadurai, 285–321. New York: Cambridge University Press, 1986.

Bean, Susan. "Gandhi and *Khadi*, the Fabric of Indian Independence." In *Cloth and Human Experience*, edited by Annette B. Weiner and Jane Schneider, 355–76. Washington, DC: Smithsonian Institution Press, 1989.

Beinin, Joel. *The Dispersion of Egyptian Jewry*. Berkeley: University of California Press, 1998.

———. "Egypt: Society and Economy, 1923–1952." In *The Cambridge History of Egypt*. Vol. 2, edited by M. W. Daly, 309–33. New York: Cambridge University Press, 1998.

———. *Was the Red Flag Flying There?* Berkeley: University of California Press, 1990.

———. *Workers and Peasants in the Modern Middle East*. New York: Cambridge University Press, 2001.

———. "A Workers' Social Movement on the Margin of the Global Neoliberal Order, Egypt, 2004–2009." In *Social Movement, Mobilization, and Contestation in the Middle East and North Africa*, edited by Joel Beinin and Frédéric Vairel, 181–201. Stanford, CA: Stanford University Press, 2011.

Beinin, Joel, and Zachary Lockman. "1919: Labor Upsurge and National Revolution." In *The Modern Middle East*. 2nd ed., edited by Albert Hourani, Philip S. Khoury, and Mary C. Wilson, 395–428. New York: I. B. Tauris, 2005.

———. *Workers on the Nile: Nationalism, Communism, Islam, and the Egyptian Working Class, 1882–1954*. Princeton, NJ: Princeton University Press, 1987.

Benjamin, Walter. "Paris, Capital of the Nineteenth Century." In *Reflections*. Edited by Peter Demetz. Translated by Edmund Jephcott, 146–62. New York: Harcourt Brace Jovanovich, 1978.

Benson, Susan Porter. *Counter Cultures: Saleswomen, Managers, and Customers in American Department Stores, 1890–1940*. Urbana: University of Illinois Press, 1986.

Berman, Marshall. *All That Is Solid Melts into Air: The Experience of Modernity*. New York: Penguin Books, 1988.

———. "The Signs in the Street: A Response to Perry Anderson." *New Left Review*, no. 144 (1984): 114–23.

———. "Why Modernism Still Matters." In *Modernity and Identity*, edited by Scott Lash and Jonathan Friedman, 33–58. Malden, MA: Wiley-Blackwell, 1992.

Berque, Jacques. *Egypt: Imperialism and Revolution*. Translated by Jean Stewart. London: Faber and Faber, 1972.

Berque, Jacques, and Mustafa al-Shakaa. "La Gamaliya depuis un siècle." *Colloque international sur l'histoire du Caire*, 67–93. Cairo: General Egyptian Book Organization, 1969.

Blattner, E. J., ed. *Who's Who in Egypt and the Near East, Le mondain égyptien et du Prôche-Orient*. Cairo: Paul Barbey Press/Imprimerie Française, 1943, 1948, 1952, 1953, 1954, 1956.

Boahen, A. Adu, ed. *Africa under Colonial Domination, 1880–1935*. Berkeley: University of California Press, 1990.

Boorstin, Daniel J. *The Americans: The Democratic Experience*. New York: Random House, 1973.

Booth, Marilyn. *Bayram al-Tunisi's Egypt: Social Criticism and Narrative Strategies*. Exeter, UK: Ithaca Press, 1990.

———. *May Her Likes Be Multiplied: Biography and Gender Politics in Egypt*. Berkeley: University of California Press, 2001.

Bourdieu, Pierre. *Distinction*. Translated by Richard Nice. Cambridge, MA: Harvard University Press, 1984.

———. "The Forms of Capital." In *Handbook of Theory and Research for the Sociology of Education*, edited by John G. Richardson, 241–58. New York: Greenwood Press, 1986.

———. *The Logic of Practice*. Translated by Richard Nice. Stanford, CA: Stanford University Press, 1990.

Bowring, John. *Report on Egypt and Candia*. London: Clowes for HMSO, 1840.

Bozdogan, Sibel, and Resat Kasaba, eds. *Rethinking Modernity and National Identity in Turkey*. Seattle: University of Washington Press, 1997.

Breen, T. H. *The Marketplace of Revolution: How Consumer Politics Shaped American Independence*. New York: Oxford University Press, 2004.

Brinton, Jasper Yeates. *The Mixed Courts of Egypt*. Rev. ed. New Haven, CT: Yale University Press, 1968.

Brown, Nathan J. *Peasant Politics*. New Haven, CT: Yale University Press, 1990.

———. "The Precarious Life and Slow Death of the Mixed Courts of Egypt." *International Journal of Middle East Studies* 25, no. 1 (February 1993): 33–52.

———. "Shariʿa and State in the Modern Muslim Middle East." *International Journal of Middle East Studies* 29 (1997): 359–76.

Brummett, Palmira. *Image and Imperialism in the Ottoman Revolutionary Press, 1908–1911*. Albany: State University of New York Press, 2000.

Burchell, G., C. Gordon, and P. Miller, eds. *The Foucault Effect: Studies in Governmentality*. Chicago: University of Chicago Press, 1991.

Burke, Timothy. *Lifebuoy Men, Lux Women: Commodification, Consumption, and Cleanliness in Modern Zimbabwe*. Durham, NC: Duke University Press, 1996.

Bushnaq, Inea, ed. and trans. *Arab Folktales*. New York: Pantheon, 1986.

Cachia, Pierre. *Popular Narrative Ballads of Modern Egypt*. Oxford: Clarendon Press, 1989.

Campos, Michelle U. *Ottoman Brothers: Muslims, Christians, and Jews in Early Twentieth-Century Palestine*. Stanford, CA: Stanford University Press, 2011.

Carruthers, Susan L. *Cold War Captives*. Berkeley: University of California Press, 2009.

Çelik, Zeynep. *The Remaking of Istanbul*. Berkeley: University of California Press, 1986.

———. *Urban Forms and Colonial Confrontations: Algiers under French Rule*. Berkeley: University of California Press, 1997.

de Chabrol, M. "Essai sur les moeurs des habitans modernes de l'Egypte." In *La descrip-tion de l'Egypte*, vol. 14. Paris: Imprimerie Impériale, 1809.

Chalcraft, John T. *The Striking Cabbies of Cairo and Other Stories: Crafts and Guilds in Egypt, 1863–1914*. Albany: State University of New York Press, 2004.

Chatterjee, Partha. *The Nation and Its Fragments*. Princeton, NJ: Princeton University Press, 1993.

———. *The Politics of the Governed*. New York: Columbia University Press, 2004.

Chawaf, Layane, and Ali Abou Chadi. "Répertoire des films." In *Egypte: 100 ans de cin-ema*, edited by Magda Wassef, 286–315. Paris: Editions Plume, 1995.

Chevallier, Dominique. "Un example de résistance technique de l'artisanat syrien aux XIXe et XXe siècles: Les tissues ikatés d'Alep et de Damas." *Syria: Revue d'art orien-tal et d'archéologie* 39 (1962): 300–24.

Chomiak, Laryssa, and John P. Entelis. "The Making of North Africa's Intifadas." *Middle East Report*, no. 259 (Summer 2011): 8–15.

Cohen, Lizabeth. *A Consumer's Republic: The Politics of Mass Consumption in Postwar America*. New York: Vintage Books, 2003.

Cohn, Bernard S. *Colonialism and Its Forms of Knowledge: The British in India*. Prince-ton, NJ: Princeton University Press, 1996.

Cole, Juan Ricardo. *Colonialism and Revolution in the Middle East: Social and Cultural Origins of Egypt's 'Urabi Movement*. Princeton, NJ: Princeton University Press, 1993.

———. "Feminism, Class, and Islam in Turn-of-the-Century Egypt." *International Jour-nal of Middle East Studies* 13 (1981): 394–407.

Cooper, Artemis. *Cairo in the War, 1939–1945*. London: Hamish Hamilton, 1989.

Cooper, Frederick. *Colonialism in Question*. Berkeley: University of California Press, 2005.

Cowan, J. M., ed. *The Hans Wehr Dictionary of Modern Written Arabic*. 3rd ed. Ithaca, NY: Spoken Language Services, 1976.

Crossick, Geoffrey, and Serge Jaumain, eds. *Cathedrals of Consumption: The European Department Store, 1850–1939*. Brookfield, VT: Ashgate, 1999.

Cumberbatch, A. N., for UK Board of Trade. *Egypt: Economic and Commercial Condi-tions in Egypt, October 1951*. London: HMSO, 1952.

Dahi, Omar S. "Understanding the Political Economy of the Arab Revolts." *Middle East Report*, no. 259 (Summer 2011): 2–6.

Dammond, Liliane S., with Yvette M. Raby. *The Lost World of the Egyptian Jews: First-Person Accounts from Egypt's Jewish Community in the Twentieth Century*. New York: iUniverse, 2007.

Daunton, Martin, and Matthew Hilton, eds. *The Politics of Consumption: Material Cul-ture and Citizenship in Europe and America*. New York: Berg, 2001.

Davis, Eric. *Challenging Colonialism: Bank Misr and Egyptian Industrialization, 1920–1941*. Princeton, NJ: Princeton University Press, 1983.

Deeb, Marius. "Bank Misr and the Emergence of the Local Bourgeoisie in Egypt." *Middle Eastern Studies* 12, no. 3 (1976): 69–86.

Dikötter, Frank. *Exotic Commodities: Modern Objects and Everyday Life in China.* New York: Columbia University Press, 2006.

Djerdjerian, Taline. "Political Consumerism and the Boycott of American Goods in Egypt." In *Cairo Contested,* edited by Diane Singerman, 393–413. Cairo: American University in Cairo Press, 2009.

Dougherty, Roberta L. "Badiʿa al-Masabni, Artiste and Modernist." In *Mass Mediations,* edited by Walter Armbrust, 243–68. Berkeley: University of California Press, 2000.

Doumani, Beshara. *Rediscovering Palestine: Merchants and Peasants in Jabal Nablus, 1700–1900.* Berkeley: University of California Press, 1995.

Egyptian Trade Index. Alexandria: Middle East Publishing, 1952, 1956–57.

Eldem, Edhem, Daniel Goffman, and Bruce Masters. *The Ottoman City between East and West.* New York: Cambridge University Press, 1999.

Elmessiri, Nur. "Cairo: Nur Elmessiri Reviews Youssef Chahine's *Cairo as Seen by Chahine.*" *Middle East Report* 202 (Winter 1996): 31–32.

Eman, André. *L'industrie du coton en Egypte: Etude d'économie politique.* Cairo: Imprimerie de l'Institut Français d'Archéologie Orientale, 1943.

Empson, C., for UK Department of Overseas Trade. *Report on Economic and Commercial Conditions in Egypt, June 1939.* London: HMSO, 1939.

Exertzoglou, Haris. "The Cultural Uses of Consumption: Negotiating Class, Gender, and Nation in the Ottoman Urban Centers during the Nineteenth Century." *International Journal of Middle East Studies* 35 (2003): 77–101.

Fahmy, Khaled. *All the Pasha's Men: Mehmed Ali, His Army, and the Making of Modern Egypt.* New York: Cambridge University Press, 1997.

———. "Modernizing Cairo: A Revisionist Narrative." In *Making Cairo Medieval,* edited by Nezar AlSayyad, Irene A. Bierman, and Nasser Rabbat, 173–99. New York: Lexington Books, 2005.

———. "An Olfactory Tale of Two Cities: Cairo in the Nineteenth Century." In *Historians in Cairo,* edited by Jill Edwards, 155–87. New York: American University in Cairo Press, 2002.

Fandy, Mamoun. "Political Science without Clothes: The Politics of Dress; or, Contesting the Spatiality of the State in Egypt." In *Beyond the Exotic: Women's Histories in Islamic Societies,* edited by Amira el-Azhary Sonbol, 381–98. Syracuse, NY: Syracuse University Press, 2005.

Fanon, Frantz. *The Wretched of the Earth.* Translated by Constance Farrington. New York: Grove Weidenfeld, 1963.

Faraj, Samir. *Nariman: Akhir malikat Misr.* Cairo: Ahram Publishing, 1992.

Fédération Egyptienne de l'Industrie. *Foreign Trade of Egypt.* Cairo: SOP, 1955.

Feldman, Ilana. *Governing Gaza.* Durham, NC: Duke University Press, 2008.

Ferguson, James. *The Anti-Politics Machine.* Minneapolis: University of Minnesota Press, 1994.

Fikri, ʿAli. *Adab al-fatah.* 3rd ed. Cairo: al-Liwaʾ, 1901.

Fleischmann, Ellen. *The Nation and Its "New" Women: The Palestinian Women's Movement, 1920–1948.* Berkeley: University of California Press, 2003.

Foucault, Michel. "Of Other Spaces." Translated by Jay Miskowiec. *Diacritics* 16, no. 1 (Spring 1986): 22–27.

Freitag, Sandria B. "Visions of the Nation: Theorizing the Nexus between Creation, Consumption, and Participation in the Public Sphere." In *Pleasure and the Nation,* edited by Rachel Dwyer and Christopher Pinney, 35–75. New Delhi: Oxford University Press, 2001.

Freund, Bill. "The City of Durban: Towards a Structural Analysis of the Economic Growth and Character of a South African City." In *Africa's Urban Past,* edited by David M. Anderson and Richard Rathbone, 144–61. Portsmouth, NH: Heinemann, 2000.

Friedman, Monroe. *Consumer Boycotts: Effecting Change through the Marketplace and the Media.* New York: Routledge, 1999.

Gallagher, Nancy Elizabeth. *Egypt's Other Wars: Epidemics and the Politics of Public Health.* Syracuse, NY: Syracuse University Press, 1990.

Gaonkar, Dilip P., ed. *Alternative Modernities.* Durham, NC: Duke University Press, 2001.

Garret, Pascal. "Les 'Marchés modernes' en Egypte." *Lettre d'information de l'observatoire urbain du Caire contemporain.* Centre d'Etudes et de Documentation Economiques (CEDEJ), nos. 41–42 (September 1995): 20–29.

Gayed, Riad. *Egypt: From Mena to Fouad, Gayed's Practical Guide to Egypt.* Cairo, 1937.

Gershoni, Israel. "The Evolution of National Culture in Modern Egypt: Intellectual Formation and Social Diffusion, 1892–1945." *Poetics Today* 13 (1992): 325–50.

Gershoni, Israel, and James Jankowski. *Confronting Fascism in Egypt.* Stanford, CA: Stanford University Press, 2010.

———. *Egypt, Islam and the Arabs: The Search for Egyptian Nationhood, 1900–1930.* New York: Oxford University Press, 1986.

———. "Print Culture, Social Change, and the Process of Redefining Imagined Communities in Egypt; Response to the Review by Charles D. Smith of *Redefining the Egyptian Nation.*" *International Journal of Middle East Studies* 31, no. 1 (February 1999): 81–94.

———. *Redefining the Egyptian Nation, 1930–1945.* New York: Cambridge University Press, 1995.

Gerth, Karl. *China Made.* Cambridge, MA: Harvard University Press, 2003.

———. "Featured Review of Frank Dikötter, *Exotic Commodities.*" *American Historical Review* 113, no. 3 (June 2008): 785–87.

Gesink, Indira Falk. "'Chaos on the Earth': Subjective Truths versus Communal Unity in Islamic Law and the Rise of Militant Islam." *American Historical Review* 108, no. 3 (June 2003): 710–33.

El-Ghobashy, Mona. "The Praxis of the Egyptian Revolution." *Middle East Report*, no. 258 (Spring 2011): 2–13.

Glickman, Lawrence B. "'Buy for the Sake of the Slave': Abolition and the Origins of American Consumer Activism." *American Quarterly* 56, no. 4 (December 2004): 889–912.

———. *Buying Power: A History of Consumer Activism in America.* Chicago: University of Chicago Press, 2009.

Goffman, Daniel. "Izmir: From Village to Colonial Port City." In *The Ottoman City between East and West,* edited by Edhem Eldem, Daniel Goffman, and Bruce Masters, 79–134. New York: Cambridge University Press, 1999.

Goldberg, Ellis. "Peasants in Revolt—Egypt 1919." *International Journal of Middle East Studies* 24 (1992): 261–80.

Goldschmidt, Arthur. *Biographical Dictionary of Modern Egypt.* Boulder, CO: Lynne Rienner, 2000.

Golia, Maria. *Cairo.* London: Reaktion Books, 2004.

Gordon, Joel. "Film, Fame, and Public Memory: Egyptian Biopics from Mustafa Kamil to *Nasser 56,*" *International Journal of Middle East Studies* 31 (1999): 61–79.

———. *Nasser's Blessed Movement: Egypt's Free Officers and the July Revolution.* 1992. Reprint, Cairo: American University in Cairo Press, 1996.

———. *Revolutionary Melodrama: Popular Film and Civic Identity in Nasser's Egypt.* Chicago: Middle East Documentation Center, 2002.

Goswami, Manu. *Producing India: From Colonial Economy to National Space.* Chicago: University of Chicago Press, 2004.

Grehan, James. *Everyday Life and Consumer Culture in 18th-Century Damascus.* Seattle: University of Washington Press, 2007.

Groff, Florence. *Guide to Cairo and Environs.* Cairo: Lavados, 1893.

Guenther, Irene. *Nazi Chic?* New York: Berg, 2004.

Al-Hakim, Tawfiq. *Yawmiyat na'ib fi'l-aryaf.* Cairo: Maktabat Misr, 1988.

Halevi, Leor. "Christian Impurity versus Economic Necessity: A Fifteenth-Century Fatwa on European Paper," *Speculum* 83, no. 4 (October 2008): 917–45.

Hampikian, Nairy. "Medievalization of the Old City as an Ingredient of Cairo's Modernization: Case Study of Bab Zuwayla." In *Making Cairo Medieval,* edited by Nezar AlSayyad, Irene A. Bierman, and Nasser Rabbat, 201–34. New York: Lexington Books, 2005.

Handley, Susannah. *Nylon.* Baltimore, MD: Johns Hopkins University Press, 1999.

Hanley, Will. "Foreignness and Localness in Alexandria, 1880–1914." PhD diss., Princeton University, 2007.

———. "Grieving Cosmopolitanism in Middle East Studies." *History Compass* 6, no. 5 (2008): 1346–67.

Hanna, Nelly. "The Urban History of Cairo around 1900." In *Historians in Cairo: Essays in Honor of George Scanlon*, edited by Jill Edwards, 189–201. New York: American University in Cairo Press, 2002.

Hansen, Bent. *Egypt and Turkey: The Political Economy of Poverty, Equity, and Growth*. Washington, DC: Oxford University Press for the World Bank, 1991.

———. "Income and Consumption in Egypt, 1886/1887 to 1937." *International Journal of Middle East Studies* 10 (1979): 27–47.

Hansen, Bent, and Girgis A. Marzouk. *Development and Economic Policy in the UAR (Egypt)*. Amsterdam: North Holland Publishing, 1965.

Hansen, Karen Tranberg. *Salaula: The World of Secondhand Clothing and Zambia*. Chicago: University of Chicago Press, 2000.

Haqqi, Yahya. *Safahat min tarikh Misr*. Cairo: General Egyptian Book Organization, 1989.

Harb, Muhammad Talʿat. *Majmuʿat khutub Muhammad Talʿat Harb basha*. 3 vols. Cairo: Imprimerie Misr, 1957/n.d.

Harvey, David. *Paris, Capital of Modernity*. New York: Routledge, 2003.

———. "The Political Economy of Public Space." In *The Politics of Public Space*, edited by Setha Low and Neil Smith, 17–34. New York: Routledge, 2006.

Hatem, Mervet. "The Enduring Alliance of Nationalism and Patriarchy in Muslim Personal Status Laws." *Feminist Issues*, Spring 1986, 19–43.

d'Hestroy, Baron E. de Gaiffier. *Egypte: Situation economique, financière et commerciale en 1907*. Brussels: Piquart, 1908.

Hill, Enid. "The Golden Anniversary of Egypt's National Courts." In *Historians in Cairo*, edited by Jill Edwards, 203–22. New York: American University in Cairo Press, 2002.

Hilton, Matthew, and Martin Daunton. "Material Politics." In *The Politics of Consumption: Material Culture and Citizenship in Europe and America*, edited by Martin Daunton and Matthew Hilton, 1–32. New York: Berg, 2001.

Hinds, Martin, and el-Said Badawi. *A Dictionary of Egyptian Arabic*. Beirut: Librarie du Liban, 1986.

Hirschkind, Charles. *The Ethical Soundscape*. New York: Columbia University Press, 2006.

Hobsbawm, Eric. "Cities and Insurrections." In *Revolutionaries*, 261–78. 1973. Reprint, New York: New Press, 2001.

Hopwood, Derek. *Egypt: Politics and Society, 1945–1984*, 2nd ed. Boston: Allen and Unwin, 1985.

———. *Tales of Empire: The British in the Middle East, 1880–1952*. London: I. B. Tauris, 1989.

Horden, Peregrine, and Nicholas Purcell. "The Mediterranean and 'the New Thalassology.'" *American Historical Review* 111, no. 3 (June 2006): 722–40.

Hourani, Albert. *Arabic Thought in the Liberal Age, 1798–1939*. New York: Cambridge University Press, 1962.

Hussein, Ahmed, and M. A. Badry. "A Statistical Report on Commercial Workers and the Effect of the Minimum Wage Scheme on Their Wages." *L'Egypte contemporaine* 44, no. 271 (January 1953): 1–8 (English summary), 1–33 (Arabic text).

Ibrahim, Saad Eddin. *The New Arab Social Order: A Study of the Social Impact of Oil Wealth*. Boulder, CO: Westview, 1982.

Idris, Yusuf. *City of Love and Ashes*. Translated by R. Neil Hewison. Cairo: American University in Cairo Press, 1999.

Ilbert, Robert. *Alexandrie, 1830–1930*. 2 vols. Cairo: Institut Français d'Archéologie Orientale, 1996.

———. "L'invention du marché: Alexandrie, 1850–1920." In *Les villes dans l'Empire Ottoman: Activités et sociétés*. Vol. 2, edited by Daniel Panzac, 357–76. Paris: CNRS Editions, 1994.

Ilbert, Robert, Ilios Yannakakis, and Jacques Hassoun, eds. *Alexandria, 1860–1960*. 1992. Reprint, Alexandria, Egypt: Harpocrates, 1997.

L'indicateur touristique d'Egypte/Tourists' Egyptian Companion, 1952–1953. Cairo: A. Karama, 1952.

International Federation of Master Cotton Spinners' and Manufacturers' Association (IFMCSMA). *Official Report of the International Cotton Congress Held in Egypt, 1927*. Manchester: Taylor Garnett Evans, n.d.

Issawi, Charles. *Egypt at Mid-Century*. New York: Oxford University Press, 1954.

———. "Egypt since 1800: A Study in Lopsided Development." *Journal of Economic History* 21 (1961): 1–25.

Jacobs, Meg. *Pocketbook Politics: Economic Citizenship in Twentieth-Century America*. Princeton, NJ: Princeton University Press, 2005.

Jankowski, James P. *Egypt's Young Rebels: "Young Egypt," 1933–1952*. Stanford, CA: Hoover Institution Press, 1975.

Jankowski, James, and Israel Gershoni, eds. *Rethinking Nationalism in the Arab Middle East*. New York: Columbia University Press, 1997.

Jayyusi, Salma Khadra. "Introduction." In *Modern Arabic Poetry: An Anthology*, edited by Salma Khadra Jayyusi. New York: Columbia University Press, 1987.

Jirousek, Charlotte. "The Transition to Mass Fashion System Dress in the Later Ottoman Empire." In *Consumption Studies and the History of the Ottoman Empire, 1550–1922*, edited by Donald Quataert, 201–41. Albany: State University of New York, 2000.

Jomard, M. "Description abrégée de la ville et de la citadelle du Kaire." In *La description de l'Egypte*, vol. 14. Paris: Imprimerie Impériale, 1809.

Juifs d'Egypte: Images et textes. 2nd ed. Paris: Editions du Scribe, 1984.

El Kadi, Galila, and Dalia ElKerdany. "Belle-époque Cairo: The Politics of Refurbishing the Downtown Business District." In *Cairo Cosmopolitan*, edited by Diane Singerman and Paul Amar, 345–71. New York: American University in Cairo Press, 2006.

Karanasou, Floresca. "Egyptianisation: The 1947 Company Law and the Foreign Communities in Egypt." DPhil diss., Oxford University, 1992.

Keddie, Nikki R., and Beth Baron, eds. *Women in Middle Eastern History: Shifting Boudaries in Sex and Gender*. New Haven, CT: Yale University Press, 1991.

Kelly, John D., and Martha Kaplan. *Represented Communities: Fiji and World Decolonization*. Chicago: University of Chicago Press, 2001.

Kerboeuf, Anne-Claire. "The Cairo Fire of 26 January 1952 and the Interpretations of History." In *Re-Envisioning Egypt, 1919–1952*, edited by Arthur Goldschmidt, Amy Johnson, and Barak Salmoni, 194–216. Cairo: American University in Cairo Press, 2005.

———. "La 'racaille' et les 'intrigants': Etude comparée de deux émeutes." *Egypte/monde arabe* 1–2, nos. 4–5 (2000–2001): 55–80.

Kerr, Malcolm, and El Sayed Yassin, eds. *Rich and Poor States in the Middle East: Egypt and the New Arab Order*. Boulder, CO: Westview, 1982.

Keshavarzian, Arang. *Bazaar and State in Iran*. Cambridge: Cambridge University Press, 2007.

Khan, Noor-Aiman Iftikhar. "The Enemy of My Enemy: Indian Influences on Egyptian Nationalism, 1907–1930." PhD diss., University of Chicago, 2006.

Kholoussy, Hanan. *For Better, For Worse: The Marriage Crisis That Made Modern Egypt*. Stanford, CA: Stanford University Press, 2010.

———. "Monitoring and Medicalising Male Sexuality in Semi-Colonial Egypt." *Gender and History* 22, no. 3 (November 2010): 677–91.

Al-Khuli, Fikri. *Al-Rihla*. 3 vols. Cairo: Dar al-Ghad, 1987–1992.

Kilani, Muhammad Sayyid. *Tram al-Qahira*. Cairo: Dar al-Farjani, 1968.

King, Anthony D. "Colonial Cities: Global Pivots of Change." In *Colonial Cities*, edited by Robert Ross and Gerard J. Telkamp, 7–32. Boston: Martinus Nijhoff, 1985.

Kitroeff, Alexander. *The Greeks in Egypt, 1919–1937: Ethnicity and Class*. London: Ithaca Press, 1989.

Kopytoff, Igor. "The Cultural Biography of Things: Commoditization as Process." In *The Social Life of Things*, edited by Arjun Appadurai, 64–91. New York: Cambridge University Press, 1986.

Krämer, Gudrun. *The Jews in Modern Egypt, 1914–1952*. Seattle: University of Washington Press, 1989.

Kupferschmidt, Uri M. *The Orosdi-Back Saga*. Istanbul: Ottoman Bank Archives and Research Centre, 2007.

———. "Who Needed Department Stores in Egypt? From Orosdi-Back to Omar Effendi." *Middle Eastern Studies* 43, no. 2 (March 2007): 175–92.

Kurpershoek, P. M. *The Short Stories of Yusuf Idris.* Leiden, Netherlands: Brill, 1981.

Lacouture, Jean, and Simonne Lacouture. *Egypt in Transition.* Translated by Francis Scarfe. New York: Criterion Books, 1958.

Landshut, Seigfried. *Jewish Communities in the Muslim Countries of the Middle East: A Survey for the American-Jewish Committee and the Anglo-Jewish Association.* London: Jewish Chronicle, 1950.

Lane, Edward. *Arabic-English Lexicon.* 1862. Reprint, New York: Ungar, 1956.

———. *Manners and Customs of the Modern Egyptians.* 1836, 1895. Reprint, London: East-West Publications, 1989.

Laskier, Michael M. *The Jews of Egypt, 1920–1970.* New York: New York University Press, 1992.

Leach, William R. *Land of Desire: Merchants, Power, and the Rise of a New American Culture.* New York: Vintage, 1994.

———. "Transformations in a Culture of Consumption: Women and Department Stores, 1890–1925." *Journal of American History* 71, no. 2 (September 1984): 319–42.

Lee, Leo Ou-Fan. "Shanghai Modern: Reflections on Urban Culture in China in the 1930s." In *Alternative Modernities,* edited by Dilip Parameshwar Gaonkar, 86–122. Durham, NC: Duke University Press, 2001.

Lemire, Beverly. "Consumerism in Preindustrial and Early Industrial England: The Trade in Secondhand Clothes." *Journal of British Studies* 27, no. 1 (January 1988): 1–24.

LeVine, Mark. *Overthrowing Geography: Jaffa, Tel Aviv, and the Struggle for Palestine, 1880–1948.* Berkeley: University of California Press, 2005.

Levy, Clement, comp. *The Stock Exchange Year-Book of Egypt.* Cairo: Stock Exchange Year-Book of Egypt, 1937, 1939, 1941, 1942, 1943, 1957.

Lewis, Bernard. *The Emergence of Modern Turkey.* 1961. Reprint, New York: Oxford University Press, 1968.

———. *What Went Wrong? Western Impact and Middle Eastern Response.* London: Phoenix, 2002.

Lia, Brynjar. *The Society of the Muslim Brothers in Egypt.* Reading, MA: Ithaca Press, 1998.

Lindisfarne-Tapper, Nancy, and Bruce Ingham, eds. *Languages of Dress in the Middle East.* London: Curzon, 1997.

Lockman, Zachary. *Contending Visions of the Middle East.* New York: Cambridge University Press, 2004.

Ludden, David. "India's Development Regime." In *Colonialism and Culture,* edited by Nicholas B. Dirks, 247–87. Ann Arbor: University of Michigan Press, 1992.

Lynch, Jeremiah. *Egyptian Sketches.* London: Edward Arnold, 1890.

Mabro, Robert. "Alexandria, 1860–1960." In *Alexandria, Real and Imagined*, edited by Anthony Hirst and Michael Silk, 247–62. Burlington, VT: Ashgate, 2004.

———. *The Egyptian Economy, 1952–1972*. Oxford: Clarendon Press, 1974.

MacPherson, Kerrie L., ed. *Asian Department Stores*. Honolulu: University of Hawaii Press, 1998.

Mahfouz, Naguib. *Autumn Quail*. Translated by Roger Allen with John Rodenbeck. New York: Anchor Books, 1985.

———. *Khan al-khalili*. 1946. Reprint, Cairo: Dar Misr li'l-Tabaʿiyya, n.d.

———. *Midaq Alley*. Translated by Trevor Le Gassick. Washington, DC: Three Continents Press, 1977.

———. *Palace of Desire*. Translated by William Maynard Hutchins, Lorne M. Kenny, and Olive E. Kenny. New York: Anchor Books, 1991.

———. *Al-Qahira al-jadida*. Cairo: Dar Misr li'l-Tibaʿa, 1945.

———. *Al-Summan waʾl-kharif*. 1962. Reprint, Cairo: Maktabat Misr, n.d.

Mansfield, Peter. *The British in Egypt*. New York: Holt, Rinehart and Winston, 1971.

Marrey, Bernard. *Les Grands magasins des origines à 1939*. Paris: Picard, 1979.

Marsot, Afaf Lutfi al-Sayyid. *A Short History of Modern Egypt*. New York: Cambridge University Press, 1986.

Mazower, Mark. *Salonica, City of Ghosts: Christians, Muslims and Jews, 1430–1950*. New York: Knopf, 2005.

McAlister, Melani. *Epic Encounters: Culture, Media, and U.S. Interests in the Middle East since 1945*. Rev. ed. Berkeley: University of California Press, 2005.

McClintock, Anne. *Imperial Leather*. New York: Routledge, 1995.

Mead, Donald C. *Growth and Structural Change in the Egyptian Economy*. Homewood, IL: Richard Irwin, 1967.

Meisami, Julie Scott, and Paul Starkey, eds. *Encyclopedia of Arabic Literature*. Vol. 2. New York: Routledge, 1998.

Meyerowitz, Joanne. *Women Adrift: Independent Wage Earners in Chicago, 1880–1930*. Chicago: University of Chicago Press, 1991.

Micheletti, Michele. *Political Virtue and Shopping*. New York: Palgrave Macmillan, 2003.

Mickelwright, Nancy. "Women's Dress in Nineteenth-Century Istanbul: Mirror of a Changing Society." PhD diss., University of Pennsylvania, 1986.

Miller, Michael B. *The Bon Marché: Bourgeois Culture and the Department Store, 1869–1920*. Princeton, NJ: Princeton University Press, 1981.

Mitchell, Richard P. *The Society of the Muslim Brothers*. 1969. Reprint, New York: Oxford University Press, 1993.

Mitchell, Timothy. *Colonising Egypt*. Berkeley: University of California Press, 1988.

———. *Rule of Experts: Egypt, Techno-Politics, Modernity*. Berkeley: University of California Press, 2002.

———. "The Stage of Modernity." In *Questions of Modernity*, edited by Timothy Mitchell, 1–34. Minneapolis: University of Minnesota Press, 2000.

Mizrahi, Maurice. *L'Egypte et ses juifs: Le temps révolu*. Lausanne, Switzerland: Imprimerie Avenir, 1977.

———. "The Role of Jews in Economic Development." In *The Jews of Egypt: A Mediterranean Society in Modern Times*, edited by Shimon Shamir, 85–93. Boulder, CO: Westview, 1987.

Moore, Austin L. *Farewell, Farouk*. Chicago: Scholars' Press, 1954.

Mostyn, Trevor. *Egypt's Belle Epoque: Cairo and the Age of the Hedonists*. 1989. Reprint, New York: I. B. Tauris, 2007.

Mulock, E. Homan, for UK Department of Overseas Trade. *Report on the Economic and Financial Situation of Egypt, March 1921*. London: HMSO, 1921.

———. *Report on the Economic and Financial Situation of Egypt, April 1923*. London: HMSO, 1923.

———. *Report on the Economic and Financial Situation of Egypt, June 1925*. London: HMSO, 1925.

———. *Report on the Economic and Financial Situation of Egypt, June 1926*. London: HMSO, 1926.

———. *Report on the Economic and Financial Situation of Egypt, May 1927*. London: HMSO, 1927.

———. *Report on the Economic and Financial Situation of Egypt, May 1928*. London: HMSO, 1928.

Al-Munjid. Beirut: Dar al-Mashriq, 1994.

Naguib, Nefissa. "Basic Ethnography at the Barricades." *International Journal of Middle East Studies* 43, no. 3 (August 2011): 383.

Najmabadi, Afsaneh. "Hazards of Modernity and Morality: Women, State, and Ideology in Contemporary Iran." In *Women, Islam, and the State*, edited by Deniz Kandioyti, 48–76. Philadelphia: Temple University Press, 1991.

Navaro-Yashin, Yael. "The Market for Identities: Secularism, Islamism, Commodities." In *Fragments of Culture: The Everyday of Modern Turkey*, edited by Deniz Kandiyoti and Ayse Saktanber, 221–53. New Brunswick, NJ: Rutgers University Press, 2002.

Nord, Phillip. *The Politics of Resentment*. 1986. Reprint, New Brunswick, NJ: Transaction, 2005.

O'Brien, Patrick. *The Revolution in Egypt's Economic System*. New York: Oxford University Press, 1966.

Owen, Roger. *Cotton and the Egyptian Economy, 1820–1914*. London: Oxford University Press, 1969.

———. *The Middle East in the World Economy, 1800–1914*. New York: Methuen, 1981.

Panzac, Daniel. "The Population of Egypt in the Nineteenth Century." *Asian and African Studies* 21 (1987): 11–32.

Papasian, E. D. *L'Egypte: Economique et financière, 1922–1923, 1924–1925.* Cairo: Imprimerie Misr, 1923, 1926.

Péron, René. *La Fin des vitrines: Des temples de la consommation aux usines à vendre.* Cachan, France: Editions de l'Ens-Cachan, 1993.

Perrot, Philippe. *Fashioning the Bourgeoisie.* Translated by Richard Bienvenu. Princeton, NJ: Princeton University Press, 1994.

Philipp, Thomas. *The Syrians in Egypt, 1725–1975.* Stuttgart: Franz Steiner Verlag, 1985.

Politi, Elie I., ed. *Annuaire des sociétés égyptiennes par actions.* Cairo and Alexandria: Imprimerie Procaccia, 1932, 1942, 1947, 1955.

Pollard, Lisa. *Nurturing the Nation.* Berkeley: University of California Press, 2005.

Powell, Eve M. Troutt. *A Different Shade of Colonialism: Egypt, Great Britain, and the Mastery of the Sudan.* Berkeley: University of California Press, 2003.

Prakash, Gyan, ed. *After Colonialism.* Princeton, NJ: Princeton University Press, 1995.

———. "The Urban Turn." In *Sarai Reader 2002: The Cities of Everyday Life,* edited by Ravi S. Vasudevan, Ravi Sundaram, Jeebesh Bagchi, Monica Narula, Shuddhabrata Sengupta, and Geert Lovink, 2–7. Delhi, India: New Media Initiative, 2002.

Prestholdt, Jeremy. *Domesticating the World: African Consumerism and the Genealogies of Globalization.* Berkeley: University of California Press, 2008.

Prochaska, David. *Making Algeria French: Colonialism in Bône, 1870–1920.* New York: Cambridge University Press, 1990.

Quataert, Donald, ed. *Consumption Studies and the History of the Ottoman Empire, 1550–1922: An Introduction.* Albany: State University of New York Press, 2000.

———. *Manufacturing and Technology Transfer in the Ottoman Empire 1800–1914.* Istanbul: Isis Press, 1992.

Qutb, Sayyid. *Al-ʿAdala al-ijtimʿiyya fiʾl-islam.* 1953. Reprint, Beirut: Dar al-Shuruq, 1975.

———. *Social Justice in Islam.* Translated by John B. Hardie with Hamid Algar. New York: Islamic Publications International, 2000.

Raafat, Samir W. *Cairo: The Glory Years.* Alexandria: Harpocrates, 2003.

Rabinow, Paul. *French Modern: Norms and Forms of the Social Environment.* 1989. Reprint, Chicago: University of Chicago Press, 1995.

Rabo, Annika. *A Shop of One's Own: Independence and Reputation among Traders in Aleppo.* London: I. B. Tauris, 2005.

Radwan, Fathi. *Khatt al-ʿataba: Hayat tifli misri.* Cairo: Dar al-Maʿarif, 1973.

Al-Rafiʿi, ʿAbd al-Rahman. *Fi aʿqab al-thawra al-misriyya.* 3rd ed. 3 vols. 1947–1951. Cairo: Dar al-Maʿarif, 1987.

Rai, Lajpat. *Young India: The Nationalist Movement.* New York: B. W. Huebsch, 1917.

Randall, Amy E. "Legitimizing Soviet Trade: Gender and the Feminization of the Retail Workforce in the Soviet 1930s." *Journal of Social History* 37, no. 4 (Summer 2004): 965–90.

Rappaport, Erika Diane. *Shopping for Pleasure: Women in the Making of London's West End.* Princeton, NJ: Princeton University Press, 2000.

Raymond, André. *Artisans et commerçants au Caire au XVIIIe siècle.* 2 vols. Damascus, Syria: Institut Français de Damas, 1973.

———. *Cairo.* Translated by Willard Wood. Cambridge, MA: Harvard University Press, 2000.

Raymond, André, and G. Wiet. *Les Marchés du Caire: Traduction annoté du texte de Maqrizi.* Cairo: Institut Français d'Archéologie Orientale du Caire, 1979.

Reekie, Gail. *Temptations: Sex, Selling, and the Department Store.* St. Leonards, Australia: Allen and Unwin, 1993.

Reid, Donald. "Syrian Christians, the Rags-to-Riches Story, and Free Enterprise." *International Journal of Middle East Studies* 1 (1970): 358–67.

Reimer, Michael J. *Colonial Bridgehead: Government and Society in Alexandria, 1807–1882.* Boulder, CO: Westview, 1997.

Reynolds-Ball, E. A. *Cairo of To-day: A Practical Guide to Cairo and its Environs.* 2nd ed. London: Adam and Charles Black, 1899.

Rich, Jeremy. *A Workman Is Worthy of His Meat: Food and Colonialism in the Gabon Estuary.* Lincoln: University of Nebraska Press, 2007.

Richards, Thomas. *The Commodity Culture of Victorian Britain.* London: Verso, 1990.

Roberts, Mary Louise. "Gender, Consumption, and Commodity Culture." *American Historical Review* 103, no. 3 (June 1998): 817–44.

Rodenbeck, Max. *Cairo: The City Victorious.* New York: Knopf, 1999.

Rosen, Christine Meisner. *The Limits of Power: Great Fires and the Process of City Growth in America.* New York: Cambridge University Press, 1986.

Ross, Robert, and Gerard J. Telkamp. *Colonial Cities.* Boston: Martinus Nijhoff, 1985.

Rossant, Colette. *Memories of a Lost Egypt: A Memoir with Recipes.* New York: Clarkson Potter, 1999.

Rossi, William A. *The Sex Life of the Foot and Shoe.* New York: Dutton, 1976.

Rowlatt, Mary. *A Family in Egypt.* London: Robert Hale, 1956.

Ruedy, John. *Modern Algeria.* Bloomington: Indiana University Press, 1992.

Rugh, Andrea B. *Reveal and Conceal: Dress in Contemporary Egypt.* Syracuse, NY: Syracuse University Press, 1986.

Russell, Mona. *Creating the New Egyptian Woman: Consumerism, Education, and National Identity, 1863–1922.* New York: Palgrave Macmillan, 2004.

———. "Marketing the Modern Egyptian Girl: Whitewashing Soap and Clothes from the Late Nineteenth Century to 1936." *Journal of Middle East Women's Studies* 6, no. 3 (Fall 2010): 19–57.

Russell, Sir Thomas. *Egyptian Service, 1902–1946.* London: John Murray, 1949.

Ryzova, Lucie. "Egyptianizing Modernity through the 'New *Effendiya*': Social and Cultural Constructions of the Middle Class in Egypt under the Monarchy."

In *Re-Envisioning Egypt, 1919–1952*, edited by Arthur Goldschmidt, Amy Johnson, and Barak Salmoni, 124–63. New York: American University in Cairo Press, 2005.

———. "'I Am a Whore but I Will Be a Good Mother': On the Production and Consumption of the Female Body in Modern Egypt." *Arab Studies Journal* 12, no. 2, and 13, no. 1 (Fall 2004–Spring 2005): 80–122.

Safran, Nadav. *Egypt in Search of Political Community: An Analysis of the Intellectual and Political Evolution of Egypt, 1804–1952*. Cambridge, MA: Harvard University Press, 1961.

Sallam, Hesham. "Striking Back at Egyptian Workers." *Middle East Report*, no. 259 (Summer 2011): 20–25.

Sanders, Lise Shapiro. *Consuming Fantasies: Labor, Leisure, and the London Shopgirl, 1880–1920*. Columbus: Ohio State University Press, 2006.

Sanders, Paula. *Creating Medieval Cairo*. New York: American University in Cairo Press, 2008.

Saul, Samir. *La France et l'Egypte de 1882 à 1914: Intérêts économiques et implications politiques*. Paris: Comité pour l'histoire économique et financière de la France, 1997.

Sawislak, Karen. *Smoldering City: Chicagoans and the Great Fire, 1871–1874*. Chicago: University of Chicago Press, 1995.

Scarce, Jennifer. *Women's Costume of the Near and Middle East*. London: Unwin Hyman, 1987.

Schanz, Moritz. *Cotton in Egypt and the Anglo-Egyptian Sudan, Submitted to the 9th International Cotton Congress*. 1913. Reprint, Greenville, CA: Dyer Press, 2007.

Schemeil, Marius. *Le Caire: Sa vie, son histoire, son peuple*. Cairo: Dar al-Maaref, 1949.

Scott, David. "Colonial Governmentality." In *Anthropologies of Modernity: Foucault, Governmentality, and Life Politics*, edited by Jonathan Xavier Inda, 23–49. Oxford: Blackwell, 2005.

Scott, James. *Seeing like a State*. New Haven, CT: Yale University Press, 1998.

———. *Weapons of the Weak: Everyday Forms of Peasant Resistance*. New Haven, CT: Yale University Press, 1985.

Seddon-Brown, N. "The Effect of the Quality of Cotton upon Costs of Production and the Quality of Cloth." In *Official Report of the International Cotton Congress Held in Egypt, 1927*, edited by IFMCSMA, 146–48. Manchester, UK: Taylor Garnett Evans, n.d.

Selous, G. H., for UK Department of Overseas Trade. *Economic Conditions in Egypt, July 1935*. London: HMSO, 1935.

———. *Report on Economic and Commercial Conditions in Egypt, May 1937*. London: HMSO, 1937.

Selous, G. H., and L. B. S. Larkins, for UK Department of Overseas Trade. *Economic Conditions in Egypt, July 1933*. London: HMSO, 1933.

Seton, Grace Thompson. *A Woman Tenderfoot in Egypt.* New York: Dodd, Mead, 1923.

Shaarawi, Huda. *Harem Years: The Memoirs of an Egyptian Feminist, 1879–1924.* Translated by Margot Badran. New York: Feminist Press of the City University of New York, 1987.

El Shakry, Omnia. *The Great Social Laboratory: Subjects of Knowledge in Colonial and Postcolonial Egypt.* Stanford, CA: Stanford University Press, 2007.

Shamir, Shimon, ed. *The Jews of Egypt.* Boulder, CO: Westview, 1987.

Sharma, Aradhana, and Akhil Gupta, eds. *The Anthropology of the State.* Malden, MA: Blackwell, 2006.

El-Sayed, Karim. "Egypt's Last Effendi: On the Government Efforts to Privatize Department Stores." *Economic and Business History Research Center Chronicles* 1, no. 4 (April–June 2006): 22–24.

Al-Sharqawi, Jamal. *Hariq al-Qahira.* Cairo: Dar al-Thaqafa al-Jadida, 1976.

Shechter, Relli. "The Cultural Economy of Development in Egypt: Economic Nationalism, Hidden Economy and the Emergence of Mass Consumer Society during Sadat's Infitah." *Middle Eastern Studies* 44, no. 4 (2008): 571–83.

———. "Press Advertising in Egypt: Business Realities and Local Meaning, 1882–1956." *Arab Studies Journal* 10, no. 2, and 11, no. 1 (Fall 2002–Spring 2003): 44–66.

———. "Reading Advertisements in a Colonial/Development Context." *Journal of Social History* 39, no. 2 (Winter 2005): 483–503.

———. *Smoking, Culture, and Economy in the Middle East: The Egyptian Tobacco Market, 1850–2000.* New York: I. B. Tauris, 2006.

———, ed. *Transitions in Domestic Consumption and Family Life in the Modern Middle East.* New York: Palgrave Macmillan, 2003.

Shehata, Samer S. "Plastic Sandals, Tea and Time: Shop Floor Politics and Culture in Egypt." PhD diss., Princeton University, 2000.

El Sherbini, Abdel Aziz, and Ahmed Fouad Sherif. "Marketing Problems in an Underdeveloped Country—Egypt." *L'Egypte contemporaine* 47, no. 285 (July 1956): 5–85.

Shirabli, Muhammad. "Al-Suq: Qalb al-madina al-islamiyya." *Al-Hilal* 96 (August 1989): 64–75.

Shlala, Elizabeth. "Mediterranean Migration, Cosmopolitanism, and the Law: A History of the Italian Community of Nineteenth-Century Alexandria, Egypt." PhD diss., Georgetown University, 2009.

Shokr, Ahmad. "The 18 Days of Tahrir." *Middle East Report*, no. 258 (Spring 2011): 14–19.

Sims, David. *Understanding Cairo.* New York: American University in Cairo Press, 2010.

Skovgaard-Petersen, Jakob. *Defining Islam for the Egyptian State: Muftis and Fatwas of the Dar al-Ifta.* New York: Brill, 1997.

Sladen, Douglas. *Oriental Cairo: The City of the "Arabian Nights."* London: Hurst and Blackett, 1911.

Smart, Alan. *The Shek Kip Mei Myth: Squatters, Fires, and Colonial Rule in Hong Kong, 1950–1963*. Hong Kong: Hong Kong University Press, 2006.

Smith, Carl. *Urban Disorder and the Shape of Belief*. 2nd ed. Chicago: University of Chicago Press, 2007.

Smith, Charles D. "'Cultural Constructs' and Other Fantasies: Imagined Narratives in Imagined Communities; Surrejoinder to Gershoni and Jankowski's 'Print Culture, Social Change, and the Process of Redefining Imagined Communities in Egypt.'" *International Journal of Middle East Studies* 31, no. 1 (February 1999): 95–102.

———. "Imagined Identities, Imagined Nationalisms: Print Culture and Egyptian Nationalism in Light of Recent Scholarship." *International Journal of Middle East Studies* 29, no. 4 (November 1997): 607–22.

Société Orientale de Publicité (SOP). *The Egyptian Directory, L'Annuaire Egyptien, al-Dalil al-Misri*. Cairo: SOP Press, 1918, 1927, 1935, 1941, 1944, 1948, 1951, 1958, 1961.

Spufford, Margaret. *The Great Reclothing of Rural England*. London: Hambledon Press, 1984.

Starrett, Gregory. "The Political Economy of Religious Commodities in Cairo." *American Anthropologist* 97, no. 1 (March 1995): 51–68.

Stillman, Yedida Kalfon. *Arab Dress from the Dawn of Islam to Modern Times: A Short History*. Edited by Norman Stillman. Boston: Brill, 2003.

Stoler, Ann Laura. *Carnal Knowledge and Imperial Power: Race and the Intimate in Colonial Rule*. 2002. Reprint, Berkeley: University of California Press, 2010.

Stowasser, Barbara Freyer. *Women in the Qu'ran, Traditions, and Interpretation*. New York: Oxford University Press, 1994.

Strong, Pauline Turner. *Captive Selves, Captivating Others: The Politics and Poetics of Colonial American Captivity Narratives*. Boulder, CO: Westview, 1999.

Tarlo, Emma. *Clothing Matters: Dress and Identity in India*. Chicago: University of Chicago Press, 1996.

Taylor, J. W., for UK Board of Trade. *Egypt: Economic and Commercial Conditions in Egypt, November 1947*. London: HMSO, 1948.

Thompson, Elizabeth. *Colonial Citizens: Republican Rights, Paternal Privilege, and Gender in French Syria and Lebanon*. New York: Columbia University Press, 2000.

———. "Sex and Cinema in Damascus: The Gendered Politics of Public Space in a Colonial City." In *Middle Eastern Cities 1900–1950*, edited by Hans Chr. Korsholm Nielsen and Jakob Skovgaard-Petersen, 89–111. Proceedings of the Danish Institute in Damascus I. Aarhus, Denmark: Aarhus University Press, 2001.

Tiersten, Lisa. *Marianne in the Market: Envisioning Consumer Society in Fin-de-Siècle France*. Berkeley: University of California Press, 2001.

Tignor, Robert. *Egyptian Textiles and British Capital, 1930–1956*. Cairo: American University in Cairo Press, 1989.

———. *State, Private Enterprise, and Economic Change in Egypt, 1918–1952.* Princeton, NJ: Princeton University Press, 1984.

Tippett, L. H. C. *A Portrait of the Lancashire Textile Industry.* New York: Oxford University Press, 1969.

Trivedi, Lisa. *Clothing Gandhi's Nation: Homespun and Modern India.* Bloomington: Indiana University Press, 2007.

Tsirkas, Stratis. *Drifting Cities.* Translated by Kay Cicellis. Athens: Kedros, 1995.

Tucker, Judith. *Women in Nineteenth-Century Egypt.* New York: Cambridge University Press, 1985.

Al-Tunisi, Bayram. *Ashʿar Bayram al-Tunisi.* Cairo: Maktabat Madbuli, 1985.

Turner, R. M., for UK Department of Overseas Trade. *The Economic and Financial Situation in Egypt, June 1929.* London: HMSO, 1929.

Turner, R. M., and L. B. S. Larkins, for UK Department of Overseas Trade. *Economic Conditions in Egypt, July 1931.* London: HMSO, 1931.

Van Nieuwkerk, Karin. *"A Trade like Any Other": Female Singers and Dancers in Egypt.* Austin: University of Texas Press, 1995.

Vatikiotis, P. J. *The History of Egypt.* 3rd ed. Baltimore, MD: Johns Hopkins University Press, 1985.

Vitalis, Robert. "On the Theory and Practice of Compradors: The Role of ʿAbbud Pasha in the Egyptian Political Economy." *International Journal of Middle East Studies* 22, no. 3 (August 1990): 291–315.

———. *When Capitalists Collide: Business Conflict and the End of Empire in Egypt.* Berkeley: University of California Press, 1995.

Wahba, Magdi. "East and West: Cairo Memories." *Encounter* 62, no. 5 (May 1984): 74–79.

Wahba, Mourad M. *The Role of the State in the Egyptian Economy, 1945–1981.* Reading, UK: Ithaca Press, 1994.

Walkowitz, Judith. *City of Dreadful Delight.* Chicago: University of Chicago Press, 1992.

Walsh, Claire. "The Newness of the Department Store: A View from the Eighteenth Century." In *Cathedrals of Consumption*, edited by Geoffrey Crossick and Serge Jaumain, 46–71. Brookfield, VT: Ashgate, 1999.

Walton, Whitney. *France at the Crystal Palace: Bourgeois Taste and Artisan Manufacture in the Nineteenth Century.* Berkeley: University of California Press, 1992.

Warf, Barney, and Santa Arias. "Introduction: The Reinsertion of Space into the Social Sciences and Humanities." In *The Spatial Turn: Interdisciplinary Perspectives*, edited by Barney Warf and Santa Arias, 1–10. New York: Routledge, 2009.

Wassef, Magda, ed. *Egypte: Cent Ans de Cinéma.* Paris: Institut du Monde Arabe, 1995.

Watenpaugh, Keith. *Being Modern in the Middle East.* Princeton, NJ: Princeton University Press, 2006.

Weiss, Gillian. "Barbary Captivity and the French Idea of Freedom." *French Historical Studies* 28, no. 2 (Spring 2005): 231–64.

Weiss, Walter M., and Kurt-Michael Westermann. *The Bazaar: Markets and Merchants of the Islamic World*. New York: Thames and Hudson, 1998.

Wells, Sidney H. "L'Industrie du tissage en Egypte." *L'Egypte contemporaine*, 4 November 1910, 578–84, and 5 January 1911, 52–73.

Westad, Odd Arne. *The Global Cold War*. New York: Cambridge University Press, 2007.

Wheelock, Keith. *Nasser's New Egypt*. New York: Praeger, 1960.

White, Luise. "Cars Out of Place: Vampires, Technology, and Labor in East and Central Africa." In *Tensions of Empire: Colonial Cultures in a Bourgeois World*, edited by Ann Laura Stoler and Frederick Cooper, 436–60. Berkeley: University of California Press, 1997.

Wilcox, R. Turner. *The Mode in Footwear*. New York: Scribner's, 1948.

Willcocks, William, and James Ireland Craig. *Egyptian Irrigation*. 2 vols. London: Spon, 1913.

Williams, Rosalind H. *Dream Worlds: Mass Consumption in Late Nineteenth-Century France*. Berkeley: University of California Press, 1982.

Wilson, Ara. *The Intimate Economies of Bangkok*. Berkeley: University of California Press, 2004.

Winegar, Jessica. *Creative Reckonings: The Politics of Art and Culture in Contemporary Egypt*. Stanford, CA: Stanford University Press, 2006.

———. "Taking Out the Trash: Youth Clean Up after Mubarak." *Middle East Report*, no. 259 (Summer 2011): 32–35.

Wissa, Hanna F. *Assiout: The Saga of an Egyptian Family*. Sussex: Book Guild, 1994.

Wright, Arnold, and H. A. Cartwright. *Twentieth-Century Impressions of Egypt: Its History, People, Commerce, Industries, and Resources*. London: Lloyd's Greater Britain Publishing, 1909.

Wright, Gwendolyn. "Boulevard Muhammad V." In *Streets: Critical Perspectives on Public Space*, edited by Zeynep Çelik, Diane Favro, and Richard Ingersoll, 225–34. Berkeley: University of California Press, 1994.

———. *The Politics of Design in French Colonial Urbanism*. Chicago: University of Chicago Press, 1991.

Zaalouk, Malak. *Power, Class and Foreign Capital in Egypt*. London: Zed, 1989.

Zakim, Michael. "Sartorial Ideologies: From Homespun to Ready-Made." *American Historical Review* 106, no. 5 (December 2001): 1553–86.

Zaydan, Jurji. *Tarajim mashahir al-sharq*. Vol. 1. Beirut: Dar Maktabat al-Haya, 1970.

Al-Zayyat, Latifa. *Al-Bab al-maftuh*. 1960; Cairo: al-Hayat al-Misriyya al-ʿAmma li'l-Kitab, 1989.

———. *The Open Door*. Translated by Marilyn Booth. New York: American University in Cairo Press, 2000.

Zubaida, Sami. "Cosmopolitanism and the Middle East." In *Cosmopolitanism, Identity, and Authenticity in the Middle East*, edited by Roel Meijer, 15–33. New York: RoutledgeCurzon, 2003.

INDEX